D0557672

Cover: Compugraphics by Pierre Bertrand

Repensando la violencia y el patriarcado frente al nuevo milenio

Nuevas perspectivas en el mundo hispánico y germánico

Rethinking Violence and Patriarchy for the New Millennium

A German and Hispanic Perspective

edited by

Fernando de Diego and Agatha Schwartz

Université d'
University of
Ottawa

National Library of Canada Cataloguing in Publication

Repensando la violencia y el patriarcado frente al nuevo milenio : nuevas perpectivas en el mundo Hispanico y Germanico = Rethinking violence and patriarchy for the new millennium : a German and Hispanic perspective.

Papers originally presented at a conference held at the University of Ottawa, Oct. 18-21, 2001, entitled Violencia y patriarcado en la leteratura y las artes = Violence and patriarchy : perspectives for the new millennium.
Includes bibliographical references and index.
ISBN 0-88927-304-9

1. German literature--20th century--History and criticism--Congresses. 2. Spanish literature--20th century--History and criticism--Congresses. 3. Violence in literature--Congresses. 4. Patriarchy in literature--Congresses. 5. Violence in motion pictures--Congresses. 6. Patriarchy in motion pictures--Congresses.
I. Diego, Fernando de, 1948- II. Schwartz, Agata, 1961- III. Title: Rethinking violence and patriarchy for the new millennium.

NX180.F4R46 2002   830.9'355   C2003-900157-1

The editors wish to thank the Social Sciences and Humanities Research Council of Canada, the Faculty of Arts and the University of Ottawa for their support of the conference and the publication of the present volume.
We would also like to thank our research assistants, Brent DeVoss, Carolina Herrera, Elizabeth Meagle and Alberto Villamandos.

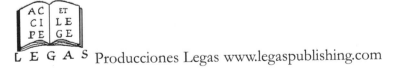

L E G A S Producciones Legas www.legaspublishing.com

For further information and for orders:

Fernando de Diego
Dept. of Modern Lang. and Lit.
University of Ottawa, Ottawa, ON K1N 6N5
Tel. (613) 562-5800 ext. 3759 Fax (613) 562-5138

Printed and bound in Canada

Contents / Índice

Fernando de Diego Pérez

Uiversity of Ottawa

Introducción

La violencia se ha manifestado a lo largo de la historia bajo formas diversas. Su relación con el patriarcado, lejos de ser exclusiva, se ha mantenido como una constante en sociedades a veces tan diferentes, a primera vista, como las hispánicas y las germánicas. El desafío principal de nuestro coloquio fue tratar de estudiar bajo perspectivas diversas la presencia en ambas culturas de elementos recurrentes que conformaran lo que podríamos llamar el paradigma de la violencia en la sociedad falocrática. El patriarcado, por su parte, no puede considerarse como propio de una cultura en particular. Su carácter transcultural, basado en la dominación de la mujer por el hombre, se evidencia a lo largo y ancho de una concepción del mundo cuya presencia permea todas las relaciones humanas.

Los estudios críticos sobre la violencia y el patriarcado desde el punto de vista feminista han denunciado las diferentes representaciones de la mujer en el imaginario colectivo definido por el paradigma antes citado. Los trabajos realizados por investigadores en los últimos años parecen coincidir en la emergencia de formas artísticas, literarias y fílmicas en el caso que nos ocupa, en las que el estereotipo del rol de la mujer se ha subvertido mediante un proceso de autoconcienciación, que conduce a una afirmación cada vez más clara de la conciencia que de sí mismas tienen las mujeres como seres humanos. La discriminación secular a que se vieron sometidas mediante una reificación constante, tanto en el dominio público como en el privado, la locura como escapatoria a un mundo cada vez más alienante, el incesto como forma de sexualidad si no aceptada al menos no reprimida, la violación como forma de poder establecida por la sociedad machista, no son más que algunos de los ejemplos que se pueden citar dentro del apartado más general que representa el binomio violencia y patriarcado.

En los trabajos de este volumen las investigadoras/los investigadores, que han participado en el coloquio, nos muestran que en los diversos productos culturales que conforman lo que se podría llamar la cultura de ambas sociedades, la presencia de la violencia si no de forma constante ni exclusiva en todas las producciones, como antes señalábamos, si ocupa un lugar destacado en ella.

La violencia está presente en muchos de los aspectos de la sociedad mexicana. El estudio de **Luzelena Gutiérrez de Velasco** relaciona la violencia que podemos llamar social y la presente en la obra literaria de

Elena Garro. La visión de esta autora, esposa por treinta años de Octavio Paz, parece establecer una paralelismo entre su vida con el futuro premio Nobel y la violencia que subyace en su relación de pareja. En este trabajo se deja entrever "la otra cara" del gran autor al presentárnoslo literariamente como un ser humano autoritario e intransigente. Por su parte **Julia Tuñón** dedica su artículo al Indio Fernández y su obra cinematográfica. Personaje violento en su vida privada y con las actrices que con él trabajaron, este director lleva a escena todo una serie de personajes estereotipados que llenaron las salas de cine en la llamada Edad de Oro del cine mexicano. Los roles masculinos en su obra responden a varones que encarnan la honra, la violencia y una vida sexual diversificada frente a mujeres marcadas por su carácter pasivo, modesto y tolerante. Julia Tuñón analiza en su trabajo las diferentes modalidades del melodrama mexicano y el papel que la mujer ha representado en él históricamente. También dentro del mundo cultural cinematográfico mexicano pero desde la perspectiva de las realizadoras mexicanas, **Maricruz Castro Ricalde** nos introduce en un cine cuyo eje temático no gira, como el de El Indio Fernández, en torno a la violencia como tal, aunque ésta aparezca de forma física o simbólica. El concepto de "violencia de la retórica" (Teresa de Lauretis) aplicado al lenguaje produce una polarización en la que "el otro es dominado y menospreciado desde y por el lenguaje", como afirma Castro Ricalde. Esta forma de expresión de la violencia, la agresión interpersonal, permite relacionarla con la estructura social en la que aparece. La visión del colonizador se denuncia en esta cinematografía marcada por una visión femenina del cine mexicano.

Los artículos de **Ana Rosa Domenella** y **Laura Cázares** se basan en novelas mexicanas escritas por mujeres en las dos últimas décadas del siglo pasado. La primera hace un estudio muy documentado del término patriarcado y su relación con la violencia desde el panteón mexicano hasta nuestros días. Partiendo de la definición de Graciela Hierro por la cual el patriarcado es "una estructura de violencia que se institucionaliza en la familia, se refuerza en la sociedad civil y se legitima en el Estado", Ana Rosa Domenella hace un recorrido de las diversas concepciones que este término tiene en Bourdieu, Bataille y Hegel para terminar con la crítica marxista. Laura Cázares, por su parte, estudia la violencia partiendo del presupuesto de Ariel Dorfman, para quien su presencia se constata tanto en la literatura como en la historia de Hispanoamérica. Su trabajo analiza la relectura de textos bíblicos, por Inés Arredondo, y la presencia de una violencia en las relaciones cotidianas y el problema de la interrelación personal en Aline Pettersen.

En lo referente a la literatura peruana, **Rocío Silva Santisteban** parte en su artículo de la estética de lo corporal, de la posición "política del cuerpo femenino en tanto locus de la articulación de una experiencia crítica en relación al logos androcéntrico", para estudiar los procesos de deslizamiento, como desterritorialización y relocalización política del corpus estudiado. El análisis de la recepción en la prensa y en la academia del debate sobre la violencia en la literatura peruana ocupa una parte central de su trabajo, y permite ver cómo a pesar de la presencia de dicho debate en los círculos hegemónicos nunca se considera en igualdad de condiciones las propuestas de género de la hermenéutica feminista ni la perspectiva de género aplicada a la crítica cultural, en palabras de la propia autora. **Paolo de Lima** analiza la obra poética de Silva Santisteban y Dalmacia Ruiz-Rosas dentro de un contexto en el que el proceso de creación poética está íntimamente relacionado con las condiciones sociales de producción.

Lady Rojas al analizar la obra de Vargas Llosa, *La fiesta del chivo*, se plantea la relación existente entre "el crimen de la violación individual como violencia política y el trauma físico-psicológico" que sufrió una parte del pueblo dominicano bajo la dictadura Leónidas Trujillo. La figura del dictador latinoamericano que tan abundante bibliografía tiene, se enriquece con esta novela del autor peruano. El trabajo de Rojas pone de manifiesto cómo mediante la ficción narrativa Vargas Llosa denuncia la evolución de la política dominicana y "cómo se modelaban los códigos socio-culturales machistas en función del gobierno de un tirano".

En los artículos que tratan de la producción cultural española, dos en inglés y otros dos en castellano, los autores nos presentan una perspectiva tanto de la relectura histórica de temas clásicos como un estudio de un cineasta reciente e imprescindible en la cultura española franquista como es Carlos Saura, y de un género que toma cada vez importancia en la narrativa escritas por mujeres: la novela policiaca.

El tema del incesto como acto de violencia aparece en el artículo de Alberto Villamandos mediante la comparación entre las obras sobre el tema de Thamar y Amnón por García Lorca y por la poeta Maite Pérez Larrumbe. La actualización del tema bíblico se estudia desde una primera perspectiva en la que hace un recorrido del mismo en la literatura española desde el romancero tradicional hasta García Lorca, analizando las variables y las recurrencias en varios autores y obras, hasta llegar a "procedimientos retóricos de más claro contenido contestatario y feminista" entre los que se encuentran como afirma Susana Reisz "la reescritura de los grandes mitos de la tradición grecolatina y judeocristiana desde una perspectiva ignorada a través de los siglos: la de las protagonistas de esas historias paradigmáticas". Desde una perspectiva en la que se estudia la ruptura del canon tradicional de la crónica, el artículo de Elizabeth Meagle va a tratar de la novela *Urraca* de Lourdes Ortiz. La novelista madrileña que trata en otras de sus obras, y en especial en *Los motivos de Circe* —colección de cuentos— sobre personajes bíblicos, míticos y pictóricos, de la reescritura de mitos, de forma recurrente a lo propuesto por Reisz, se ataca en esta novela histórica a un personaje femenino, Urraca reina de Castilla, mediante la construcción de un sujeto histórico enunciador de un discurso sobre el poder que no puede dejar de lado la subjetividad propia del personaje. El proyecto estético e ideológico que Ortiz lleva a cabo en su novela le permite la relectura de una historia de la que quedan pocas huellas en las crónicas, mediante un discurso en primera persona, deudor de la autobiografía ficticia, en el que expone la teoría del poder y la exclusión de la mujer del mismo.

El trabajo de Shelley Gosdlan se interna en un género poco desarrollado en la novelística española de mujeres hasta un pasado bien reciente. Las "mujeres malas", las mujeres criminales, representadas en estas obras de ficción se estudian como una respuesta al discurso genérico de la violencia. Estas novelas son una forma de narrativa que "(…) belongs to several sub-genres: the Spanish re-formulation of the hard boiled model known as the *novela negra*", que Godsland asocia a una respuesta cultural en los primeros años de la Transición española. Lo interesante de este artículo está en las posibilidades que abre y los caminos que traza para una investigación sobre este tipo de novelística considerada tradicionalmente al margen del canon y de la academia.

Por último, la reflexión de Georg Schmid sobre tres películas de Carlos Saura, *Ana y lobos* (1972), *Deprisa, deprisa* (1980) y *Taxi de noche* (1997) pone de manifiesto la relación existente entre la violencia encarnada por los estereotipos producto del fascismo y su conducta social dentro de una sociedad marcada por el machismo institucional, en la que el papel de la mujer estaba destinado a mantenerse en los márgenes del poder real. La evolución de los personajes femeninos en las películas de Saura se conforman de acuerdo con la evolución propia de la sociedad española en las casi tres décadas que cubren los tres filmes.

Los trabajos del presente volumen, creemos presentan un panorama amplio, con estudios puntuales y concretos, de cómo la violencia y el patriarcado han marcado el panorama cultural del mundo hispánico. Además, pensamos que aparte del interés que pueden suscitar los análisis que los textos presentan, la problemática del congreso no hace si no abrir una vía a nuevos trabajos de investigación sobre el tema.

Agatha Schwartz
University of Ottawa

Rethinking Violence and Patriarchy for the New Millennium: A German and Austrian Perspective

With the September 11 terrorist attacks in the US, the topic of violence and patriarchy became frighteningly relevant during the preparation of the conference "Violence and Patriarchy: Perspectives for the New Millennium" held at the University of Ottawa in October 2001. Although most conference participants had already defined and more or less finalized their presentations by the time of the deadly event, it gave our discussions during the conference a sharper angle regarding the significance of patriarchy and the degrees of its manifestation in different cultures at the beginning of the 21st century; the ways in which the ideology of patriarchy, either explicitly or implicitly, allows for and contributes to violence in its various forms; and finally, how visual and literary representations conform to or challenge our perception of the connection between patriarchy and violence, notably in the German and Hispanic cultural contexts.

Patriarchy can be defined, according to Marielouise Janssen-Jurreit, as "jedes Gesellschatssystem, das Männern in ihren verschiedenen sozialen Rollen konkrete oder normative Macht über Frauen einräumt, in dem Männer über die weibliche Existenz zu ihren Gunsten verfügen können" (Janssen-Jurreit 105).[1] Sociobiology has claimed that men's domination over women is rooted in human physiology, and that therefore women have "naturally" always been subordinate to men (cf. Goldberg qtd. in Lee and Daly 30). By presenting anthropological research that proves the contrary, Richard Lee and Richard Daly refute such statements as essentialist and ahistorical. They arrive at the following conclusion: "The question of male dominance is a sociological and cultural question, a product not of animal instincts, but, rather, of human history" (Lee and Daly 42).

Janssen-Jurreit links the origins of patriarchy to male control over female sexuality and fertility through history. Women's less advantageous social status is therefore a necessary outcome of their reproduc-

---

[1] "every social system which grants men in their various social roles concrete or normative power over women, a system, in which men can dispose of women's existence to their own advantage."

tive functions in a male-dominated system. The separation, especially, of male children from their mothers through rituals of manhood and the rule of elderly men in human communities leads to the exclusion of women from most decision-making processes and eventually locks them into a system of dependency (cf. Janssen-Jurreit 124). It is therefore no surprise that the first women's movement already at the end of the 19th century recognized that the woman question was an economic question.[2] In this matter little has changed, given that women still own only about 1% of the total wealth in the world. Looking at women's situation worldwide, not just in the two "camps" of those fighting an ideological as well as physical war against each other, we can recognize various degrees of women's dependency and the control over their sexuality and reproductive functions, be it through open abuse in once Taliban-controlled Afghanistan, genetic mutilation in many African countries, or the perennial debate regarding abortion laws in Europe and North America.

The need to dominate and control women in a patriarchal system proves to be a primary source of various forms of violence: "The field in which the triad of men's violence is situated is a society, or societies, grounded in structures of domination and control" (Kaufman 6). According to Kaufman, and contrary to what sociobiology would like to assert, we cannot know with certainty whether male violence has or does not have any biological roots; it is therefore much more important a question to ask "what societies do with the violence," how violence is "socially sanctioned or socially tolerated" (4), and, we would like to add: how violence is put into place and maintained, how it is *legitimized* in different societies. Spousal and sexual violence, for instance, may be tolerated to various degrees in an agrarian society, whereas in an industrial one it loses its legitimacy, since legal protection may exist for women who are victims of such violence (cf. "Symposium" 360).

An important, if not *the* most important way for the perpetuation of patriarchy and its values, which allow for various culturally accredited forms of violence, is the internalization of patriarchy and its myths. The image of woman as victim is one of those patriarchal myths which are based on binary oppositions, such as active-passive, connoted with the male and female sexes respectively. Maintaining the designation of the passive category "victim" for women who suffer male violence hinders their possibility of resistance and agency. It is one of the prime examples of how patriarchy and its discourse become internalized. Sharon Lamb has stressed that female victims of sexual abuse are con-

---

[2]One only has to mention Charlotte Perkins Gilman's famous study *Women and Economics* which was translated into several other languages.

structed and silenced for the sake of the accepted and acceptable image that a patriarchal society wants to maintain: that of the weak and suffering victim whose agency and ability to heal are doubted and taken away from her, "because they reproduce a notion of girlhood and womanhood that we would like to preserve: the helpless female — slight, airy, voiceless — who needs reviving (as with Ophelia) or rescuing" (Lamb 113).

The topic of "woman as victim" vs. "woman as perpetrator," along with the related question of male versus female aggression, has been reconceptualized in the past few decades by authors from different disciplines using various approaches. In the mid-eighties, German feminist psychoanalyst Margarete Mitscherlich wrote on women's aggressive behaviour. She came to the conclusion that women are not by nature any more peaceful than men are. However, through their upbringing in a society operating on gender roles based on binary oppositions and thus favouring the image of the passive and docile female, girls are discouraged from outwardly expressing aggressive tendencies; their energy of aggression is thus turned inward and often manifested as masochism. Yet unlike Freud, for whom female masochism was a "natural" part of the development of female sexuality, Mitscherlich considers it to be socialized: "On est en droit de penser que c'est leur position séculaire d'opprimées dans la société et dans la famille qui fait que tant de femmes ont des fantasmes masochistes" (Mitscherlich 211).[3] More recently, North American feminists, such as Naomi Wolf, confirmed Mitscherlich's findings regarding women's aggressive tendencies. Wolf, arguing against what she terms "victim feminism," also sees in women's socialization, not their nature, the reason for their generally less aggressive behaviour: "But the fact that women were relegated by force into creating a tradition of nurturing does not mean that women are themselves naturally better than men, or that they hold the patent on kindness, holistic thinking, or care for others" (Wolf 148). Reflecting along the same lines, Claire Renzetti concludes that it is the negatively connotated image of the "bad woman" which may play a crucial role in women downplaying their aggression (Renzetti 49).

The contributions in the present volume discuss how all of the above is reflected in literary and cinematographic representations, how German and Austrian literatures and film construct and/or deconstruct concepts of violence and patriarchy. The text of the plenary lecture by Verena Stefan, "The Roaring Inside Her," gives, from the point of view of a writer who adheres to cultural feminism, a general introduction on

---

[3] "It is justified to think that women's secular position of the oppressed in society and in the family is to blame for the fact that so many women have masochistic fantasies."

the topic and offers some reflection on how women are capable of reclaiming their power and resisting the violent forces of patriarchy.

Sophie Boyer in "Temporality and Subversion in Marlen Haushofer's *The Wall*" analyses the abolition of linear time as a measurable category and the very basis of a patriarchal system in this novel by Haushofer. The author interprets the violence with which the female protagonist's spatio-temporal system "beyond time" is brutally abolished, and which forces her to respond with violence thereby retreating into patriarchy, as a possibility for a dystopian reading of the novel.

Jonathan J. Long in "The Lost Gender Politics of *Katharina Blum*; or, 'Wie Gewalt entstehen und wie sie verführen kann" offers an innovative interpretation of Heinrich Böll's narrative *The Lost Honour of Katharina Blum* and its film adaptation by Volker Schlöndorff and Margarethe von Trotta. In what the author calls "the seduction of violence," he demonstrates not only the connection between violence and sexuality, but also that the film, while claiming to criticize violence done to the female protagonist, actually reaffirms it by offering a voyeuristic pleasure to the audience.

Julia Neissl in "Violent Male Language in Austrian Women Writers' Discourse on Sexuality: Examples in Elisabeth Reichart, Elfriede Jelinek and Elfriede Czurda" compares three contemporary narratives by Austrian women writers: Elisabeth Reichart's *Fotze*, Elfriede Jelinek's *Lust*, and Elfriede Czurda's *Die Giftmörderinnen*. She examines the persistence of the active-passive paradigm in relationships, be it heterosexual or lesbian, and the different ways in which, through language, the texts deconstruct sexual violence.

Audrone Willeke in "Healing the Split Self: Women's Incest Narratives in Postwar German Literature" discusses the topic of father-daughter incest in three narratives by women writers from last decades of the 20th century: Ingeborg Bachmann's *Malina*, Alissa Walser's "Geschenkt", and Elisabeth Reichart's "La valse." She demonstrates the different attempts of the three female protagonists to come to terms with their incest-memories and thus deal with their victimization. Whereas Bachmann's protagonist remains internally split and Walser's builds a façade of an idealized masculinity to protect her wounded femininity, Reichart's character actively confronts her past and thus takes a first step toward healing.

Reinhild Steingrover in "Violent Acts: Comic Savagery in the Theater of Kerstin Hensel" treats (former) GDR-writer Kerstin Hensel as a playwright who exposes violence in human relationships in the context of economic and political realities which alienate the characters to the point of inability of any emotional response. It is precisely through such unsentimental depiction of violence, Steingrover argues, that Hensel tries to provoke her audience's intellectual or emotional response.

Although Gabrijela Mecky Zaragoza's "A Note on the Containment of Female Aggression: Judith the Murderess in Early 19th Century German Literature" takes us back by one century, her topic is not any less actual today. Based on the treatment of the character of the biblical Judith in three examples of German dramatic literature, the author illustrates how female aggression as one possible manifestation of female agency may be manipulated so as to serve different ideological purposes and suit a particular socio-historical need.

Sigrid Schmid-Bortenschlager in "Violence and Women's Status of Victim: Changing the Role Model or Being Caught in the Trap" analyses different paradigms of dealing with female violence in the works of three contemporary women writers. Whereas Elfriede Czurda's heroines, even as perpetrators, remain "caught in the trap" of the victim position, both Ingrid Noll's and Lilian Faschinger's murderesses move into the perpetrator position while managing to escape punishment. While the author criticizes the lack of plot and moral justification for such an outcome in Noll's *Der Hahn ist tot,* she argues that Faschinger's *Magdalena Sünderin* not only successfully deconstructs patriarchal myths of femininity, but connects sex, violence, and religion on a deeper level.

Christopher Jones in "Giving the Public What It Wants? Editorial Policy at Ariadne" deals with crime novels by women writers, a genre that has flourished in German literature of the 1990s,[4] and examines the socio-cultural function of this genre. His analysis demonstrates that women's crime fiction, as opposed to men's, not only does not idealize violence but also presents more differentiated motivations for crime. This is also reflected in the editorial policy of the publisher Ariadne, which is based on providing crime fiction that will be both thought-provoking and entertaining rather than depicting brutal violence for violence's sake.

Violence and patriarchy at the end of the 20th century, as seen by German and Austrian writers and filmmakers discussed in the contributions, offer a variety of interpretations and strategies of resistance. Although the manifestations of the success or failure to resist and reconceptualize violence, be it through the characters' actions or the use of language, relate to a specifically West and East German or Austrian cultural context, we can recognize patterns of male and female violence compatible with cross-cultural theories of violence and patriarchy as they are discussed in the Hispanic section of the present volume.

---

[4] Geoffrey G. Howes discusses the growing interest in female violence in the 1990s in "Therapeutic Murder in Elfriede Czurda and Lilian Faschinger," *Modern Austrian Literature* 32 (1999.2): 79-93.

Works Cited

Janssen-Jurreit, Marielouise. "Die Grundlagen des Patriarchats — Thesen zu einer Theorie des Sexismus." *Mythos Frau: Projektionen und Inszenierungen im Patriarchat.* Ed. Barbara Schaeffer-Hegel and Brigitte Wartmann. Berlin: Publica, 1984. 104-27.

Kaufman, Michael. "The Construction of Masculinity and the Triad of Men's Violence." *Beyond Patriarchy: Essays by Men on Pleasure, Power, and Change.* Ed. Michael Kaufman. Toronto, New York: Oxford UP, 1987. 1-29.

Lamb, Sharon. "Constructing the Victim: Popular Images and Lasting Labels." *New Versions of Victims: Feminists Struggle with the Concept.* Ed. Sharon Lamb. New York: New York UP, 1999. 108-38.

Lee, Richard and Richard Daly. "Man's Domination and Women's Oppression: The Question of Origins." *Beyond Patriarchy: Essays by Men on Pleasure, Power, and Change.* Ed. Michael Kaufman. Toronto, New York, Oxford UP, 1987. 30-44.

Mitscherlich, Margarete. *La femme pacifique: Étude psychanalytique de l'agressivité selon le sexe.* Traduit de l'allemand par Sylvie Ponsard. Paris: Des femmes, 1988.

Renzetti, Claire. "The Challenge of Feminism Posed by Women's Use of Violence in Intimate Relationships." *New Versions of Victims: Feminists Struggle with the Concept.* Ed. Sharon Lamb. New York: New York UP, 1999. 42-56.

"Symposium: Männlicher Narzißmus und weiblicher Ich-Zerfall: zum Gewaltverhältnis zwischen Mann und Frau." *Mythos Frau: Projektionen und Inszenierungen im Patriarchat.* Ed. Barbara Schaeffer-Hegel and Brigitte Wartmann. Berlin: Publica, 1984. 354-62.

Wolf, Naomi. *Fire With Fire: The New Female Power and How It Will Change the 21th Century.* Toronto: Random House of Canada, 1993.

Plenary Lecture

Verena Stefan, Author

The Roaring Inside Her

I am grateful for your request that I speak to you tonight, not only because you honour me with this request, but because I have to write, I have to create an order on the page, and as always I wish it to be a poetic order.

While I have been working on this talk about violence and patriarchy, the world has moved into war mode or, more accurately, the Western world has moved into yet another war mode. What did I think of telling you before the events of September 11, 2001? My notion of time is warped. Something happened. Something happened that asks for full attention and comprehension.

To think of either violence or patriarchy immediately depressed me. A leaden tiredness fell over me, and boredom. To engage in that frame of reference would mean to focus on male violence, male dehumanization, male terror, torture and war. I don't like that language. My profession is writing, translating (between languages as well as between worlds), teaching creative writing and giving lectures. I also like to garden, cook and practice a few other skills. But writing is the heart of my life and has been for almost as long as I have existed.

I could also say that my profession is to find out things; and as a complete autodidact, I have drawn from many sources. I am a writer with a passion for the analysis that propels truth, but I am also a writer with a picture-book mind. Text offers itself to me through images, and the images approach me when I daydream, when I walk, when I drive, when I read, when I sleep. Text, texture and context happen in the course of the writing. Whenever I get stuck, I start wandering around, looking at books or at trees, reading a lot at first, then not at all. I never listen to news in the morning æ the voices of radio speakers disrupt the poetry between night and day, the residues of sleep and dream, what Audre Lorde calls "the woman's place of power." She writes in "Poetry Is Not a Luxury:"

> These places of possibility within ourselves are dark because they are ancient and hidden; they have survived and grown strong through that darkness. Within these deep places, each one of us holds an incredible reserve of creativity and power, unexamined and unrecorded emotion and feeling. The woman's place of power within each of us is neither white nor surface; it is dark, it is ancient, it is deep. (Lorde 36)

As I move well into the writing of this speech, the United States of America attacks Afghanistan. It is Sunday afternoon, October 7, 2001. I turn on the radio to listen to "Writers and Company," but there is special coverage on the war. On TV, in the middle of a Canadian Thanksgiving Sunday afternoon, CBC, ABC, RDI, Radio Canada, Fox, PBS, are reporting on war and seem to have been doing so for hours. When did it start? When did the media prepare their shows? I am distraught and outraged all at the same time. I am afraid of war. The precision of the targeting has improved since the Gulf War, they say. The Emmy awards, which have been postponed from September 16 to this night, are cancelled for good: a historical first. The media channels are steeped in war; like on September 11, the whole world is forced to watch war. In the midst of it all, this much I know: it is the deep dark place between night and day that I want to keep alive.

Long-ago chants, lyrics, phrases drift through my mind: "Make Love, Not War;" "Give Peace a Chance;" "All across the nation / such a strange vibration / people in motion / there's a whole generation / with a new explanation;" "Imagine there is a war and nobody comes ..."

On the contrary, a shift into war gear in the Western world has taken place, though people across half the world have been living under exactly the same menace since WWII. I suspect, in fact, that WWII never ended. On September 11, the most powerful nation in the world was attacked at home, and in a way hitherto known only in disaster movies. On October 7, the most powerful nation struck back in a familiar way. The attackers from September 11 then announced there would be no more security anywhere for the people of the most powerful nation of the world and its allies. And it is true: though we in the Western world continue our daily lives the best we know how, everyday life is not the same.

I feel the rupture. Some of the thinking and feeling trails of my mind and my heart are already deserted. Some are equipped with a sign that reads "Stay away from the area because of a war-in-progress" or "Don't hike here: you won't need this path anymore." Linear thinking has never been attractive to me, but now, to fashion a text, I have to spin and spiral around as if I were an acrobat.

On September 11 while I stared at the TV screen, at the crumbling towers, listening to shocked voices, screaming voices, soon to be followed by jingoistic voices demanding revenge and taller, stronger, more triumphant towers, two passages from literature flashed through my mind — the first having to do with poetry; the second with high buildings, individual killing and the crushing of wings.

In *The Life of Poetry*, American poet Muriel Rukeyser gives us an account of the outbreak of the Spanish Civil War she witnessed in 1936 Barcelona. She talks about a boat ride at night, a boat ride that carried foreigners away from Spain toward a peaceful shore, and how, amidst the many voices talking about war and fear and bloodshed, one man suddenly asked, "And poetry — among all this — where is there a place for poetry?" (Rukeyser 3).

A few years earlier, about 1925, Lily Everit, the young girl in Virginia Woolf's story "The Introduction," feels herself sliding away from the centre of her world the moment she follows Mrs. Dalloway through a roomful of party guests. She had left home in an elated mood: her essay on the character of Dean Swift had been marked with three red stars. Mrs. Dalloway, "remembering that Lily was the clever one, who read poetry," decides to introduce her to a young man down from Oxford "who would have read everything and could talk about Shelley." Lily Everit feels like a flower that has opened in ten minutes or like a butterfly torn from her chrysalis. The shock of being all of a sudden in a public space fills her with alarm. Until her first party, she has preferred "to run and hurry and ponder on long solitary walks, climbing gates, stepping through the mud, and through the blur, the dream, the ecstasy of loneliness" (Woolf 180).

I remembered Lily Everit's story so clearly because of the recurrent images it contains of "high solemn buildings" (the towers of Westminster, churches, parliaments) that symbolize public space for her. Still staring at my TV screen, I saw something like a triple exposure. One exposure framed Lily Everit, a young man and a fly; the second one, Lily Everit's own mind-picture of civilization with the towers of her time. And in a third exposure, the towers of the World Trade Center crumbled while Lily Everit asked herself: "What had she to oppose to this massive masculine achievement? An essay on the character of Dean Swift!" (Woolf 180).

In "The Introduction," the young man Mrs. Dalloway had chosen for Lily turned around and said to her:

> "And I suppose you write ... poems presumably?"
> "Essays," Lily replied. And then, in her mind's eye, she saw the churches and parliaments and flats and telegraph wires — "all, she told herself, made by men's toil" — together with the young man — "in direct descent from Shakespeare" — and she determined that "she would not let this terror, this suspicion of something different, get hold of her and shrivel up her wings and drive her out into loneliness. But as she said this, she saw him — how else could she describe it — kill a fly. He tore the wings off a fly, standing with his foot on the fender, his head thrown back, talking insolently about himself, arrogantly, but she didn't mind how insolent and arrogant he was to her, if only he had not been brutal to flies. (Woolf 181)

But why not? Lily Everit continues to ask herself:

"(…) why not, since he is the greatest of all wordly objects? (…) But he talked; but he looked; but he laughed; he tore the wings off a fly. He pulled the wings off its back with his clever strong hands, and she saw him do it; and she could not hide the knowledge from herself. But it is necessary that it should be so, she argued, thinking of the churches, of the parliaments and the blocks of flats, and so tried to crouch and cower and fold the wings down flat on her back. (…) In spite of all she could do her essay upon the character of Swift became more and more obtrusive and the three stars burnt quite bright again, only no longer clear and brilliant, but troubled and bloodstained… (…) and, as he turned away from her, he made her think of the towers and civilization with horror, and the yoke that had fallen from the skies onto her neck crushed her (…). (Woolf 182)

"The greatest of all worldly objects," as Virginia Woolf ironically describes Mr. Brinsley, puts poetry into the same feminine category as Lily Everit, the female. His assumption exudes condescension, belittlement: poetry isn't grand, doesn't reach far, has no influence in the world. In his eyes poetry is without consequence. It is as little his equal as Lily Everit herself. Poetry and women don't expand, don't conquer, don't colonize, don't reach into the sky with tall buildings.

But what happened to the Roaring Inside Her? I asked myself as I began to wander along bookshelves in my apartment and in libraries and to walk city streets. I spoke with friends, exchanged e-mail messages, made phone calls to Germany and Switzerland, and read old and new books: *The Demon Lover, Three Guineas, Sister Outsider, Bread Out of Stone, The Straight Mind, China Men, Mrs. Dalloway, Hiroshima in America, Cassandra, The Handmaid's Tale, Why History Matters, Land To Light On,* Wyslava Szymborska, *Possessing the Secret of Joy, The Life of Poetry, The Lonely Hunter, The Member of the Wedding.*

I thought about women and nature, about human vulnerability, about the Montreal massacre on December 6, 1989, about despising and dehumanization, about the exploitation of the earth. Yes, I had to think through the whole list of atrocities again: female genital mutilation, foot binding, the European witch hunts, rape, abuse, obliteration. I thought about the female names we don't hear in the news, about the poems that don't appear on the screen. I thought about the names we keep in our mind as we inform ourselves of what is going on in the world. (Consider those long lists of names: names of leaders, of ministers, of what Virginia Woolf called the processions of educated men; names of rulers, terrorists, companies, weapons, countries where a new war starts, countries where old wars go on. We are able to memorize those long lists, to recite them like poems, like litanies — but they are not poems. They are lethal lullabies.) And I thought of Robin Morgan's magic line from the seventies: "I want a woman's revolution like a lover." Yes, I want it more than ever before. Finally I asked myself these questions: What is the centrepiece of patriarchy? What is the Roaring Inside Her? To whom does history belong? What do I know about war?

What Is the Centrepiece of Patriarchy?

The "other." A fiction. The invention of the category "the other." Men define individuals and groups as other than themselves, and take this as an excuse for superiority, exploitation, cruelty and warfare. That is, men define who is predator and who is prey.

Anything male or masculine is by definition more valuable than anything female or feminine. Women have, longer than any other human group, been defined as the "other." Woman herself is the classical Other with a capital O.

The "other" belongs to the female category — whether the "other" be a non-white or lesbian or gay or transgendered or old or ill person or a male who doesn't prove to be masculine enough.

Nature is the Other, the wild one and, of course, the fly in Mr. Brinsley's hands. For the longest time, women and nature seemed to belong together more closely than men and nature, and men took it as an excuse to exploit both. Some women took it as an excuse to feel superior.

The invention of the category "Other" is a cruel act. An endless chain of the things that divide us results from the initial cruelty.

Grappling with the sticky mess of violence and patriarchy, I read a quite remarkable book that lifted the leaden dullness I had first felt. A male clinical psychologist writes a personal account of what he knows of the male code of violence, "to break the silence," as he says. Joseph A. Kuypers' book *Man's Will To Hurt: Investigating the Causes, Supports and Varieties of His Violence* is a relief because, for once, a male voice does not add to the denial. His book could be the beginning of the end of denial. He tells the boys' club secrets: that men learn (from other men) to inflict pain, that men benefit from inflicting pain, that men get their way by inflicting pain, because they *can do it* and get away with it: "We men know our will to hurt in sports, sex, religion, politics and business," (Kuypers 17) he states laconically before he debunks the whole spectrum of popular and scientific beliefs: No, male violence is not necessary to guide evolution; no, it is not the result of testosterone nor childhood abuse nor poverty; it is not genetic nor survival of the fittest. He translates the "women-do-it-too!" argument into "don't blame me: "This argument ignores the realities of politics and family, both of which are based on male control and domination" (Kuypers 19).

If men started to unravel the connection between hurting and masculinity, there could be a ray of hope. "In the final analysis," he writes, "men's awareness of how they use their power to hurt may give rise to a profound shame. (…) And we may find in our hearts the ability to apologize for the damage we have done" (Kuypers 120). Meanwhile he suggests small and effective changes. Stop gender blindness in language, for example: "Men who drop bombs are more than pilots or soldiers. They are male pilots and male soldiers who are dropping bombs made by men, sold to men by other men, all made possible by the research and scientific discoveries of other men!" (Kuypers 114).

Stop using passive constructions too, I add. Consider the phrase violence against women, for example. WHO is violent? There is no agency, no responsible subject, in this formulation. The same is true for the phrase domestic violence. Who is violent in the house? The cat? Who is at home? Still, it is more frequently women with children than men with children. Are the children violent? Maybe. But if we want to refer to the fact that it is predominantly adult males who beat and abuse spouses and children at home, then we should stop speaking of domestic violence and start speaking of men who beat, men who rape, men who abuse at home. Violence in itself is neither domestic, nor public, nor extraterrestrial, urban or rural. Violence occurs with humans (or animals) who act.

What Is the Roaring Inside Her?

The Roaring Inside Her: It is the deepest memory in females of not wanting to live in a cage. It is everything rough, wild and free in females. It is the female's capacity to defend herself. It is her capacity to fight. Her power to step outside of the category of the "other." It is Nature's power to create earthquakes, floods and hurricanes.

In literature, "The Roaring Inside Her" is the subtitle of Susan Griffin's classic *Women and Nature* and refers to a fable in that book entitled "The Lion in the Den of Prophets:"

> She swaggers in. They are terrifying in their white hairlessness. She waits. She watches. She does not move. She is measuring their moves. And they are measuring her. Cautiously one takes a bit of her fur. He cuts it free from her. He examines it. Another numbers her feet, her teeth, the length and width of her body. She yawns. They announce she is alive. They wonder what she will do if they enclose her in the room with them. One of them shuts the door. She backs her way toward the closed doorway and then roars. "Be still," the men say. She continues to roar. "Why does she roar?" they ask. The roaring must be inside her, they conclude. They decide they must see the roaring inside her. They approach her in a group, six at her two front legs and six at her two back legs. They are trying to put her to sleep. She swings at one of the men. His own blood runs over him. "Why did she do that?"

the men question. She has no soul, they conclude, she does not know right from wrong. "Be still," they shout at her. "Be humble, trust us," they demand. "We have souls," they proclaim, "we know what is right." They approach her with their medicine, "for you." She does not understand this language. She devours them. (Griffin 189)

Audre Lorde puts it another way: "The white fathers told us: I think, therefore I am. The Black mother within each of us — the poet — whispers in our dreams: I feel, therefore I can be free" (Lorde 38).

The Roaring Inside Her is the beast that is not separated from the beauty. It is my only hope.

To Whom Does History Belong?

In a situation of assault, violation, attack, conquest or war, the defeated person — be they female or male — or the defeated group or nation is put into the female, inferior category. The winner reclaims superior male status.

On September 11, 2001, the most powerful nation in the world experienced a moment of defeat and was put into the lower, female category. Not only had the USA proven to be vulnerable at home, they had been outwitted by people they considered inferior: a double humiliation.

But there is too much linear narrative here, too much conventional storytelling. Attack-retaliation-punishment, the story goes. Good and evil are heavily pronounced. And, sure enough, there has been a plot, a great deal of suspense, fear, menace and loss. Governments and terrorist groups fashion the succeeding plots with more suspense, fear, menace, loss and bereavement to come. Each plot annihilates the previous ones: Hiroshima, seventy thousand killed in one minute; Baghdad, more bombs in one night than during the whole war over Dresden; the firestorm of Dresden — who remembers it anyway — Rwanda, the list of pain goes on: Rwanda, Bosnia, Kosovo, Iraq — each name deeply attached to the United States of America — either by their willful absence or by too much carpet-bombing presence.

The shock of the attack against the World Trade Center is already glued over by the war against Afghanistan. Linear progress prevails. Go on! Next move! Imperious compulsion. That odd thinking: more, more, more. I have experienced great trouble throughout my life in understanding the principle of progress — the fact is, I never did understand it. That is why it is difficult for me to memorize the representatives of linear narrative and politics, to recite the litany of their names that are leaden with the despising of other people's cultures, with killing fields and with the denial of the killing fields. My mind takes every opportunity to step aside, to follow sidetracks. Every dot on a line is thrilling, an invitation to leave the path. Could the straight line discover a memory of bending, and begin to meander rather than continue to shoot forward?

A war story between two rival male gangs is going on. The politicians and the military in our part of the world are mostly white middle-aged and old men. The storytellers in the media are younger, and there are women too. The heroes are male. Did we hear of women firefighters? Did we hear of any heroic acts of women? I have no doubt that they took place, but this, too, depends on how one defines heroism.

Is there day-after-day coverage about the endurance, the courage, the strength, the brilliance of Afghan women who have survived twenty years of war? These are not women who have been buried in the burqua. They dare to run clandestine schools for girls, which does not require simply knowing how to teach girls to read and write. It requires resistance, brilliance, alertness, an imaginative and knowledgeable mind. They are heroines, survivors, inheritors of their own history and traditions as women and girls, rather than passive creatures of a terror regime.

Memorizing poems was life-saving for many Jewish prisoners in the death camps. Ruth Klüger, an Austrian-born Jewish-American scholar and writer, recalls in her autobiography *weiter leben* (*A Holocaust Girlhood Remembered*) how she survived Auschwitz by memorizing poems during endless hours of inspection and how she, a twelve-year-old girl at the time, wrote poems herself. Later in life, she had the experience of people denying her ordeal. A friend of hers, a German intellectual, gave a talk on Auschwitz. When she reproached him with not having first asked her to recount her experiences, he said he hadn't remembered that she had been in Auschwitz. Theresienstadt, yes, but not Auschwitz. He couldn't bear it, she concluded, that a girl owned an experience that in his mind was reserved for adults, preferably men.

Years later the situation occurred again with her husband, a Berkeley historian whose curriculum included Nazi Germany. She offered to give a talk in his classes on the situation in the death camps. His face went blank. He had served as an American soldier and identified with the battle of good against evil. He often mentioned how piercingly cold the winter of 1944-45 had been. Once she talked back, telling him that she too remembered that cold, especially since she hadn't benefited from warm army blankets and clothing and sufficient food rations. He lost his temper because her recollections, only a girl's recollections, competed with his. There she learned, she writes, that wars belong to men.

Her boys boasted at school that their mother had escaped from a Nazi camp. The other children ridiculed them and called them liars, since they knew from films that only men were capable of such heroic deeds. A girl, no. Your dad, OK. But not your mother. Wars are the property of men, Ruth Klüger concludes, and the recollections of war, too.

Do you remember Frankie Addams? Carson McCullers created her during WWII. She is the heroine of *The Member of the Wedding*. Frankie is preoccupied with soldiers for specific reasons. In her twelfth summer, in 1944, the world seems shattered and torn, and it turns around way too fast, at a thousand miles an hour. The war in Europe is also happening so fast that Frankie Addams can't keep up. War images and world images swirl in her head, overlapping each other, getting all mixed up together. The only people who regularly come into town from the outside and then leave it again are soldiers from the nearby barracks. For Frankie, they embody the big world, the whole world. Soldiers can be sent into any country on earth; they have entry everywhere. But how can she go out into the world, produce a connection? She dreams of going into the Marines and being honoured with gold insignia, but doesn't know how this dream might be realized. Finally, it occurs to her how she might participate in the Second World War: she will give blood. She won't bleed on the battlefield, although she is full of bloodthirsty ideas and attacks of rage and possesses a considerable arsenal of weapons. She will give her blood to those who go to battle, to the soldiers. In her mind she hears the doctors say that her blood, the blood of Frankie Addams, is the richest, reddest blood they have ever seen, and she dreams of it flowing on in the veins of all the possible soldiers in the whole world. And after the war the soldiers will thank her and address her, not as "Frankie," but in soldierly style as "Addams." But she is not allowed to give her blood; she is still too young. For everything, it seems, she is either too old or too young.

Frankie owns a stolen knife with three blades and a file she uses to sharpen the knife and also to file her fingernails, when they're long enough. Once she shot bullets on the playing field with her father's revolver. But when she commits a sin in the garage with the boy next door, she is unarmed, unsure, and doesn't know what's happening to her, what it is they're doing. Something that makes her feel sick to her stomach. Before falling asleep, when the scene appears to her again, she imagines that she is sticking a knife between the boy's eyes. She packs her suitcase. Where should she go? Everyone else knows where they belong: her father to his jewellery business, the soldiers to the army, Bernice, the housekeeper, with her family and the church. Frankie's brother wants to marry, and only Frankie is completely alone. There seem to be but two options for her in order to enter public space and travel the world: war or love. Her rite of passage begins when she decides to join her brother and his fiancée on their honeymoon trip.

She walks through town like a queen, no longer separated from the world, although everything seems distorted to her: the unexpected doesn't surprise her and the familiar seems strange. For the first time she looks a soldier on the street calmly in the eye, without envy and bitter jealousy in her heart. Instead she feels a kind of recognition in his look; in her opinion this is how free travellers look at each other. She interprets all encounters now out of this feeling, and when a drunken soldier takes up with her and asks whether they should go to her place or his, she is proud to be treated as an equal, as a traveller in a foreign country. She goes for a beer with him to the Blue Moon, a flophouse for soldiers and other adults who do as they please.   Here, Carson McCullers has the twelve-year-old girl speaking in sentences she has picked up from adults — "They say Paris has been liberated. In my opinion, the war will be over next month" (McCullers 66) — an eager, grotesque-sounding attempt to talk politics with the soldier without being able to give the sentences she speaks her own meaning. Finally, the author's voice filters out the babble and names the girl's situation on the threshold of the world:

> Nor would he talk about the war, nor foreign countries and the world. To his joking remarks she could never find replies that fitted, although she tried. Like a nightmare pupil in a recital who has to play a duet to a piece she does not know, F. Jasmine did her best to catch the tune and follow, but soon she broke down and grinned until her mouth felt wooden. (McCullers 128)

One can hardly imagine a more fitting description for the situation of the female stranger in the world. Like Lily Everit, Frankie wants to participate in worldly affairs with her own knowledge. She simply wants to have a decent conversation with an equal. But the scenario McCullers describes is crazy-making, a game of confusion in which only one thing is certain: it's a nightmare, and there's no telling if one will wake up from it.

Many of the girls I have found in literature are lonely hunters, solitary runners — like Frankie Addams, seeking and creating a ritual of transition without the company or support of adult women or other girls. With their experience of ten, twelve years, they preserve an archaic female wisdom. They know what female freedom is; unlike adult feminists, they don't have to reclaim it. The stress of becoming a woman, a REAL woman, doesn't eat them up yet. Rather, they determine their own vagabond freedom, their own rhythm, their own life-preserving aggressivity. Theirs is a wild, unruly, primitive response, comprising day and night, the woods, every road of the world and of the mind, magic power, the stars and the aspiration to fulfil one's dreams, to use one's potential as a human being. Neither fish nor fowl... they defy the expectation that they unlearn their liberty. Then they discover that these are not the right traits for the true women they are meant to become, that only boys can inherit the world.

Still in the altered state of her lonely initiation, Frankie accompanies the soldier to his room. This time she recognizes the danger in the sudden silence, which reminds her of the silence in the garage. Immediately she turns to go, he prevents her, and without thinking, she bites his tongue with all her strength. When he goes after her again, she reaches for the nearest object and hits him over the head with a glass pitcher. With one blow, with her blow, she has broken the silence, averted danger. The soldier's head sounds hollow like a coconut.

That night, distraught, she asks her father if one can kill a person by hitting them over the head with a glass jug. As usual, the father isn't listening. She persists, and he takes the reality out of her question when he says he's never done such a thing and consequently she hasn't either. In his friendly way he confirms the adult principle: children are not to be believed. Beyond that his distracted answer says: you could not do anything that lies outside of my ability to imagine.

Frankie's vision is that humans could and would meet as free travellers, not as women, not as men, throughout their lives, throughout the world. That she should be put into the category of the Other is beyond her imagination. I like to look at her as somebody talking to us about fundamental aspects of the human condition. Like other young heroines, she conveys messages to us from a time when the girl is still a human being, before she mutates into a woman.

What Do I Know About War?

A friend whom I haven't seen for thirteen years comes for breakfast. Our conversation sparks through the kitchen and weaves into a brilliant mellow September morning. The phone rings. My lover, who knows I don't listen to the news in the morning, leaves a message about the attack in New York City. At noon, by myself again, I turn on the TV, stare at a plane that enters into a tower and leaves it on the opposite side. Though I have never lived with a TV before, never witnessed a war "live" on the screen, and don't watch horror movies either, the image bears an eerie familiarity. Has this been the last conversation before World War III? I ask myself. Then I feel the ocean, the immensity of the Atlantic Ocean between North America and Europe. It eludes the conceptual mind. How did anybody ever manage to cross it? It is vast, infinite, cold. The void. I am cut off from Europe. The mind jumps again. The towers keep crumbling like sandcastles. Berlin... Berne...

there are invitations to teach and to read. But I don't want to get stuck over there either, is the third flash in my mind. I want to come back to Montreal.

In moments of shock the body's memory speaks out. The reptilian brain shoots its "fight or flight" reaction through my system. War has been close to me since I was conceived. One of my deepest emotions before falling asleep is: *Nicht auf der Flucht. Not while fleeing.* Then I sigh. Tonight I am safe. The emotion is linked with physical delight: I am in a dry place, it is not humid, I am not freezing. But always have the bags ready. Better to be prepared.

Some things about war I learned from my mother: losing a house, fleeing, being bombed, being on a train full of refugees, fear of rape, hope for protection by state authorities, being turned down, being trapped on a train, becoming a prisoner of war, defying the enemy with her mother tongue, empowering herself by her mother tongue to a degree that defied rape. It comes to my mind now that it was she, in our family, who had a heroic war story — not Father.

She wants to leave Prague with her two little boys to head for Switzerland. She has already left behind their Berlin home of six years. My father was drafted with the pitchfork troops only for the last shabby battle. The Prague railway station is overcrowded with scurrying people. Were the gilded spheres on the roof, the magnificent glass dome, still shining? May 1945, and the Russian Army arrives. Everybody German or speaking a Germanic language instantly becomes a prisoner. She is arrested with hundreds of people in a cinema. The rapes start immediately. After two weeks they are transported to a camp in the countryside where they have to work in the fields for Czech farmers. The rapists, both Russian and Czech men, come every night to pick some of the women and girls. I got so furious, she would tell us. You can't imagine how indignant I suddenly felt when a soldier tapped my foot one night, ordering me to follow him. It was out of question. Night after night we would lie there, our hearts hammering. But now I heard myself yelling at him in Bernese German with all my strength. The words just broke out of me. Never before in my life had I told anybody to go to hell, let alone called them a bastard. The soldier, baffled by a vernacular he didn't know and that wasn't the enemy's language, let her be.

Her story of the power of language belongs to my life like a recurring tune of which one doesn't remember the beginning. It transmits the secret of gutted language, of being outraged to the point of NOT giving permission to let rape happen, of the hysterical use of language in the true sense of the word.

Finally, behind all my questions about patriarchy and violence and the stories of women and girls, I see Artemis, whom we know from

Greek mythology as the great huntress, the guardian of animals, woods, rivers, plains and mountains. Today we would say she is the keeper and guardian of the ecosystem. She not only protects and balances the ecological system, she immediately takes revenge against anyone who is disrespectful or hurtful toward nature and animals. It is said that she is also the great midwife, capable of soothing labour. Hers is a soothing influence too for those who die; her arrows of death are said to be swift and gentle. She dictates the appropriate way to kill an animal, and the rituals of dissection, preparing, sharing and disposing of inedible parts. Young creatures, including human creatures and especially girls, enjoy her unconditional love and attention. Last but not least, she offers a protected area to all those who seek refuge. If they reach her territory, they are safe.

Artemis is a recluse and protective of her privacy and her rhythm. In the central vignette of her story, we find her deep in the woods at the river, ready to take a bath. Actaeon, the hunter, comes along, following his hounds that have found her. He is watching her, though he knows it is a sacrilege. She transforms him into a stag, and his own hounds chase him to death. There is much speculation about this myth. Some say the violent ending of Actaeon's life refers to an early stage of patriarchy during which a king still served a queen or a goddess and had to die after a year or two of governing. He is reminded that he is but a mortal creature in her universe and that it is she who decides about life and death. Later in history, the king would go on living but would have to relinquish power to his successor after a year. And even later, as we know, the king would insist on staying in power for as long as possible, and if he could, he would prefer to be immortal.

In the short story "The Maiden Artemis," by British writer Sara Maitland, Artemis is on center stage deep in the woods, as she continues to undress and to prepare for her bath. She neither returns Actaeon's gaze nor rejects it nor puts a spell on him. There is nothing that has to do with menace or war in this meeting. The image is much older. It is so old, that it takes me quite a while to understand that she is not engaged in the predator-prey game as we know it. She is not busy deciding whether she should engage in it, whether she should mobilize extra energy to protect herself or defend herself or pass unseen. She continues to undress to take her bath. My eyes meet Her original gaze. It is not fixed on a predator's next move. She neither slides away from the center of her world nor neglects her own rhythm. There is a sentimental account of her in every version of Greek mythology that goes somewhat like this:

As a three year old, she sat on the president's lap while he asked her, what would you like, my child? The president's name at the time was Zeus. He was in a jovial mood that afternoon. Three-year-old Artemis knew exactly what she wanted: To be forever a virgin, bow and arrow, sixty sea nymphs, twenty river nymphs, all the mountains of the world and every town you would like to give me, but one would do, for I will prefer to spend most of my time in the mountains. President Zeus agreed. He seemed amused —why, what a cute little daughter with such extravagant ideas!— fulfilling all her wishes in a generous mood, but also because he didn't take her too seriously. And then, wouldn't she add to his pantheon, where all the goddesses were neatly matched with the opposite sex (except for Pallas Athene but this is yet another story) and give it an eccentric flair?

So off she went to live happily in the woods, surrounded by countless nymphs.

I sometimes wonder that her story didn't get lost over the centuries, that it hasn't been completely silenced. It certainly changed many times and is probably mutilated, a marginalized picture in mythology and psychology. But she remained The Roaring Hidden Twin in every female soul, a beautiful barbarian, who survived because she nurtured the imagination of poets and writers.

Monique Wittig writes in *Les Guérillères*:

> {...} il y a eu un temps où tu n'as pas été esclave, souviens-toi. Tu t'en vas seule, pleine de rire, tu te baignes, le ventre nu. Tu dis que tu en as perdu la mémoire, souviens-toi. (...) Tu dis qu'il n'y a pas de mots pour décrire ce temps, tu dis qu'il n'existe pas. Mais souviens-toi. Fais un effort pour te souvenir. Ou, à défaut, invente." (Wittig 126)[1]

In whichever version, the Artemis story evokes questions about violence, cruelty, self-defense, resistance and women before and during patriarchy — questions that would be thrilling to ponder. Meanwhile — Two male leaders are pushing the world with equal frenzy deeper and deeper into horror and cruelty. Both stress that good and evil are separate and that it is the other who is evil. This in itself is a patriarchal axiom. In reality, good and evil belong together as does everything in the world. That we are interconnected is not an idea that spread with the internet, it is the most ancient fact. There are so many unpleasant consequences of our interconnectedness that we prefer to sort things again into separate compartments. For our interconnectedness means that we are also connected to Mr. Bush and to Mr. Bin Laden, that the veiled women of Afghanistan are not pitiful creatures *over there* but part

---

[1] (...) There was a time when you were not a slave, remember that. You walked alone, full of laughter, you bathed bare-bellied. You say you have lost all recollection of it. Remember. The wild roses flower in the woods. (...) You say there are no words to describe this time, you say it does not exist. But remember. Make an effort to remember. Or, failing that, invent." (Wittig 89)

of our lives and our mind, our whole being. It also means that Western women with the civil rights they have achieved are part of the Afghan women's reality.

I miss a reference to the planet itself in the present cacophony of voices. How much more male leadership can the human race endure? someone asked the other day. None, it seems to me. But this question is still an androcentric angel. Even if we wish to diligently manage natural resources in order to survive, we don't include the planet herself in our view. It is her body in the first place that is sliced open, parched, trampled upon and devastated in the ongoing wars, not just our future crops.

Were my talk the introduction of a creative writing workshop I would give you the quotations I used as prompts for your own writing, and I would add another one, a poem by Alice Walker:

> We have a beautiful
> Mother
> her green lap immense
> her brown embrace
> eternal
> her blue body
> everything we know. (Walker 460).

Works Cited

Griffin, Susan. *Women and Nature. The Roaring Inside Her*. San Francisco: Sierra Club Books, 1987.

Klüger, Ruth. *weiter leben*. Göttingen: Wallstein Verlag, 1993.

—. *A Holocaust Girlhood Remembered*. New York: Feminist Press, 2001.

Kuypers, Joseph A. *Man's Will to Hurt: Investigating the Causes, Supports and Varieties of His Violence*. Halifax: Fernwood Publishing, 1992.

Lorde, Audre. *Sister Outsider*. Freedom, CA: The Crossing Press, 1984.

Maitland, Sara. *Telling Tales*. London, West Nyack: The Journeyman Press, 1983.

McCullers, Carson. *The Member of the Wedding*. New York: Bantam, 1958.

Rukeyser, Muriel. *The Life of Poetry*. Ashfield, MA: Paris Press, 1996.

Woolf, Virginia. "The Introduction." *The Complete Shorter Prose*. Ed. Susan Dick. London: Hogarth Press, 1973.

Wittig, Monique. *Les Guérillères*. Paris: Les Éditions de Minuit, 1969.

—. *Les Guérillères*. Trans. David Le Vay. London: Owen, 1971.

Sophie Boyer

Bishop's University

Temporality and Subversion in Marlen Haushofer's *The Wall*

In the novel *Vendredi ou les limbes du Pacifique* (1967; English as *Friday*), French author Michel Tournier summarizes the challenges that time inflicts on the recluse. As the sole survivor of a shipwreck, Robinson is confronted with the following dilemma: should he implement a spatiotemporal system that stems from centuries of patriarchal domination and domesticate "his" untamed island, Speranza, or should he give in to the telluric "savage" rules of the island? The protagonist discusses this battle with time in his logbook:

> I live day-to-day; I let myself go, let time slip between my fingers, waste my time, waste away. Basically, time lies at the heart of the problem of this island and it's not a coincidence that — sinking even deeper — I began to live as though I was living outside of time. By putting my calendar back up, I regained control over my own destiny. (Tournier 60)

The heroine of *The Wall* (*Die Wand*, 1963) by Austrian author Marlen Haushofer's finds herself in a strikingly similar dilemma; but in this case, the reader is presented with a female version of the story of Robinson Crusoe.[1] In the form of a narrative, quite like a diary, a widow in her forties and mother of two describes the events that led her to spend more than two years in the Austrian Alps. Although the narrator had originally intended to spend a single weekend in the mountains with her cousin and her cousin's husband, the day after her first night[2] she finds herself the sole survivor of a nuclear catastrophe. She does not know what caused this incident, nor the extent of the damage it has

---

[1] For further discussion on the literary tradition of the robinsonades and Haushofer's feminine version, refer to Irmgard Roebling's article ("Ist *Die Wand*"). It shows how *The Wall* deviates from the traditional model since the heroine's period of isolation is not a test ("Bewährung") which comes before the ultimate reintegration into social order, but an end in itself.

[2] An important detail which is absent in the critique, but which is quite meaningful is the fact that the night during which the invisible wall emerges in the forest is none other than the *Walpurgisnacht*, the eve of April 30th. It is no coincidence that the catastrophe occurs during the night of Walpurgis, a ritual during which evil forces are evoked and celebrated.

caused. While trying to meet up with the others who stayed in the village, she comes up against a transparent and invisible wall, which naturally allows her to see some of the other inhabitants of the area, who appear to be petrified by this unknown weapon. This wall, which seems impassable, imprisons the woman. Inside this closed space, as though trapped in a glass bubble, the woman, who remains unnamed for the entire story, must watch over herself and the animals that are under her protection. Two years pass without any human interaction, until one day a man suddenly appears from the forest and slaughters the heroine's dog and bull with an axe. In the ultimate act of defence, the woman shoots the man. In order not to sink into total despair, she begins to write about the events that occurred since the nuclear catastrophe, and the reason for her "shipwreck" in the countryside.

This act of remembrance allows the narrator to go back in time, to provide a chronological account of the events, and demonstrates her desire to take control of an unravelling situation: confronted by the murderous madness of the intruder, the narrator, for the lack of finding an explanation or comfort with an other, sees no other option but to write down a long monologue as a way of passing the time during the dreary winter afternoons and to kill time. However, the reader soon witnesses a subtle loss of control over the spatio-temporal dimension of the narrative. This loss of control is written like a watermark in the text;[3] it is but the stage preceding the appearance of a new order, most notably that of a concept of time "beyond time." While this gradual shifting towards a new order takes place, the protagonist undergoes a physical and psychological metamorphosis, which further estranges her from the woman she was before her imprisonment behind the wall.

Let us make it clear, however, that it would be futile to attribute any type of radical feminist ideology to Haushofer's work to ensure the author a place among feminist writers. Indeed, Marlen Haushofer, who was born in 1920 and died of bone cancer in 1970, belonged to a generation of female writers who were still rooted in the established literary tradition. Despite the many prestigious literary prizes awarded to Haushofer during her lifetime, her work was forgotten for more than a decade. The book, which Haushofer herself considered to be her most important novel,[4] finally achieved considerable success posthumously

---

[3] Indeed, parallel to the fictional time, the two years during which the majority of the story unfolds, runs the narrative time, which is the shorter period of the two since the actual writing of the diary takes place between precisely November 5 to February 25. Despite the heroine's efforts to fit her story into some kind of chronological or linear framework, she still breaks the stream of the narrative —briefly, linear time— with philosophical digressions, flashbacks, and prolepses.

[4] During an interview with the journalist Elisabeth Pablé, Marlen Haushofer replied without hesitation to the following question: "Was halten Sie für Ihr wesentlichstes Buch?":

upon republication in 1983 — twenty years after its first release. This late rediscovery can be explained by the fact that the novel was republished at a time when people were preoccupied by the nuclear arms race. If the story of *The Wall* tugged at the heartstrings of the Western imagination, it, nevertheless, did not produce the same agreement regarding its form. Thus, a large part of the criticism of Haushofer is due to her lack of innovation in the elaboration of a language that, in order to be consistent with the personal growth of the protagonist in *The Wall*, should mark a definitive break with patriarchy. Joachim von der Thüsen notes in his article "Die Stimme hinter der Wand" (The Voice Behind the Wall) that the protagonist's new life experiences are hardly reflected in new ways of expression. The images that are evoked to translate the new contact with nature do not go beyond the frame of a traditional romantic sensibility: "Es wird eigentlich kaum der Versuch gemacht, neue Formulierungen für neue Erfahrungen zu finden. So bedient sich der Blick zu den Sternen, in die grüne Weite und hinüber zu den Tieren des traditionellen empfindsamen Vokabulars" (Thüsen 163).[5]

Isolde Schiffermüller, for her part, notes the formal failure that *The Wall* represents: no place is made for the development of a language which would allow for the freedom of creativity and imagination. As a consequence, the language simply sticks to a plot dominated by the hopelessness and existential emptiness of the times. Schiffermüller's criticism is twofold: not only does Haushofer fail to express herself in her own language —"Marlen Haushofer gelingt es nicht, [...] zu einer eigenen Sprache vorzustoßen" (Schiffermüller 149)—, but she is also not able to provide an alternative to the traditional social order. From this angle, her novel remains basically a dystopia: "[...] die weibliche Gegenutopie, die Marlen Haushofer jenseits der 'Wand' entwirft, wird zum Ausdruck einer spezifisch weiblichen Entfremdung, der Identätslosigkeit und Selbstverleugnung des weiblichen Subjekts auf einem hypothesierten Standort jenseits von Gesellschaft und Geschichte" (Schiffermüller 149).[6] Yet, it is precisely the concept of the rupture of

---

"*Die Wand,* und ich glaube nicht, daß mir ein solcher Wurf noch einmal gelingen wird, weil man einen derartigen Stoff wahrscheinlich nur einmal im Leben findet" (Pablé 129; "Which of your books do you consider to be the most important? *The Wall*; and I don't think that I will ever again be capable of writing such a powerful book because you only stumble upon this kind of material once in a lifetime. ")

[5] "The author hardly ever tries to find new ways for the novel experiences that she expresses. Thus, the gazing at the stars, the forest, and the animals is expressed with a traditional pre-Romantic vocabulary."

[6] "The feminine dystopia Marlene Haushofer develops beyond the 'wall' expresses a specifically feminine alienation, the lack of identity and the self-denial of the female character in a hypothetical location above and beyond society and history." Ricarda Schmidt comes to the same acknowledgement of failure when she concludes her analysis of *The Wall* with the following remarks: "Bei Haushofer [...] gibt es [...] keine poli-

time, the indication of a time unconnected to history, that is rampant in *The Wall*. This seems to give the novel the feeling of a utopia and calls for an urgent questioning of the innate tools of violence and destruction of our society.

The protagonist's reflections and personal growth related to imaginary and narrative time are inextricably joined to a loss of identity and the birth of a new identity, which is largely influenced by her contact with nature. Unable to know the exact date when she began writing her story, the narrator indicates from the start of the novel that it is difficult for her to create a linear temporal referential framework for the events:

> Today, the fifth of November, I shall begin my report. I shall set everything down as precisely as I can. But I don't even know if today really is the fifth of November. Over the course of the past winter I've lost track of a few days. I can't even say what day of the week it is. But I don't think that's very important. (Haushofer 1990: 1)

It is on this premise that she begins her story, which goes back more than two years. After discovering the invisible wall the day after her arrival at the cottage, the protagonist tries to mark the boundary of this glass wall. She thus begins to survey the area, which will henceforth become her home. However, this willingness to discover the land does by no means reveal an unconscious desire to own and control it as was the case of Michel Tournier's Robinson. Indeed, Robinson decides that everything that exists on the island and destabilises the order of men must "henceforth be measured, proven, certified, mathematical and rational" (Tournier 67). He goes so far as to create a "Conservatory of Pounds and Measures" so that the teeming, untamed natural world might be "contained" by the act of writing, fixed in a register. It must be stated that although the protagonist of *The Wall* is driven by something

---

tisch-gesellschaftliche Perspektive zur Überwindung der männlichen Ordnung und der weiblichen Entfremdung. [...] Es ist charakteristisch für die Zeit vor dem Beginn der zweiten Frauenbewegung, daß in diesem Roman auf dem positiv beschriebenen Weiblichen keine alternative Gesellschaftsordnung aufgebaut wird: Das weibliche Ich kann sich nur auf sich selbst und die Natur beziehen und sich an ihr abarbeiten." (Schmidt 177; "According to Haushofer, there is no politico-social point of view which could overcome the masculine order of things and feminine alienation. It is characteristic of the period before the beginning of the New Women's Movement that in this novel, no alternative social order is constructed from the feminine element which is positively connotated: the feminine 'I' can only refer to herself and nature and is worn out by its contact with the latter.") However, it would be unfair and incorrect to limit our examination of critical literature to a single point of view, which sometimes appears to be judged on mere intent. We should note that a more recent review focuses on an interpretation which is far less reductionist in approach. Thus Hugo Caviola's essay convincingly emphasizes the aesthetic complexity of *The Wall*. His postmodernist interpretation of the novel shows the subtle and fluctuating relationship between intimacy and hostility that occurs between the narrator and the reader. (Caviola 107ff).

similar to Robinson's desire for control, her purpose is different, in that she wishes to subdue the very hostility of the wall, a product of man's destructive efforts, whose presence disturbs the natural order of things. Moreover, it is this order of nature that interrupts the narrator's delimitation of the wall: a cow that strays from its herd and survives the catastrophe requires immediate care and definitively moves the narrator from the wall. Nature is a superior force to which she no longer has any choice but to submit: "So there I was in a wild and strange meadow in the middle of the forest and suddenly I was the owner of a cow. I was quite plain that I couldn't leave the cow behind" (23).

Like Robinson, who decided to create a water clock to avoid the "mire" which threatened to transform him into a total savage, the protagonist imposes the ancient order of things on her new life:

> I also resolutely decided to wind the clock daily and cross off each day in the diary. At the time it struck me as very important; I was practically clinging to the meagre remnants of human routine left to me. [...] I don't know why I do that, it's as if I'm driven by an inner compulsion. Maybe I'm afraid that if I could do otherwise I would gradually cease to be a human being, and would soon be creeping about, dirty and stinking, emitting incomprehensible noises. (34)

Yet, the distinction drawn here between man and animal does not imply superiority of one over the other; rather it clearly reveals the reality of the human condition, which weighs down on it like an inevitable burden: "Not that I'm afraid of becoming an animal. That wouldn't be too bad, but a human being can never become just an animal; he plunges beyond, into the abyss" (34). However, the wall that separates her from humanity, and moreover her proximity to or fusion with nature, will impose upon her a gradual — yet irreversible — metamorphosis. In an aside, characteristic of her writing style, the narrator explains the physical transformations that affect her body. It is these transformations that help her to create a new identity in constant flux:

> The womanliness of my forties had fallen from me, along with my curls, my little double chin and my rounded hips. At the same time I lost the awareness of being a woman. My body, more skilful than myself, had adapted itself [...] Sometimes I was a child in search of strawberries, or a young man sawing wood, or, when sitting on the bench [...] I was a very old, sexless creature. Today the peculiar charm that emanated from me back then has left me entirely... I'm more like a tree than a person... (68-69)

A mental transformation, which changes her relationship with time, accompanies the physical metamorphosis. Thus, contrary to the woman that she was in the beginning of the fictional time, who still was anchored in a traditional order of time, the narrator of the story explains how, after a fever that rendered her half-conscious for several days, she lost track of time: "My watch and my alarm-clock had stopped, and I knew neither what day nor what time it was" (219). For want of anything better, she thus decides to set her watch by the daily flight of the crows over the hunting-lodge and to strike off a week from the diary. Slowly, however, she notices the extent to which she "gradually started to break free of [her] past and find a new way of organizing things" (220). She sways into this new order of things a few days later when her alarm-clock stops ticking away and she is overcome by a "new silence" (228). She subsequently misplaces her wristwatch and thus loses the only instrument that she had left with which she could tell time. In spite of this, she changes her daily rhythm of life to "crow's time" (219). From then on "artificial human time" (52) is put on hold.

The narrator first experiences a new temporal dimension when she spends some time in the "Alm" (alpine pasture); she decides to spend the second summer of her captivity in the mountains so her cow and her calf can have access to better grass and fresher air. This place, according to the narrator herself is appealing — in almost a dangerous manner — because "the *Alm* lay outside of time" (158). Life on the pasture involves little organization and few pressures, which leads her to sink into a state of contemplation where she finds inner freedom. Life at the hunting-lodge in the valley, on the other hand, requires her to carry out daily tasks, which remind her of her human condition, overwhelming and heavy in the utmost sense. In the end, the pasture is perhaps simply a place of her inner rite of passage, a magical threshold which separates the past from the future, the *hic et nunc* of an identity in transformation:

> I find it hard to separate my old self from my new self, and I'm not sure that my new self isn't gradually being absorbed into something larger that thinks of itself as "We." It was the *Alm*'s fault. It was almost impossible, in the buzzing stillness of the meadow, beneath the big sky, to remain a single and separate Self, a little, blind, independent life that didn't want to fit in with a greater Being. (161)

In his article on *The Wall*, François Venter interprets this sense of being at one with nature, this harmony with the changing of the seasons as an obvious marker of a *feminine writing*. He bases his analysis on theories by Julia Kristeva from *Le Temps des femmes* and emphasizes the rejection of a linear, historical time and the adoption of a cyclical time, which is feminine in essence and subversive in itself (Venter 62-64). However, although the heroine of the novel, in order to survive, must succumb to nature's rhythm, the linearity of time may be momentarily suspended, but it is never totally abandoned. Thus, Venter's conclusions seem to overzealously slot *The Wall* into the category of *feminine writing* — a category that is all the more problematic because it threatens quite often to sink into a reductionist essentialism. However, if there is a literary work which is irreducible to any one category, it is, par excellence, Marlen Haushofer's *The Wall*, this highly complex and rare text, in which even the narrator avoids the pitfall of a partial thought:

> I was no longer in search of a meaning to make my life more bearable. That kind of desire struck me as being almost presumptuous. Human beings had played their own games, and in almost every case they had ended badly. And how could I complain? I was one of them and couldn't judge them, because I understood them so well. (184)

Thus, if it is possible to talk, like Venter, about subversion of the temporal order, it is by no means in the sense of a radical ideology, but rather a temporary transgression which the heroine herself considers to be both fascinating and dangerous. Rather than keeping to the concept of a cyclical notion of time, the subversion stems from the notion of a time "beyond time" or at least the impression of a time "beyond history."

As previously noted, the narrator considers the pasture to be "outside of time." It is in the mountain pasture where she, thanks to her many hours spent contemplating the sky full of stars, momentarily transports herself to somewhere far beyond the terrestrial world, to a place where time no longer exists:

> Every fine evening I sat on the bench in front of the house [...] and watched the red glow of evening spread across the western sky. Later I saw the moon rising and the stars flashing. [...] I didn't think, I didn't reminisce, and I wasn't afraid. I just sat quite still, leaning against the wooden wall, tired and awake at the same time, and looked at the sky. I got to know all the stars; although I didn't know their names they soon grew familiar. The only ones I knew were the Plough and Venus. All the others remained nameless, the red, green, bluish and yellow ones. If I narrowed my eyes to slits I could see the infinite abysses opening up between the constellations. Huge black hollows behind dense star-clusters. (166)

Should we infer from her introspective stargazing and the poetic description of black holes that a fourth dimension of time, the so-called space-time continuum, does exist?[7] One thing is certain: the narrator has a mystical, sacred experience when she observes the Milky Way.

---

[7] In her analysis of the concept of time in matriarchal societies, Heide Göttner-Abendroth explains how places of worship were made in a spiral form to represent the movement of the planets and stars. She rejects the notion of both cyclical and linear time, which

Suspended between Heaven and Earth, she is literally in state of *ecstasy*, having an out of body experience. On this patch of land, the heroine, beyond being obligated to look after herself, discovers a way to communicate with a higher entity: Heaven. In his book *Le sacré et le profane*, Mircea Éliade uses the concept of *axis mundi* to describe this experience. The mountaintop pasture, like a sacred circle, places the heroine at the centre of the world on an infinite vertical axis, an infinite axis of eternal presence, which links her to the cosmos:

> If something sometimes vaguely disturbed me, it was that everything had gone so well. We were all healthy, the days stayed warm and fragrant, and the nights were filled with stars. Finally, since nothing else happened, I got used to this state [...] Past and future washed around a little warm island, the here and now. I knew it couldn't stay that way, but I didn't worry about it at all. (186-187)

Yet the sacred experience soon reminds her of her experience with the profane events of daily life: the heroine's deep thoughts about the constellations always seem to turn back at the reality of human life on Earth. In fact, it is when she realizes that "the great game of the sun, moon and stars seemed to be working out" that she concludes that "human beings had played their own games, and in almost every case they had ended badly" (184). Is it a coincidence that the place which threatens to rob her of her sense of self and separate her from humanity also becomes the place that throws her violently back down to earth? The "mystical aura" of the pasture actually turns into an apocalyptic vision when, at the end of the novel, an unknown murderer trespasses and brutally kills her bull and dog. In turn, the narrator, without giving it a second thought, shoots the murderer, and with this bullet she destroys what was left of the old world order, a world where violence and the spirit of destruction led to human petrification.

Is *The Wall* a dystopian novel? In light of the terrorist attacks on September 11, 2001 and the United States military's eagerness, the lesson this novel may teach us seems to be more about utopia. If we listen carefully to the words of the narrator, she speaks about an ideal to be attained, the ideal of a new world awaiting its dawn:

> I often look forward to a time when there won't be anything left to grow attached to. I'm tired of everything being taken away from me. Yet there's no escape, for as long as there's something for me to love in

---

indicate "ideological constructions." (Göttner-Abendroth 112) With the developments of modern physics and Einstein's theories, the linearity of time is denied: it is possible to observe the different stages of time in space through a telescope. This simultaneity in the observing of the cosmos is very similar to the matriarchal concept of "spiral time."

the forest, I shall love it; and if some day there is nothing, I shall stop living. If everyone had been like me there would never have been a wall […]. But I understand why the others always had the upper hand. Loving and looking after another creature is a very troublesome business, and much harder than killing and destruction. It takes twenty years to bring up a child, and ten seconds to kill it. (140)

In light of this noble praising of the supreme act — love — how should the heroine's counter-attack toward the intruder's violence be interpreted? Her action that ends the stranger's life is cold, mechanical and is neither premeditated nor impassioned, but a necessary deed:

I dashed into the hut and tore the rifle from the wall. It took a few seconds [...] I aimed and fired [...] The man dropped the hatchet and collapsed with a strange spinning motion.[...] I knew he must be dead, he had been such a big target that I couldn't have missed. I was glad he was dead. (240-241)

To violence, the heroine responds by violence: an eye for an eye, a tooth for a tooth. The law of retaliation stands here as one among the numerous biblical references written into *The Wall* (cf. Roebling "Drachenkampf:" 300). Perhaps it is exactly in this reference that we may read the ultimate subversion of the temporal order; although through her action, the heroine seems to adopt a law which is inherent in a society based on violence and revenge, by that very same action she establishes the very principle of an order before-the-time. Thus if *the* Book, the Bible, begins with the Genesis and ends with the Apocalypse, *The Wall* reverses this order: first the appearance of the wall and later of the intruder only precede the motion toward a lost paradise, a time-before-time, before humans and their history. For it *is* a motion, and its outcome is evoked in the possibility of a form of expression which resembles prehistoric cave paintings:

In my dreams I bring children into the world, and they aren't only human children; there are cats among them, dogs, calves, bears and quite peculiar furry creatures. [...] It only looks off-putting when I write it down, in human writing and human words. Perhaps I should draw these dreams with pebbles on green moss, or scratch them in the snow with a stick. But I can't yet do that. I probably won't live long enough to be so transformed. Perhaps a genius could do it, but I'm only a simple person who has lost her world and is on the way to finding a new one. That way is a painful one, and still far from over. (207-208)

The heroine remains alone with her female animals, resigned to endure her human condition until the very end — and here she ends her story and history.

Works Cited

Caviola, Hugo. "Behind the Transparent Wall: Marlen Haushofer's Novel *Die Wand.*" *Modern Austrian Literature* 24/1 (1991): 100-12.

Éliade, Mircea. *Le sacré et le profane.* Paris: Gallimard, 1965.

Göttner-Abendroth, Heide. "Urania æ Time and Space of the Stars : The Matriarchal Cosmos through the Lens of Modern Physics." *Taking Our Time: Feminist Perspectives on Temporality.* Ed. Frieda Johles Forman. Oxford: Pergamon Press, 1989. 108-19.

Haushofer, Marlen. *The Wall.* Transl. Shaun Whiteside. San Francisco: Quartet Books, 1990.

Pablé, Elisabeth. "Marlen Haushofer oder die sanfte Gewalt: Ein Gespräch mit Elisabeth Pablé." *"Oder war da manchmal etwas anderes?" Texte zu Marlen Haushofer.* Ed. Anne Duden et al. Frankfurt a.M.: Neue Kritik, 1986. 127-31.

Roebling, Irmgard. "Ist *Die Wand* von Marlen Haushofer eine weibliche Robinsonade?" *Diskussion Deutsch* 20 (1989): 48-58.

—."Drachenkampf aus der Isolation oder Das Fortschreiben geschichtlicher Selbsterfahrung in Marlen Haushofers Romanwerk." *Amsterdamer Beiträge zur neueren Germanistik* 29 (1989): 275-332.

Schiffermüller, Isolde. "Weibliche Utopie und Selbstverleugnung: Zu den Widersprüchen in Marlen Haushofers Roman *Die Wand.*" *Quaderni di lingue e letterature* 13 (1988): 139-49.

Schmidt, Ricarda. "Frauenphantasien über Frauen und Natur." *Germanisch-Romanische Monatsschrift* 38 (1988): 168-84.

Thüsen, Joachim von der. "Die Stimme hinter der Wand: Über Marlen Haushofer." *Amsterdamer Beiträge zur neueren Germanistik* 21 (1987): 157-70.

Tournier, Michel. *Vendredi ou les limbes du Pacifique.* Paris: Gallimard, 1972.

Venter, François. "Marlen Haushofers Roman *Die Wand* als écriture féminine." *Acta Germanica* 22 (1994): 57-66.

Translated from French by Kelli Fraser

Jonathan J. Long

University of Durham, UK

The Lost Gender Politics of *Katharina Blum:* or, 'Wie Gewalt entstehen und wie sie verführen kann'

Introduction

When Heinrich Böll's short narrative *Die verlorene Ehre der Katharina Blum* (*The Lost Honor of Katharina Blum*) was published in 1974, it became an immediate bestseller and sold 150,000 copies within six weeks (Rainer 160). The film of the same name, directed by the husband-and-wife team of Volker Schlöndorff and Margarete von Trotta, was premiered a year later in October 1975. By 1977, 1.25 million viewers had seen the film, making it the most successful film of the New German Cinema (Gast 127). An outline sketch of the plot might throw some light on the reasons for this phenomenal success.[1] Events are set in motion by the chance encounter between the main character Katharina Blum and a suspected terrorist called Ludwig Götten. They meet at a carnival party in Cologne and return to her flat. The following morning, having learned that Götten is under police surveillance, she enables him to escape from her flat unseen. As a result of her involvement with Götten, Katharina is interrogated by police, and continually libelled by the gutter press, until eventually she arranges an interview with a tabloid journalist whom she shoots dead when he suggests that they have sex together.

In addition to the sensational — even melodramatic — nature of the story in itself, it also possessed considerable contemporary relevance. The political context in which the book appeared was the increasing hysteria in West Germany about the threat allegedly posed to the state by the terrorist activities of the Baader-Meinhof Group and the Red

---

[1] An interesting point of comparison here is Peter Schneider's *...schon bist du ein Verfassungsfeind* (*...and before you know it, you're an Enemy of the State*. Berlin: Rotbuch, 1975, which deals with the "Radikalenerlaß." This was a decree passed by the German government in 1972, which excluded from public service all members of organisations deemed to be hostile to the constitution of the Federal Republic ("verfassungsfeindlich") and its effects on an individual teacher. The plot is unspectacular, and reveals the shocking abuse of power by those in authority by unpacking the paradoxes inherent in the implementation of the decree. Schneider's text, though, enjoyed considerably less commercial success than Böll's. By 1976, the print-run (not sales) totalled only 45,000 copies (*...schon bist du ein Verfassungsfeind*, 4).

Army Faction. This perceived threat led to extreme measures on the part of government and the security forces. At the same time, the press, most notoriously exemplified by Axel Springer's tabloid *Bild*, resorted to a combination of irresponsible sensationalism and a witch-hunt mentality. In the media at large, the word "Sympathisant" (sympathiser) was applied to anyone suspected of holding radical political views, and became a highly effective term when it came to drawing the boundaries between those who were of the "correct" political persuasion and those who were not. Böll experienced this political pigeonholing himself. In 1972, in a now-famous article for the news magazine *Der Spiegel* entitled "Will Ulrike Meinhof Gnade oder freies Geleit?" ("Does Ulireke Meinhof want mercy or safe conduct?"), he had been publicly critical of the *Bild* newspaper's prejudicial reporting of suspected terrorist actions. He was subsequently vilified in the Springer press, being labelled, among other things, a "Schreibtischtäter" (one who commits crimes from behind his writing desk) and a "salonanarchistischer Sympathisant" (middle-class anarchist sympathiser).[2] He also had first-hand experience of illicit collusion between the police and the press: in a farcical episode in 1974, a police raid on Böll's son's Berlin apartment was reported in the Springer Press before it had even taken place.

The political and autobiographical context surrounding the publication of *Katharina Blum* has had a considerable influence on the way in which the book has been read by critics over the past twenty-five years. In general, the text has been seen as a response to Böll's own experiences at the hands of the Springer press and as a critique of collusion between the police, the church, the media, and representatives of industry and politics. The text's subtitle *Wie Gewalt entstehen und wohin sie führen kann* (*How violence originates and where it can lead*) has also directed critics' attention to the representation of violence, not only the physical violence of the murder, but the linguistic and structural violence that, as Nigel Harris writes, is "latently present in the institutions of an unjust society and manifests itself when those in positions of power act (usually surreptitiously) in such a way as to perpetuate social inequality and injustice and thus damage the well-being and potential of others" (Harris 202).

Alongside this dominant trend in the criticism on *Katharina Blum*, there has been a trickle of studies that have addressed the text from a feminist point of view. As early as 1976, Charlotte Ghurye's short study

---

2 Schlöndorff, too, was branded a "Baader-Meinhof-Sympathisant" by the *Bild-Zeitung* in 1976 (John Sandford, *The New German Cinema*. London: Oswald Wolff, 1980. 44). For an account of the language of media discourse on West German terrorism, see Andreas Musolff, *Krieg gegen die Öffentlichkeit: Terrorismus und politischer Sprachgebrauch* (Opladen: Westdeutscher Verlag, 1996. 140-220). Musolff points out that "Sympathisant" became a "pivotal stigmatic word in the terrorism debate" (165).

The Writer and Society focused, with remarkable prescience, on issues that were later to become central objects of study in the humanities and social sciences, namely class and gender. Böll's text, she argues, represents a patriarchal society in which Katharina's status as both a woman and member of the working class makes her a legitimate target for various forms of sexual aggression. Ghurye implies, however, that this aggression is not intended to meet with reader approval, because all the men whose desire Katharina rejects are prejudiced stereotypes and highly unsympathetic. The only one who is not represented as predatory and exploitative is Götten — the alleged criminal! Dorothee Römhild adds that sexual violence need not be physical, but can be linguistic. By insisting, in her police statement, on the distinction between "Zudringlichkeit" (forwardness) and "Zärtlichkeit" (tenderness), for example, Katharina "kritisiert [...] das herrschende Gewaltpotential einer Vulgärsprache, die Obszönitäten mit Liebe gleichsetzt" (Römhild 152)[3]. Katharina is dehumanised and objectified, and turned into a marketable press commodity: the lecherous whore (153). Linguistic violence is shown, in *Die verlorene Ehre der Katharina Blum*, to be a gender-specific problem, in that it both affects only women, and is unmasked by women (156).

The central issue of violence and patriarchy, then, has already been addressed to a certain extent by commentators on Böll's work. I will argue below, however, that feminist studies have not gone far enough in exploring the link between Böll's critique of violence and the critique of patriarchy that this entails. As far as the film of *Katharina Blum* is concerned, the whole issue of gender has been largely ignored by critics, and where it has been briefly mentioned, it has been glossed over. The reason for this is that a reading that takes gender politics into account threatens to blow apart interpretations that attempt to show how the film mobilises audience sympathy in order to put across its critical

---

[3] "criticises the pervasive latent violence of a vulgar language that equates obscenities with love." My discussion of Römhild concentrates on her treatment of violence. Her main argument, however, concerns Katharina's dual status as "Ms. Average" and as a vehicle for Böll's utopian "Liebesideal." She has to be seen as a "Durchschnittsbürgerin" for her victimisation by the press to inspire reader sympathy. At the same time, she has to represent a solution to this victimisation, which is a quasi-religious conception of romantic love that "redeems" her. Römhild's analysis is mostly quite insightful, but she ends up judging the novel according to the rather bizarre criterion of "realism:" Böll has not managed to abandon his ideals in favour of a "realistic" portrait of woman (162). Quite what "woman" might be, however, remains unexplored. A considerably less useful discussion is Aleidine Kramer Moeller's book *The Woman as Survivor: The Evolution of the Female Figure in the Works of Heinrich Böll* (New York: Lang, 1991). Moeller's aim is the rather pointless one of demonstrating Katharina's "saintliness." Her analysis relies exclusively on the discourse of morality (virtue and vice, good and evil), and manages to pay absolutely no attention to formal, social, and ideological questions.

"message." My title "The Lost Gender Politics of *Katharina Blum,*" then, refers in the first instance to the absence of gender in the critical discussions of Schlöndorff, and von Trotta's film. By paying particular attention to the representation of violence and patriarchy in Böll's novel and then examining the same problematic in its filmic adaptation, I shall elucidate a second meaning of my title, namely that one aspect of Böll's text that "gets lost" in the process of adaptation is, precisely, the critique of gender politics under patriarchy.

Terrorism and Sexuality in the Novel and Film of *Katharina Blum*

Despite the immediate context of the terrorist threat in West Germany in the mid-1970s, the suspected terrorist in both versions of *The Lost Honor of Katharina Blum* makes only a fleeting appearance, and a woman is left to cope with the aftermath. The way Katharina is subsequently treated by tabloid journalists, police interrogators, and even her own neighbours actually has very little to do with terrorism and a lot to do with sex. She is termed a "Räuberliebchen" in the press, an untranslatable term that casts her in the dual role of terrorist sympathiser and whore.[4] Both the police and the *ZEITUNG* repeatedly insinuate that she is involved not only in terrorist activities, but in some form of prostitution. The anonymous hate-mail that she receives consists of a similar conflation of sexual and political insults. Katharina's prudery is stressed in both the novel and the film, and her nickname "die Nonne" ("the nun") repeatedly mentioned. And so her transformation, in the press and in the public consciousness, into a whore is clearly a projection of (primarily male) anxieties: fear of terrorism is reconfigured in terms of a rapacious and threatening female sexuality.

The rhetorical purpose of this projection becomes clear if we take into consideration the social reality that formed both the context and the subject-matter of Böll's narrative. One problem the West German authorities faced was ignorance about the size of the RAF and the Baader-Meinhof organisation. In "Will Ulrike Meinhof Gnade oder freies Geleit?" Böll himself suggested that by 1972 the core Baader-Meinhof group had shrunk to a mere half-dozen individuals, making the so-called "Stadtguerillakrieg" (urban guerilla warfare) an uneven contest of six against sixty million. There was also concern that a potentially tiny group within the Federal Republic could openly declare an urban guerrilla war on German society and yet evade capture for over a year. This led to terms such as "Sympathisant," "Bande," and "Metastase" (sympathiser, gang and metastasis) entering the public discourse on ter-

---

[4] Römhild has pointed out the crassness with which Katharina undergoes a change of status from the "nun" stereotype to the "whore" stereotype.

rorism (Musolff 165). The huge but nebulous network of accomplices implied by these terms at once explained the security forces' failure to capture any suspects, and constructed a social menace that was everywhere and nowhere, highly visible in media discourse but invisible in everyday social reality. In the light of this, the substitution of female sexuality for terrorism allows press, police and public to pin down an identifiable "culprit," thereby reducing a complex set of issues within the body politic to the intimate body politics of a single individual. That individual then becomes a legitimate object of surveillance, investigation, discipline, and, if necessary, annihilation.

The substitution of sexuality for terrorism is ultimately enabled by a four-part homology: terrorism is to capitalism what female sexuality is to patriarchy. The latter is in each case the dominant term. The former terms are construed as the "other," and therefore possess subversive potential. It is in part the capacity of female sexuality and political "subversives" to undermine the very foundations of the dominant order that explains the obsessive zeal with which they have been traditionally policed by, respectively, patriarchal and capitalist societies. At the same time, however, the fear and anxiety attached to female sexuality and political violence are accompanied by an element of *desire*. This is an uncontentious point as far as "woman" is concerned. In classical psychoanalysis, the "woman as other" is both an erotic object for the desiring male *and* a bearer of the lack that gives rise to castration anxiety. In Böll's text, the combination of lust and aggression that Katharina provokes provides a vivid illustration of this duality. With regard to terrorism, the situation is more complex. What I do not wish to suggest is that the ordinary citizens of West Germany secretly wished to become either the perpetrators or the victims of terrorist attacks. But *The Lost Honor of Katharina Blum* shows that the act of combating and condemning terrorist violence often employs surveillance measures, investigative techniques, and journalistic rhetoric that are themselves forms of violence.[5] What is more, this violence is outside the rule of law, and evinces scant concern for its (innocent) victims. What emerges in the ZEITUNG reports and the activities of its journalists is a form of indiscriminate, illegal, and politicised violence that bears striking structural similarities to the terrorist aggression it claims to combat.

The substitution of sexuality for terrorism and the subsequent violation of the female "suspect" are common to both the novel and the film of *Katharina Blum*. The difference between the two versions lies in

---

[5] This problem is not limited to the right; the persistence of symbolic violence in the political discourse of anti-fascist organisations and the Green Party in post-war Germany has been subjected to trenchant analysis and critique in Uli Linke's book *German Bodies: Race and Representation after Hitler* (New York: Routledge, 1999) 153-216.

the discourse through which the facts of the represented world are mediated, and this is the focus of the remainder of this article.

Violence and Irony:
Böll's narrative *The Lost Honor of Katharina Blum*

The German term "Gewalt" that occurs in the subtitle of Böll's text has a much greater semantic range than the English "violence," encompassing also power, in the sense of power over people. This immediately broadens the relevance of the text. It is not merely a study of the violence inflicted on and by an individual citizen, but an exploration of how violence against individuals serves the material interests of those who exercise power ("Gewalt") over others in political, economic, and sexual terms. This presented Böll with a serious representational problem: how to write about violence when violence itself has been co-opted by the culture industry and turned into a commodity whose commercial function is the production of pleasure, and whose ideological function is to naturalise and legitimise state repression or aggression?[6]

The narrator of *Katharina Blum* offers a solution to this problem. He refuses to write about blood, and directs those seeking gratification of their bloodlust to the products of the entertainment industry: film, television, and musicals (Böll §3/ 9).[7] Physical violence in the text is, as Nigel Harris points out, deliberately de-sensationalised, its importance and interest restricted to a minimum. Indeed, the narrator is reluctant to describe specific acts of physical brutality at all. Harris argues that the narrator deals with violent events in a laconic and detached way in order that other, subtler forms of violence might emerge more clearly (Harris 203).[8] It is not merely the narrator's detachment that is of relevance here, but, more importantly, the fact that this detachment is a crucial strategy in the creation of irony. By means of irony, the narrator impedes an *un*critical "consumption" of the text, and opens up the possibility of a *critical* engagement with violence and its representation.

Whilst there are many acts of violence in *The Lost Honor of Katharina Blum*, the critique of patriarchy emerges most clearly at those points

---

[6] Some particularly transparent examples of this tendency are crime dramas, Westerns, and Cold War thrillers. The representation of often extreme violence is coupled with representational techniques that both force the reader or spectator into a position of acquiescence, and align him or her with the representatives of the state apparatus.

[7] All references are to Heinrich Böll, *Die verlorene Ehre der Katharina Blum, oder: Wie Gewalt entstehen und wohin sie führen kann* (Munich: dtv, 1976). Since there are numerous German and English editions available, I refer to section numbers as well as page numbers. All translations are my own.

[8] Harris's article is the most systematic and extensive discussion of the various forms of violence that manifest themselves in Böll's text.

where Katharina is herself the object of violence. Interestingly, the degree of physical violence she suffers is small. She is, however, subjected to numerous forms of "structural violence" whose aim is to perpetuate existing power-relations, be they economic or gender-related, and hence to "damage the potential and well-being" of those not already in positions of power. Katharina's treatment at the hands of the gutter press and the linguistic means by which her character is assassinated have already formed the subject of several studies and need not be rehearsed here.[9] My concern is with those moments in the text where violation of Katharina is simultaneously implied and criticised by means of the narrator's irony.

When the police invade her flat on the morning after her meeting with Götten, for example, Katharina is "allowed" to get dressed in her bathroom in the presence of policewoman Pletzer. The narrator adds, "Doch durfte die Badezimmertür nicht ganz geschlossen werden; sie wurde von zwei bewaffneten Beamten schärfstens bewacht" (Böll § 13/ 18).[10] The word "bewachen," normally translated as "to guard," refers grammatically to the door, but the feminine pronoun "sie" contains the possibility of ambiguity: it could also refer back to Katharina. In addition, "be*wachen*"—from the same root as the English "watch"— implies relations of *looking* in a way that "guard" does not, a reading that is supported by the word "schärfstens," a common modifier of verbs of *perception*. ("To watch over" would be a possible equivalent.) So what appears to be a neutral description of security measures actually implies that Katharina is the victim of voyeuristic looking on the part of the police. The fact that the two policemen are armed also needs interpretation, since we already know that the officers who raided the flat are armed (Böll §11/16), and the detail is therefore redundant. I would suggest here that the common metaphor "phallus=weapon" is operative, highlighting the aspect of sexual aggression implicit in the act of looking without being seen.[11] Later, in police custody, Katharina insists on paying herself for a snack, "obwohl einer der jungen Beamten, der am Morgen ihre Badezimmertür bewacht hatte, während sie sich anzog, bereit war, 'ihr einen auszugeben'" (Böll §16/ 25).[12] Although it remains unstated, there is an implied causal link here between the guarding of

---

[9] In addition to Römhild, see in particular Eberhard Schieffele, "Kritische Sprachanalyse in Heinrich Bölls *Die verlorene Ehre der Katharina Blum*," Basis 9, 1979: 169-87.

[10] "But the bathroom door was not permitted to be closed; it/she was observed with the closest attention by two armed officers."

[11] According to this logic, it is only by taking possession of the gun/phallus that Katharina can intervene in the patriarchal society that oppresses her, which is, of course, precisely what she does.

[12] "although one of the young officers, who had watched over her bathroom door that morning, offered to 'stand her one.'"

the bathroom and the offer to buy Katharina a snack, adding to the impression that "extremely attractive Blum" (Böll §12/ 18) must have been spied on as she got dressed.

The desire that manifests itself in the above act of voyeurism emerges repeatedly throughout the text. Indeed, Katharina becomes an object of desire for almost all the men with whom she comes into contact. One of the first things she is asked when her flat is raided is "Hat er dich denn gefickt,"[13] a question that is utterly unmotivated in terms of the criminal investigation, and betrays instead an uncontrollable sexual jealousy. It remains unclear whether this question was posed by Inspector Beizmenne or Public Prosecutor Hach, but the latter is deemed the more likely culprit, since he is widely regarded as a lecher and would have liked to indulge in "die so grob definierte Tätigkeit" with her himself (Böll § 12/ 18).[14] Desire also manifests itself in the advances that Katharina has to endure from priests (Böll § 24/ 44), her former employer Dr Kluthen (Böll § 15/ 21), drunken friends of her current employer (Böll § 17/ 26), and Sträubleder. Even Beizmenne's young assistant, Walter Moeding, becomes erotically attracted to Katharina by the end of her first interrogation (Böll § 20/ 30). Ultimately, even Blorna begins to neglect his appearance and personal hygiene after her arrest, and insists on a pathetic ritual of hand-holding when he visits her in prison (Böll § 57/ 117-8).[15] Charlotte Ghurye sees Katharina as exerting an "almost mysterious charm" on men (Ghurye 67), but this argument misses the point because it turns the question of agency back onto Katharina. The fact that practically *every* man in the book appears to lust after Katharina represents a moment of comical excess that serves to ironise male desire, especially since Katharina resolutely rebuffs all advances.

Behind the comic excess, though, a more serious point is being made. Every male-female relationship is seen as one of latent sexual aggression, especially when that relationship is framed by an institutional context: in a police station, the workplace, or church. Institutions are shown to perpetuate power-relations that keep women in positions of inferiority by reducing them to objects of desire. This is what Harris means by "structural violence," and Böll's critique of institutions has to be seen simultaneously as a critique of the patriarchal society that these institutions represent.

---

[13] "Did he fuck you then?"

[14] "the activities so coarsely described"

[15] It becomes clear that even this ostensibly harmless handholding is a form of violation. The narrator stresses that this "Händchenhalten" is "eine vollkommen einseitige Sache" ("a perfectly one-sided matter", Böll § 57/ 118), which echoes Katharina's own definition of "Zudringlichkeit" ("forwardness") as "eine einseitige Handlung" ("a one-sided act") during her police interviews (Böll § 18/ 27).

The Seductions of Violence: Schlöndorff and von Trotta's Film
The Lost Honor of Katharina Blum

The film version of *The Lost Honor of Katharina Blum* was a co-production between the television station Westdeutscher Rundfunk (WDR), Schlöndorff's company Bioskop, and a German subsidiary of the American production and distribution company Paramount Orion. This alone meant that the political and economic pressures on Schlöndorff were not the same as those faced by Böll and his publishers. The fact that the film was partly funded by a public-service broadcaster resulted in the modification of the disclaimer at the beginning of Böll's text so as to remove all references to the *Bild* newspaper. More importantly, the involvement of a large commercial distributor meant that emphasis was inevitably going to be placed on box-office success, the exigencies of which necessarily exert a considerable influence on film form.[16]

Böll's ironic narrator and his multiperspectival narrative techniques thus give way to a linear narrative made in what Bordwell and Thompson describe as "a classically straightforward style" (Bordwell 487). Despite sharply diverging opinions as to the political import and aesthetic adequacy of the extensive changes made by Schlöndorff and von Trotta in adapting *The Lost Honor of Katharina Blum* for the screen, critics agree that the film's mode of address is primarily emotional where Böll's text had been cerebral. The main effect is to create audience sympathy with Katharina's plight. Martha Wallach's characterological study, for example, shows how Katharina corresponds in large measure to "German" (i.e. capitalist and patriarchal) fantasies of the ideal citizen and the ideal woman. She argues that Katharina's subservience is emphasised in the film, exaggerating the extent of her victimisation and turning her into "a heroine with whom the German reading public could identify" (Wallach 66-9). Robert C. Reimer points out that the numerous shot-reverse shot sequences and close-ups of Katharina herself mean that "viewers come to identify with all the indignities Katharina has to endure" (Reimer 65).[17] For Lester Friedman, motivic repetition is the key device: crosses show that Katharina and her friends are constantly "targeted," while the visual symbolism of windows and mirrors imply that they are "almost literally encased in glass," unable to "protect themselves from constant, insidious surveillance" (Friedman

---

[16] The only critic to mention the potential political effects of production is Jack Zipes in "The Political Dimensions of *The Lost Honour of Katharina Blum*." Zipes links Schlöndorff's courting of a commercial distributor to the lack of developed left-wing culture in the Federal Republic, and points out the contradiction in trying to enlist established corporations and institutions in order to point to the need for opposition to the political status quo.

[17] Cf. also Wolfgang Gast, Knut Hickethier and Burkhard Vollmers.

247). The clear division of characters into "good" and "bad" and the concomitant simplification of moral issues are mentioned by several critics, most impressively in Anna K. Kuhn's essay "Schlöndorffs *Die verlorene Ehre der Katharina Blum*: Melodrama und Tendenz."[18] For Kuhn, the film reduces Böll's aesthetic experiment to an impassioned polemic against yellow journalism, and becomes a tendentious melodrama in which the audience is impelled to identify with the positive characters' suffering.

Despite widespread agreement among critics that identification with Katharina takes place, however, the means by which this is created has not yet been fully explored. A detailed reading of looking relations within the world of the film will allow us to understand precisely how identification with the heroine is encouraged.

The Lost Honor of Katharina Blum is, to a very large extent, structured around linguistic exchange rather than action, and so it is unsurprising that the shot-reverse shot sequences noted by Reimer should be so prevalent. This alone, however, cannot account for the phenomenon of identification, since any shot-reverse shot sequence involves constant shifting from one character's optical point of view to another's. Point of view has to be considered in conjunction with acting: the gestures and inflections of voice that give looks their meaning.

Two contrasting examples of looking are provided by Katharina and Götten on the one hand, and Katharina and public prosecutor Peter Hach on the other. As Götten enters the party at the beginning of the film, the camera is just behind him, with the result that the spectator and Götten first see Katharina at the same moment. Katharina comes towards the camera and walks past, holding Götten's gaze and looking back at him as she walks down the corridor. Shortly afterwards, the camera is behind Katharina's left shoulder as she looks at Götten through a glass door. He returns the look with an expression of benignancy, and the same exchange of looks is repeated soon afterwards, just before the pair begin to dance. The interesting thing about this relay of looks is that it implies reciprocity of desire by emphasising Katharina as an *active* participant in the exchange, and this is later reinforced during a flashback, as Katharina thinks back to the night of the party. For the only time in the film, the two heads are photographed in profile, facing each other and filling the whole of the frame, implying not only intimacy, but equality within the exchange of looks.

Katharina's first encounter with Hach, however, is quite different. Once her flat has been ransacked, a shot from Katharina's point of view shows Hach coming towards her and recollecting that he has seen her somewhere before. When Katharina points out that he was often pre-

[18] Cf. also Zipes 410-11.

sent at parties held by her employers, the Blornas, he tells her that appearing before the police in such scanty clothing (she is in her dressing gown) does not create a favourable impression. As he says this, a further shot from Katharina's point of view allows us to witness Hach as he looks her up and down with the stereotypical male gaze of proprietorial erotic appraisal. Hach's aggressive speech and gestures make it clear that looking relations here are fundamentally one-sided: the public prosecutor is the bearer of the gaze, and the woman its powerless object.[19] Furthermore, because Hach's act of looking Katharina up and down is represented from *her* point of view rather than his, the spectator is sutured into the film as victim rather than bearer of the objectifying male gaze.[20] This in turn encourages identification with the humiliation suffered by the screen protagonist.

Identification and, consequently, emotional involvement with the heroine, then, are created by the relays of looks between characters, and are the primary means by which Schlöndorff and von Trotta attempt to convey the critical moment of Böll's story. If, however, we bring a consideration of spectatorship to bear on the question of violence and patriarchy, the film of *Katharina Blum* emerges as much more problematic. The aspect of spectatorship on which I wish to focus is the way in which the structure of the film addresses spectators, positioning them physically, psychically, and ideologically in relation to the world represented on screen.[21]

In an early and highly influential contribution to the study of cinema spectatorship, Laura Mulvey pointed out that cinematic apparatus places the spectator in the position of a voyeur, of one who enjoys not only the pleasure of looking without being seen, but also the power that accrues to the bearer of the gaze.[22] Schlöndorff and von Trotta's *Katharina Blum* is concerned to a high degree with the relationship between voyeurism and power. Several critics have pointed out that the footage from surveillance cameras turns the film spectator into a voyeur and implicates him or her in the police's guilt.[23] But the thematisation of

---

[19] This is the first in a series of exchanges that show Hach to be obsessed with sex. It is he, for example, who always asks sex-related questions during Katharina's interrogations.

[20] For a discussion of suture in film theory, see Kaja Silverman, *The Subject of Semiotics* (New York: Oxford UP, 1983) 194-236.

[21] Judith Mayne's classic study *Cinema and Spectatorship* (London: Routledge, 1993) gives a lucid critical account of various approaches to spectatorship.

[22] Mulvey goes on to relate the voyeuristic pleasure of the cinema to Lacan's mirror phase and the formation of the ego, but the complexities of her analysis are not of direct relevance to the current argument.

[23] See e.g. Friedman 246; Kuhn 137. Reimer also makes a passing reference to this aspect of the film (63).

voyeurism permeates *Katharina Blum* to a much greater extent. It is an element of the film that has not yet received systematic attention, partly because it undermines the arguments concerning identification with Katharina Blum, which, as we have seen, are so prevalent in the existing critical literature.

Acts of voyeurism are repeatedly dramatised within the represented world of the film, and the female body is repeatedly constituted as the object of the voyeuristic gaze. As Katharina is being escorted to a police car after her arrest, she is pursued by numerous photojournalists and has her head held forcibly back by a policewoman so that the press photographers might get a view of her face. The power of the gaze is shown not only to be intimately linked to institutional power, but to constitute a form of violence in itself. More importantly, we later see the published photograph, from Katharina's point of view, on the front page of the ZEITUNG, making it clear that institutional power is mobilised in order to turn Katharina into a media spectacle. At a later stage, the journalist Werner Tötges hands Beizmenne the Blum family album, and a shot from their point of view depicts two portraits of Katharina as a young woman. Tötges's quasi-erotic stroking of the picture makes clear the component of desire in this look, and the power relations involved are implied when Tötges offers to give the photograph of Katharina to Beizmenne. Again, Katharina has become a spectacle, an image for exchange. The obsession of the police with the secret accumulation of images is made apparent throughout the film by the backdrop of the photoboard in the police station. When Katharina arrives for interview, she witnesses close-ups of Götten being attached to the board, and numerous later scenes take place against this photographic reminder of the ubiquity of police surveillance.

It may be an overstatement to claim that these examples of voyeuristic looking *create* a critical spectator-position, but they certainly offer the possibility of such a position. In the case of the press photographers, this is due to the fact that the voyeurs are themselves represented in the act of looking, and their looking is predicated on actual physical violence being perpetrated against Katharina. When we see the resulting press photograph from Katharina's optical point of view, the viewing situation is influenced by our foreknowledge of the violation that preceded the photograph. This blocks uncritical consumption of the media image and encourages critical reflection on the relationship between violence and the gaze. A similar point can be made about the moment where Katharina becomes aware of the police photographs of Götten. Structures of identification have already aligned the spectator firmly with Katharina, with the result that he or she shares Katharina's alarm at the extent of police incursion into the privacy of individuals. Conversely, both Beizmenne and Tötges are established as villains.[24] So

although the photographs of the young Katharina are seen from Beizmenne's point of view, the film's structures of identification allow the
spectator to adopt a detached or critical attitude towards the voyeuristic gaze.

Other representations of voyeuristic looking, however, are more
ambiguous in the spectator position they imply. The very title sequence
of the film involves a plain-clothes police officer taking black-and-white
footage of Götten as he crosses the Rhine on a flat-bottomed car ferry.
The surveillance cameras provide secondary footage at other points in
the film as well, for example when Götten and the party guests are
being trailed by a police car, or when Katharina and Götten return to
her flat after the party. In all of these cases, the spectator is forced to
occupy the position of the surveillance cameraman and, as we have
already seen, is implicated in police voyeurism as a result. This link
between the spectator and the police is underscored by an episode of
the film in which we see a group of detectives being briefed in a minia-
ture cinema, with the surveillance footage being shown on a screen in
front of them. The situation of the characters on screen replicates the situation of the cinematic spectator, and functions as a kind of *mise-en-
abyme* of the act of viewing.

Admittedly, the use of surveillance footage in the title sequence
does represent the cameraman in the act of filming. But rather than
opening up the possibility of a critical spectator-position, the sequence
actually encourages identification with the forces of law and order. This
is firstly because no clear structures of identification are in place beyond
the contrast between Götten's rugged good looks and the staid, middle-
aged cameraman who is clearly a victim of the 1950s *Freßwelle*. Secondly, the first thing that Götten does is to steal a car. Contravening the ideology of private property and the values of consumer society makes
him a criminal, and renders him —provisionally at least— a thorough-
ly legitimate object of observation in the eyes of the law-abiding spectator. Instead of criticising this form of structural violence, then, the film
appears to endorse it. This is further illustrated by the footage of Katharina and Götten returning to her apartment, where a slow zoom into a
super-close-up of the lovers kissing turns the spectator into a voyeur of
the most crass kind: one who looks without being seen at the erotic
activities of others. It is notable that as the couple embrace, Götten has

---

[24] Several theorists have examined spectatorship in relation to intertextuality, demonstrating, for example, that structures of identification are in part dependent on familiarity with the earlier roles and media personality of the actors concerned. (See Mayne,
chapters 3 and 6 for a survey of such approaches.) Mario Adorf, who plays Beizmenne
in the film of *The Lost Honor of Katharina Blum*, had established himself in the 1950s as a
screen villain, and this would clearly have affected audience reaction to the character of
Beizmenne, one of Katharina's main antagonists.

his back to the camera, while Katharina's face is fully exposed, thus constituting her once again as a spectacle.

A further complication is that what appears to be surveillance footage is in fact incompatible with the technology that would have been used to shoot films of this kind. This can be ascertained even without recourse to the history of surveillance cameras. In the first sequence, for example, there is a jump-cut as Götten drives past the camera position, and a rapid shift in camera angle and height of framing. The image remains in black and white, the central cross indicates that the film is notionally being taken through the viewfinder of a cinecam. But the rapid shift in camera position would be impossible if Götten were indeed being filmed by the detective. Similarly, the sequence in which Katharina and Götten arrive at her apartment and enter the lift involves complex camera movements including crane shots with backward tracking, panning, and zooming. The equipment necessary to achieve such footage would be so bulky that no covert cameraman could possibly conceal himself. Observations of this kind are pointless if they serve merely to bolster naive arguments concerning filmic realism. The point I wish to make, however, is more serious. Although we appear to be merely "eavesdropping" on footage whose intended audience are characters within the film, the elaborate cinematography in these sequences means that the *actual* address must be to a spectator *outside* the represented world. Thus the issue of voyeurism cannot be reduced to police surveillance activities; rather, it is a directorial strategy whose primary function is to constitute the spectator as a voyeur.

This strategy recurs at numerous points throughout the film. We have seen above that the narration of the episode in which Katharina is forced to get dressed with her bathroom door ajar is highly ironic in Böll's text, and implies voyeurism on the part of the police whilst providing no opportunity for erotic gratification on the part of the reader. The narration of this episode in the film, however, has a rather different effect. Katharina and Frau Pletzer go into the bathroom, leaving the door open. To the left of the screen stands one of the armed policemen, while the camera focuses on Katharina's undressing and undergoing what is euphemistically called a "full body search." In typical Hollywood fashion, the height of framing corresponds roughly to eye-level, but the camera cannot be equated with the optical point of view of any particular character. Rather, it constitutes a disembodied look, suturing the spectator into the events on screen by forcing him or her into the role of voyeur.[25] Meanwhile, the policeman looks dutifully outward,

---

[25] The aspect of seeing without being seen is doubled by the presence of a mirror behind Katharina, which gives the spectator access to the side of her that is turned away from the camera. Claims by critics that the view through the bathroom door intensifies the

and is thereby exculpated. His later offer to buy Katharina a snack correspondingly appears as nothing more than a "nice gesture," and is unmotivated by the wider thematics of the text.

There are further sequences that construct the naked female body as a spectacle and hence a legitimate object of the voyeuristic gaze. The first of these is the shower scene, which is utterly unmotivated by the plot or the demands of the adaptation. Close-ups of Katharina's face beneath the jets of water are reminiscent of one of the two typical addresses of soft-core pornography, namely the "private masturbatory fantasy in relation to which the spectator is situated as voyeur" (Annette Kuhn 114).[26] The second sequence is arguably more troubling, and concerns the depiction of Katharina washing her mother's corpse in the hospital morgue. The camera is placed obliquely behind the laid-out body, and the mise-en-scène is such that despite the presence of four nurses and Katharina around the table, the naked corpse is fully accessible to the viewer's gaze. The camera occupies the position of a disembodied observer, suturing the spectator into the scene as, yet again, a voyeur.

The implications of all this from the point of view of violence and patriarchy is that the film repeatedly constitutes the female body as something to be looked at by a controlling (male) gaze. This is particularly evident in the dressing scene, where the spectator is firmly situated within the same physical *and institutional* space as the police officers. But the other sequences, too, offer the possibility of seeing without being seen, which emphasises the element of power inherent in such structures of looking. Two of the key terms in the definition of structural violence given above were its latent institutional presence and its surreptitious deployment in such a way as to perpetuate social inequality. One of the institutions in which structural violence can be witnessed is the cinema, and this is illustrated by the film of *Katharina Blum* whose mode of address compels the spectator to take part in scopophilic acts that constitute violations of privacy and perpetuate power relations in which women are forced into the role of the passive object of a gaze that is often equated with institutionally powerful males.

The critique of violence and patriarchy that can be discerned in Böll's narrative, then, gives way to something much more ambiguous in Schlöndorff and von Trotta's film adaptation of the text. On the one

---

audience's sense of victimisation (Wallach 68) or that the mirrors reflect "both [Katharina's] humiliation and indignation" (Reimer 248) ignore the mode of address that this sequence creates.

[26] Reimer's point that Schlöndorff and von Trotta's film titillates viewers even as they feel outrage at the mistreatment of the heroine (Reimer 63) hits the nail squarely on the head, but is not explored further in his own analysis.

hand, cinematography and excellent acting allow a differentiated portrayal of looking relations within the represented world in order to distinguish between "Zudringlichkeit" and "Zärtlichkeit," between desiring gazes that represent, respectively, sexual aggression and mutual erotic attraction. At the same time, however, the critical potential of this technique is subverted by numerous sequences in which the spectator-position constructed by the cinematic apparatus is that of a voyeur, of one who sees without being seen and reaps the pleasure inherent in such looking and the power that results therefrom.

It is at this point that we can return to the substitution of female sexuality for terrorism discussed earlier. We have seen that the primary function of this substitution is to provide an identifiable "perpetrator" who then becomes the legitimate object of disciplinary measures carried out by patriarchal institutions. The manifold ironies of Böll's novel imply that what masquerades as an anti-terrorist investigation is in fact motivated by patriarchal institutions that have an interest in perpetuating existing gender relations. At one level, the film ostensibly reproduces this aspect of Böll's text by encouraging strong identification with Katharina and hence criticism of the forces that oppress her. At another level, however, it repeatedly constructs a spectator-position that allies the spectator with the forces of oppression and repression. Furthermore, the naked female body is turned into either a spectacle of erotic contemplation or a corpse to be examined by the gaze. Schlöndorff and von Trotta's film of *The Lost Honor of Katharina Blum*, then, itself *performs* the very acts of objectification, surveillance, and discipline that Böll's text sets out to criticise.

It is in this sense that it is possible to speak of the "lost gender politics of *Katharina Blum*." Schlöndorff and von Trotta's film cannot avoid the seductions of violence, which in turn leads them away (another sense of "verführen") from the criticism implied by Böll's text and towards a mode of cinematography that reinforces rather than undermines the pervasive link between violence and patriarchy.

Works Cited

Böll, Heinrich. *Die verlorene Ehre der Katharina Blum, oder: Wie Gewalt entstehen und wohin sie führen kann.* Munich: dtv, 1976

Bordwell, David and Kristin Thompson, *Film Art: An Introduction.* 4th ed. New York: MacGraw Hill, 1993.

Friedman, Lester. "Cinematic Techniques in *The Lost Honor of Katharina Blum.*" *Literature/Film Quarterly* 7 (1979): 244-52.

Gast, Wolfgang, Knut Hickethier and Burkhard Vollmers. "Die verlorene Ehre der Katharina Blum." *Literaturverfilmung.* Ed. Wolfgang Gast. Bamberg: Buchners, 1993. 126-33.

Ghurye, Charlotte W. *The Writer and Society: Studies in the Fiction of Günter Grass and Heinrich Böll.* Bern: Lang, 1976.

Harris, Nigel. *"Die verlorene Ehre der Katharina Blum*: The Problem of Violence." *The Narrative Fiction of Heinrich Böll: Social Conscience and Literary Achievement.* Ed. Michael Butler. Cambridge: Cambridge UP, 1994. 198-218.

Kramer Moeller, Aleidine. *The Woman as Survivor: The Evolution of the Female Figure in the Works of Heinrich Böll.* New York: Lang, 1991.

Kuhn, Anna K. "Schlöndorffs *Die verlorene Ehre der Katharina Blum*: Melodrama und Tendenz. *Literaturverfilmung.* Ed. Wolfgang Gast. Bamberg: Buchners, 1993. 134-41.

Kuhn, Annette. *Women's Pictures: Feminism and Cinema.* London: Routledge and Kegan Paul, 1982.

Linke, Uli. *German Bodies: Race and Representation after Hitler.* New York: Routledge, 1999.

Mayne, Judith. *Cinema and Spectatorship.* London: Routledge, 1993.

Mulvey, Laura "Visual Pleasure and Narrative Cinema." *Visual and Other Pleasures.* Basingstoke: Macmillan, 1989. 14-26.

Musolff, Andreas. *Krieg gegen die Öffentlichkeit: Terrorismus und politischer Sprachgebrauch.* Opladen: Westdeutscher Verlag, 1996.

Nägele, Rainer. *Heinrich Böll: Einführung in das Werk und die Forschung.* Frankfurt am Main: Fischer Athenäum, 1976.

Reimer, Robert C. "Applause and Volker Schlöndorff and Margarete von Trotta's *Die verlorene Ehre der Katharina Blum.*" *Crime in Motion Pictures.* Ed. Douglas Radcliff-Umstead. Kent: Kent State UP, 1986. 63-67.

Römhild, Dorothee. *Die Ehre der Frau ist unantastbar: Das Bild der Frau im Werk Heinrich Bölls.* Pfaffenweiler: Centaurus, 1991.

Sandford, John. *The New German Cinema.* London: Oswald Wolff, 1980.

Schieffele, Eberhard. "Kritische Sprachanalyse in Heinrich Bölls *Die verlorene Ehre der Katharina Blum.*" *Basis* 9 (1979): 169-87.

Schneider, Peter *...schon bist du ein Verfassungsfeind.* Berlin: Rotbuch, 1975.

Silverman, Kaja. *The Subject of Semiotics.* New York: Oxford University Press, 1983.

Wallach, Marta. "Ideal and Idealized Victims: The Lost Honor of the Marquise von O., Effi Briest, and Katharina Blum in Prose and Film." *Women in German Yearbook* 1, 1985: 61-75.

Zipes, Jack. "The Political Dimensions of *The Lost Honour of Katharina Blum.*" *Perspectives on German Cinema.* Ed. Terri Ginsberg and Kirsten Moana Thompson. New York: G.K. Hall, 1996. 401-412.

Julia Neissl

University of Salzburg, Austria

Violent (Male) Language in Austrian Women Writers' Discourse on Sexuality: Examples in Elisabeth Reichart, Elfriede Jelinek and Elfriede Czurda

The innumerable forms of violence present in patriarchal systems orig-inate in their hierarchical structures and the binary codes that these imply (female/male, weak/strong etc). Men's ostensible superiority gives them gender-based power and therefore authority over others, including women. In this case, I use the word "violence" not only to indicate an action against the will of another, but also the reproduction of the violence inherent in social structures (cf. Ohms 18). This view is shared by many, for example, Van Aaken (8) believes "dass sich die 'Männlichkeit des Mannes' durch die Lust ausdrückt, andere zu unter-werfen und dem eigenen Willen gefügig zu machen, — eine Männ-lichkeit, die sich zuerst gegenüber Frauen behauptet" (Van Aaken 8).[1]

In her historical analysis of the origins of the patriarchal system, Gerda Lerner refers in particular to the decisive role played by the exchange value of women in the development of patriarchal social forms. She connects this idea, as formulated by Lévi-Strauss, with the component of sexuality. Woman as exchange object "ist in sehr unter-schiedlichen Formen denkbar, etwa als gewaltsame Entführung der Frauen aus ihrem eigenen Stamm (Brautraub), als rituelle Defloration oder Vergewaltigung, auch als durch Verhandlungen arrangierte Ver-mählung" (Lerner 71).[2] When love, emotional ties and sexuality are conceptualised, women's supposedly natural inferiority plays a central role: the woman must be available to the man — otherwise he can claim his "right" with violence. In her analysis Van Aaken even goes so far as to say that in the majority of patriarchal societies, most marriages began with a rape (i.e. the marriage arrangements made for the daughter by the parents; cf. van Aaken 295). Lerner also points out the connection

---

[1] "'man's masculinity' expresses itself in the desire to subjugate others and force his will upon them — a masculinity which asserts itself towards women first of all."

[2] "takes on many different guises, for example, as the violent abduction of women from their own tribe ("Brautraub"), as ritual defloration or rape, as marriages arranged through negotiations."

between subjugation by (sexual) violence and its consequences, i.e. pregnancy that bound the woman to the man and his family not just physically but also psychologically, compelling her to be loyal: "Wieder einmal machte ihre biologische Funktion die Frauen anpassungsfähiger im Hinblick auf diese neue, kulturell geschaffene Rolle als Unterpfand" (Lerner 72).[3]

At the symbolic level, the relation of the trinity patriarchy-sexuality-violence is made clear through the "weapon" which men use. The phallus principally means the maintenance of the status quo and signifies male potency; as such it serves both to delineate the "other" and as an "executive instrument" in the sexualised forms of violence with which women are often confronted (cf. Ohms 1993). For example, Thürmer-Rohr writes in her text on women accomplices: "Der Mann verschafft sich die Erfahrung, Macht gegenüber einer Frau zu spüren, zu sehen, auszuprobieren, auszukosten — über sein kardinales Männlichkeits — und Machtsymbol, seine Sexualität. Er verschafft sich selbst den Machterweis, indem er — mit Körperkraft und zumeist strammen Penis — der Frau den Ohnmachtserweis erteilt und Unterwerfung erzwingt" (Thürmer-Rohr 25).[4]

As can be seen from the above, on the one hand one can establish a clear historical connection between violence, sexuality and the origins of patriarchal social forms. On the other, the primacy of violence in all kinds of relationships becomes apparent even in today's society when we consider that after thirty years of the New Women's Movement, issues of sexual abuse, violence in relationships, the need for therapy and "safe zones" such as safe houses for women are still central concerns of women's politics.

In the last two decades of the twentieth century this combination of patriarchal social structures and ideas of sexuality along with their (violent) manifestations has been thematised on a linguistic level by several Austrian women writers. Sexuality becomes the central sphere of female experience in literature, in which confrontation with the male (symbolic) order is inevitable. There is a very close link in these texts between a critique of the language that the authors have at their disposal and the social system that has produced this language. My contribution concentrates on three works by Austrian women writers: Elisabeth Reichart's *Fotze* ("Cunt," 1993), Elfriede Jelinek's *Lust* (1989) and Elfriede Czurda's *Die Giftmörderinnen* ("Murderesses by Poison," 1993).

---

[3] "Once again, their biological function made women more adaptable to this new, culturally created role of a pledge."

[4] "The man's experience of what it is to have power over a woman to feel, see, try and taste power — comes from his primary symbol of masculinity and power, his sexuality. He proves his power — with physical strength and mostly an erect penis æ by proving the woman her lack of power and forcing her to submit."

Critique of language becomes apparent as the protagonist of Elisabeth Reichart's *Fotze* sets out on a search for female identity at the limits of available words and with it of liveable possibilities, only to discover that this identity exists exclusively in the form of male definitions with violent connotations. Long passages of the text are concerned with finding a name for her sexual organs, which she has never known what to call: "Er hat mir ein Wort zurückgegeben für mein Geschlecht und meine Erregung aufgefangen mit Berührungen, in seinem Mund spüre ich meinen Orgasmus, und die Hände dringen durch den Schweiß bis zu ihm und mir. Er ist in mich gedrungen mit seinem Wortrausch" (Reichart 7).[5] Actual physical contact and the arousal caused by naming the sexual organs are mixed here. The "nameless existence" is given the name "Fotze." This term has several meanings in German: "mouth," "slap," and "vagina" ("cunt"). Thus the component parts of the text are present from the very beginning: a nexus of language, violence and sexuality (cf. Fliedl 85). The naming of the female sex organs is one of the protagonist's first steps in her search for identity. For a while, this first experience blinds her to the male power of definition, which lies behind it. The protagonist only realises the link between power and sexuality when the "virtual man" (with whom she has only had telephone sex up to this point) appears in her reality. Now the word "Fotze" sounds "used up," ("verbraucht") it tastes "nach Herrschaft, ich wollte nicht beherrscht sein" (Reichart 95).[6] Having realised her continuing dependence on male (linguistic) structures, the protagonist offers resistance by refusing to speak: "Ich entziehe ihm die Bezeichnung für sein DING, nenne es nicht mehr bei dem von ihm gewünschten Namen" (29).[7]

The strength of male expression is contrasted by female speechlessness/wordlessness, the man is unmasked as word-powerful and dominant (43). "Aneignung der männlichen Gewaltsprache durch eine Frau [zeigt] die Verbindung von Sexualität und Gewalt, Eroberungszwang und Krieg. Nach und nach wird über die Suche nach einer weiblichen Sexualität ein Defizit der Sprache, weibliche Sprachlosigkeit, erfahren" (Pfeiferovà 46).[8] The male position is also made clear at a grammatical

---

[5] "He's given me back a word for my sex and caught up my arousal with touch, in his mouth I feel my orgasm, the hands penetrate through the sweat to him and me. He has penetrated me with his ecstasy of words."

[6] "like domination, I didn't want to be dominated."

[7] "I take away from him the designation for his THING, I don't call it by the name he wants any more."

[8] "Appropriation of violent male speech by a woman [shows] the link between sexuality and violence, the compulsion to conquer and wage wars. Over and over, the search for a female sexuality leads to the discovery of a deficit in language, of female speechlessness."

level in the text, when the female first-person narrator, who is trying to become a subject, realises that her sisters' sentences do not contain a subject. Their communication behaviour has reduced them to the status of object. The ("male"/female) first-person narrator discovers: "bei mir fing jedoch jeder Satz mit Ich an, austauschbares Ich, omnipotentes Ich, es richtete Schaden an" (Reichart 116).[9] There is a clear link between the missing word for the woman's own sex organs and her uncertainty about sex, as well as the suppression of desire which she connects with her mother. The mother appears almost like a nightmare during the sexual act, to strengthen the daughter in her submissive behaviour: "'Beiß die Zähne zusammen, alles geht vorbei, brave Tochter,' hörte ich deine Stimme, während ich zusah, wie ich für Männer nur aus Brust und Geschlecht bestand" (90).[10] In the long run, this unsatisfying sexual life makes the woman rebel and turn to forms of physical defence and resistance. However, a positive solution to the dilemma cannot be found, as, despite her knowledge about the role of violence in relationships, historically reoccurring images of sexual relations and "dreams of Prince Charming" remain stronger. "Fotze ist Reicharts radikalster, konsequentester und damit auch riskantester Versuch, sich mit einer hämmernd brutalen, stellenweise pornographisch vulgären Sprache, mit einer metaphorischen Deterrioration in das Zentrum des Knotens (NS)Gewaltgeschichte-Frau-Sprache-Krieg hineinzuschreiben" (Slibar 23).[11] The polysemantic title is already expressive of these wider implications. In the text, sexuality is unmasked as one of the fundamental violent structures in patriarchal society. It makes it impossible for a first-person female anchored in language to exist. The woman searches for a female identity, she wants to become a subject, not to remain stuck in object status like the women of her parents' generation or even her own sisters. To this end she identifies with her father. However, she fails in the attempt to appropriate his language discovering instead that the language always remains "male;" in the end, this realisation leads to her self-destruction.

In Elfriede Jelinek's novel *Lust* (1989), the male perspective on discourse about sexuality is brought into the foreground emphatically. This anti-pornographic text uses language itself to unmask the violent

---

9 "I on the other hand began every sentence with I, interchangeable I, omnipotent I, it caused damage."

10 " 'Grit your teeth, nothing lasts forever, good girl,' I heard your voice while I saw how for men I was only made up of breasts and sex organs."

11 "*Fotze* is Reichart's most radical, coherent and therefore also riskiest attempt to write herself into the centre of the thematic knot [...] Nazi-Violence-History-Woman-Language-War, by using a pounding, brutal and at times pornographically vulgar language and metaphoric deterioration."

conditions prevalent in heterosexual relationships. A mimetic survey of male discourse unmasks its structures of power and violence, which also manifest in sexuality. The roles in the text are distributed according to the traditional scheme: the man feels desire that he wants to/must satisfy, the woman is the subservient, passive victim, the "used" one. The author herself described the function of the text as follows:

> In dem was ich schreibe, gibt es immer wieder drastische Stellen, aber die sind politisch. Sie haben nicht die Unschuldigkeit des Daseins und den Zweck des Aufgeilens. Sie sollen den Dingen, der Sexualität ihre Geschichte wiedergeben, sie nicht in ihrer scheinbaren Unschuld lassen, sondern die Schuldigen benennen. Die nennen, die sich Sexualität aneignen und das Herr/Knecht-Verhältnis zwischen Männern und Frauen produzieren. Im Patriarchat ist es auch heute noch so, dass nicht Männer und Frauen gleichermaßen genießen, wie sie genießen wollen. Ich will dieses Machtverhältnis aufdecken. (Jelinek in Nagelschmidt 245)[12]

The text is made almost unbearable for the reader by the description of violent sexuality. The primary elements are the innumerable, ever intensifying variations on sexual exploitation and rape of the woman. Sexuality is represented as an exclusively male physical need and negatively connotated. Jelinek not only unmasks patriarchal claims of power in this way but also the misogynistic character of language. The binary character of language, the "phallocentric" system (cf. Lindhoff 97), as Jacques Derrida says, is upheld in all metaphoric areas. Thus progressive-sounding technical vocabulary is reserved for the description of the male genitalia, whereas the female remains bound to ideas of darkness and caverns. For example, "his weapon," the "elec. cable" or "the express train, which thunders along" for the penis, whereas the female genitalia are described as "holes," "tunnels and cavities" or "reeking foxholes." Conventional pornographic language and myths are used to describe the sexual act: the lusting man and the fragmented woman who is broken up into openings (cf. Höfer 106). The violence of the sexual act is continually present and is intensified through innumerable repetitions: "Er zieht in ihren Arsch ein und schlägt ihr Gesicht gegen den Wannenrand. Sie schreit noch einmal" (Jelinek 27).[13]

---

[12] "In all that I write there are always drastic passages, but they are political. They do not have the innocence of being and the purpose to turn the reader on. They are meant to give things and sexuality their history back, not to leave them in their seeming innocence but rather name the guilty parties. I name those who appropriate sexuality as their own and produce the master/servant relationship between men and women. In patriarchy it is still the case today that men and women do not enjoy to the same extent or to the extent they want. I want to uncover these power structures."

[13] "He rams into her arse and hits her face against the edge of the bathtub. She screams once again."

Elfriede Jelinek is not interested in the individual but in the illness in society. Thus her figures are mostly just stereotyped ciphers who fulfil their sexually demarcated roles: "Sie erzählt nicht lediglich von und spricht über Gewaltverhältnisse, sondern sie sucht sie in der Sprache selbst bloßzustellen und entlarvt durch Montage, Verzerrung und Verfremdung die harmonische Lügenhaftigkeit der Sprech- und Denkweisen" (Nagelschmidt 246).[14] The phallus is the only symbol which gives structure both to the discourse of the sexes and their life in society; it is the ultimate active authority (cf. Vinken 13).

The text is also interesting regarding the historical aspects of rape. As mentioned earlier, rape was the departure point in the history of patriarchy, where women were treated as subservient objects. Patriarchy thus even precedes the idea of slavery (cf. Lerner). The constellation of the female protagonist's marital and extra-marital relationships clearly demonstrates a male alliance: on the one hand there is a gang-rape by her lover, a young student, in front of his male and female friends (the complicity of other women is more prominent in the text than any kind of solidarity); on the other hand, husband and lover maintain eye-contact during the marital rape. This act clearly reinstates the husband's position as "owner," but also serves the sexual satisfaction of both male parties. While one masturbates at home, the other rapes his wife in the car — the woman is reduced to the role of exchange object (cf. Baackmann 188).

Jelinek has already commented on whether and to what extent these links between patriarchy and violence are still relevant in 21st century literature. Although her latest novel *Gier* ("Greed," 2000) is thematically no longer exclusively about sexuality as the central aspect of the prevailing conditions of violence, it is nevertheless a continuation of *Lust* in more than its title. Although "Greed" is more about money than sexual satisfaction, claims of possession are woven into the substance of sexual relationships here as well. The subservient role of women and their desire to experience themselves as victims is directly addressed in the text: "Es kann grundsätzlich alles mit Frauen gemacht werden, als hätten sie etwas angestellt und wollten bestraft werden. Und was mit ihnen noch nie gemacht worden ist, das machen sie dafür umso lieber" (Jelinek 2000: 41).[15]

Since the 1980s, Elfriede Czurda's texts have also dealt with the connections between patriarchal violence and sexuality. In contrast to

---

14 "She does not just describe and tell of violent relationships, but instead tries to reveal them in language itself and unmasks the deceptive harmony in our ways of thinking and speaking with montage, distortion and alienation."

15 "Basically you can do anything with women, it's as if they'd done something wrong and wished to be punished for it. And if it's something that's never been done before, they're all the more willing."

her novel *Kerner* (1985), which thematizes the sexual abuse of a child and the perpetrator-victim complex, *Die Giftmörderinnen* (Murderesses by Poison, 1993) describes heterosexual and lesbian relationships in which women at least attempt to break out of their respective life situations, despite patterns of dependence and repression mechanisms being represented as unavoidable. Czurda has often thematised sexual relationships and illusions of love "hervorgerufen durch Wort-gaukeleien" (Classen 2).[16] *Die Giftmörderinnen* is interesting as it represents more or less a variation on the texts I have already discussed. The author describes a short-lived escape from frustrating everyday marital life for two women, one with a dreadful stepmother, the other with a violent husband. Their short-term rebellion takes the form of a lesbian relationship. However, ultimately they do not manage to break free of restrictive structures: after the oppressed wife has poisoned her husband, her girlfriend deserts and betrays her. The author's intention was to leave no illusions standing, therefore even the "alternative" homosexual relationship is negatively judged and its sexuality linguistically unmasked.

In the heterosexual relationship, the sexual act is described as follows: "Hans zerrt Else ins Bett. Da kann Else nichts machen. Nur Hans tut was [...] Da! Da ist eine Hand. Sucht die Schenkel. Wird sie gleich finden. Hat fünf schreckliche Finger zum Wühlen. Hat Finger, die bohren. Wie Maul Würfe. Wie Würmer. [...] Hans schnauft. Hans hechelt. Hans zittert. Hans schwitzt" (Czurda 32).[17] In the lesbian relationship, the egocentric perspective and role distribution according to binary codes is represented in the roles of the active and passive sexual partner: "Komm Erika, sagt Else, ich will dir mit der Hand unter den Rock schlüpfen. [...] Else schlüpft, Ach Else, sagt Erika. Erika beginnt zu schnaufen. Es geht in die Geschmacks Richtung von Erika. Erika fällt mitten in ihrem Schwarm. Sie stöhnt. Else geht mit Erika die ganze Arithmetik durch. [...] Sie hakeln sich an und kuppeln sich fest. Stimmt genau. Diese Zwinge hält. So ist die Liebe" (107).[18]

As far as the heterosexual act is concerned, the striking elements are the distribution of the active and passive roles as well as the rape images and the destruction of the woman resulting in her rejection of

---

[16] "conjured up by word tricks."

[17] "John pulls Else into bed. Else can't do anything about it. Only John does something [...] There! There is a hand. Looks for the thighs. Finds them straight away. Has five dreadful fingers to burrow with. Fingers which dig. Like moles. Like worms. [...] John pants. John gasps. John quivers. John sweats."

[18] "Come Erika, says Else, I want to slip my hand under your skirt. [...] Else slips, oh Else, says Erika. Erika begins to pant. It goes according to Erika's taste. Erika falls into her craze. She moans. Else goes through all the arithmetic with Erika. [...] They hook unto each other and couple themselves tight. Perfect fit. This clasp holds. Such is love."

her own body. Male activity is connected with physical but also verbal violence, expressed above all through the modulation of language. The devaluation of the woman is made clear for example in word chains such as "Losinsbettmitdirdustreunendesluder" (32).[19] Thorpe describes this writing strategy as an "attack on the noun." In comparison with Verena Stefan's Häutungen (Shedding, 1975), which looks for female speech in metaphors of nature, she discovers: "Czurda's effort is by far the more radical of the two and holds out hope for a new way of using language by deconstructing words, nouns in particular, into their constituent parts, similar to building blocks in order to expose their underlying meaning" (Thorpe 498).

The lesbian variant contains the activity of both women, but a closer inspection reveals clearly that Else often concentrates on living up to Erika's sexual expectations. Erika is in a position of power over Else, she is the language user, she uses the same tactics as Else's husband to make Else dependent on her. In her letters the violent component becomes visible, for example when she writes: "Liebste Elsefee Liebste was für ein Rausch mit den Sinnen braust mit einer Leidenschaft ohne Besinnung und Gesang, [...] daß ich nicht mehr von dir laß so wie du nie mehr fortkommst von mir in der größten Liebe, ob du es möchtest oder nicht. [...] So rammt Erika ihren Denk Zettel in den Ehe Ausgleich" (Czurda 51).[20] Although lesbian sexuality also seems compulsive, satisfaction is possible for both women. Here the text uses the plural, both of them roll groaning on the ground. However, needless to say, even on the linguistic level, the binding, restrictive nature of the relationship is omnipresent.

Similar to the unmasking of the petit-bourgeois ideology of marital heterosexual relationships, the seeming escape into homosexuality fails as an alternative. Accordingly, critics have focussed on this negative aspect of the lesbian relationship. This relationship between two women shows little solidarity — on the contrary, as Lettner says: "Die lesbische Liebesbeziehung zwischen Erika und Else scheidet als programmatische Alternative aus, weil die Gewaltverhältnisse der Liebe, die Verquickung von Begehren und Unterwerfung und die Machtstrukturen in ihr nicht aufgehoben werden können" (Lettner 129).[21] This realisation has less to do with a homophobic structure of the text

19 "Intobedwithyouyouwhore."

20 "Dearest Else-elf, dearest what an ecstasy of senses roars with a passion without thoughts or song [...] I will never leave you just as you will never get away from me in the greatest love, whether you want it or not [...] Thus Erika shoves her lesson into the marriage-compensation."

21 "The lesbian love relationship between Erika and Else does not constitute a programmatic alternative, as it cannot abolish the violence in love, the connection between desire and submission nor the power structures."

than with the author's intention to characterise social relationships as destructive and potentially violent. The homosexual variant is just as functionalised here as the affair with the young student in Jelinek's *Lust*, for example: both are illustrations of yet another shattered illusion. Parallels are to be seen not just in the polarity of violence and love, but also in the nature of the language used by Czurda, which was partly inspired by Jelinek.

The three texts I have referred to were all written in the last two decades of the 20th century. All in all they do not show much optimism as far as sexual relationships and the relationship between the sexes is concerned. They all take sexuality as the crucial point for the thematisation of relationships between women and men. Their specifically Austrian character lies in their combination of a critique of language and social criticism (cf. Gürtler 271).

If we take into account the Lacanian theory which sees the phallus as the most important signifier in the symbolic order (cf. Lindhoff 80), the vicious circle in the writing of female authors becomes clear: the "exclusion" of women from patriarchal social systems leads —in relation to language— to the absence of femininity in the same. Through language learning and the (active) entry into the symbolic order, the mother-child relationship is disturbed, and the father, who stands for law and authority, is experienced as a powerful opponent (cf. Lacan 128). The relation between possessing language and the powerful sex, which means the father and as a result all men, is a decisive factor above all in Elisabeth Reichart's text. The search for a female identity in the male linguistic system is at first satisfied through a strong identification with the father. Identity and power over language are closely linked here: the daughter looking for identity emulates her father and builds with him his "Vaterhäuser" ([male] family homes; Reichart 22). Only gradually does the woman realise that relationships to men and their linguistic power can never be "female" and can only mean new dependency and a continuation of the "history of violence" in the relationships between the sexes. The author therefore concentrates on the search for a female identity through language while unmasking its violent structures and drawing the necessary consequences from this linguistic "non-existence" of the feminine.

Jelinek's and Czurda's texts are dominated by a critique of social relationships and the structures of violence associated with them. They are therefore, unlike Reichart, less interested in individual searches and more in the behaviour of men and women in sexual relationships which they view as a consequence of the social system as a whole. In this web of perpetrators and sufferers of violence, the woman always takes on the part which history has given her: "Denn Überleben bedeutet, geringstmögliche Beschädigung und geringstmögliche Dauer der Qual.

Ums Überleben kämpfen heißt auch hier, ein auf den Mann, auch auf den Mann als Mißhändler gerichtetes, an seinen Handlungen orientiertes, auf ihn aufmerksames, auf ihn reagierendes, taktierendes Verhalten, immer mit dem Ziel, die eigene Schädigung nicht zu vergrößern" (Thürmer-Rohr 29).[23]

The fact that women have taken part in these oppressive structures for such a long time before choosing resistance is partly due to the social norm of living together, of living with men, as Thürmer-Rohr explains (30). Jelinek's and Czurda's critique of language takes the form of a mimetic approach to the text, as described and demonstrated by Luce Irigaray. By discovering the empty spaces and the missing feminine, traditional male discourse is displaced and uncovered. The method works by writing into and questioning as well as writing and thinking further, so that the blind spots which arise from the suppression of the unconscious are illuminated from another, gender-critical perspective (cf. Irigaray 173). The potential for catastrophe and violence inherent in the gender structures and the discourse of love becomes clear in the authors' appropriation of patriarchal discourse. Thus Elfriede Jelinek's *Lust* becomes a repulsive anti-porno, which demonstrates power relationships and dependency in relationships in umpteen descriptions of the sexual act. In Czurda's work, the hierarchical and therefore phallocentric order of relationships of every kind stands to the fore, as here not only the heterosexual, but also the lesbian relationship is characterised by structures of violence and binary divisions into an active and passive, a powerful and subservient partner.

Works Cited

Baackmann, Susanne. *Erklär mir die Liebe. Weibliche Schreibweisen von Liebe* in der deutschen Gegenwartsliteratur. Hamburg: Argument, 1995.

Classen, Albrecht. "Elfriede Czurda.". In: *Kritisches Lexikon der Gegenwartsliteratur.* München: Text +Kritik, 1990.

Czurda, Elfriede. *Die Giftmörderinnen.* Reinbek: Rowohlt, 1993.

Fliedl, Konstanze. "Wortschande." In: *Literatur und Kritik* 277/278 (1993): 85-86.

Gürtler, Christa. "Zum Paradigma der Frauenliteratur in Österreich. über die (Un)-Möglichkeit der Erregung öffentlicher Aufmerksamkeit." *Konflikte — Skandale— Dichterfehden in der österreichischen Literatur.* Ed. Wendelin Schmidt-Dengler et al. Berlin: Erich Schmidt, 1995. 267-279.

Höfer, Günther. "Sexualität und Macht in Elfriede Jelineks Prosa." *Modern Austrian Literature* 23 (1990): 99-110.

[23] "Survival means the least damage possible and the shortest duration of suffering. Here, to fight for survival also means tactically adjusting one's behaviour to the man, even the one who is an abuser, orienting oneself after his actions, being attentive to him, reacting to him, always with the aim of minimising the damage done to oneself."

Irigaray, Luce. *Speculum. Spiegel des anderen Geschlechts*. Frankfurt: Suhrkamp, 1980..

Jelinek, Elfriede. *Lust*. Reinbek: Rowohlt, 1989.

———. *Gier*. Reinbek: Rowohlt, 2000.

Lacan, Jacques. *Schriften II*. Weinheim-Berlin: Quadriga, 1991.

Lerner, Gerda. *Die Entstehung des Patriarchats*. Frankfurt-New York: Campus, 1995.

Lettner, Natalie. "Anderes Geschlecht – andere Räume? Zu (Hetero-)Topologie des Weiblichen. Textanalysen zu Marlen Haushofer und Elfriede Czurda." Diplomarbeit, University of Salzburg, 1993.

Lindhoff, Lena. *Einführung in die feministische Literaturtheorie*. Stuttgart: Metzler, 1995.

Nagelschmidt, Ilse. "Schreiben kann jeder, der denken kann. Der ferne analytische Blick der Elfriede Jelinek." *Gewalt der Sprache – Sprache der Gewalt*. Ed. Angelika Corbineau-Hoffmann and Pascal Nicklas Hildesheim: Olms, 2000. 243-264.

Ohms, Constanze. *Mehr als das Herz gebrochen: Gewalt in lesbischen Beziehungen*. Berlin: Orlanda, 1993.

Pfeiferová, Dana. "Über die Tödlichkeit des Schweigens." *Script* 17 (1999): 44-49.

Reichart, Elisabeth. *Fotze*. Salzburg: Otto Müller, 1993..

Slibar, Neva. "Von Opfern und ihrer Sprache. Elisabeth Reicharts transgenerationelle weibliche Rollenprosa." *Script* 6 (1994): 21-23.

Stefan, Verena. *Häutungen: Autobiographische Aufzeichnungen, Gedichte, Träume, Analysen*. Frankfurt a.M.: Fischer Taschenbuch, 1994 (1975).

Thorpe, Kathleen. "Selbst-Gespräche; Häutungen by Verena Stefan and Die Giftmörderinnen by Elfriede Czurda." *Frauen: MitSprechen. MitSchreiben*. Ed. Marianne Henn and Britta Hufeisen. Stuttgart: Akademischer Verlag, 1997. 490-99.

Thürmer-Rohr, Christina. "Frauen in Gewaltverhältnissen. Zur Generalisierung des Opferbegriffs." *Mittäterschaft und Entdeckungslust*. Ed. Christina Thürmer-Rohr. Berlin: Orlanda:, 1990. 22-36.

Van Aaken, Vera. *Männliche Gewalt. Ihre Wurzeln und ihre Auswirkungen*. Düsseldorf. Patmos, 2000.

Vinken, Barbara. "Das Gesetz des Begehrens. Männer, Frauen, Pornographie." *Die Versuchung der Pornographie*. Ed. Drucilla Cornell. Frankfurt: Suhrkamp, 1997. 7-26.

Audrone B. Willeke
Miami University, USA

Healing the Split Self: Women's Incest Narratives in Postwar German Literature[1]

The theme of father-daughter incest in postwar German literature deals with a type of violence in which the power relationship between two individuals is most uneven: an adult male misuses the authority inherent in his role as guardian to abuse the body of a young female. This betrayal of trust, as much as the physical violation, has long-term consequences for a woman's sense of self and for her relationship to others. I will discuss identity formation in three postwar incest-narratives by German and Austrian women authors: Ingeborg Bachmann's novel *Malina*, Alissa Walser's story "Geschenkt" (Gifts), and Elisabeth Reichart's narrative "La Valse;" I will also suggest theoretical paradigms that may serve as useful tools for such an analysis.

The discourse on incest, both in its clinical and literary versions, has long been dominated by Freudian theory. When Freud developed his Oedipal theory to explain the incest narratives of his female patients, he colluded with the societal forces that protected the authority of the father. Freud could not give credence to the reality of the women's stories, for they revealed to an embarrassing degree the extent of male abuse of power. Freud's legacy led to underestimating the frequency of father-daughter incest, or when the facts were indisputable, to a shift of responsibility to the daughter, who "seduced" the father, or to a collusive, inadequate mother, who did not prevent it. As a result, the daughter has been subjected to multiple silencing; society's dismissal of her experiences as imaginary, trivial, or self-provoked leaves her to deal alone with the after-effects of incest. These external silencing mechanisms — in Ingeborg Bachmann's words, the "tearing out of the tongue" — are compounded by internal ones: shame, guilt, a sense of powerlessness, ambivalent feelings toward the perpetrator, and the burden of knowing that the relative stability of one's family depends on silence.

The women's movement of the 1960s and 70s in North America and in Europe empowered increasing numbers of incest survivors to speak

---

[1] For a more extensive discussion of this topic, see Audrone B. Willeke, "'Father Wants to Tear Out My Tongue:' Daughters Confront Incestuous Fathers in Postwar German Literature," *German Life and Letters* 55 (January 2002): 100-116.

openly and women authors to treat the topic in their writings. However, in German-speaking countries the opening of incest discourse to women's narratives has proceeded more slowly. The first significant work to depict the devastating after-effects of paternal incest, Bachmann's novel *Malina*, received negative reviews at its appearance in 1971 from (male) critics who read it as a self-exhibitionist autobiography.

By the 1980s, however, *Malina* had become a key text for feminist scholars who approached this novel predominantly through the lenses of French poststructuralism as defined by Lacan, Derrida, Kristeva, Irigaray, and Cixous. In effect, feminist theory, utilizing deconstruction techniques, turned Freud's Oedipal theory on its head: whereas for Freud the daughter's sexual fantasies serve to exonerate and sustain paternal authority, for feminist scholars, female desire represents a potential challenge to the patriarchy, an oppositional, subversive force. Poststructural readings of *Malina* have foregrounded the novel as cultural criticism: an abstract patriarchy suppresses the female Other; feminine subjectivity is destroyed by masculine logocentrism. Thus, the father figure who torments the daughter-narrator in *Malina* represents the God-father of patriarchy, while the incest experience is understood symbolically as an expression of female subjugation in general.[2] The primary mode of resistance to patriarchy in the novel, according to this approach, is a linguistic subversion that deconstructs the authoritarian social structures symbolized by the father.[3]

Despite the provocative and insightful perspectives that the feminist poststructural approach has provided, its scope of questions is limited by its assumption of a binary opposition between masculinity and femininity. This assumption, according to Sara Lennox, leads to a "mono-causal analysis of women's situation" as victims of an "abstract, generalized, monolithic, and all-embracing patriarchy or phallogocentrism" (Lennox 104). From another direction, the feminist activist Alice Schwarzer rejects poststructural criticism because she believes that it glosses over the pain and trauma of incest. While I am not sympathetic to Schwarzer's reading of *Malina* as a straightforward autobiographical

---

[2] For instance, Charlotte van Praag identifies the father as "die Vatergottheit, die Verkörperung des Numinosen" (God the Father, the embodiment of the numinous) and states categorically, "hier [wird] keineswegs der irdische Vater gemeint" (no earthly father is meant here; Praag 115-6.) Similarly, Gudrun Kohn-Waechter interprets the incest-dreams as a "selbstmörderische Fixierung der Ich-Erzählerin an eine allmächtige Gott-Vater-Figur" (a suicidal fixation of the I-narrator on an all-powerful figure of God the Father; Kohn-Waechter 101).

[3] For a sensitive reading of linguistic resistance in *Malina*, informed by Lacan and Kristeva, see Margaret McCarthy, "Murder and Self-Resuscitation in Ingeborg Bachmann's *Malina*."

confession, I agree with her that the specific nature of the incest experience has been often overlooked.

The deficiencies of the Freudian and the limitations of the post-structural paradigms suggest that we need to find a new theoretical basis from which to understand the identity issues reflected in incest narratives by women. I suggest that we take into account the wealth of clinical studies on incest produced by psychotherapists since the 1970s, along with the theories of personality development based on this data. The experience acquired from therapy has encouraged psychiatrists to develop theories of women's identity formation after incest, such as the theory of split personality proposed by Janet Liebman Jacobs in her book *Victimized Daughters* (1994). According to Jacobs, the daughter's conflicting emotions toward the abusive father create a split in her identity between a powerless female victim and a masculinized façade self that identifies with the father (Jacobs 12). The process begins with alienation from the mother, by whom the daughter feels betrayed. The mother appears weak and ineffectual, unable or unwilling to stop the abuse; thus, the daughter comes to regard her, and all women, including herself, with contempt. With the weakening of the mother-daughter bond, the abused daughter looks for an ego ideal in the more powerful parent. As a result, she may develop a "fraudulent" identity, imitating and modeling the father to the exclusion of the mother, accompanied by fantasies of maleness (77).

According to Jacobs, the needs of the father, his demands for love and compliance, are at the center of the abused daughter's emotional life, "resulting in the development of an empathic bond in which the feelings of the perpetrator take precedence, displacing the child's emotional connection to the violated self" (62). In this special alliance with her father, the daughter learns to associate love/sex with violence, suffering and sacrifice, a lesson in masochism that leaves her open to repeat victimization throughout her life. Jacobs believes that empathy for the perpetrator prevents the creation of a positive female identity, thus it is necessary above all for the daughter to disengage emotionally from the father (147).

Jacobs proposes that an incest victim can resolve the split by embracing a female self that is "true," while rejecting a set of contradictory feelings and values as "false." In her dualistic model, one aspect of the self must be repudiated in order to strengthen the other. I propose to modify this scheme by introducing a second theoretical model that I call the "inclusive self." Sheinberg and Fraenkel, in *The Relational Trauma of Incest*, work with a concept of the self derived from Kenneth Gergen's notion that the self is not dualistic, but rather flexible and fluid. Since every person holds a complex web of contradictory loyalties and ambivalent feelings, fragmentation is a natural condition of selfhood. Thus, according to Sheinberg and Fraenkel, the traumatized daughter can create relative inner cohesion by means of a life narrative that interprets and integrates contradictory emotions and painful experiences in a way that is meaningful for her (Sheinberg and Fraenkel 81). These rival models of identity, the split self and the inclusive self, provide a conceptual framework for my examining of the incest narratives by Bachmann, Walser, and Reichart.

The consequences of the incest experience, as depicted in Bachmann's *Malina*, conform closely to the processes described by Jacobs. In my analysis, I focus on the second of the three chapters, entitled "Der dritte Mann" (The Third Man), in which the female I-narrator describes a series of nightmares to her male alter ego, Malina, and discusses them with him. The nightmares depict an all-powerful and sadistic father who rapes and torments his daughter. Bachmann herself commented in an interview that the dreams contain the narrator's pre-history — stories that the I-narrator was not permitted to tell but which, disguised as dreams, explain her destruction (or near-destruction) (Bachmann 1983: 89).[4]

In the novel, the mother-daughter attachment is weakened by betrayal; for though the mother is aware of the incest, she remains silent and passive. In a symbolic expression of this betrayal, the mother holds three flowers representing her daughter's life, one of which she throws to the father in a gesture of sacrifice (cf. Boa 134). He, however, tramples on all three flowers as though they were bugs ("Wanzen"). What follows is reminiscent of Gregor's demise in Kafka's *Die Verwandlung* (*The Metamorphosis*): "Meine Mutter fegt die zertretenen Blumen, das bißchen Unrat, weg, stumm, um das Haus rein zu halten" (Bachmann 1971: 188-9).[5] The mother's complicity with the father models for the daughter female passivity in the face of male authority, a passivity that the daughter reproduces in her responses to the father and later to her lover, Ivan.

Under circumstances of abuse, idealization of the father can also take the negative form of demonization, whereby the father is perceived

---

[4] In a later interview, Bachmann emphasized the significance of the dream chapter: "Das Traumkapitel ist für mich wichtig; denn wir erfahren ja nichts über den Lebenslauf dieses Ich oder über das, was ihm zugestoßen ist — all das ist in den Träumen, teils versteckt, teils auch ausgesprochen. Jede erdenkliche Art von Folter, von Verderben, von Bedrängtwerden [...]" (Bachmann 1983: 97). (The dream chapter is important for me, because we learn nothing about the life of this 'I' or about what happened to her; all of that is partly hidden and partly expressed directly in the dreams; every possible type of torture, corruption, pressure.)

[5] "My mother silently sweeps away the trampled flowers, the bit of garbage, in order to keep the house clean."

as all-powerful for both good and evil — he is both caregiver and tormentor. In *Malina*, such a reverse form of idealization takes place: the narrator constructs the monstrous father-image of the dreams by intertextual references to mythological, literary, folkloric, and historical examples of brutality. For instance, to silence his daughter when she says "no" to him, the father tries to tear out her tongue (184), as in the incest-myth of Philomela. The father's sexual aggression is accompanied by demands for nurturing and sympathy from a daughter who is socialized to be dutiful and obedient. The daughter responds by empathizing with the emotional and physical needs of the abuser, thus an ambivalent attachment develops. For instance, after a scene of domestic violence, the I-narrator not only protects her drunken father from the police but she also lies down on the floor next to him — "denn hier ist mein Platz, neben ihm, der schlaff und traurig und alt schläft" (215).[6] The daughter is an emotional hostage whose situation is expressed metaphorically by the key that the father takes away and which she cannot get back — he holds the "key" to her inner life (236).

In response to these contradictory emotions — empathy, guilt, fear, hate — the daughter develops a split identity that in the novel takes the form of two characters: she is a debased, victimized self (the female I-narrator) with a male ego ideal (Malina). The I-narrator as "violated body" (Jacobs 165), betrayed by both mother and father, loses the ability to trust and is incapacitated by fears and anxieties. Powerless to resist repeated invasions on her body, she casts herself in the role of permanent victim, identifies with persecuted Jews, and believes that resistance is futile. The incest trauma produces a debased sense of self that predisposes the novel's I-narrator to repeat victimization, as in her relationship with Ivan. In Ivan she finds a man who is similar in his narcissism to her father — he humiliates, uses and abandons her.

In the novel's dichotomized representation of self, Malina incorporates the desired father-protector qualities of emotional stability, rationality, efficiency, and competence. When discussing her dreams, Malina, the self-as-subject, urges the I-as-object to take responsibility for her life. Although Malina functions as the guardian of the helpless I-narrator, he also acts as a rational censor and interrupts the narrator's stories — he forms a shield between her present self and her memories. In Bachmann's novel, the actual experience of sexual abuse is never admitted into consciousness. To be sure, in the dream chapter, in the presence of both father and mother, the daughter names the deed: "Blutschande, es war Blutschande" (188).[7] However, the hellish scenes of her nightmares are not the actual memories of abuse but the manifest content of

---

[6] "for here is my place, next to him who is sleeping — so feeble, sad, and old."

[7] "Incest, it was incest."

the repressed memories. The disorienting sequence of dream images is a narrative device that replicates the protagonist's inability to form a coherent and continuous life story. In the I-narrator's own words, she is a "Karikatur… im Geist und im Fleisch" (349).[8]

Bachmann's novel traces the unsuccessful struggle of the daughter-narrator to establish emotional autonomy. The fantasized confrontations with her father take place at the dinner table. While the father eats greedily, the daughter begins to hurl various objects at him. However, her defiance is futile, even comical — she merely splatters food on her father's face (242-45). Instead of reasserting her devalued female self, the narrator capitulates to her male alter ego, Malina. The I-narrator's split identity is replicated by the image of the split in the wall of her room. Unable to shed her victim identity, the female "I" shrinks to nothingness as she steps into the cracked wall. What remains of the truncated self in the guise of the masculine Malina is indeed merely a façade, a "shadow" self without access to memories of sexual abuse. The narrative resolves the problem of the split self in line with the either/or paradigm proposed by Jacobs. However, in contrast to Jacobs, the novel's protagonist prefers the masculine ego ideal to the insecure, anxiety-ridden female. As Elizabeth Boa points out, "the title of *Ich*'s autobiography, which is not *her* name, strikingly signals her failure to establish a unified identity" (Boa 134).

Some twenty years later, two short stories appeared that again deal with father-daughter incest from the daughter's point of view — Alissa Walser's "Geschenkt" (Gifts) and Elisabeth Reichart's "La Valse." In contrast to the I-narrator of *Malina,* the first-person narrators of these later stories are not incest victims but rather incest survivors. The difference between victim and survivor lies in the meaning an individual gives to the experience and its aftermaths. While victims comply with the social expectation to remain passive, survivors, according to Rosaria Champagne, "move to a place where they reject the demand to remain politely silent" (Champagne 2). In Walser's and Reichart's stories, the daughter-narrators are confident enough to confront the father as equals.

In a fitting twist of fate, Alissa Walser received the Ingeborg Bachmann Prize for "Geschenkt" in 1992, the year in which Elisabeth Reichart also published "La Valse." First published in the magazine *Der Spiegel* (28/1992), "Geschenkt" attracted attention above all due to the suspicion of family scandal. In a number of interviews, Alissa Walser sought to dispel this suspicion, stating emphatically that the story was not a portrayal of the relationship between herself and her famous

---

[8] "a caricature… in mind and body."

father, Martin Walser.[9] Nonetheless, as with the initial *Malina* reception twenty years earlier, some reviewers rejected this text as pornographic and exhibitionistic — an airing of dirty linen in public.[10] More interesting than the issue of autobiography is Alissa Walser's unusual narrative voice which one reviewer describes as "Kalter Schick glitzert neben uneingestandener Trostlosigkeit" (*Süddeutsche Zeitung*).[11] Her first-person narrator moves in an emotional vacuum in which sexual encounters are reduced to an exchange of body fluids, as indifferent as eating and drinking.

The brutal violence of *Malina* is absent in Walser's "Geschenkt." On the eve of her eighth birthday, the narrator's father had slept with her in the same hotel bed; at that time she did not understand his sexual arousal nor that he was masturbating. In keeping with the title of the anthology in which this story appeared, *Dies ist nicht meine ganze Geschichte* (This Is Not My Whole Story), the narrative withholds as much as it reveals, leaving open the exact nature of the eroticized relationship between father and daughter. The adult daughter feels violated by the father's erotic possessiveness — he attempts to control her over the years through gifts of money and through insistent questioning about her relationships to other men. "Manchmal glaube ich, er hat mich markiert, wie der Hund einen Baum" (Walser 8),[12] thinks the daughter as she visits him on his sixty-second birthday which comes a day before her thirty-first. "Immer will er wissen, wo ich gewesen bin, wer mit mir war, was wir gemacht haben, und was noch" (11).[13] She knows that behind these questions are others that he dares not ask, such as: "[W]ie geht es deiner Fotze, lohnt es sich, wird sie gut bezahlt, […]?" (ibidem).[14] For the father, the prying questions provide vicarious sexual excitement, replacing the earlier physical contact. For the daughter, the questions that bore into every aspect of her life are incestuous violations of her private space, negations of her autonomy. She understands that the prying and the money are instruments of power and coolly determines to put a stop to it. Returning home, she uses some of the money he gave her during the birthday visit to hire a callboy. When

---

[9] Interviews with Alissa Walser on this topic have appeared in *Süddeutsche Zeitung* (March 19, 1994) and in *Bunte* (May 25, 2000).

[10] The unsigned review in the *Frankfurter Allgemeine Zeitung* (March 19, 1999) labeled this and the other short stories in Alissa Walser's first anthology as: " …deutlich[es] pornographisch[es] Sagen" (clearly pornographic narration; Feuilleton: 28).

[11] "Cold glamour glitters alongside unacknowledged despair."

[12] "Sometimes I think he has marked me like a dog marks a tree."

[13] "He always wants to know where I was, with whom, what we did, and what else."

[14] "How is your cunt, is it good, does it get paid well, […]?"

the father telephones her and as usual begins to ply her with questions, she tells him, "Ich habe mir einen Jungen gekauft" (12).[15]

In Alissa Walser's story, the streetwise daughter turns the tables on the father when she imitates his actions, claiming the same "male" sexual privileges for herself. With the callboy, she recreates a similar relationship of money, power, and dependency that had enabled her father to manipulate her through the years. During the erotically tense telephone conversation with her father, she notices that he has moved to her room and lain down on her bed where she is afraid he may be masturbating. When her father falls silent, she gently hangs up the telephone, "ganz leise, ganz sachte, so sachte, wie man die Tür zu einem Kinderzimmer schließt, wenn es dort endlich still geworden ist" (20).[16] As she metaphorically closes the door on him, it is the incestuous father who appears childishly naïve and helpless.

The division of consciousness is not projected onto two separate characters in Walser's story, as was the case in the *Malina* novel. Instead, the "split" appears here as the protagonist's inability to integrate her emotions with sexual intimacy. By imitating her exploitative father, the daughter protects herself from him, but pays a high price: estrangement from her feelings. Living in an emotional vacuum, she experiences sex with the callboy as a totally depersonalized act, indifferent yet awkward, like a hand in someone else's pocket (20). In her condition of psychic numbness, sex is nothing more than a power game. The resolution of the incest trauma also follows the either/or pattern in *Malina*: the vulnerable self in this story has been displaced by a sovereign but emotionally stunted façade.

Elisabeth Reichart's short story "La Valse" is structurally related to Bachmann's *Malina* in so far as it expresses the split consciousness of the incest survivor by means of two separate characters: the I-narrator Briscilla and her dead sister Hanna, whose voice Briscilla has internalized. The split differs from the one in *Malina*, however, because here the two aspects of the self are not gendered as feminine/masculine; rather, Hanna represents the voice of defeatism in Briscilla's struggle toward autonomy. Briscilla's monologues, some in the form of imaginary dialogues with Hanna, occur during the last seven days of her father's life, as he is dying of cancer. The biblical allusion to the seven days of creation underscores Briscilla's struggle to recreate herself — to heal the inner split by working through the contradictions in her relationship to her father: scorn and anger, but also pity and hope for reconciliation.

15 "I bought myself a boy."
16 "as gently as we close the door to a child's room, when it finally becomes quiet in there."

As a young girl, Briscilla depended on her father and loved him, despite the sexual abuse. When he shifted his attention away from her to Hanna, he turned the sisters into rivals (Reichart 34). As an adult, Hanna had been unable to confront her father; instead, she turned her aggression inward, mutilating her body before she hanged herself (cf. Blume). Hanna's suicide instigated Briscilla's reckoning with her father, which she undertakes by actions rather than words. Briscilla "speaks out" by demonstrating in public what the father had taught her to do for his private pleasure: swinging her hips to mimic a prostitute, she strolls past her father and his business associates. Briscilla is convinced that this acting-out of promiscuous behavior caused not only shock and humiliation but also his fatal illness. Now that the power relationship is reversed and the dying father totally dependent on her, Briscilla feels obliged to play the role of the dutiful daughter (Reichart 8): she brings him home from the hospital and puts him into her own bed, the same bed in which he had raped her. However, Briscilla's compliant behavior masks a complexity of emotions that erupts in the course of the narrative.

Briscilla exhibits the attributes of a divided self, with one part actively engaged in freeing herself from emotional bondage to the father, while the other part, speaking with Hanna's internalized voice, is trapped in the role of self-hating victim who calls for vengeance. Body memories of rape intrude on her daily activities, even teeth brushing is a difficult chore — she gags involuntarily when she sticks her toothbrush into her mouth. Briscilla is aware that her experience of childhood sexual abuse makes her vulnerable to repeat victimization. Suffering from low self-esteem, she sees herself as ugly, spoiled for men, nothing but a sex object — a "hole," a "nothing." Dissociated from her own emotions, like the narrator in "Geschenk," she thinks: "Jetzt müßte ich wohl irgendetwas fühlen. Abscheu wahrscheinlich" (11).[17] Briscilla's emotional paralysis and mistrust cripple her ability to develop intimate relationships with other men. Speaking to her comatose father, she admits a terrible truth: he still retains sexual ownership of her.

However, Briscilla struggles to transform herself from victim to survivor by a narration that encompasses conflicting aspects of the incest experience. While in *Malina* the trauma of sexual abuse is expressed in dream-like images of persecution, Reichart's narrator gives voice to the terrifying memories themselves. When she finally confronts her father, overcoming the silence that led to Hanna's death, Briscilla stands naked in front of him, for her body itself is the accuser: "In dieses Fleisch hast du dich gekrallt und hineingebissen, und in dieses Loch hast du deinen

---

[17] "I should be feeling something now. Disgust probably."

Schwanz gesteckt, [...]" (37).[18] Moreover, Briscilla accuses not only her father, but also the societal structures that give men power over women's bodies. Referring to the biblical story of Lot and his daughters, she challenges the assumption underlying that text, namely that daughters are the property of the father. As Juliet Wigmore has noted, "Briscilla's reading of this story, from the vantage point of her own experience of abuse, subverts Lot's position and with it the ethics and authority of the original" (Wigmore 491).

On day seven, Briscilla dreams that her father's death has set her free; however, in the same dream she knows that undetected "plastic bombs" are traveling with her on her flight (Reichart 42). With this image of hijacking and terrorism, Briscilla expresses the realization that she will never be secure, for the memories inscribed on her body can erupt at any time. Nonetheless, after pronouncing judgment on her dead father with the single word "Scheiße" (shit; 44), Briscilla is prepared to take a first step toward psychic freedom. By silencing the internalized voice of defeatism and despair, she affirms her identity as an autonomous woman who can remember her past and can begin to shape her own future: "Ich kann also gehen. Ich bin jetzt frei" (44).[19] By presenting an incest survivor who recognizes her ambivalent feelings toward her abuser, Reichart's narrative offers the possibility for healing, whereas Bachmann's and Walser's protagonists remain internally split between a rejected female self and an idealized masculine façade.

Works Cited

Bachmann, Ingeborg. *Malina*, Frankfurt/M.: Suhrkamp, 1971.

—. *Wir müssen wahre Sätze finden: Gespräche und Interviews.* Ed. Christine Koschel and Inge von Weidenbaum. Munich and Zurich: R. Piper, 1983.

Blume, Sue. "The Incest Survivors' Aftereffects Checklist." *Secret Survivors: Uncovering Incest and Its Aftereffects in Women.* New York: Ballantine Books, 1990. xviii-xxi.

Boa, Elizabeth. "Women Writing about Women Writing and Ingeborg Bachmann's *Malina.*" *New Ways in Germanistik.* Ed. Richard Sheppard. New York. Oxford: Munich: Berg, 1990. 128-44.

Champagne, Rosaria. *The Politics of Survivorship: Incest, Women's Literature, and Feminist Theory.* New York and London: New York UP, 1996.

"Interview with Alissa Walser." *Bunte* May 25, 2000: 60-61.

Jacobs, Janet Liebman. *Victimized Daughters: Incest and the Development of the Female Self.* New York and London: Routledge, 1994.

Kohn-Waechter Gudrun *Das Verschwinden in der Wand: Destruktive Moderne und*

18 "You clawed and bit your way into this flesh, and you stuck your tail into this hole."
19 "I guess I can go. I am free now."

Widerspruch eines weiblichen Ich in Ingeborg Bachmanns "Malina." Stuttgart: Metzler, 1992.

Lennox, Sara. "The Feminist Reception of Ingeborg Bachmann." *Women in German Yearbook* 8 (1992). Ed. Jeanette Clausen and Sara Friedrichsmeyer. Lincoln and London: U of Nebraska P, 1993. 73-111.

Liebman Jacobs, Janet. *Victimized Daughters: Incest and the Development of the Female Self.* New York and London: Routledge, 1994.

McCarthy, Margaret. "Murder and Self-Resuscitation in Ingeborg Bachmann's *Malina." Out From the Shadows: Essays on Contemporary Austrian Women Writers and Filmmakers.* Ed. Margarete Lamb-Faffelberger. Riverside, CA: Ariadne, 1997. 38-54

Praag, Charlotte van. *"Malina* von Ingeborg Bachmann, ein verkannter Roman." *Neophilologus* 66:1 (1982): 115-6.

Reichart, Elisabeth. "La Valse." *La Valse: Erzählungen.* Salzburg: Otto Müller, 1992.

Schwarzer, Alice. "Schwarzer über *Malina." Emma* (February 1991): 16-20.

Sheinberg, Marcia and Peter Fraenkel, *The Relational Trauma of Incest: A Family-Based Approach to Treatment.* New York and London: The Guilford Press, 2001.

Süddeutsche Zeitung. Unsigned review. March 17, 1994.

—. Interview with Alissa Walser. March 19, 1994.

Walser, Alissa. "Geschenkt," *Dies ist nicht meine ganze Geschichte.* Reinbek bei Hamburg: Rowohlt, 1994. 7-20.

Wigmore, Juliet. "Elisabeth Reichart's 'La Valse' and the Text of Abuse." *German Life and Letters* 49.4 (October 1996): 491.

Willeke, Audrone B. "'Father Wants to Tear Out My Tongue.' Daughters Confront Incestuous Fathers in Postwar German Literature." *German Life and Letters* 55 (January 2002): 100-116.

Reinhild Steingrover

Eastman School of Music, University of Rochester, USA

Violent Acts: Comic Savagery in the Theater of Kerstin Hensel

Kerstin Hensel is best known for her prose and poetry. Her novels *Tanz am Kanal* (1994) and *Gipshut* (1999) have won her critical praise and prestigious literary prizes. Her poetry collections were published in the early 1980s in the GDR when she was still in her early twenties. Yet, she has dated her beginnings as a writer with a theater visit: "Merkwürdigerweise habe ich mit 17 angefangen mit Dramatik, nicht wie andere mit der Lyrik. Das lag daran, daß mich das Theater faszinierte — die 'Faust' Inszenierung von Drescher in Karl Marx Stadt sah ich mit 16. Das war so ein Erlebnis, nach dem ich meinte, man müsse unbedingt Dramatik schreiben" (Hensel/Trauth 59).[1]

She began writing plays and published her first dramatic text *Ausflugszeit* in the GDR journal *Theater der Zeit* in 1988. This first play, "Ausflugszeit," was greeted with much interest but also serious trepidation: "Konfus oder genial?" was the surprised response of one critic (Millich qtd. in Hensel/Trauth 59) to what Hensel herself later classified as a beginner's piece, but one that already contained all of the important aesthetic devices for her later dramatic writing.[2] Since then she has written nine plays, five of which have been staged at theaters in Ingolstadt, Greifswald, Cottbus, and Mannheim. Among her most recent plays is *Atzenköfls Töchter*, which was commissioned by the city of Ingolstadt in 2001 to commemorate the 100th birthday of Marieluise Fleißer.

This essay seeks to analyze the depiction of violence in Hensel's dramatic works, especially *Atzenköfls Töchter* and its intertextual relationship with Fleißer's works. Hensel's dramatic strategy alternates between parodistic humor and the performance of slapstick absurdities on the one hand and the unsensational staging of acts of violence that are shocking precisely because of their complete lack of emotionality on

---

[1] All translations of German quotes are mine. ("Interestingly I began writing plays at age 17, not poetry like many others. I was fascinated by the theater – I saw Drescher's production of 'Faust' when I was 16 in Karl Max Stadt. After that experience I was convinced that I had to write plays.")

[2] "Es war ein Anfangswerk. Zumindest steckt in 'Ausflugszeit' ästhetisch alles das, was sich später in meinem Theaterschreiben fortgesetzt hat." ["It was a beginners' work. At least 'Ausflugszeit' contained everything aesthetically that I have developed in my later dramatic writing."] (Hensel 1996: 86-7) Critic Johannes Birgfeld assesses this early play as her most political and daring one (Birgfeld 46-63).

the other. This dramatic strategy thematizes the dynamics of class and gender with references to specific social and political issues. Moreover, Hensel alludes to literary predecessors and engages dramatic genres such as Brecht's epic theater and Fleißer's *critical Volksstück,* but creates her own dramaturgical response to the changed world of global capitalism.

Hensel makes frequent use of violent acts: rape, exploitation of subordinates, psychological or emotional cruelties and finally murder. Human interactions in all social spheres of Hensel's fictional worlds are characterized by violence. Brutality and exploitation are not hidden or taboo but performed matter-of-factly and without any melodramatic impact on the reader/viewer, since the plays' characters are not shaped for audience identification. Rather than presenting evolving characters, Hensel's figures are prototypes, such as unconscionable capitalists, small-minded petit bourgeois employees, pompous doctors, crude soldiers, frustrated housewives, evil parents and disoriented children. With such a grim but often surprisingly comical line-up, the author explores large topics such as the individual and society, (German) history experienced from the fringes of society, globalization from a very local perspective, sexuality and gender relations, and the act of writing itself.

The use of violence as a structural element in all human interactions in her plays reflects the author's view of the political and economic context that situates them. According to Hensel, a class society provokes the poet to write from a position of resistance. When asked about her position as a writer during the aftermath of German unification she stated the following:

> Mein Schreiben hat sich in keiner Weise geändert. Deutschland hat sich von seiner üblichen Seite gezeigt, für mich ist nirgends ein humanitärer Fortschritt zu sehen. Die Menschen sind die gleichen geblieben: Fanatismus, Spiessigkeit, Abhängigkeit und was sonst noch so Themen in meinem Schreiben waren — das Panoptikum, das für ein paar Wochen zu fallen sich anschickte, hat sich in genauso kurzer Zeit restauriert. In einer Klassengesellschaft wird sich das Amt des Dichters wohl nie ändern; er wird immer im Widerstand sein. (qt. in Baume 66)[3]

This resistance manifests itself in Hensel's plays in a particular way: the author exposes the everyday violence in decidedly unemotional terms. In *Müllers Kuh,* for example, murder is discussed unemotionally between victim (the grandmother) and perpetrators (her children)

---

3 "My writing hasn't changed at all. Germany has shown itself from its usual side and I cannot detect any humanitarian progress. People are still the same: fanaticism, petit-bourgeois attitudes, dependency and whatever else used to be my topics — the panopticum that seemed to fall for a few weeks has restored itself quickly. The poet's task will never change in a class society: he will always be in the resistance."

because the old woman has become economically dispensable. The application of economic analysis to human relations contains its own horrific logic, to which the stage characters show no emotional response. Hensel leaves it to the audience to respond emotionally and/or intellectually to this unsentimental display.

The same strategy can be found in regard to sexual violence. The rape of the daughter in *Atzenköfls Töchter* is performed in the presence of her father without his protest or hindrance. Instead, the rapist boyfriend and the father ("der Ernährer") calmly continue the discussion of their card game.

> *Ralle stößt Ernährer weg, vergewaltigt Berta*
> Berta: Gott! Gott! Erlöse mich!
> Ralle: Fullhouse! *Knöpft sich sofort zu.*
> Ernährer: Noch ein Spielchen? Beim Poker hau ich dich nieder.
> Ralle: Keine Zeit Schmidt. *Zu Berta* Der Mann muß weiter. Er ist nun mal keine
>   Frau. (Hensel 2001: 39)[4]

This succinct three-way conversation exemplifies Hensel's staging of violent acts as commonplace and unsensational: Ralle's "Fullhouse" addresses the father in reference to their on-going card game *and* Berta in reference to the brutal rape. The economy of language displayed here underscores the dual oppression of Berta (by her father and "lover") as well as her absence from the scene. In this rape scene, as in others in Hensel's work, the victim has no voice. The rape is clearly an act of power rivalry between the two men and has nothing to do with sexual desire.

Hensel's earlier play *Müller's Kuh, Müllers Kinder* stages a parallel scene to the above, but in this instance, the rape is contextualized by ideologies of global capitalism, more specifically the transformation of the formerly communist East German economy to Western style capitalism. A personified "Kommherzbank" shows father and mother how to act in the new economy. He appears just after the daughter Minna has transformed herself successfully from her former farmer-daughter-self into an "Asian sex slave" named Pham Thai. The father immediately greets his daughter with xenophobic slurs, fearing she will take away his job:

> Vater: Sie nimmt mir meinen Posten weg! Sie will Melkvorsteher im Müller-
>   Milch Konzern werden, ich seh ihr das an!
> Kommherzbank (*vögelt Pham Thai*): Bleiben Sie cool Mann. Ich bin gekommen,
>   um Ihnen den Übergang vom Kommunismus zum Kapitalismus zu er-

---

4 "*Ralle pushes Ernährer to the side, rapes Berta*/ Berta: God! God! Redeem me!/ Ralle: Full-house! *buttons himself up immediately*/ Ernährer: Another game? In poker I'll knock you down/ Ralle: No time, Schmidt. *To Berta* Man has to move on. He is not a woman after all."

leichtern... (*erleichtert sich*)... das war das erste. (*Knöpft sich zu*) Und nun das eigentliche. Pham Thai, was kannst du? (Hensel 2000: 14)[5]

In both scenes the rape itself is not mentioned directly but performed matter-of-factly as socially acceptable. The stage characters do not reflect on this violence as they do in the plays by other contemporary playwrights. Gesine Danckwart's recent play *Täglich Brot*, where the characters muse throughout the play about various forms of oppression and the consequences on their lives, is an example of a different dramaturgical use of violence. Elfriede Jelinek's plays of excess and exaggeration physically stage this violence which Danckwart's characters contemplate. Jelinek's early plays bear some resemblance to Hensel's in their strategy of staging graphic violence matter-of-factly and in casting prototypes. In contrast, however, Jelinek's language is often saturated with philosophical quotations from the works of Barthes, Beaudrillard, Hegel, Heidegger as well as pop culture, while Hensel's working class cast is unable or unwilling to reflect on its situation. Her characters become both the victims and perpetrators of violent acts by acting according to purely economic considerations. Audience compassion and identification is not Hensel's aim. We observe the logical dynamics of capitalism as a spectacle rather than a tragedy on stage. Hensel's strategy betrays not a lack of compassion for the fate of the oppressed but a lack of confidence in the effectiveness of the dramaturgy of identification and catharsis.

Critic Johannes Birgfeld was the first to survey Hensel's dramatic output sketching her development from a political and very experimental beginning to a more conventional dramatic strategy. Birgfeld traces the influences of the popular Viennese comedy (Ferdinand Raimund's *Alpenkönig* in regard to *Hyänen*) and the postmodern theater of Heiner Müller (*Germania II* in relation to *Ausflugszeit*). He sums up:

> Sie [her plays] arbeiten intensiv mit bewußten Brüchen und Verknappungen, sind zersplitterte, lückenhafte und scharfkantig ausgreifende Bilderbögen, kaleidoskopartige Kommentare zur gegenwärtigen Lebenswelt, die in ihrer Kombination von abgründiger Komik, fatalistischer Weltsicht, Lust am Bühnenspiel und dem Spaß am Verschrecken auf der deutschen Bühne recht einmalig sind. (Birgfeld 62)[6]

[5] "Father: She's taking my job away! She wants to become the milking supervisor in the Müller Milk Coporation, I can tell!/ Kommherzbank (*screwing Pham Thai*): Stay cool, man. I have come to relieve you in the transition from communism to capitalism ... (*relieves himself*)...that was the first thing. (*buttons up*) And now to the real business. Pham Thai, what are your qualifications?"

[6] "Her plays work intensively with conscious breaks and minimalisms, consist of series of images that are fragmented, elliptical, and rough around the edges. They are kaleidoscopic commentaries on the contemporary world and unique for the German stage

Among Hensel's most recent plays is the aforementioned *Atzenköfls Töchter,* which is subtitled: "Schauspiel, Zum Gedenken an Marieluise Fleißer" (Play to the Memory of Marieluise Fleißer). It clearly shows traces of the encounter with the older writer's work, about whom Günter has written: "So einfach ihre Menschen sind, was sich an ihnen zeigt, ist der höchst komplizierte Zusammenhang von Milieu, Erziehung, Psyche, Fremdbestimmung, Rollensucht und Hemmung, Gruppenzwang und individueller Verlorenheit" (Rühle 60).[7] *Atzenköfl* indeed makes many references to the life and work of Fleißer, beginning with her childhood experience in the Catholic boarding school, run by nuns, which becomes a *Töchterschule*[8] in Hensel's play. The teacher Ms. Atzenköfl herself represents the hypocritical, abusive, authoritarian, at times magical and increasingly insane force of such schooling that drives two of the three "daughters" in the school commit suicide with their teacher at the end of the play. The figure of Atzenköfl demonstrates that women participate as much in the brutalization of their inferiors as do men. Both Fleißer and Hensel have a tradition of casting women characters in such roles.

Hensel's play consists of 27 connected scenes and presents the figures of three girls, Berta, Meta and Christel and their vague hopes to find love, happiness and freedom for themselves. From their early experiences in Atzenköfl's school to their interactions with the soldiers Kolbe and Schlesack, Berta's father, who is referred to only as "Ernährer" (another reference to Fleißer's play *Tiefseefisch* in which the character Laurenz refers to himself as "Ernährer"), and the (con-)artist Ralle, the play traces their repeated unsuccessful attempts to emancipation. Only Berta has a vague idea of what her goal in life might be, namely to write for the theater (again an allusion to Fleißer's biography as well as Hensel's). Meta and Christel are neither content with life in the small town of Oberbichl, nor are they able to envision alternatives: Meta marries the very first man whom she encounters, Christel clings to her life as a shopkeeper. Before following Atzenköfl in her suicide she sadly summarizes: "Es hat mich kein Mensch auf dieser Welt gewollt. Und ich habe auch keinen gewollt. Wißt ihr wie schrecklich es ist, nichts zu wollen..." (Hensel 2001: 59).[9] Meta on the other hand acknowledges

---

in their combination of deep comedy, fatalistic worldviews, and their pleasure in the dramatic play and the fun of provocation."

[7] "As simple as her human figures are, they show the highly complicated context of milieu, education, psyche, determination from outside, desire to be someone or inability to be someone, group pressure and individual loneliness."

[8] A traditional school for girls from a good family. It did not offer an education that prepared for entry into a university but prepared girls for their traditional roles in society.

[9] "Nobody wanted me in this world. And I didn't want anybody either. Do you know how terrible it is, to want nothing."

a life of disappointment and alienation when she exclaims: "Ich bin nicht losgekommen von diesem ewiggleichem Leben. Und ich habe nix gemerkt. Hörst du Berta, nix gemerkt!" (59).[10]

Berta nevertheless refuses to give up, and despite numerous and life-long failures to free herself from the oppressions of her small-town environment, she resolves to leave for the metropolis: "Hier mach nicht ich das Licht aus. Ich kaufe mir jetzt eine Fahrkarte nach München. Und dann weiter nach Berlin, und dann..." (61).[11] The final sentences of the play return the reader/viewer to the beginning, when Atzenköfl had admonished Berta as a child: "Du mußt noch viel für dich tun, Berta Schmidt. Zeit läuft!" (4).[12] These words from the first scene are meant to force Berta into passive subordination, aiming for a suppression of all passions (sexual and otherwise), but when Berta repeats them in the very end she takes them literally as an act of empowerment to become her own woman. This might indicate an attempt to overcome the life-long oppression, but can also be seen as an ironic sign of continued imprisonment in the inability to find her own words. Hensel has deliberately concluded with ambivalence, neither optimistic nor fatalistic in tone. The double-meaning of the final words in the play convey clearly that writing in itself will not be the road to liberation.

Moreover, the remark "Zeit läuft!," also echoes a statement by Berta in the beginning of the play in which she expresses a profound sense of being an outcast in her social environment as well as in her historical context: "Die Zeit ist eine wahnsinnige Maschine, die schneller läuft, als ich existiere" (10).[13] The image conveys Berta's sense of being out of step with her time, sensing its passage and finding herself unable to shape even her own "herstory." Her feeling of urgency to accomplish something, to be somebody, is not matched by the reality of her conformity and confinement. Ultimately then, this is the plays' most profound violence: the recognition of being superfluous, unnoticed by history, unfulfilled by lifetime achievements or love. The underlying economy of valuing people like goods and services for their market worth, their popularity, strength or power is the reflection of a society that is uninterested in humanism, emotion and morality.

Like other contemporary playwrights who can be loosely grouped under the rubric of *critical Volkstück* (cf. Cocalis) such as Kerstin Specht and Elfriede Müller, Hensel employs a dramatic structure that depicts

---

[10] "I didn't get away from this life of sameness. And I didn't understand anything. Do you hear, Berta, didn't understand anything!"

[11] "I will not turn off the light here. I will buy myself a ticket to Munich now. And then to Berlin, and then..."

[12] "You have yet to do a lot for yourself, Berta Schmidt. Time's running!"

[13] "Time is an insane machine that runs faster than I exist."

working class characters speaking in their local vernacular about their daily struggles and experiences of escalating violence and domestic tragedy. Susan Cocalis defines the *critical Volksstück* as a genre which "should deliberately shock the audience through the deployment of brutal, violent, or obscene acts, which it would present as the truly natural, and thus sincere basis for everyday life" (Cocalis 113). In Fleißer's play *Purgatory in Ingolstadt* e.g. an illegitimate pregnancy is the catalyst for a string of brutalities. This popular genre on German stages in the 1920s and 30s was revived in the 1960s and 70s when Fleißer's work was rediscovered by writers such as Rainer Werner Fassbinder and Frank Xaver Kroetz. Hensel's allusion to this form is parodistic.

Hensel returns loosely to the form of the *critical Volksstück* in *Atzenköfl*, in order to provoke contemporary audiences with the extremely understated depiction of rape or murder. The very casual occurrence of violence is part of her plays' normality, indeed as normal as lunch or intercourse. Hensel thus mimics the form of the *critical Volksstück*, and pays homage to Fleißer's dramatic forms and themes. She simultaneously undermines this historical subtext by normalizing extremely violent human interaction as socially acceptable behavior and thus confronting audiences with the human effects of a world devoid of true affection and kindness. While this dramatic strategy is inherently political it questions the definition of political theater. Absurd humor and slapstick violence have displaced earnest melodrama or appeals to reason.

Consider this scene from *Atzenköfl* in which the main character Berta meets the artist Ralle. Alluding to the encounter between Brecht and Fleißer, Hensel's Berta begins to articulate her hopes of becoming involved with the theater. But her excitement is quickly disappointed when Ralle declares: "Eine Frau kann nur etwas darstellen, nicht sein" (Hensel 2001: 24).[14] He therefore demands that she should abandon the idea of writing for the theater and become an actress for his own plays instead. In order to prove his point he forces Berta to perform how she can escape from the provincial imprisonment of her hometown. He asks her to climb over an imaginary wall while yelling: "Die Zeiten sind furchtbar, diese Stadt ist eine Hölle, aber wir krallen uns an der glatten Mauer hoch" (25).[15] Instead Berta repeatedly runs against the (imaginary) wall. This farcical absurdity is pursued even further after Ralle

---

14 "A woman can only represent not be something." Compare Jelinek's play *Clara S.*: "Wahrscheinlich ist die Frau doch eher das nichts. Das Nichts! Man kann sie im Grunde nicht berühren. Lieber die reine Flamme studenlang anschauen als sich in die Frau hineinarbeiten."["Probably woman is nothing after all, Nothingness! One can essentially not touch her. Better to stare for hours into the pure flame than to work oneself into woman."] (Jelinek 84).

15 "Times are terrible, this city is hell, but we shinny up the slick wall."

makes clear that she has failed as an actress. Adding insult to injury he comments: "Zwecklos. Aber trösten Sie sich: jeder Mensch hat seine eigene Wohlgeratenheit, hat in seiner Begrenzung auch seine Vollendung" (25).[16] He announces that she'll make a fine secretary for his own work. Instead of dumping him Berta clings to the hope of escape that he represents and begs him to let her be his equal. Ralle reacts swiftly and rapes her while making notes to himself: "Das wirtschaftliche Verhältnis der Liebe besteht im Abstand den der Mensch zu ihm einnimmt. Und der Mann bestimmt ihn" (27).[17] Berta's response follows as prompted and mechanically: "Berta: *erschrocken parierend*: Es war schön, Ralle" (27).[18] This scene is typical for Hensel's writing of absurd slapstick situations which can be effectively visualized on stage and their sudden intensification through a cold-blooded, non-sensational depiction of violence, for example, rape.

This description of gender relations as power relations characterized by brutality is common in Hensel's work. Unlike earlier plays, however, the gender roles in *Atzenköfl* are stereotypical and clichéd: Ralle is absurdly powerful, although clearly identifiable for the audience and for Berta as a hoax. Surprisingly his sexist platitudes do not fail to dominate and nearly destroy Berta. Unlike earlier plays such as *Grimma* where the oppressed women simply fight back or *Hyänen* where Elly bites off her murderous fiancé's tongue, Berta is provocatively docile. Hensel's refusal to write her main character as a more emancipatory one frustrates contemporary desires for bolder and brasher females but has to be seen again as a reference to Fleißer's unsuccessful struggles for artistic and personal autonomy.

Hensel incorporates direct quotations from Fleißer's plays, albeit in critically modified contexts. Fleißer's strategy of showing women as exchangeable commodities, whose desire and individuality is negated by their sexist environment is utilized again by Hensel to demonstrate the commodification of Berta as a woman and a writer. Hensel quotes Fleißer's plays *Tiefseefisch* and *Pioniere in Ingolstadt* almost verbatim for her purpose. In *Tiefseefisch* (1930) the writer Laurenz, who is modeled after Brecht dictates his girlfriend Gesine a few rules for their relationship: "Sie möchte es unterlassen die Gedanken von Laurenz denken zu wollen" (Fleißer 301).[19] Hensel's poet Ralle reprimands Berta for her success after her theatrical debut by stating: "Ich mag das nicht, wenn

---

[16] "Useless. But console yourself: each person has his own good form, has his perfection in his limitations."

[17] "The economic relationship of love consists in the distance of humans to it. And man determines it."

[18] "Berta (*responds as prompted in terror*): It was beautiful, Ralle."

[19] "She is asked, not to think the thoughts of Laurenz."

du dich ungefragt an meinen Gedanken bedienst" (Hensel 2001: 34).[20]

From Fleißer's play, Hensel takes the disappointment present in Berta's attempt to claim her own desire along with Gesine's failure to maintain artistic autonomy, and combines them into the fate of her own Berta-figure while expanding the depiction of the "gender war" into a critical farce that exposes the commodification of love and writing, emotional and sexual desire. Twenty-five years after Fleißer's death this gender war is still raging. Hensel pays tribute to the lasting validity of Fleißer's work through these intertextual references. Her specification of the play's location (Oberbichl) and time "Gestern im Heute" ("yesterday in today") emphasize this continuity.

In all her writings Hensel has expressed ironic criticism of political and social issues but has rejected literary forms that are motivated by didactic goals. Hensel's hope for social change is not tied to a belief in the theater as a "moralische Anstalt." She uses the stage for an often surreal theatricality and sometimes confusing spectacle of events, quickly changing scenes, songs and poems and a disregard for the laws of time and place. In *Müllers Kuh*, for example, the former East German farmers suddenly take off from their dining room in an imaginary airplane to inspect a plantation in Thailand. In *Atzenköfls Töchter* a soldier is shot only to reappear in a later scene and then to die again. In *Grimma* the four main characters are cannibalizing a dead jogger, whose role in the play is unclear to begin with, under a yodeling sky. These examples illustrate the irreverent and admittedly very dark humor with which Hensel stuns and provokes her audience. Hensel's topics of German unification, global capitalism and authoritarian education, to name but a few, form the serious sub-text, onto which these visual images are crafted with great sarcasm, ironic wit and an often physical humor.

Hensel thus is not interested in genres such as documentary or naturalistic theater but consistently points to the playful and theatrical character of her dramas. Instead of explaining analytically of how violence is created and how humans can morally respond to oppressive super-structures she designs performances of violent acts that are staged by objectified types in role-play scenarios. This strategy is a compelling mix of Jarry's pre-surrealist Ubu-plays and a critical engagement of Brechtian epic theater to which Hensel playfully alludes. For example Berta's Brechtian *moritat*-like song in the middle of *Atzenköfls Töchter* where she chants "Am Leben ist der Tod nur echt!" (Hensel 2001: 34)[21] stages Hensel's grotesquely cynical portrayal of Berta's hopeless attempt at the theater. Berta's ambition for artistic self-expres-

---

[20] "I don't like it, when you help yourself to my thoughts without asking."

[21] "Death is the only real thing in life."

sion quickly ends in the sober realization that the stage is not the place for social criticism, when the audience members respond to Berta's desperate and insulting song with loud applause making it clear that they have not listened. The use of the Brechtian *moritat* ("In dieser /Oder jener Welt/ In diesen oder jenen Tagen")[22] alludes to Brecht's theory of epic theater, but Berta's failure to literally employ the alienation effect and to create distance to her performance humorously mimics Hensel's skepticism in the effectiveness of the Brechtian project. The above mentioned rape scene in *Müllers Kuh* contains several hints to various Brecht plays as well. The change from Minna to Pham Thai on stage is reminiscent of *Der gute Mensch von Sezuan* (*The Good Person of Sezuan*). Wheres Brecht's Shen Te/Shui Ta character is depicted in an unsolvable moral dilemma, Hensel's figure changes herself deliberately into a sex slave as a career move, demonstrating the seemingly outdated nature of moral categories altogether. In contrast to Kerstin Specht's play *Lila,* in which a mail-order bride is imported from Thailand to a village in Germany, Minna's career move in Hensel reflects her understanding of the new economy in which fortunes can be distributed as randomly as the titles' allusion to a popular children's rhyme (Abzählreim) suggests: "Müllers Kuh, das bist du" (Müller's cow that's you).

In introducing the plays of Marieluise Fleißer to an English speaking audience Sue Ellen Case wrote: "Where Brecht staged class, Fleißer staged gender, and where he demystified labor relations, she demystified emotional/sexual ones. Fleißer rendered visible and specific the material operations of emotional and sexual experiences, thus opening them to change" (Case 28). In her many parodistic allusions to Brecht and Fleißer, Hensel addresses both gender and economic conditions. However, in the world of global capitalism the expectation of social change through theater seems hopelessly anachronistic.

In an essay on Jelinek's *Krankheit oder Moderne Frauen* Sigrid Berka reflects on Jelinek's concept of intertextuality "that the life of a work of art depends on the digestion of dead texts, that is, on the transformation and new contextualization of quotes" (Berka 375). Hensel's use of Fleißer's texts transforms the earlier material from the exploration of the causes of brutalities among youngsters in the repressive milieu of a small town into a farcical spectacle. Shocking behavior and tragedy can no longer take place because of the absence of true emotions. In the globalized capitalized world the law of profitability is absolute, exploitation is freed of moral bondage and everything and everybody is corrupt. The resulting quintessential emptiness is expressed in several of Hensel's plays. Elly, the failed artist in *Hyänen* sums it up paradig-

---

[22] "In this or that world/ in these or those days."

matically: "es ist wie ein innerer Drang, so schrecklich sein zu müssen, und doch sehnt man sich nach einem wirklichen Leben" (Hensel 1999: 15).[23]

Hensel uses powerful metaphors to express this lack of authentic experiences or relationships. Elly's artistic creations, for example, consist of cut-out collages from mail-order catalogues. She calls her resulting book "Das bunte Buch des Lebens."[24] This hugely successful bestseller is reminiscent of Ralle's enterprise as traveling salesman. He offers maps, history books, scissors and glue in a type of do-it-yourself-kit to create history anew: "Die Geschichte neu schaffen, das hat Zukunft" (Hensel 2001: 19).[25] Unlike Jelinek, who positions her gender critique in relation to "poststructuralist discourses on femininity" (Berka 384), Hensel contextualizes her gender wars within the contemporary experience of a global market economy that oppresses men and women. Women however, even if they are participating in the exploitation (the mother in *Müllers Kuh* or the teacher Atzenköfl) can be doubly exploited by either being forced into traditional gender roles or reduced to sex objects.

In the case of *Atzenköfl*, Hensel thus transforms the historical subtext, consisting of Fleißer's biography, literary texts as well as her concern for analysis of how social contexts produce behavioral violence between the genders into a post-Brechtian critique of capitalism, where violence is too pervasive and random to be productively analyzed. Morality and human kindness are absent in Hensel's violent acts. Her theater is not mourning this absence with pedagogical intentions but performs this grotesque new world with clever inventiveness, physical humor, and an often minimalist language that is effective precisely because of its unsentimental tone. Hensel's dramaturgy of casual depictions of violence is as surprising as it is provocative in its unsentimental brutality and surreal escapades.

Works Cited

Baume, Brita."Mein Thema war nie die DDR." *Ich will meine Trauer nicht leugnen und nicht meine Hoffnung.* Ed. H. Grubitzsch et al. Bochum: Winkler, 1994. 57-69.

Berka, Sigrid. "Das bissigste Stück der Saison: the Textual and Sexual Politics of Vampirism in Elfriede Jelinek's *Krankheit oder Moderne Frauen.*" *The German Quarterly* 68.4 (Fall 1995): 372-88.

Birgfeld, Johannes. "Zwischen Groteske und Menschentheater. Zur Dramatik." *Kerstin Hensel.* Ed. Beth Linklater and Birgit Dahlke. Swansea: Wales UP, 2001. 46-63.

[23] "It is like an inner force to be so terrible, and yet one longs for the real life."
[24] "The colorful book of life."
[25] "To create history anew, that has future."

Case, Sue Ellen, ed. *The Divided Home/Land: Contemporary German Women's Plays.* Ann Arbor: University of Michigan P, 1992.

Cocalis, Susan. "The Politic of Brutality: Toward a definition of the Critical Volksstück." *The Divided Home/Land, Contemporary German Women's Plays.* Ed. Sue Ellen Case. Ann Arbor: U of Michigan P, 1992. 106-130.

Danckwart, Gesine. *Täglich Brot.* Frankfurt: Fischer, 2001.

Fleißer, Marieluise. *Gesammelte Werke.* Vol 1. Ed. Günther Rühle. Frankfurt a. M.: Suhrkamp, 1972.

Hensel, Kerstin. *Atzenköfls Töchter.* Köln: Projekt Theater und Medienverlag, 2001.

—. "Ausflugszeit." *Theater der Zeit* 9 (1988): 61-64.

—. *Grimma.* Köln: Projekt Theater und Medienverlag, 1995.

—. *Hyänen.* Köln: Projekt Theater und Medienverlag, 1999.

— and Volker Trauth. "Indem ich schreibe, suche ich eine Antwort." *Theater der Zeit* 9 (1988): 59-60.

—. *Müllers Kuh, Müllers Kinder.* Köln: Projekt Theater und Medienverlag, 2000.

—. "Überall ist Grimma: Kerstin Hensel im Gespräch mit Ronald Richter." *Theater der Zeit* 7/8 (1996): 86-7.

Jelinek, Elfriede. *Clara S.* Köln: Prometh Verlag, 1984.

Rühle, Günther. "Leben und Schreiben der Marieluise Fleißer aus Ingolstadt." *Marieluise Fleißer. Gesammelte Werke.* Vol 1. Frankfurt: Suhrkamp, 1972. 7-60.

Specht, Kerstin. *Das glühend Männla. Lila. Amiwiesen.* Frankfurt: Verlag der Autoren, 1990.

Gabrijela Mecky Zaragoza

University of Toronto, Canada

A Note on the Containment of Female Aggression: Judith the Murderess in Early 19th Century German Literature[1]

"Un mansevo aj en la gera / Mučača es, mansevo no,"[2] Spanish Jews sing in the 15th century. *Pregoneros Van I Vienen*[3] is the title of the song that the singers carry with them to their new home country. The song is about a "mansevo" on the battlefield who — to the wholehearted horror of all — turns out to be a "mučača," a very belligerent "mučača" whose convincing handling of the sword creates less turmoil than the loss of her helmet in the heat of the battle: a loss that puts a hairy end to the anatomical hide-and-seek. With the image of its courageous *tomboy-mučača*, the song anticipates a need that, especially in modern times, has a belated renaissance: the need to dissipate diverse fears along with the help of wonderful tales about wonderful Jewish heroines.

Although fear[4] is a fundamental experience of human existence, the psychological and physical expressions of fear have not presented themselves in a constant, ahistorical manner throughout time, but instead were subject to social and psycho-historical change (Arnold-de

---

[1] This note is a short introduction to the topic of my master's thesis (*"Frau mordet Mann* oder die Frage nach der Legitimation und Realisation weiblicher Aggression in ausgewählten Judith-Dramen," U Waterloo 1999). I wish to thank Agatha Schwartz and Marija Euchner for their help with the translation of this document. The original German text is available from me upon request.

[2] "Un mancebo hay en la guerra / Muchacha es, mancebo no." ("A youth came to the battlefield, No boy it was, but a girl"). For the Spanish and English translation, see Schwartz 158-161.

[3] Schwartz translates the title as "La Doncella Guerrera" ("The warrior woman").

[4] Kierkegaard makes a distinction between "Angest" ("fear") and "Frygt og lignende Betegnelser" ("fright and similar feelings"), see Bergenholtz 66. With his philosophical approach, however, Kierkegaard clearly refers to lexical discourses of the 18th century. In Adelung's *Wörterbuch* from 1793, for example, fear is described as "Unlust über ein bevorstehendes Übel" ("reluctance caused by an impending evil"), whereas fright is described as "Beklemmung in der Brust" ("a feeling of oppressiveness in the chest"), see Begemann 5. In this note, however, it is not necessary to make this heuristic distinction (Begemann 4) between the phenomenon of "fear" (defined as an indistinct emotional reaction) and the phenomenon of "fright" (defined as a more concrete, object related emotional reaction).

Simine 56). One thing, however, has remained constant: a strong desire to control fear. One possible way to achieve this fear-control is by means of literary production and its reception. Literature or, in Aristotle's words, *poiesis* processes reality. Not only is *poiesis* a means to realise all kinds of desires, but it is also a process through which one comes to terms with the world of reality. In dramatic texts in particular, the two main conditions of *poiesis* — *techné* and *mimesis* — prepare the foundation on which *eleos* and *phobos* can develop their healing effects and culminate in the so-called *katharsis*. Literary or, more precisely, dramatic representations of fear are useful for a specific purpose: they provide an opportunity to experience fright without any real danger and thus enable a safe pleasure (Erdheim 297). This voyeuristic appropriation of fear, this amorphous emotion, is often related to the construction of gender.

With respect to the concept of gender, cultural scholars distinguish between socio-culturally determined arrangements between the sexes and the raw material of sexual anatomy. Most scholars would now agree that gender is not a natural but rather a potent social and ideological category (Loster-Schneider 29). "All societies, it appears now, manifest some gender asymmetry — that is, men and women have different roles [...] — but the qualities, roles, and tasks accorded to men and women vary enormously across time and culture" (Lennox 158). Three theoretical assumptions are important for my argument: that the gender conceptions of a society are represented in its cultural productions; that — in the opinion of cultural materialists — culture is not a unity but an arena where the social contradictions are manifested (165); and finally, that cultural productions, including literature, have certain functions in a society. Literary concepts of gender, in particular, act as containers for fantasies of both desires and fears. According to German psychoanalyst Christa Rohde-Dachser, gender models for women consist of those parts which are excluded from the male self-definition (Rohde-Dachser 145): the *feminine* bears the repressed or, in other words, it brings forward that which has been rejected in a culturally acceptable form in order to make it controllable and disposable.

If one follows this train of thought, it is not "strange," as Virginia Woolf claims (Woolf 76), that, since the era of the ancient Greeks, countless female figures have found their place in literary texts. On the contrary, fictional women are often allowed to do what real women are forbidden to: they may leave the narrow, domestic boundaries of female existence; they may overcome the object status, and they are given the opportunity to become historical subjects. They act either as personifications of an ideal *femininity*, i.e. they love, nurture, heal, and sacrifice themselves — in short, they do good; or they invoke fear by intriguing, seducing, robbing, or even murdering. As different as the figures and their stories may be, they all have one thing in common: they are controlled by the text. This means that the Megaera, this terror of all males, is allowed to misbehave, to sharpen her knife but only if the omnipotent creator of the literary creation can subdue her at the end. According to this hypothesis, the representation of female action and aggression resembles a voyeuristic appropriation of the *Other*, which is ultimately the uncanny. Female aggression, according to this reading, becomes a farce, an absurd spectacle of male demonstrations of power. This also seems to be the case with representations of Judith the Murderess.

The book of the Apocrypha *Judith*[5] has received a variety of treatments in art, literature, and music throughout the centuries. Christian and Jewish scholars mutually agree that the short narrative was written in Palestine around 150 BC (Hanig 5). In the early Christian Church, the Jewish tale becomes well known through Greek and Latin translations and is often quoted, not in a canonical fashion, but rather as an edifying example, e.g. by Clement of Rome, Clement of Alexandria, Origen, Tartullian, Ambrose, and Augustine (Hanig 10). The earliest literary texts that appear to have been inspired by the Jewish narrative are the short Anglo-Saxon poem *Judith* and the first German poem of the troubadours, the so-called *Ältere Judith*. The latter gives us a short overview of the main plot of the Jewish story: the villainous "olofern" wants to conquer a beautiful Jewish "castle," but is prevented by the virtuous widow Judith: "durch des wîbis klûgi / er wart des wînis mûdi [und sie] sluch [ihm] daz houbit von dem buchi" (Diemer 117-123).[6] Although the theme of Judith the man-killer is subsequently taken up in German literature, it has its heyday during the 19th century.[7]

The 19th century shows Europe in a state of great upheaval: the pre-industrial society is being transformed into a civil one (Witzig 66). The early decades prepare the foundation for the growth of both specific and unspecific fears. The rapid process of modernization seems to be based on internal constraints, thereby provoking a change in mentalities and creating indistinct fears in people (Elias 445). Also, apart from the ambiguous nature of progress itself, certain political and social events in Germany create uneasiness among many people. Many historical sources show several types of fear which never appeared before (cf. Begemann 165). Such an increased potential for fear naturally seeks for outlets and finds them, among other literary figures, in the figure of Judith.

Within a short period of time, three texts about Judith are written: in 1809 by Heinrich Keller, in 1818 by an anonymous author, and in 1841

---

[5] My source for the Greek text of Judith is the bilingual edition of Enslin and Zeitlin.

[6] Judith inebriates Holoferne and slays him.

[7] For an overview, see Purdie, Baltzer, and Fitz-Gerald.

by Friedrich Hebbel.[8] The three texts illustrate two things: on the one hand, the texts show how different fears provoke different gender models and thus determine how female aggression is legitimised and manifested in the texts; on the other hand, they also show how these literary-aesthetic conceptions of gender themselves help to overcome, in a playful manner, a murderous event as well as the murderess herself. Although the strategies to overcome the *feminine* differ, they have one thing in common: in each case, the fictional woman is eventually confined to the traditional bourgeois fantasies of femininity.[9]

In 1809 Heinrich Keller creates a text about Judith that carries textual strategies of idealising the female protagonist on multiple levels. The form itself, the strophic rhyme, which lends a poetic touch to the story (Purdie 87), strongly corroborates this strategy. One can surmise that the historical context had decisively contributed to this idealised perception of the Jewish murderess. The play was written between the reign of Napoleon I and the Wars of Liberation. The patriotism with which the men enter the battlefield at the very end of Keller's play can be read as a fictional answer to Fichte's *Reden an die deutsche Nation* (*Addresses to the German Nation*), published in 1808. In times of real threat, violent actions by women seem to be legitimised through literary production, albeit under very special circumstances. These circumstances, however, throw a different light on the idealisation strategy.

Judith's decision to enter the political stage is legitimised by the representation of the Jewish men as enamoured wimps on the one hand; and by the fact that she is the personification of ideal *womanhood* on the other. She resembles a personified idea, burdened with ideology, rather than a real character. This idea is based on a split image of womanhood which is inherent in patriarchal thinking. Judith represents the stereotype of Theweleit's "white woman," which is to say, she is the greatest, the purest, the strongest, and the most beautiful woman. The sun functions as a keyword: Judith's whole being is associated with it

---

[8] I wish to point out that Keller's text and the anonymous one from 1818 were never discussed in detail before my master's thesis. The two texts, however, were mentioned in the following works: Keller's text is quoted in Goedeke's *Grundrisz zur Geschichte der Deutschen Dichtung* (471-472), in Heinsius' *Bücherlexikon* (Vol. 3, 301), in the lexica of Kosch (1035) and Killy (274 f.), in Grimm's *Kleineren Schriften* (9-11), and in Wyss' (50), Purdie's (87-89), and Baltzer's (33-34) works. The anonymous text is quoted in Heinsius' *Bücherlexikon* (Vol. 5, 69), in Kosch's *Theaterlexikon* (928), in Frenzel's *Stoffe der Weltliteratur* (372), and in Purdie's (89), and Baltzer's (42) works.

[9] The German bourgeois gender model for women as it is represented in the literary discourses of the time is deeply divided. On the one hand, writers like Wilhelm von Humboldt, Friedrich Schlegel, and Friedrich Schiller celebrate the ideal of the "schöne Seele," the beautiful, home-loving, pure soul; and on the other hand, they engage in horror scenarios of furious, bloody, revolutionary women. A good example is Schiller's poem *Das Lied von der Glocke*.

(126, 154, 184) — a metaphor for the Divine, for the soul's purity, for insight, for justice (de Vries 400), and for what in the Song of Solomon is called "electa ut sol."[10] Judith represents the light, and it is only this light that may win the victory over the darkness which oppresses Bethulia. But there are more expressive symbols. In this text, the destructive mania of Holoferne and his soldiers causes a life and death struggle. Holoferne, the representative of a negative male power, wants to injure the Earth, the "Mutterschoos," ("the womb of the mother") and wants to flood the ground with blood, with "Purpurwogen" (64). One can venture to say that only an ideal embodiment of the female principle, a woman who is wearing the purple gown of the Virgin Mary (135),[11] can liberate the world of this plague and heal the wounds of Mother Earth. Although Judith is associated with nature — in the text used in a broader sense as the endangered Earth —, the purple gown of the Virgin Mary implies that the male killing can be stopped only by a woman who has successfully overcome her own nature. A pure, divine idea can be realised only by a pure soul. Judith enters the political stage as an internally desexualised being: "[k]ein Mann verdient die Gottheit zu besitzen" (121).[12] She uses her intoxicating beauty which enthralls men of all ages —"Jeder schreyt: Ich will sie haben! / [...] Greise, Männer, Jüngling, Knaben" (38)[13] — as a tool to turn her *femininity* into a weapon: upon divine order, she transforms herself externally into Theweleit's sexual "red woman." She succeeds in melting Holoferne's heart of stone without sacrificing her chastity. The discrepancy between her murderous plan and her hypocritical declarations of love to Holoferne does not provoke a tragic conflict in this text, because Judith is irrefutably legitimised by God's will and her love for the Jewish people. Keller's heroine is deeply engrossed in her role as a divine servant. Therefore, the female warrior merely seems to be breaking out of the traditional female role: by adhering to the image of the sacrificing woman, she fulfils the very patterns from which she seems to have escaped on the surface. In fact, Keller's protagonist is rewarded for her role-conformity by being referred to as "Goddess" by Eliab, the only hero among all the anti-heroes (24).

The literary-aesthetic realisation of the act of killing also serves the idealisation strategy. Everything takes a smooth course: the defeat of the brute Holoferne is a full success without Judith losing her virtuous

---

[10] See the *Biblia Sacra Latina* (6:10).

[11] In Greek and Byzantine art of the 4th to the 8th century BC, Godmothers' gowns are often painted in these colors; see Schmidt 202, 222. Heinrich Keller wrote his text in Rome in 1807.

[12] "No man deserves to possess the Goddess."

[13] "Everybody is shouting: 'I want her' – elderly men, men, youths, and boys."

glory. The scene of Holoferne's death suggests that a woman cannot act without the help of the divine Father: not only does she need his guidance to be sufficiently charming, but she also depends on his aid to enable her to strike with her sword. The few things we learn about the murderous act appear to be pure and holy — *kosher*. There is hardly any blood on the stage, nor do the characters display any outward signs of disturbing emotions. The head of the dragon, "the one with the terrible look in his eyes," as Holoferne is called in the text, has come into the possession of God's female avenger, suddenly and quietly. The reminder of the heroic deed — "das schnöde Haupt" ("the vile head" 187) — disappears in the same inconspicuous way into the bag of the servant.

One can conclude that in Keller's text, female aggression is legitimised only if the protagonist thinks and behaves in an ideal way, if she acts exclusively for God and her people. Considering the historical context, it can be said that the protagonist's unconditional will to sacrifice herself seems to be a call upon the French conquerors to stop their fury. Yet in a broader sense, Judith's murderous deed serves the aims of a male cause. This deed is idealised as a feat that serves as a model to rouse from their lethargy not only fictional, but also real battle-weary men. Female aggression becomes an instrument of textual legitimisation and realisation. It is domesticated — and thus overcome in a playful manner.

The anonymous text of 1818 *Judith und Holofernes* is entirely different. Judith's character as well as her action and motivation are demonised. Misogyny and anti-Semitism are dominant characteristics of the text. Here as well, the historical context seems to be important: the text was written after the Wars of Liberation at the time of the Congress of Vienna. The first line of interpretation seems to be clear: Napoleon is on Elba, thus the willingness to legitimise the historical actions of a woman decreases. Yet, there exists another, a complementary line of interpretation. The "Nation," as stated in the preface, can be realised only if Judaism is overcome, if the "bösen talmudischen [...] Grundsätze mit unseren weit bessern christlichen rühmlichst vertauscht [werden]" (4).[14] The text thus exemplifies how, in times of a changing society and government, pictures of the enemy — the so-called *Other* — are developed to guarantee the community ties and to assert, in this case, the Christian-German subject. In addition, the murderess is Jewish herself. It is obvious that in the anonymous text, the fact that she belongs to the so-called second sex (Beauvoir) is even more fatal than the fact that she belongs to a group of corrupted people.

---

[14] "the evil principles of the Talmud are gloriously replaced by our much better Christian ones."

Although the Jewish men are harshly criticised by the narrator, they do not have to suffer in hell at the very end. In contrast to Judith, they are still allowed to engage in victorious celebrations in what is called the Jewish "Wildniß" ("wilderness" 77): "Mer hoben gesiegt! [...] Jou, jou! Rauben! Beute machen! Dos wölln mer!" (81-83).[15]

The plot of this drama can be interpreted on two different, closely related levels. On both levels, it tells a story of temptation. On the textual level, external forces in form of the devil seduce Judith; on the subtextual level, internal forces as manifested in her sexual drive compel her. Yet, *womanhood* is permanently associated with everything opposed to God's word, to the Logos of the fathers; it is associated with nature in a broader sense, with demonic forces, and with a chaotic rage of destruction.

The plan to murder Holofernes is introduced as an illegitimate devilish act. Therefore, all other attempts of legitimisation are stripped of any basis. Judith, the woman with doubtful qualities — among others the effect she has on men, leaving them impotent and sick[16] — craves the fruits of glory. Caught in mental and physical desires of all kinds, she overlooks not only the cloven hoof, but also the "horns" and the "red eyes" of the angelic apparition in her dream, associating it with "Adonai" and following its call blindly: Nein, das war kein Traum æ Das war ein wahres Gesicht æ Gesehen von Angesicht zu Angesicht hab' ich ihn wirklich / den göttlichen Uriel / kleine Hörner, wie Moses, und rothe Augen, wie der Shilo, hatte er ja / Ach, und in ein allerliebstes Shabbesröckel war er gekleidet [...] Reine Wahrheit hat er mir [...] gesagt." (58)[17]

This Judith, too, embraces her role as a servant of a male authority, but unfortunately, she serves the wrong side. Without being aware of it, she allows herself to be made a false prophet by a demon, even though she believes until the very end that her murderous act was legitimate. Only after Judith loses her virginity on Holoferne's carpet — and with it the last highly symbolical protection against evil — and the unholy union has been sealed between her and the new object of her desire, is she confronted with her error:

---

[15] "We won! Let us rob and steal! This is what we want to do!"

[16] Judith is "Madje" ("virgin") and "Wittib" ("widow") at the same time. Her husband, as Abra tells us, was an "erbärmlicher Knirps [und] wor krank [und] konnt' nischt vollziehn die Hochzeit von anen Shabbes zün anern Shabbes" ("wimp and was ill and could not fulfil his matrimonial duties from one sabbath to the next," 70). He died under mysterious circumstances. A similar lot falls to his successor.

[17] "No, it was no dream / It was a real face / I really saw him from face to face / the divine Uriel / with little horns, like Moses, and red eyes, like Shilo / Oh, and he wore a charming shabbes-jacket [...] and told me nothing but the truth."

> Also vereinigt sind wir nun [...] auf ewig! [...] ich besitze [...] unter
> dem Herrscher der untersten Welten [...] ein Reich von erstaunlicher
> Größe [...] Doch gehet der Weg nicht Aufwärts zum Himmelreich,
> sondern nur abwärts ein wenig [...] Adramelech heiß' ich, bin erster
> Minister der Hölle, Satans verfinsterten Reiches, und aller Verworfe-
> nen! (105-108)[18]

At the very moment of her *anagnorisis*, she is sent on a journey with
no return. Adramelech's driver —"der Kutscher"— takes his duties
very seriously. Judith is banished to the place where, according to the
text, winged sows are awaiting her.

The literary-aesthetic realisation of the act of killing, or more precisely, its omission, also reflects that the act is a profoundly illegitimate
one. The scene of Judith and Holoferne is reduced to a minimum of four
pages (out of 108). This fact reveals the text's true intention: it is above
all about conveying a general idea of Judith's and her people's bad
character. In all secrecy, in night's darkness, the female agent of evil
strikes successfully and kills, with Satan's powers, Holoferne, "den
Edelmüthigen," the betrayed representative of civilisation. Judith, the
female "Bestie" ("beast") will soon be severely judged by the Assyrians
who represent the good side. They reach the unanimous agreement that
she belongs in hell.

One can conclude that in this anonymous text from 1818, the historical action by a woman is represented as an aberration. Obviously,
she has to set an example as to what happens to those women who
leave their domestic boundaries; who believe in acting on divine orders
and become warriors; who act for the enemy, the non-Christian side;
and who seal a pact with demons to create a hellish spectacle that leads
to bloody destruction. The hellfire they started will finally engulf them.
Female aggression is clearly negated here; it is demonised and eternal-
ly damned — and thus overcome in a playful manner.

With *Judith* by Friedrich Hebbel (1841), a second and this time final
rupture in the adaptation of the tale of Judith takes place. In contrast to
the text from 1818, in which Judith is accused of using Satan's powers,
Hebbel stresses the psychological motives of a supposedly heroic deed.
The text illustrates the difficult process of female individuation. It is
impossible for the heroine to live within the fixed categories of her pre-
determined space; therefore, she espouses a patriotic mission and transgresses the boundaries of so-called female *nature*. Yet, she must learn
that the deed destroys her rather than bring her glory.

---

[18] "Thus we are reunited forever. I possess under the lord of the underworld a kingdom
of astounding dimensions. Yet the road does not lead up to Heaven, but downward a
little. Adramelech is my name, I am the Prime minister of Hell, of Satan's dark kingdom
and of all who are depraved."

Here as well, it seems to be important to take into account the historical context. Hebbel's drama was written in a period of restoration. At this time, the bourgeois society is already established. The separation into a public male and a private female world prevails (Witzig 69); the dichotomous gender model — and with it the ideal of passive *womanhood* — enables the functioning of the new social order. Hebbel's text reflects the ideology of the sexes of his time by presenting a horrific example of what happens to women who want to leave their traditional space. In Hebbel's text, too, the political action of a woman is doomed to failure. The message of the text seems to be that a woman cannot move rationally on the male stage of world politics, because her female *nature* will betray her.[19]

Judith's resolution to ban the Assyrian threat with weapons of her *femininity* is depicted as subjective and illegitimate. All subsequent attempts of legitimisation are therefore called into question. Deeply frustrated by a husband who tries to avoid any physical (i.e. symbiotic) encounters with her — whenever he tries to overcome his phobia, he feels desperately dominated by the female principle itself, the dark sides of Mother Earth —[20] she tries to forget her matrimonial nightmares and searches extensively for new challenges. Therefore, it is not surprising that the widowed virgin perceives Holoferne's politics of expansion as a potential change to show the world and, more importantly, herself that she is much more than an infertile housewife. "Ich mögt' ihn sehen," (20)[21] is her first reaction to Ephraim's growing feelings of doom. Unfortunately, Hebbel's Judith, too, thinks that she needs an external, male authority to sanction her desires. She needs it so badly that she is willing to turn Jesus' painful cries for help — "My God, my God, why did you leave me" (Matthew 27:46) — into a very personal order: "Gott! Gott! Mir ist, als müßt' ich Dich am Zipfel fassen, wie Einen, der mich auf ewig zu verlassen droht" (25).[22] After three nights of hypocritical and somewhat self-righteous prayers for release — from bad memories as well as from her meaningless life — she finally releases herself. Slowly, her personal needs take on the dimension of a divine-patriotic mission:

---

[19] Mirza brings it to the point: "A woman should give birth to men, never should she kill them."

[20] "[E]s war, als ob die schwarze Erde eine Hand ausgestreckt und ihn von unten damit gepackt hätte [...] 'Ich kann ja nicht,' antwortete er dumpf und bleiern, 'Ich kann nicht!'" ["It was as if the black Earth had reached out with her hand and had grabbed him from below. 'I cannot,' he answered with dullness and heaviness, 'I cannot!'"] (17).

[21] "I want to see him."

[22] "God! God! It is as if I had to grab you like someone who wants to leave me forever."

Nur ein Gedanke kam mir, nur Einer, mit dem ich spielte und der
immer wiederkehrt; doch, der kam nicht von Dir. Oder kam er von
Dir? — [...] Er kam von Dir! Der Weg zu meiner That geht durch die
Sünde! [...] Dank, Dank Dir, Herr! (25-26)[23]

It is obvious that Judith falls prey to a multi-layered *hamartia* of
which she becomes aware only after the murder. Little by little, the
"Nebelschleier" ("the fog") that has been covering her unconscious disappears, and little by little, she has to learn that — contrary to her belief
— God did not choose her to be the saviour of her people. In fact, only
the combination of Manassa's restrained and Holoferne's unleashed
sexual drives turns her into a murderess. Raped by a womaniser, who
wants to conquer the world in order to take possession of as many
women as possible, Judith avenges her violated self by striking with the
sword. But she cannot live with the discovery that she was mainly driven by her own thirst for revenge. After her failed attempt to escape
into word games[24] as well as into insanity,[25] she has to acknowledge
that she has not only committed an illegitimate murder, but that she has
also lost her lover, in her opinion, the archetypical superman, the first
and last man on earth (79). She becomes a tragic figure by giving way
to self-destructive inclinations: "Dank? Wer will den? [...] sie [die Tat]
zermalmt mich [...] Was Gott nur dazu sagt, wenn er morgen früh
herunterschaut und sieht, daß die Sonne nicht mehr gehen kann und
daß die Sterne lahm geworden sind" (72-73).[26] Yet, it is through this
unconditional acceptance of her guilt and the renunciation of her own
life that she partly accepts her guilt: her deed is re-legitimised to a certain degree. However, the price is high, for it is Judith herself.

In this text, unlike the previous two, the scene of the murder is
depicted in detail. The aesthetic realisation reflects the heroine's inner
strife. Judith battles with herself; her emotional outbreaks and reflections, her partly hesitant, partly hectic moves show that God and her
people no longer seem to exist for her during important moments. The

---

23 "I had only one thought that I played with and that keeps returning; but it didn't come
from you. Or did it? It did come from you! The path to my deed leads through sin.
Thank you, thank you my Lord!"

24 Like Kleist's Penthesilea (100), she tells her maid about her deed in the subjunctive
mood: "dies Erblassen Deines Gesichts könnte mir einreden, ich habe das Unmen-
schliche gethan" ["Your face turning pale could convince me that I have done something inhuman.] (71).

25 "Komm, wir wollen wieder spielen [...] Eben war ich ein böses Weib [...] Hu! Sag' mir,
was ich nun sein soll!" ["Let us play again [...] I was a bad girl just now [...] Hu! Tell
me what I have to be now."] (73).

26 "Thankfulness? Who needs it? It [the deed] is eating me up inside. What will God say
if he looks down tomorrow morning and sees that the sun cannot shine any more and
that the stars are frozen."

scene illustrates that she can kill only if she is in a state of profound despair.

One can conclude that in Hebbel's text, female aggression is legitimised to a certain extent under one circumstance only. A woman who murders is, unlike the biblical Judith, not allowed to celebrate her bloody deed. She is not allowed to anoint herself with olive oil for the festivities, nor is she permitted to live to be a hundred and five years of age (177). She is not idealised as a "Wunder der Natur" ("wonder of nature"); instead, she has to acknowledge the unnaturalness of her deed. A woman who kills has to end tragically: she will ultimately be destroyed by the hellish fire of her own conscience. In Hebbel's text, female aggression is deprived of its *raison d'être*; it is strangulated — and thus overcome in a playful manner.

In this analysis, I have shown that all three texts deal with the revolutionary act of a woman killing a man. At the same time, this revolutionary act is less revolutionary than it seems to be. In fact, the effect of this purported transgression is undermined by several factors:

• The three heroines are shown in traditional female roles: they either appear as serving women (Keller/Anonymous) or/and as love-stricken women (Anonymous/ Hebbel).

• The plots express literary judgements about female behaviour-patterns that emphasise the age-old Eve-Maria-stereotypes: the altruistic woman is rewarded (Keller), whereas the egocentric maid in the service of Uriel alias the Prime minister of hell is severely punished (Anonymous). The loving woman who is controlled by her lustful feelings — in the anonymous text that happens after she has "abused a holy love" (4) — and/or the (somehow) self-confident woman who is driven by the wish to overcome the female object status (Hebbel) have to fail.

• The plot's anti-revolutionary effect is corroborated by the underlying depiction of the misogynistic relationship between womanhood and *nature* — where *nature* traditionally plays a negative role — with the exception of Keller's white super-heroine who is able to overcome it.

• The fact that the apocryphal figure of Judith is used for different purposes in the texts can tell us something about the self-serving functions that female gender models in literary texts by male authors have. Keller's Judith is supposed to stir tired men; in the anonymous text, Judith helps to set up the picture of the Jewish *Other*; and in Hebbel's text, Judith helps to affirm the dichotomous bourgeois gender model.

In all three texts, the legitimisation and realisation of female aggression leads to the overcoming of a cruel event. Every woman who transgresses traditional boundaries, who dares to murder a man without having a divine mission, is sent to hell: either to an external one where all kinds of beasts wait for her, or an internal one which is even more terrible. Only the woman whose pride is broken is allowed to survive, as states the priestess shortly after Penthesilea's death in Kleist's drama. In the Christian context, this is the woman who has at least submitted to the heavenly patriarch in order to lifelessly execute his orders — a dead woman, "eine Abgestorbne" (Kleist 103), one who, despite a murder, does not provoke fear. The overcoming of fear seems to be what all three texts have set as their ultimate goal.

One could argue that at least some fear of the *feminine* should have vanished after these three literary attempts. The figures of Judith in the 20th century, however, give rise to doubt. The battle against the Jewish murderess on the textual battlefield seems to go on: in Kaiser's and Giraudoux's texts behind the curtains of Holoferne's bedroom, in Castellanos' text in Chiapas, in "una tierra llena de sepulcros" (Castellanos 167); and in Dürrenmatt's role plays of 1986 on a stage of double identities — Jeanne d'Arc in the role of Judith — where his heroine (Jeanne/Judith) is yearning for hellish tortures after the murder of Napoleon/Holoferne. The heroic "mučačas" of the past have vanished; they appear to have left the stage forever, in order to make room for their sisters who long to die.

Works Cited

Aristoteles. *Die Poetik. Griechisch / Deutsch.* Trans. Manfred Fuhrmann. Stuttgart: Reclam, 1982.

Arnold-de Simine, Silke. "Die Lust an der Angst. Zur Schauerliteratur von Autorinnen um 1800." *Geschlecht — Literatur — Geschichte I.* Ed. Gudrun Loster-Schneider. St. Ingbert: Röhrig, 1999. 55-79.

Baltzer, Otto. *Judith in der deutschen Literatur.* Berlin, Leipzig: de Gruyter, 1930.

Die Bibel. Nach der deutschen Übersetzung von D. Martin Luther. Berlin: Lutherisches Bibelhaus, 1966.

Begemann, Christian. *Furcht und Angst im Prozeß der Aufklärung. Zur Literatur und Bewußtseinsgeschichte im 18. Jahrhundert.* Frankfurt a. M.: Athenäum, 1987.

Bergenholtz, Henning. *Das Wortfeld Angst. Eine lexikographische Untersuchung mit Vorschlägen für ein großes interdisziplinäres Wörterbuch der deutschen Sprache.* Stuttgart: Klett-Cotta, 1980.

Biblia Sacra Latina. Ex Biblia Sacra Vulgatæ Editionis. London: Bagster & Sons, 1970.

The Book of Judith. Greek Text with an English Translation. Ed. Morton S. Enslin and Solomon Zeitlin. Philadelphia: Brill, Leiden, 1972.

Castellanos, Rosario. *Poesía no eres tu; obra poética: 1948-1971.* México: Fondo de Cultura Económica, 1975. 145-167.

Diemer, Joseph. *Deutsche Gedichte des elften und zwölften Jahrhunderts*. Darmstadt: Wissenschaftliche Buchgesellschaft, 1968. 117-123.

Dürrenmatt, Friedrich. *Die Wiedertäufer. Eine Komödie in zwei Teilen. Urfassung*. Zürich: Diogenes, 1980.

Elias, Norbert. *Über den Prozess der Zivilisation. Soziogenetische und psychogenetische Untersuchungen*. Vol. 2. Bern, München: Francke, 1969.

Erdheim, Mario. *Die Psychoanalyse und das Unbewußte in der Kultur. Aufsätze 1980-1987*. Frankfurt a. M.: Suhrkamp, 1988.

Fichte, Johann Gottlieb. "Reden an die deutsche Nation." *Johann Gottlieb Fichte's sämtliche Werke*. Vol. 7. Ed. J. H. Fichte. Berlin: de Gruyter & Co, 1965. 257-516.

Fitz-Gerald, John D. "La historia de Judit y Holofernes en la literatura española." *Hispania* XIV (1931): 193-96.

Frenzel, Elisabeth. *Stoffe der Weltliteratur. Ein Lexikon dichtungsgeschichtlicher Längsschnitte*. Stuttgart: Kröner, 1976. 371-373.

Giraudoux, Jean. *Judith. Tragédie en trois actes*. Paris: Grasset, 1932.

Goedeke, Karl. *Grundrisz zur Geschichte der Deutschen Dichtung*. Vol. 6. Leipzig, Dresden, Berlin: Ehlermann, 1886. 471-472.

Grimm, Jacob. *Kleinere Schriften VI. Recensionen und vermischte Aufsätze*. Vol. 3. Hildesheim: Olms, 1965. 9-11.

Hanig, David Daniel. "Three transformations of the Judith Story: A comparative study of Hebbel, Kaiser, and Giraudoux." Diss. Indiana U, 1965.

Hebbel, Friedrich. *Sämtliche Werke. Historisch-kritische Ausgabe*. Vol. 1. Ed. Richard Maria Werner. 3. Ed. Berlin: Behr's, 1911-13. 1-81.

Heinsius, Wilhelm. *Allgemeines Bücher-Lexikon*. Vol. 3 / 4 und Vol. 5 / 6. Leipzig 1812 and 1817. Graz: Akademische Druck- und Verlagsanstalt, 1962. 301 and 69.

Judith und Holofernes. Ein Drama in fünf Akten. Zerbst: Andreas Füchsel, 1818.

Kaiser, Georg. "Die jüdische Witwe. Bühnenstück in fünf Akten." *Gesammelte Werke*. Vol. 3. Berlin: Kiepenheuer, 1931. 245-425.

Keller, Heinrich. *Judith. Schauspiel von Heinrich von Itzenloe, Hofpoet bey Kaiser Rudolf II. Aus einer alten Handschrift*. Zürich: Orell, Füßli u. Companie, 1809.

Killy, Walther. *Literatur Lexikon. Autoren und Werke deutscher Sprache*. Vol. 6. München: Bertelsmann, 1989. 274-275.

Kleist, Heinrich von. *Penthesilea. Ein Trauerspiel*. Stuttgart: Reclam, 1994.

Kosch, Wilhelm. *Deutsches Literatur-Lexikon. Biographisches-Bibliographisches Handbuch*. Vol. 8. Bern, München: Francke, 1981. 1035.

___ . *Deutsches Theaterlexikon. Biographisches und bibliographisches Handbuch*. Vol. 2. Wien, Klagenfurt: Kleinmayr, 1960. 928 and 977.

Lennox, Sara. "Feminist Scholarship and Germanistik." *The German Quarterly* 61, 2 (1989): 158-170.

Loster-Schneider, Gudrun. "Wer hat Angst vor Virginia Woolf? Gender-wissenschaftliche Paradigmen in den historischen Kulturwissenschaften." *Geschlecht – Literatur – Geschichte I*. Ed. Gudrun Loster-Schneider. St. Ingbert: Röhrig, 1999. 9-32.

Mecky, Gabrijela. "'Frau mordet Mann' oder die Frage nach der Legitimation und Realisation weiblicher Aggression in ausgewählten Judith-Dramen." U of Waterloo, 1999.

Purdie, Edna. *The Story of Judith in German und English Literature*. Paris: Librairie Ancienne Honoré Champion, 1927.

Rohde-Dachser, Christa. *Expedition in den dunklen Kontinent. Weiblichkeit im Diskurs der Psychoanalyse*. Frankfurt a. M.: Fischer, 1997.

Schiller, Friedrich. *Gedichte. Eine Auswahl*. Ed. Gerhard Fricke. Stuttgart: Reclam, 1980.

Schmidt, Heinrich. *Die vergessene Bildersprache christlicher Kunst. Ein Führer zum Verständnis der Tier-, Engel- und Mariensymbolik*. München: Beck, 1981.

Schwartz, Stephan. "Yo soy una Rosa / I am a rose. Judeo-Spanish Texts from Bosnia." *Journal of Croatian Studies* 31 (1990): 158-161.

Theweleit, Klaus. *Männerphantasien I. Frauen, Fluten, Körper, Geschichte*. Reinbek: Rowohlt, 1980.

Vries, Ad de. *Dictionary of Symbols and Imagery*. Amsterdam, London: North Holland Publishing Company, 1974.

Witzig, Heidi. "Historische Dimensionen weiblicher Aggressivität." *Starke Frauen – Zänkische Weiber? Frauen und Aggression*. Ed. Elisabeth Camenzind and Kathrin Knüsel. Stuttgart: Kreuz, 1992. 61-80.

Woolf, Virginia. *A Room of One's Own*. Toronto: Mc Clelland & Stewart, 1929.

Wyss, Bernhard. *Heinrich Keller: der Züricher Bildhauer und Dichter*. Diss. U Zürich, 1891. Frauenfeld: Huber, 1891.

Sigrid Schmid-Bortenschlager

University of Salzburg, Austria

Violence and Woman's Status as Victim: Changing the Role Model or Being Caught in the Trap?

It has been something of an unofficial dogma in the new women's literature — at least in German language women's literature — that violence was something women suffered but never perpetrated themselves. Literature was hence perpetuating the image of women as passive victims, thus leaving the role of activity, including violence, to men.

It could therefore be considered an emancipatory step that in the 1980s a few books appeared in which women were depicted as inflicting psychological — and physical — violence: the common denominator of these books was that violence was inflicted by mothers on their daughters. I am thinking here of Elfriede Jelinek's *Klavierspielerin* (1983; *The Piano Teacher*, 1999), made into a successful film that won several prices at the 2001 Cannes Film Festival; Waltraud Mitgutsch's *Die Züchtigung* (1985; The Punishment) and Claudia Erdheims *Bist Du wahnsinning geworden?* (1984; Have you gone mad?). Women were finally taking up the motif of the intergenerational conflict, which had been a motif so dear to mainstream literature opposing fathers and sons, especially in the *Sturm and Drang* period and in expressionism.

Elfriede Czurda went a step further when she published *The Giftmörderinnen* (Murderesses by Poison) in 1991, taking a contemporary real-life crime — two lesbians who killed the husband of one of them in Itzehoe, Germany — and transforming it into a very artificially and skilfully constructed novel about the relationship of power and language, in which, in the end, the murdering women turn out to be the real victims of society, once again.

We have to consider this background of violence enacted by women as some kind of a literary taboo to explain the refreshing surprise and the success of the novels by Ingrid Noll, starting with *Der Hahn ist tot* (*Hell has no fury*) in 1991, followed by *Die Häupter meiner Lieben* (My Beloveds' Heads), *Die Apothekerin* (The Woman Pharmacist) in 1994 and *Röslein rot* (Little Red Rose) in 1998, all published by Diogenes not in their highly esteemed mystery collection,[1] but in the regular fiction program.

---

[1] The German translations of Patricia Highsmith's novels are published here.

In Noll's books we do not only encounter a woman writing crime stories — which is a venerable British tradition going back to Agatha Christie — but a woman who describes a murderess, moreover, paints her very sympathetically and does not let her get caught by the police.

Contrary to the journalistic stories about the aging little housewife who became a bestseller author, Ingrid Noll is a highly intelligent and cultured woman: she has a doctorate in German literature and art history and she knows her literary techniques. The story is told by the murderess herself, a woman over fifty, more or less successful in her career (although she has not finished her university studies), yet unsuccessful in her private and love life. In her fifties she falls madly in love for the first time, and it is this love that makes her kill three women and the policeman who is on the verge of finding her out. What makes the book extraordinary is the detached and slightly ironic way in which the narrator, Rosemarie Thyra Hirte, looks at herself and her passion, and how coolly and "normally" she becomes a murderess. The murders themselves — three of them rather impulsive, the first and the last by gunshot, one by throwing an electric dryer into the bathtub and ultimately drowning the unconscious victim, and one premeditated: pushing her best friend down a tower — are described in more or less graphic detail; Rosemarie is genuinely sick afterwards, and her fainting, throwing up, getting diarrhea etc. are described in sympathetic detail. But although the physical reaction to her deeds is violent, she soon regains control of herself and her practical and moral reactions are much more calm and level-headed. In the course of events she discovers that power, the power to kill, is at least as satisfactory a passion as love. As the story unfolds and she realizes that her beloved Witold is a vain and weak man, more than trying to seduce him she enjoys reminding him how she witnessed him shooting his wife and only finished the job for him. She blackmails him into helping her to dispose of the murdered policeman; in the process Witold is permanently maimed in the exploding car, a fact that leads the police to consider him to be the murderer.

Nevertheless, in the end justice and morality prevail, although it is not human justice, but fate. Rosemarie Hirte is diagnosed with cancer of the colon; she is saved but severely handicapped by having an artificial anus, and she spends the rest of her life visiting her beloved — with whom contact never went further then a friendly kiss — twice a week in the asylum, where the brain-damaged and paraplegic Witold is taken care of. It remains ambivalent whether she comes in order to take care of him or to control him.

The book has been acclaimed for its dry humour and psychological insights, and it still makes entertaining reading. If we consider the depiction of violence, the problems inherent in this first novel become more apparent in the following ones. In the second novel, *Die Häupter meiner Lieben* (My Beloveds' Heads), two young girls, Maja and Cora — both sixteen years of age in the beginning and going into their twenties at the end — use murder as a problem-solving device, the problems being jealousy toward a nasty brother, boredom with an annoying husband or attempted blackmail by a young lover. In this and the following novels mere greed replaces love as a motivating power for killing. In *Die Apothekerin* (The Woman Pharmacist) it is an idiosyncratic rich grandfather, in *Röslein rot* (Little Red Rose) a boring rich husband with a heart condition who both find a premature end at the hands of the legal heirs. The heirs show no regret whatsoever and the police do not suspect anything. In *Röslein rot* it is a woman friend of the murderess who detects the truth — only to turn her knowledge to her own financial advantage.

In Noll's novels the problematic combination of psychological realism and ironic use of a literary cliché becomes obvious. In the first novel the heroine's cancer, as a sort of *deus ex machina,* solves the problem of guilt and punishment — the latter being integral elements of the pattern of the classical detective story. When this element is absent, the psychological realism of the texts leaves two possible interpretations: either murder is actually reduced to a practical and successful problem-solving device, a device as to how to become rich by getting rid of "useless" people (aging grandparents, sick husbands and wives), which is surely problematic from a moral point of view; or we have to read the novels as a kind of dream-fulfilment of attaining wealth and independence through murder, a wish that is, if not reflected on in any way, no less dubious on a social and moral level.

What can be done on a literary level with the motif of the happy and unpunished murderess is shown in Lilian Faschinger's *Magdalena Sünderin* (*Magdalena the Sinner*) from 1995 (English translation in 1997). The title itself alludes to the Bible, to sin and forgiveness, and this allusion is amplified in the text (cf. Greiner). The heroine, a young independent woman on a motorbike abducts a Roman-Catholic priest in order to confess to him the seven murders of her seven lovers. The abduction was necessary as nobody wanted to listen to her story. The story is told from the perspective of the priest, who in the course of the three-day confession becomes her new lover. Magdalena's confession is rendered in direct speech, so we actually have two first-person narrators, a female one — who remains her old self —, and a male one who changes from condemning priest and victim of Magdalena's violence to understanding and loving accomplice and who, in the end, is very unhappy about being freed by the police and his virtuous sister Maria and very happy about the successful flight of his lover Maria Magdalena.

Similarly to Noll's novel, in *Magdalena the Sinner* the murders are associated with sex, but whereas the elderly Rosemarie kills her (real or imagined) female rivals in order to gain Witold's love, Faschinger's heroine kills her lovers to end relationships that had begun very promising but have, in various ways, turned unsatisfactory for her. Just like Rosemarie, Magdalena is never detected. Only once is she suspected of murder, not by the police but by friends of the deceased. She uses seven different kinds of murder (drowning, burning, poisoning, stabbing, shooting, strangling, pushing over the cliff), and some of the acts are described in rather gruesome detail. We also find the whole range from spontaneous murder to well-planned execution. What the reader will find missing — in comparison to Noll's narrative — is the feeling of guilt and its physical syndroms on the part of the murderess. Magdalena's acts of killing are acts of either compassion or of self-defence; her feeling afterwards is always one of liberation.

The biblical allusions and the number seven has lead reviewers to make the connection with the seven deadly sins, a parallel that is not supported by a closer analysis of the text. The seven lovers — and the seven murders just as the seven relationships — can be read as real-life types of male-female relationships, or, to be more precise, as different forms of women's victimizations, and /or of literary or filmic prototypes of female-male relationships.

The first lover, the Friesian represents the prototype of the melancholy hero. Magdalena meets him in catacombs; he is lying in a coffin and is depicted as holding a skull in his hand. His various suicide attempts are all unsuccessful, and while sinking ever deeper into his depression, he leaves breadwinning and all practical matters totally to Magdalena. Her compassion for him is deep and he takes advantage of it to the utmost, but in the end she realizes that she must rid herself of him if he is not to draw her down with him. Drowning is the method she chooses to kill him — the literary couple Hamlet and Ophelia are recalled but in a role reversal: from victim, Ophelia turns into murderess.

Igor, the second lover, an Ukrainian living in Paris, plagues her eventually with his jealousy and his drunkenness. She ends this relationship by fire, with which it had also begun, and moves on to the Spanish dance-instructor Pablo who, a real Don Juan, shares his love for her with practically every other woman he meets. The novel thus moves from the extreme of Igor's jealous monogamy to absolute promiscuity — on the part of the man, not the woman. Magdalena's answer to it is poison, which she gets from the British *clochard* Jonathan Alistair Abercrombie, with whom she moves from Paris to London. Whereas up to now she has provided or shared in providing (with Pablo) the material means of existence, Jonathan provides for her, but he uses her up physically, turning out to be, literally and metaphorically, a vampire: he drinks her blood and uses her as a model for his sculptures. Bram Stoker, countless film versions up to Roman Polanski, and feminist interpretations of the vampire myth (cf. Jelinek and Bronfen) are clearly recognizable. The vampire has to be stabbed, and although the next lover, Michael from Transsylvania, offers Magdalena the correct tool, a wooden stick, she prefers to enact Hitchcock's *Psycho*, stabbing Jonathan in the shower with a knife — female-male roles being reversed once again.

The sexual abstinence Michael imposes upon her is motivated in various ways: Magdalena has to re-enact his mother (another Hitchcock parallel) by wearing her clothes, and he also imposes his religious fervor upon her by turning her into an active member of Jehovah's Witnesses. When she accidentally finds out that the religious sublimation, which he has imposed upon their relationship, is fake and that he has a homosexual relationship with one of his "brothers," she shoots him and has to leave London. Back on the continent she meets, in the casino in Baden-Baden, the aged and very rich Baron Otto who invites her to live with him, read to him from Dante's *Divina Comedia* and de Sade,[2] and finally asks her to enact sado-masochistic scenes from de Sade, once again reversed, with him in the role of the masochist and her in the role of the domina. Everything goes well until the baron finds out about her "natural" and very satisfying sexual relationship with his Austrian chauffeur Clemens who is consequently sent away. Magdalena can stay on, but the lavish presents she used to receive for her services up to now are transferred to the Bohemian cook who is about to replace her also in her sexual function. Therefore she plays one of the games to the end, strangles Otto and makes it look like suicide.

Constricting family ties had been one of the reasons for Magdalena's initial flight from Austria. At this point, they start to encroach on her again with Clemens' plans to marry her and with one of her sisters having found her in Baden-Baden and extorting money from her. Planning to flee to Prague she looses — the unconscious at work — her way and ends up in Munich, and finally with her next lover, Karl in Garmisch-Partenkirchen, in Bavaria, dangerously close to Austria. Like Baron Otto, Karl takes care of her financially, although at a much lower level of expenses. He soon begins to engulf her with his family history, his three former wifes and six children, some of whom move into the house, call all the time etc. Karl tries to make her into a composite of his former wives through a combination of their singing, cooking, and sportive abilities, which results in the "ideal woman:" physically and sexually attractive, artistically gifted, and with all the qualities of a good

---

[2] Let's recall here the film *La Lectrice* by Deville with Miou Miou in the role of the reader, but also, via the connection Baden-Baden, Claude Miller's superb *Mortelle Randonnée*, in which Isabelle Adjani plays a multiple murderess.

housekeeper and mother. While Magdalena complies with his require-
ments to sing and cook for him, the physical presence and the demands
of understanding his large family become too much for her: on a mountain hike she pushes Karl down a precipice, whereupon she returns to
Austria to confess her adventures to the ever more understanding
priest.

Contrary to Noll's story, in *Magdalena the Sinner* there is no moral
ending; Faschinger's novel has an open ending: on her motorbike, Magdalena succeeds in her flight from the Austrian police and can assume
an independent life and live (and maybe kill) happily ever after. As I
have already pointed out previously, Faschinger cites and deconstructs
various images of women as victims in a playful, postmodern way. The
story cannot be read as a realistic depiction of actual life. Psychology
does enter into the picture, but only to be treated in the very same way
as the other literary, filmic or general myths and images about women
and sexuality. The heroine does call for identification, but on a level
which is repeatedly broken and thus can never be taken completely
seriously. Murder here certainly is neither a problem-solving device nor
a wish fulfilment. The book offers the possibility, so often claimed by
films and books depicting violence, of purging oneself of aggressive
tendencies by channelling them into a game, which never looses its
character of being only a game, a story told all over again. It is this conscious storytelling that brings us back to an earlier novel by Faschinger,
Die neue Scheherazade (The New Sheherazade), a re-telling of the *Tales of
1001 Nights*, where, just like in psychoanalysis, talking and storytelling
are used as a device and method for female survival.[3]

Over and over again, Faschinger's heroines happen to be forced
into the role of woman as victim, but Magdalena manages to turn things
around: in the end, her lover becomes just another corpse and she can
move on, albeit only to soon find herself caught in a similar predica-
ment. But as Faschinger's novel does not aspire to realism, as Noll's
novels definitely do, this series of Magdalena's misfortunes can also be
interpreted as working through the models of male-female relationships offered by literature. Thus her returning home to Austria does not
necessarily have to be read as a defeat but rather as hope for a new

---

[3] In Faschinger latest novel, *Wiener Passion* (1998; *Vienna Passion*, 2001), this storytelling
does not save the murderess from being executed; but her story, found accidentally and
read by her great-granddaughter, enables her to change her life: she refuses to be bossed
around and controlled by her lover. Instead, she liberates her singing-teacher from the
dominance of his dead mother and enters into a relationship with him where she plays
the active role. What sounds like a realistic novel when condensed into one sentence is
certainly not that: the heroine, whose father is an Afro-American, is supposed to star as
Anna Freud in a Broadway musical. Once again, it is a story re-told, slightly out of
focus.

beginning; after all, her relationship with the priest does not end in murder as all her previous relationships did. His celibacy kept him ignorant and innocent of the social rules and regulations governing sexual relationships and thus he may be read as a model for a "new man."[4]

Noll's novels, on the other hand, end on a less positive note. True, Thyra Hirte escapes legal punishment for her murders, but her illness and her visits to her paraplegic wished-for lover make her life worse than it had been at the beginning of the novel. Her life has become richer only for the experience of passion (love and power), which she cannot enjoy anymore. Noll's other novels end on a less grim note: her heroines end up wealthy and unencumbered by husbands or male relatives. Still, the fairy tale-like ending of "she (not they) were rich and lived happily ever after" does not sound quite convincing: on the one hand it contrasts with the psychological and social realism of the stories; on the other hand it opens up a rather dull future since the heroines have no specific interests, projects or desires to fill the time ahead of them.[5] Noll's novels do depict women as protagonists who act violently; what she has to offer her heroines is an independent and solitary life, but the financial means for such independence have to be stolen from men by force. Hope for a working relationship between men and women does not exist.

Works Cited

Bronfen, Elisabeth. *Nur über ihre Leiche. Tod, Weiblichkeit und Ästhetik.* München, 1993.

(English as): *Over Her Dead Body: Death, Femininity and the Aesthetic.* New York: Routledge, 1992.

Faschinger, Lilian. *Magdalena Sünderin.* Köln: Kiepenheuer & Witsch, 1995.

——. *Magdalena the Sinner.* New York: Harper & Collins,1997.

——. *Die neue Scheherazade.* München, 1986.

——. *Wiener Passion.* Köln: Kiepenheuer & Wietsch, 1998.

——. *Vienna Passion.* New York: Harper & Collins, 2001.

Greiner, Ulrike. "Religionskritik in der jüngeren deutschen Literatur: Religionssoziologische Differenzierung und theologische Überlegungen." *Religions et littérature en Autriche au XXe siècle.* Ed. Arlette Camion and Jacques Lajarrige. Bern: Lang, 1997. 129-46.

Jelinek, Elfriede. *Krankheit oder moderne Frauen.* Köln: Prometh, 1987.

---

[4] This type of positively connotated sexually innocent man is also found in *Vienna Passion,* where it is not the celibacy enforced by the Catholic Church, but the dominance of the mother which has preserved the hero's innocence.

[5] One exception is the heroine of *Röslein rot* whose future as an artist is shortly mentioned.

Noll, Ingrid. *Der Hahn ist tot.* Zürich: Diogenes, 1991.

———. *Die Häupter meiner Lieben.* Zürich: Diogenes, 1993.

———. *Die Apothekerin.* Zürich: Diogenes, 1994.

———. *Röslein rot.* Zürich: Diogenes, 1998.

Christopher Jones

Manchester Metropolitan University, UK

Giving the Public What it Wants? Editorial Policy at Ariadne

Introduction

This paper considers editorial policy at Ariadne, one of Germany's best known publishers of *Frauenkrimis*, crime fiction written by women for a mainly female readership. In particular it examines the attitudes to violence in the *Frauenkrimis* accepted for publication: "Wie schon von Anfang an in den Ariadne-Krimi-Nachwörtern erläutert, hat die Ariadne-Redaktion sehr starke Vorbehalte gegen diejenigen Bestandteile feministischer Kultur, die Gewalt ästhetisieren oder Selbstjustiz als gesellschaftliche Lösung propagieren wollen" (AF2 72).[1] This examination will reveal that there is a divergence of opinion between editors and some readers, the former closely monitoring the violence in the *Frauenkrimis* which they publish and the latter wanting to vicariously live out revenge fantasies, principally against men. This dichotomy will be illuminated by:

- highlighting the editorial criteria with which Ariadne works before placing them in a context of clear social aims;
- presenting examples from readers' comments which make clear what some readers want from a *Frauenkrimi*;
- examining selected texts as case studies.

Central to this study will be the social responsibilities of authors and editors, as well as a consideration of how effective (popular) culture can be as an agent of social change.

What is a *Frauenkrimi*?

Else Laudan, one of the editors at Ariadne, gives the following definition of a *Frauenkrimi*: "Ein Krimi mit weiblicher Hauptfigur, wo eine oder mehrere Frauen im Zentrum stehen, wo Frauenalltag und Frauenproblematiken zumindest vorkommen, wo der Blick auf die Verhält-

---

[1] There have been five issues of Ariadne's journal *Ariadne Forum*. In this paper references to them are made by the abbreviation AF followed by the issue number.
"As explained from the very beginning in the epilogues to the Ariadne crime books, the Ariadne editorial team has very strong reservations about those elements of feminist culture which seek to aestheticise violence or to propagate vigilante justice as a solution to social problems."

nisse ein weiblicher ist" (AF1 19).[2] Why should there be a need for this type of literature? Frigga Haug, co-founder of Argument (Ariadne's parent publisher) follows in the footsteps of Antonio Gramsci by saying: "Im Niedergang auch der Frauenbewegung gilt es, Bücher für Frauen zu verlegen, die ihren Hoffnungen und Sehnsüchten folgen, die vergnüglich sind und die zur Handlungsfähigkeit beitragen" (AF3 7).[3] To what extent Ariadne has been successful in this endeavour is a question which will be considered in the conclusion.

Why Ariadne?

Texts from the German publisher Ariadne have been chosen because many of the views and opinions of the editorial team have entered the public domain and because of the clearly stated criteria which make violence acceptable or unacceptable in works that are chosen for publication. The potential of *Frauenkrimis* as a catalyst for raising social awareness is something which the team at Ariadne are keenly aware of. In an interview, Laudan made the conjecture, "daß das Lesen von Krimis und Literatur eine Möglichkeit bietet, Frauen für politische Kultur zu interessieren und ihr Interesse zu unterstützen" (AF2 41),[4] echoing also the debt to Gramsci's work on hegemony.

There is currently only a very small pool of original German language *Frauenkrimis* published by Ariadne; of the approximately 130 titles published so far less than ten are German language originals. The texts chosen for this study are: Kim Engels' *Zur falschen Zeit am falschen Ort* (In the Wrong Place at the Wrong Time), Dagmar Scharsich's *Die gefrorene Charlotte* (The Frozen Charlotte), Lisa Pei's *Die letzte Stunde* (The Last Lesson), and Ann Camones' *Verbrechen lohnt sich doch!* (Crime Does Pay!). These books will be examined in the order in which they were published so as to make clear the development in Ariadne's most recent publications.

Women's Crime Fiction & Violence

The presence of violence in crime fiction may be regarded as indispensable since the story is usually predicated on an act of violence, namely a murder. Nevertheless, in recent years a programmatically feminist

---

[2] "A work of crime fiction in which the main character is a woman, where there are one or more women as the focus, where the ordinary lives of women and their sorts of problems at least make an appearance, and where the point of view is a female one."

[3] "Given the decline of the women's movement it is also a question of publishing books for women that will follow their hopes and wishes, be entertaining to read, and that will assist in making women able to act for themselves."

[4] "the fact is that reading crime fiction and literature is one way of getting women interested in political culture and supporting that interest"

approach to writing genre fiction has entailed a re-evaluation of many of the fundamentals. Therefore before going on to consider how the publishing programme at Ariadne has been influenced, it is worth reviewing previous work in the field of women's crime fiction which has paid particular attention to the use of violence. In considering the differences between male and female authored crime fiction, Marion Frank explains: "The female version has discarded the typical cliches of its male counterpart, such as the concept of the detective as hero and loner, and *the idealization of violence*" (Frank 106, my italics). However, it is not that female authored crime fiction has chosen to do without violence, it is rather that any possibility of its glorification has been rejected. In discussing "loners and hardboiled women," Maureen Reddy comments:

> None of the women detectives usually takes pleasure in violence and none initiates it, as the male detectives often do; however, these books suggest that violence may sometimes be the only possible response to a violent milieu and all of the detectives are able to hold their own in a fight. These women refuse the conventionally feminine role of victim, fighting back against those who would victimize them and thereby preserving themselves. (Reddy 113)

The work of American authors Grafton, Muller and Paretsky is often used paradigmatically to illustrate this point as Ann Wilson does in her essay "The Female Dick and the Crisis of Heterosexuality" commenting that

> the heroines never initiate the violence, and respond violently only when it is clear that inaction on their part would result in death either for themselves or for someone who is defenseless. Their violent actions, cast as the only possible actions if the lives of the innocent are to be preserved, seem to involve an almost maternal instinct to protect those incapable of protecting themselves. (Wilson 149)

This notion of protecting the weak seems central to a permissible use of violence in female authored crime fiction and Reddy uses Barbara Wilson's *Sisters of the Road* to make the point "that, regardless of what one wants to believe, violence may sometimes be the only option that does not require one's own death" (Wilson 143). Brigitte Frizzoni has looked at the translated texts which Ariadne publishes and again it is the extreme reluctance of women to turn to violence that is singled out for comment: "Kritischer ist auch ihr Umgang mit Gewalt, reflektierter als ihre männlichen Vorläufer setzen sie sich mit ihrer eigenen latenten Gewaltbereitschaft auseinander" (Frizzoni 93).[5] Finally, it is

---

[5] "They also have a more critical way of tackling violence; in contrast to their male predecessors they have a more considered approach to dealing with their own latent willingness to commit acts of violence."

worth citing Sally Munt's views on the absence of large numbers of revenge fantasy texts with the following suggestion: "On a mundane level it may be that the reader's interest in an investigation in which she is constructed to connive with the feeling that the murder is justified, will inevitably wane. Perhaps the murder of patriarchs is not a functionable convention" (Munt 149).

Editorial Policy at Ariadne

Through comments in the books which they publish, through the irregular journal *Ariadne Forum*, and most recently through the publication of *Das Wort zum Mord — Wie schreibe ich einen Krimi?* (A Word about Murder — How do I Write Crime Fiction?), Ariadne have sought to establish a dialogue with their many readers. As an inevitable or possibly even intentional side-effect of this dialogue many of the criteria which the editorial team employs to make its decisions to publish or reject have become common knowledge. A good example is the Ariadne questionnaire which has to be completed by prospective authors:

> Da die Redaktion der Ariadne Krimis nicht nur stilistisch-qualitative, sondern auch klare inhaltliche Kriterien bei der Manuskriptauswahl heranzieht, hat sich gezeigt, dass ein Exposé üblicher Machart dem Lektorat meist wenig nützt wir haben daher einen Fragebogen entwickelt, der gezielt nach den uns bewegenden Aspekten von Personen- und Hintergrundkonstruktion, Rahmen und Handlung fragt. (Kemmerzell & Laudan 140)[6]

This close monitoring of the social milieu in which their fictions are set is a clear reflection of Ariadne's sociopolitical mission to provide material for critical thought as well as entertainment. This is a difficult balancing act to achieve and the types of violence that are portrayed must walk the tightrope characterised by Frizzoni as follows: "Gewalt wird somit weder verniedlicht, wie das im traditionellen englischen Rätselkrimi oft geschieht, noch zu Unterhaltungszwecken in exzessiven Bluträuschen ausgemalt, wie das in brutalen Thrillern betrieben wird" (Frizzoni 106).[7] The extent to which their readers have been satisfied with this approach is something which has formed part of the lively exchange of ideas in the letters pages of the *Ariadne Forum* journal.

---

[6] "As the editorial team for the Ariadne crime fiction series does not employ merely stylistic and qualitative criteria but also ones relating to the content when making decisions about the acceptability of a manuscript, it has become clear that a normal plot outline of the book is of little help. For this reason we have developed a questionnaire which asks targeted questions about the aspects of the construction of the characters and of the background, the framework and the plot which are of relevance to us."

[7] "Violence is not turned into something cute as often occurs in the traditional English puzzle-based detective story, nor is it portrayed in excessive frenzies for the purposes of entertainment as is the case in brutal thrillers."

The Readers

In order to better anticipate this heated dialogue which has characterised the exchange of views between the editorial team and its readers and which shall be a feature of the discussion of the four selected texts below, it is useful to quote from two readers. Firstly: "Warum über Gewalt und Brutalität hinwegschreiben, wenn sich so die Leserin zumindest gedanklich damit auseinandersetzen kann. Ohne Gewalt kein Krimi!" (AF3 22),[8] and secondly: "Also, natürlich mag ich es am liebsten, wenn das Opfer ein Mann ist, und als sadistische Phantasie gefällt mir die Mordmethode in Sabine Deitmers *Dominante Damen* ausgesprochen gut!" (AF4 76)[9] These letters reveal succinctly the broad spectrum of uses to which readers put popular fiction, ranging from the intellectual to the visceral.

Zur falschen Zeit am falschen Ort

Nicole Décuré makes the following point with regard to Sue Grafton's *"A" is for Alibi*: "C'est un positionnement différent de celui des hommes. On ne tue pas à la légère chez les femmes. C'est toujours une cause d'angoisse, de souffrance, de regret. Et qu'il s'agisse d'autodéfense ne change rien. Tuer est grave" (Décuré 44).[10] These words could be applied equally well to Ariadne's first original German *Frauenkrimi*, Kim Engels' *Zur falschen Zeit am falschen Ort* which reveals in an exemplary fashion all the points raised above in analyses of violence in women's crime fiction in America.

The story concerns a group of women who, after a chance encounter with another woman, find themselves holidaying at an out of the way place in Spain. Here they witness a murder, and end up on the run, partly because of what they have witnessed and partly because of a notebook which they took from the scene of the crime. What follows is a highly predictable tale of female bonding where all men are bad and not to be trusted. Nevertheless, Engels is able to create an atmosphere of panic and paranoia with superb accomplishment, but sadly readers have found the characters difficult to empathise with. The solidarity amongst women is dealt with in a realistic fashion as are the attempts to escape pursuit which take the friends across Europe to a women's

[8] "Why write without violence and brutality, which would at least afford the reader an opportunity to consider the matter from an intellectual point of view. You can't have crime fiction without violence!"

[9] "Well, of course I like it best if the victim is a man, and the sadistic imagination behind the murder method in Sabine Deitmer's *Dominant Dames* is something I particularly like!"

[10] "It's a point of view which is different to men's. Women do not kill lightly. It is always a source of anguish, suffering, regret. And even if it's in self defence, that changes nothing. Killing is a serious matter."

refuge in Italy and then on to a friend in England. However, interwoven between these elements are the decidedly unrealistic visions and dreams of Sahra, one of the friends, which form the basis for many of the group's decisions. It is particularly interesting to note the presence of this dimension in the light of the "Stoner-Debatte" (Stoner Debate). This was a discussion instigated by the decision by Ariadne to cease publishing Sarah Dreher's hugely popular series starring Stoner McTavish partly on account of the increasing level of New Age mysticism. Haug justified this decision "weil unser politischer Standpunkt unter anderem den Gedanken enthält, daß die Welt des Irrationalen keine Unterstützung braucht, sondern umgekehrt, daß wir in der allgemeinen Verzweiflung beteiligt sein müßten am Bau von Wällen gegen solche Strömungen" (AF1 9).[11] It is therefore difficult to understand the group's reliance on Sahra's intuitions, particularly as the story does not need them as a propelling force.

Frank's comments about the "idealization of violence" in male-authored crime fiction finds its counterpart here in the manner in which Engels depicts Beatrice's killing of Diba: "Plötzlich stand Diba vor ihr. Er starrte sie erstaunt an. Bevor er reagieren konnte, schlug sie zu. Es gab einen dumpfen Aufschlag, als er zu Boden fiel. Blut lief über sein Gesicht. Beatrice biß sich in die Hand. 'Nicht schreien,' wiederholte sie. 'Nicht schreien'" (Engels 104).[12] This is certainly no revenge fantasy, the actions are described mechanically, drained of any emotional content, leaving no opportunity for vicarious thrill-seekers to gain satisfaction. Indeed the other members of the group decide to lie to Beatrice, telling her that Diba survived the blow, but even so Beatrice asks aloud: "Warum fühle ich mich dann so mies?" (112).[13] Her actions haunt her throughout the story, even going so far as to cause her problems with her health. Maria explains that it is not exhaustion which is the cause: "Nein, es ist das Wissen, daß sie einen Menschen getötet hat, auch wenn er ein Schwein und selbst ein Mörder war" (165).[14] As Décuré says "Tuer est grave." Beatrice's friends work hard to convince her that her actions were justified in these circumstances of extreme danger: "Wenn du daran kaputtgehst, war alles umsonst, dann hättest du dich von

---

[11] "because our political position is based on, amongst other things, the view that the world of the irrational needs no support; indeed on the contrary, out of a general sense of despair, we should be involved in building barriers against such trends."

[12] "Suddenly Diba was standing in front of her. He stared at her in surprise. Before he could react she struck him. There was a dull thud as he hit the ground. Blood poured over his face. Beatrice bit her hand. 'Don't scream,' she repeated, 'don't scream.'"

[13] "Then why do I feel so rotten?"

[14] "No, it is the knowledge that she has killed someone, even if he was a pig and a murderer himself."

Diba erschießen lassen können, und uns gleich mit" (194).[15] This aspect of the story certainly seems overstated, yet the real problem most readers have had with the book is the behaviour of the characters. One reason for this may lie in the fact that the notebook which the group finds at the start of the story is all but forgotten. This is one of the key reasons that the group are being hunted down. Echoing a potential reader's disbelief, one of the other characters shouts "Wie kann man das vergessen" (205).[16] This facet means that the story itself is less than satisfying and that the characters are not treated with the respect one would normally accord survivors of such a (wo)manhunt. One reader responded to the characters as follows: "seine Heldinnen führen sich auf wie gescheuchte Hühner, nicht wie erwachsene Frauen in Gefahr" (AF2 9)[17] to express her dissatisfaction with the characters.

Die gefrorene Charlotte

One of Ariadne's best known *Frauenkrimis* has been Dagmar Scharsich's *Die gefrorene Charlotte*, perhaps partly because it sets its crimes and investigations against the background of the last few weeks of the German Democratic Republic. As civil unrest manifests itself in demonstrations on the streets of Berlin, the tellingly named Cora Ost (Cora East) has to deal with at least one terrible murder and the disappearance of a fabulously valuable collection of antique dolls. The book chronicles real life events with careful attention to detail and attempts to dovetail Cora's own development with the political development of her country. This is not the only aspect of the novel which is clearly in keeping with Ariadne's editorial policy. The attitude to violence also reveals a careful approach designed to keep Cora firmly on the side of peaceful resistance. Although she has lost at least one member of her family to a rogue Stasi[18] operative (Trautmann), she harbours no feelings of revenge and when her lover Markus Behnesch makes plans to take the law into his own hands and kill Trautmann for his crimes, Cora's reactions are unambiguous: "Mir wurde übel. Um mich her fing das Zimmer an, sich zu drehen. Ein grüner Schleier legte sich über meine Augen. Mein Herz dröhnte in meinen Ohren und machte sie taub" (Scharsich 356).[19] Her shock manifests itself as nausea and as a

---

[15] "If it finishes you off then everything has been in vain; you might as well have let Diba shoot you and us as well."

[16] "How can anyone forget that."

[17] "the heroines behave like frightened chickens not like grown women in danger"

[18] *Stasi* is the abbreviation for *Staatssicherheitsdienst*, which was the name of the secret service in the GDR.

[19] "I felt sick. The room started to spin around me. A green veil descended over my eyes. My heart roared in my ears and made them deaf."

psychosomatic attempt to seal herself off from his revelation through self-induced deafness.

Her sensitive nature, her desire to protect her relatives, her work in the hospital, are all aspects of her character which seek to prepare the reader for this extreme reaction to the possibility of physical violence. This is clearly far removed from the revenge fantasy approach to writing crime fiction which "may provide a therapeutic release for readerly outrage" (Munt 65) or the sort of *Frauenkrimi*, where a hard-won readiness to commit acts of violence is seen as a step on the road to female independence.[20] Nevertheless Cora's overtly physical reaction does have the unfortunate effect of shifting focus away from someone making an intellectual or moral decision to someone who is merely squeamish. For this reason the rejection of revenge does not have the same import here that it can have in other *Frauenkrimis*. Frizzoni's study of the translated Ariadne texts has lead her to conclude: "Aber auch wenn Rache zum Ziel führt, wird Selbstjustiz — als verständliche Verzweiflungstat — letztlich doch nicht goutiert" (Frizzoni 105)[21] æ a view which can be applied equally well to Lisa Pei's *Die letzte Stunde* which is discussed below.

Die gefrorene Charlotte has also received negative feedback from readers who focus mainly on the treatment of the central character, Cora Ost. A few examples will give the picture: "Die Hauptfigur ist dermaßen dumm, naiv, unselbständig und noch vieles mehr, dass es wirklich weh tut. KEINE Frau von 30 Jahren ist derart auf den Kopf gefallen!!!" (AF5 105),[22] or: "Die Heldin ist so naiv, daß sie schon eher wie eine Karikatur wirkt" (AF3 13).[23] The response from the editorial side (Laudan in this case) was: "Die dafür gewählte Figur der Cora Ost scheint mir so karikaturenhaft nicht. Eher würde ich sagen, sie ist — leider — weitaus repräsentativer für eine sehr große Anzahl 'ganz normaler' Frauen in unserer Kultur als beispielsweise unsere starken Berufsdetektivinnen aus den USA" (AF3 13).[24] This is a highly revealing statement as it highlights the fact that Ariadne's realistic approach does not always meet with the approval of its readership.

---

[20] As in Christine Grän's short story "Tausendundeine Nacht" [Arabian Nights], for example.

[21] "Even if revenge provides a path to the goal, it is still the case that vigilant justice — as an understandable act of desperation — remains unacceptable."

[22] "The main character is so stupid, naïve, dependent and so much more that it really hurts. NO women of 30 is such a big fool!!!"

[23] "The heroine is so naïve that she is more like a caricature."

[24] "The character of Cora East who was chosen for this purpose does not seem to me to be such a caricature. I'd be more tempted to say that she is — unfortunately — far more representative of a very large proportion of 'perfectly normal' women in our society than, for example, our strong professional women detectives from the USA."

Die letzte Stunde

Although *Die letzte Stunde* begins with the violent image of a photograph that bears needle holes through the eyes and heart, most of the
novel goes little further than this depiction of simulated violence.
Instead the author, Lisa Pei, seeks to establish an atmosphere of hidden
danger through the threatening activities which hound the day to day
life of the headmaster at a school in Cologne. These are for the most part
malicious pranks which result in the damage of property, such as the
large Z which is scratched into his car. However, a second narrative
interwoven into the main flow of the novel presents a brief biography
of a character who is known simply as Flämmchen (Little Flame) on
account of her red hair. This biographical sketch details the life of a
young girl after she is orphaned and has to move in with her abusive
uncle. The descriptions of sexual abuse are far less explicit than in *Verbrechen lohnt sich doch!* but they do tempt the reader into trying to discover how they relate to the events at the school. This task is made more
difficult by the fact that the names of the girl and her uncle are hidden,
although it is revealed that her uncle is a teacher. Indeed he refers to the
abuse to which he subjects Flämmchen as her last lesson of the day,
hence the title *Die letzte Stunde*.

As Flämmchen grows up and chooses for herself the career of
teacher there can be little doubt that the Cologne school has become the
location for a final battle, with the headmaster, Rheinstauff, as the most
likely candidate to be the uncle. Still the mystery remains as to which of
the female members of staff is the grown-up Flämmchen. By a series of
twists the reader is thrown off the scent, as it is revealed firstly that Rheinstauff had raped one of his staff and secondly that one of the teachers,
Juliane, is actually a police officer who has gone undercover. Nevertheless, by the end of the novel Juliane is revealed as Flämmchen who has
been brought in by her uncle to investigate the events at his school. She
had been trained as a teacher but then undertook a career change to
become a police officer. The various assaults on his property are shown
to the reader to be the work of Christine, the teacher that Rheinstauff
had raped. But when Juliane refuses to inform Rheinstauff of the identity of his tormentor his anger takes over and he orders her away: "Dein
Unterricht ist beendet. Für dich ist das hier die letzte Stunde" (Pei
284).[25]

For Juliane/Flämmchen this is of course a trigger phrase, and the
previously supressed memories of the abuse which she suffered with
her uncle come flooding back: "Der Vorhang riß. Das Bild war da. Sie

---

[25] "Your teaching is over. For you this is the last lesson."

sah es vor sich" (284).[26] With a great irony Rheinstauff never has the opportunity to say anything else and "die letzte Stunde" becomes the last phrase that he will ever utter because Juliane grabs the scissors from his desk and kills him with them. Although most readers will have few problems with this quick death for a serial abuser and rapist, it is not portrayed as a viable means of achieving justice. Juliane commits suicide by throwing herself from a bridge. Her last words to her uncle, "Es ist für uns beide die letzte Stunde" (284),[27] spoken at the moment that she kills him, ensure that there can be little satisfaction for the reader in his death. The suicide also becomes ambiguous as it remains unclear whether Juliane kills herself because she has betrayed all that she stands for as a police officer, whether she would rather avoid prison (as she states on 285), or whether she feels unable to live with the newly resurfaced memories of her terrible childhood experiences. This ambiguity gives the novel a bitterness which it is difficult to ignore, as whichever interpretation one chooses, Juliane seems to have been totally destroyed by her uncle. In contrast Ann Camones' novel *Verbrechen lohnt sich doch!* presents a tale of child abuse in which the girl refuses to be a victim and fights both her abuser and her own feelings successfully.

Verbrechen lohnt sich doch!

The squeamishness displayed by Cora Ost in *Die gefrorene Charlotte* is also to be found in a very different context in Ann Camones' *Verbrechen lohnt sich doch!* On the one hand it is to be found in the lead character's reactions to violence, but also to the reader's reactions to the descriptions of sexual abuse. These are made even more disturbing because they are delivered via a narrative technique which, although in the third person, takes the reader very close to the point of view of the child being abused. This approach garnered some shocked comments from readers, prompting the editorial team to respond with: "Wir fanden, daß gerade die grauenhafte Zumutung bei der Beschreibung aus der Perspektive des Kindes das Buch gut macht. Geschwiegen wird doch viel zuviel! Und daß die kleine Heldin sich nicht unterkriegen läßt, sollte eigentlich ermutigen" (AF4 86).[28]

This is true not just of the explicit descriptions of the sexual abuse to which Erzi, the main character, is subjected. It is an attitude which permeates the book as a whole. Although only a young girl, Erzi is

---

26 "The curtain tore. The picture was there. She saw it in front of her eyes."

27 "For both of us this is the last lesson."

28 "We felt that it was in particular the terrible provocation caused by the descriptions from the child's point of view that made it a good book. There is after all far too much that is kept quiet! And the fact that the little heroine doesn't let it grind her down is something which should give cause for courage."

feisty and independent enough to function as a role model for others who find themselves under threat or in difficult situations, and if Erzi can survive her ordeals and flourish then her fictional adventures can surely serve as an example to others. Camones leaves the reader in no doubt about Erzi's determined character right from the very beginning. Her characterisation of Erzi involves an attitude to violence which needs to be examined carefully. Erzi is certainly prepared to use violence as a means of self defence, such as in this scene from the first few pages of the book:

> Als er [Erzi] mit der Stichflamme seines Feuerzeugs bedrohte, so daß ihr teures Plaste-Löchershirt von Adidas beinahe Feuer gefangen hätte, wehrte sie sich, wie Bruno es ihr gezeigt hatte, mit dem Kopf, den sie blitzschnell gegen seinen stieß, als sei der eine Art Fußball. Volltreffer, Phillip hatte sich auf die Zunge gebissen. Der würde ihr nicht mehr zu nahe treten, das wäre soweit geklärt." (Camones 22-23)[29]

Phillip is two years older than Erzi which makes the confidence with which she is able to deal with his antics admirable, yet the humorous "Volltreffer" (Goal!) establishes a tone far removed from the ponderous seriousness of the texts that have been examined previously.

However, Erzi is also prepared to use violence as a means of furthering her criminal career. What Laudan has called a "kindlich-unmoralische Schläue" (AF4 113)[30] is not so easy to dismiss, as Erzi actually chooses a life of crime for herself. Beginning with the non-violent kidnapping of some garden gnomes, Erzi soon finds herself having to deal with more serious matters. Plunged headlong into the gang-warfare of the school playground Erzi has to make difficult decisions, which are made easier for her by her almost total lack of morals. This enclosed environment puts *Verbrechen lohnt sich doch!* into the venerable Germanic tradition of using the school as a microcosm of later life, such as in Robert Musil's *Die Verwirrungen des Zöglings Törless* (*Young Törless*) or Hermann Hesse's *Unterm Rad* (*Under the Wheel*). But Erzi's employment of violence is not just for self-defence as her mutilation of Figuero makes all too clear: "Aber das Schlimmste kam jetzt: Sie sprühte etwas von dem Vereisungsspray an sein linkes Ohr, zog die Gummihandschuhe über, flämmte die scharfe Klinge des Teppichmessers mit dem Feuerzeug ab, und schnitt sein Ohrläppchen ab [...] und kämpfte tapfer

---

[29] "When he threatened Erzi with the tongue of flame from his lighter so that her expensive Adidas shirt with its synthetic mesh almost caught fire, she defended herself in the manner which Bruno had shown her, by knocking her head at lightning speed against his, as if it were a type of soccerball. Goal! Phillip had bitten his tongue. He wouldn't get too close to her again, that had been taken care of."

[30] "a child's immoral cunning"

gegen Übelkeit und Reue an" (129-130).[31] Admittedly, she shares similar physical reactions to Beatrice in *Zur falschen Zeit am falschen Ort* or Cora in *Die gefrorene Charlotte*, but this action has been taken of her own free will. The significant fact, presumably from an editorial point of view, seems to be that it is not merely revenge: "Es war schließlich nicht Rache, jedenfalls nicht an ihm, sondern Notwendigkeit" (132).[32] Indeed when Erzi has real cause for feelings of revenge she fights against them. Immediately after Schnippler has abused her she feels "In diesem Moment hätte sie ihn umbringen können" (208),[33] but two paragraphs later she is already trying to get over these feelings: "Erzi blickte schnell weg und kämpfte eisern gegen ihre Rachegefühle an" (ibidem).[34] This struggle is far more effective than the approach adopted in *Zur falschen Zeit am falschen Ort* as Erzi is someone who is capable of physical violence faced with a very understandable feeling for revenge. The fact that she does not give in to that temptation is a far greater indication of her genuine moral fibre.

Later in the book Schnippler is killed, not by Erzi but by Bernadette. The killing is not presented to the reader only explained after the event, thereby making any opportunity for a vicarious revenge fantasy impossible. Indeed the realism of the situation is undermined by Erzi's precociously self-reflective comments to Bernadette: "Du mußt alle Beweise verschwinden lassen, wie im Krimi" (274).[35] Nevertheless, Ariadne's claim to dislike publishing *Frauenkrimis* that seek to portray violence as a tool to achieve worthwhile ends is thrown into doubt when we read Bernadette's admission: "Nein, Notwehr war das nischt mehr, sondern irgendwie eine Art Erkenntnis über ihn, nämlisch, daß wir erst vor ihm Ru'e 'aben, wenn er tot ist. Deshalb mußte isch ihn umbringen" (281).[36] Given the graphic descriptions of Erzi's abuse most readers will have few problems with this. Some readers clearly want even more:

> Endlich!, denkt die Leserin, das Schwein ist entsorgt, er hat seinen Tod wahrhaft verdient. Autorin Ann Camones hatte mit ihrem Mord an dem „Schleimlolli," wie die achtjährige Erzi aus *Verbrechen lohnt sich doch!* diesen Perversling nennt, nicht das geringste moralische Prob-

---

31 "But the worst came now: she applied a little of the freezing spray to his left ear, put the rubber gloves on, put the sharp edge of the carpet-knife through the flame of the lighter, and cut his earlobe off… fighting bravely against nausea and regret."

32 "It was in the final analysis not revenge, at least not against him, but necessity."

33 "At this moment she could have killed him."

34 "Erzi looked away quickly and fought hard against her feelings of revenge."

35 "You've got to make all the evidence disappear like in a crime novel."

36 {With a French accent:} "No, it wasn't self-defence anymore, but rather a kind of realisation that he would only leave us alone once he was dead. That's why I had to kill him."

lem. Ich auch nicht! Im Gegenteil: Mir war sein Tod, hervorgerufen durch einen Schürhaken, viel zu human. Eine qualvollere Todesart, beispielsweise durch schleichendes Gift, hätte ich noch mehr genossen. (AF5 5)[37]

But in the final analysis *Verbrechen lohnt sich doch!* presents individuals in an extreme situation who must turn to extreme measures to ensure the safety of Erzi as well as Schnippler's own daughters. There is no question of bloodlust or pleasurable revenge, but an honest analysis of a very difficult and unusual situation. Few readers will ever find themselves faced with a similar problem, and so the novel cannot function as a condonation of violence in general and certainly not for revenge purposes. Bernadette's speech makes it clear that she acted not with respect to past events which would have been revenge, but with regard to safeguarding the children's future. Although the reader cited above wanted a more painful death for Schnippler it is interesting to note that when they dispose of the corpse Erzi's thoughts try to remember the good things about him: "Sie versuchte sich an seine Körperwärme zu erinnern, an sein manchmal so bezauberndes Wesen, seine zärtliche Fürsorge, seine Heiligenscheinhaare" (Camones 295).[38] This gives the outcome a complexity which lifts it high above a simple tale of violent revenge. Instead it provides ample food for thought about a society in which individuals, in this case women and children, have to break the law in order to have the freedom from abuse which should be theirs by right. As such it represents a breakthrough text amongst the German Ariadne *Frauenkrimis* which is able to fulfil the potential of popular culture to educate and inspire without being tiresomely self-righteous. It also avoids crossing the line into violent revenge fantasies which, aside from their dubious morality, run the risk of dissipating the reading public's outrage by feeding them material for a thrillingly vicarious solution to problems. This outrage could be transformed into a greater social awareness.

Conclusion

I hope to have made it clear that in my view there has been a development amongst the German *Frauenkrimis* published by Ariadne. This

---

[37] "At last!, thinks the reader, the pig has been disposed of, he had really deserved his death. The author Ann Camones had absolutely no moral problems with the murder of the 'Slimeball,' as this pervert is referred to by the eight-year-old Erzi in *Crime does Pay!* Me neither! On the contrary: his death, which was caused by a poker, was far too humane. I would have enjoyed a more painful type of death, such as with an insidious poison, even more."

[38] "She tried to remember the warmth of his body, his personality which could be so charming at times, his tender care, his halo-like hair."

development has involved a move away from the programmatic approach to dealing with violence to one which allows the individual authors more freedom to tackle such matters in their own way. The problematic characterisation of the group of women in *Zur falschen Zeit am falschen Ort* or the irritating naivety of Cora in *Die gefrorene Charlotte* have given way to Erzi's determination to make her own way through life without jettisoning all notions of right and wrong. Other recent German *Frauenkrimis* from Ariadne have also borne testimony to a desire to reach a wider audience with the publication of almost mainstream texts such as Monika Geier's *Wie könnt ihr schlafen* (How can you sleep) and the acquisition of Martina Bick's serial detective Marie Maas in *Blutsbande* (Blood Bonds). Indeed *Wie könnt ihr schlafen* went on to win the Marlowe award in 2000. Surely such successes can only make it easier for publisher Haug to achieve her goals: "So erweist sich aus der verlegerischen Praxis, daß richtig ist, was Gramsci in den Gefängnisheften als politisch notwendig herausarbeitete: nicht *gegen* den Zeitgeist zu arbeiten, sondern ihn zu verändern" (AF3 9).[39]

Works Cited

Bick, Martina. *Blutsbande*. Berlin, Hamburg: Argument, 2001.

Camones, Ann. *Verbrechen lohnt sich doch!*. Hamburg: Argument, 1995.

Décuré, Nicole. "Pleins feux sur les lumières anglo-américaines: 30 ans de féminisme, 15 ans de polar." *Les Temps Modernes* 52 (1997): 35-52.

Engels, Kim. *Zur falschen Zeit am falschen Ort*. Berlin, Hamburg: Argument, 1991.

Frank, Marion. "The Transformation of a Genre: The Feminist Mystery Novel." *Feminist Contributions to the Literary Canon*. Ed. Susanne Fendler. Lewiston, Queenston, Lampeter: Edwin Mellen, 1997. 81-108.

Frizzoni, Brigitte. "Mordsfrauen". *Schweizerisches Archiv für Volkskunde* 95 (1999): 87-112.

Geier, Monika. *Wie könnt ihr schlafen*. Berlin, Hamburg: Argument, 2000.

Hesse, Hermann. *Unterm Rad*. Frankfurt a.M.: Suhrkamp, 1982.

____. *Under the Wheel*. Transl. Michael Roloff. New York: Farrar, Straus, and Giroux, 1968.

Kemmerzell, Anja and Else Laudan, eds. *Das Wort zum Mord: Wie schreibe ich einen Krimi?* Hamburg: Argument, 1999.

Munt, Sally. *Murder by the Book?* London: Routledge, 1994

Musil, Robert. *Die Verwirrungen des Zöglings Törleß*. Reinbek bei Hamburg: Rowohlt, 1974. (1906)

____. *Young Törless*. Transl. Eithne Wilkins and Georg Kaiser. Harmondsworth: Penguin Books, 1961.

---

[39] "So the experience of publishing has shown that Gramsci was correct in his *Prison Notebooks* when he established that it was a political necessity to change the spirit of the times and not work against it."

Pei, Lisa. *Die letzte Stunde*. Berlin, Hamburg: Argument, 1995.

Reddy, Maureen T.. *Sisters in Crime*. New York: Continuum, 1988.

Scharsich, Dagmar. *Die gefrorene Charlotte*. Berlin, Hamburg: Argument, 1993.

Wilson, Ann. "The Female Dick and the Crisis of Heterosexuality." Ed. Glenwood Irons. *Feminism in Women's Detective Fiction*. Toronto: U of Toronto P, 1995. 148-156.

Luzelena Gutiérrez de Velasco

PIEM - El Colegio de México

Violencia constante más allá del amor en *Mi hermanita Magdalena* de Elena Garro

La violencia es la imborrable marca de nuestra época. La hemos visto desplegarse en los ámbitos político, económico, social y en el más íntimo círculo de lo familiar. Sin duda, hemos advertido sus graves consecuencias en la formación de las sociedades, en los obstáculos para la instauración de las democracias, en la expoliación contra los países débiles, en los terribles miedos en el seno de las relaciones humanas, en las resquebrajaduras que separan a los hijos de los padres, y a las mujeres de sus parejas. Ningún espacio queda exento de sus embates y nadie puede ufanarse de no haber sido violento. Así, la violencia nos circunda y lo sabemos ahora con certeza.

Una modalidad sumamente preocupante de este fenómeno es la violencia hacia las mujeres, que ha sido definida como "todo acto de violencia que tenga o pueda tener como resultado un daño o sufrimiento físico, sexual o psicológico para la mujer, inclusive las amenazas de tales actos, la coacción o la privación arbitraria de la libertad, tanto si se produce en la vida pública como en la privada". (Naciones Unidas, Programa de Acción de la Conferencia de Derechos Humanos). Las estadísticas nos ofrecen datos alarmantes sobre los altos índices de violencia en contra de las mujeres en el ámbito familiar. En todo el mundo se observan comportamientos violentos que afectan a las mujeres y ningún país escapa a sus efectos. Así, en Estados Unidos, donde se realizan estudios sistemáticos sobre violencia de género, se calcula que un 29% de las mujeres han sido maltratadas en su relación conyugal alguna vez, y para Canadá, según el estudio de 1993 de Lori Haskell y Melanie Randall, *The women's safety project: summary of key statistical, findings*, se establece la cifra de 27%. Para el caso de México, se señala el 33% de mujeres que han vivido relaciones violentas y en su gran mayoría (75%) recibieron el maltrato por parte de sus parejas, como registra Elizabeth Shrader y Rosario Valdez en "Características y análisis de la violencia doméstica en México" (1987)[1]. Estos datos nos sirven para comparar solamente a los tres países participantes en el TLC y establecer un criterio para advertir la gravedad del problema.

---

[1] Estos datos fueron tomados del estudios comparativo que Marta Torres incluye en *La violencia en casa* (México: Paidós, 2001) 181-210.

Sabemos también que en las cuestiones de violencia hacia las mujeres y la violencia familiar existe un impresionante subregistro, dado el temor a las represalias, la inconsistencia legislativa, la ambigua impartición de justicia y las justificaciones culturales de esas conductas. Asimismo, tenemos conciencia de los importantes avances que se han realizado en torno a este problema, en lo relativo a las modificaciones de la legislación de los países, a raíz de las Conferencias Mundiales de la Mujer y los Acuerdos Internacionales y Continentales, como es el caso de la Convención de Belém do Pará, signado por la mayoría de los países de América.

Aunado al problema del subregistro, debemos señalar que muchas formas de violencia en contra de las mujeres son castigadas de manera leve e incluso perdonadas —como en algunos casos de hostigamiento sexual en que no se tienen pruebas contundentes—, debido a los patrones de masculinidad imperantes. Todo esto a pesar de los esfuerzos de muchos grupos de mujeres y organizaciones sociales que se niegan a perpetuar esos modelos de conducta, basados en principios de desigualdad e inequidad genérica. En ese contexto, centro nuestra atención en la violencia invisible, la que no deja huellas externas, es decir, el maltrato emocional. Marta Torres, en el libro *La violencia en casa*, señala que: "durante mucho tiempo se pensó que la violencia era exclusiva o fundamentalmente física y se ignoraba cualquier otra consecuencia que no pudiera apreciarse en el cuerpo" (113). Sin embargo, el maltrato psicológico, la humillación, la burla, el trato irónico, el silencio que aísla van dejando marcas en la esfera emocional y lastiman profundamente la integridad psíquica de las personas. No quedan huellas visibles, pero la persona se resquebraja.

Tras este largo preámbulo, necesario para enmarcar el fenómeno de la violencia emocional, conviene ya abordar el caso de Elena Garro (1916-1998). Esta escritora mexicana, famosa no sólo por su rica obra literaria, por ser la autora de textos de indudable importancia como las novelas *Los recuerdos del porvenir* (1963), *Testimonios sobre Mariana* (1981), *Reencuentro de personajes* (1982), de cuentos como los de *La semana de colores* (1964) y de obras dramáticas como *Un hogar sólido* (1958) y *Felipe Ángeles* (1967), sino famosa también por su matrimonio con Octavio Paz y por la multitud de rumores que se difundieron sobre su conflictiva relación con el poeta.

En sus obras, la descripción de la violencia física y política es un componente que aparece de manera recurrente y con intensidad. Así, Garro aborda la violencia durante la Guerra Cristera en México (1924-1929) en su novela más connotada, *Los recuerdos del porvenir*, y pone de manifiesto la crueldad institucional en contra de los huelguistas ferrocarrileros, que transparentan a los jóvenes participantes en el movimiento estudiantil de 1968, en la novela *Y Matarazo no llamó...* (1991). En ellas, Garro destaca la violencia del poder y los poderosos sobre los grupos indefensos y los débiles. Marca así el peso de una justicia poética que los alcanza a todos, al General Rosas y a Isabel, como también al despistado Eugenio Yánez. Sin embargo, Garro dedicará muchas páginas al particular tratamiento de la violencia en la vida de pareja, en el ámbito familiar. Como ocurre en el sojuzgamiento de Mariana en *Testimonios sobre Mariana*, en el despojo y muerte de Consuelo en *La casa junto al río* (1983) y culmina con el caso extremo del personaje Inés de la novela homónima de 1995. Esa mujer es sometida y torturada por los miembros de una corporación multinacional.

En los últimos años de su vida, la escritora decidió (por necesidades económicas) dar a la publicidad múltiples textos que había guardado y escondido en su mítico baúl. Ejerció la autocensura muy probablemente debido a un prurito literario, o bien por el temor que le causaba hacer públicas una serie de obras en las que ponía de manifiesto los defectos y crueldades de su ex esposo, a quien nunca le escatimó una gran admiración literaria. Aprovechó Garro la reelaboración de un registro autobiográfico para volver sobre los primeros años de su vida matrimonial y legarnos dos obras de calidad dispar.

Una de ellas excelente, de carácter testimonial, en la que se mezclan el registro autobiográfico, las memorias y las viñetas sobre la Guerra Civil española: *Memorias de España 1937*, (1992), en la que relata sus recuerdos de ese viaje de novios que se convirtió en conciencia y también su versión de esa guerra, cruel para ambos bandos.

El otro texto, peculiar por haber sido editado como la "única novela inédita de la gran narradora mexicana" apareció en 1998, en el año de la muerte de Elena Garro, con un prólogo de Patricia Rosas Lopategui, quien también había publicado en 2000 *Yo sólo soy memoria*, una biografía visual de Garro. Nos queda la pregunta sobre si la escritora se hubiera decidido a permitir la edición de *Mi hermanita Magdalena*. Tal vez no. Quizá, debido a ser ésta una novela 'informe' o bien porque los personajes transparentan demasiado a las personas reales que son los referentes en esa historia.

Con todo, podemos afirmar que *Mi hermanita Magdalena* es una novela significativa en la producción de Elena Garro y que de su lectura podemos extraer conclusiones valiosas para entender el proceso de constitución del texto y, por otra parte, recobramos datos sobre un registro autobiográfico que ha sido deformado y exagerado por los rumores y por las expresiones de la autora misma, vertidas en entrevistas o comentarios.

Octavio Paz quiso olvidar que se había casado con Elena Garro y dejar en una *terra incógnita* los casi 30 años de convivencia con la escritora. Elena Garro quiso no olvidar su matrimonio con Paz, y lo reconfigura en memorias y textos de ficción para mostrar otra faceta del hombre ilustre, su cara oscura; o al menos para hacer descender al prohombre a su mera condición de hombre.

En el texto autobiográfico, incluido en las cartas que Elena Garro dirigió a Emmanuel Carballo[2], se describe el momento en que ella conoció a su futuro esposo como una situación de violencia: "junto al piano había algunos jóvenes que cuchicheaban y se miraban. Uno se acercó a invitarme a bailar. 'No bailo', dije. Me tiró del brazo: 'La conozco muy bien. Es usted una puritana y ahora viene con el pastor protestante de su parroquia', dijo con insolencia. No pude bailar con Pedrito y nos fuimos después de la agresión. El agresor era Octavio Paz" (Carballo 503). Vale la pena resaltar que en ese primer encuentro, como lo relata o fantasea Elena Garro, hay una indudable violencia física y emocional de él hacia Garro. No podemos probar si la historia relatada es verídica o si Elena Garro quiere dejar un testimonio que nos comunique esa fuerza agresiva del escritor. Lo cierto es que, poco tiempo después, según ella recuerda: "Un día me casé, abandoné a mis maestros" (Carballo 504). La unión no prometía ser feliz y para ella representa una ruptura.

La novela *Mi hermanita Magdalena*[3] nos transmite, como disparador de la acción, el relato de la boda y la desaparición del personaje Magdalena, a partir de datos que podemos asemejar a la boda 'real' de Elena Garro. En 1937 ella contrajo nupcias con el poeta, en secreto, con testigos que ella no conocía y sin la autorización de sus padres. El relato reconfigura esa boda y el viaje que los novios realizaron hacia la España en guerra. Las circunstancias y los detalles son transformados por la autora para ficcionalizar el inicio de una relación difícil. Elige los espacios de París y Ascona (Suiza) y sitúa las acciones en los años 60.

Con referencia al carácter 'informe' de esta novela, debe señalarse que si le exigimos criterios de cohesión y progresión narrativa, el texto resulta sumamente fallido, porque el suspenso planteado en el inicio del relato se desvanece. La desaparición de Magdalena deja de funcionar como un acicate narrativo y el suspenso se transfiere a otras secuencias del relato.

La novela plantea en sus cuatro capítulos momentos diversos de la vida de Magdalena, en una progresión cronológica lineal. Cada capítulo parece perder la conexión con el anterior, pero en ellos persiste la voz narradora de Estefanía que acompaña a su hermanita y relata las aventuras de ambas. Estefanía y Magdalena son los personajes que consiguen dar unidad a un relato que se dispersa y disgrega en múltiples microhistorias, que giran en torno al tema de la violencia.

---

[2]Elena Garro elabora un relato autobiográfico en las cartas que le hace llegar a Emmanuel Carballo, "Elena Garro" en *Protagonistas de la literatura mexicana*, 2a. ed. (México: SEP-Ed. Del Ermitaño, 1986) 490-518.

[3]Carballo 490-518.

Así, en un primer acercamiento, nos parece enfrentar cuatro novelas distintas, unidas por tenues hilos narrativos. Con todo, si recordamos los procedimientos elegidos por la autora para conformar textos como *Andamos huyendo Lola* o *La semana de colores*, y tal vez *Testimonios sobre Mariana*, descubriremos que, en el caso de *Mi hermanita Magdalena*, se trata también de cuatro novelas cortas concatenadas, en tanto cada una conserva su independencia narrativa, con un espacio y una constelación de personajes específicos, y sólo en el capítulo final se interconectan los eventos del relato.

La trama gira en torno a la misteriosa desaparición de Magdalena en México. En el primer capítulo Magdalena es una ausencia siempre presente, porque persiste en las reflexiones y andanzas de sus hermanas, Estefanía y Rosa. Se descubre paulatinamente que Magdalena, tras su matrimonio secreto con Enrique, es forzada a irse con él a París: "Magdalena se fue llorando. Su marido la sacó a empellones y nadie pudo impedírselo" (19). Aclarar este misterio sirve como eje para impulsar el relato porque, según narra Estefanía: "Puedo afirmar que mi familia era una familia feliz, moderada, discreta, cortés y espartana (...) ¿Cómo explicar la gran catástrofe de la desaparición de Magdalena? No había explicación y decidimos callar mientras encontrábamos a mi hermanita" (13). Las hermanas eligen una lectura inspiradora y guía en su búsqueda, que es *Crimen y castigo* de Dostoievski, y vuelven hacia ciertos hechos de la historia, Robespierre por ejemplo, para encauzar su labor de investigación. Enrique y Magdalena son los ausentes y obligan a dos búsquedas paralelas: las hermanas van tras las noticias de Magdalena, y Justa desea saber sobre su hijo Enrique.

Esta última búsqueda da paso al relato de una modalidad de violencia familiar que consiste en la presión que las suegras ejercen en el ámbito doméstico. A Elena Garro le interesaba explorar este tema, porque en su vida había padecido la compleja relación personal con su suegra, doña Pepa, madre de Octavio Paz. Así, en *Mi hermanita Magdalena*, Justa se convierte en una representación de la maldad. Se instala todos los días en la mesa de la familia de Magdalena y genera una atmósfera de terror callado, sin amenazas explícitas. Pero su sola presencia produce miedo, tristeza y todos van perdiendo el apetito. Estefanía la describe así:

> Llevaba pendientes de diamantes, zapatos con tacón muy alto, que parecían incapaces para sostener su enorme corpachón. Un perfume espeso se desprendía de su persona, sus labios estaban cargados de carmín y sus párpados untados de carbón azul. Doña Justa era muy voluminosa. He pensado que quizá no era ni tan alta ni tan gorda, pero daba la impresión de llenar la casa. Se diría una planta carnívora devoradora de sus interlocutores y del aire que respiraban. Cerca de ella nos sentimos minúsculos y estúpidos (25).

Su amenaza es silenciosa y transforma la vida de la familia de Magdalena, al grado de involucrar al padre en un crimen. El relato de ese acoso es puntual y ascendente. Los lectores percibimos la angustia que genera la intromisión de esa mujer. En el entorno se producen otras situaciones de violencia concomitante a esta: las sirvientas sufren el acoso de un hombre que las persigue por la calle y golpea a Marta, una de ellas. Entre tanto Estefanía y Rosa, convertidas en detectives, siguen a Justa para descubrir sus misterios. Advierten que Justa vive una vida doble y que, tras su apariencia de madre preocupada por Enrique, se oculta un relato sórdido. La mujer se relaciona con un grupo mafioso en la calle de Santo Domingo. Y, en ese contexto, Dostoievski hará que las hermanas imaginen planes múltiples para matar a doña Justa: "Por primera vez el homicidio nos pareció normal. Suprimir a un ser malvado era legítimo y la verdadera víctima resultaba el asesino" (33).

Justa se casa con Luis María, un personaje siniestro, y éste manda golpear y matar a su esposa Raquel, para no tener obstáculos en su nueva boda: "La encontraron con el pescuezo rebanado en tamaño charcazo de sangre", dice un vecino. Toda la violencia descrita en el primer capítulo enmarca el relato omitido de la relación entre Magdalena y Enrique. Sólo al final del capítulo, un mensaje de Magdalena: "Papá ruégote mandes inmediatamente París una hermana Stop Hotel Royal Stop Tengo miedo Stop no avises a nadie viaje Stop" (62), nos informa sobre la sensación del temor que ella siente en París.

A la violencia de la suegra Justa y la de su entorno, el segundo capítulo añade el relato de la violencia en París. Estefanía y Magdalena se reencuentran e inician una vida de aventuras. El correlato histórico es ahora la casa de Marat, oscura y en reconstrucción, porque ha sido comprada por Magdalena. En la ciudad se despliegan las fuerzas del F.L.N. y la O.A.S., ya que, mediante un anacronismo histórico, Elena Garro sitúa los hechos de la guerra de Argelia en los años sesenta. La vinculación con México se establece mediante las cartas que Rosa les escribe a sus hermanas.

Debemos destacar algunas cuestiones. Magdalena huye del marido amenazante, por lo que Enrique se encuentra ausente del relato y sólo aparece al final del capítulo, cuando se reúne con Estefanía y la lleva a su casa.

Enrique no interactúa con Magdalena, sin embargo la vida de la mujer es regida por lo que ese hombre piensa. Los amigos y conocidos de Enrique le transmiten a Magdalena los mensajes del marido y sirven como la conciencia que constriñe los actos de Magdalena. No logramos enterarnos de las causas ciertas de la disputa matrimonial. Sólo existe el antecedente de un suicidio cometido por una modelo, que escribe el nombre de Enrique en el espejo. Magdalena escucha también que su esposo quiere 'dormirla', en sentido criminal.

Entonces se plantea una amenaza silenciosa, como en el caso de doña Justa. Magdalena se oculta de Enrique, pero él siempre sabe dónde está ella. Por otra parte, no conocemos el origen de los recursos económicos de Magdalena, que gasta sin parar (compra la casa de Marat, paga el hotel, comen y pasean por París). Se sugiere que es dinero que recibió de Enrique. Éste se encuentra envuelto en negocios turbios, que Magdalena no conoce. A la atmósfera de guerra soterrada en las calles de París, se suma el temor de las hermanas a verse enfrentadas a un grupo que contrabandea con armas. Entonces Estefanía resume su miedo con estas palabras: "Nunca saldríamos de esa casa abandonada. Me pareció ver a mi hermanita convertida en un esqueleto polvoriento sentado en el diván. El pavor me impidió hablar" (81).

Interesa mostrar que la violencia en este segundo capítulo no es una acción directa contra el cuerpo de la mujer, sino la creación de una atmósfera que la reduce a la inmovilidad y a un comportamiento infantil. Entendemos así el por qué la hermana menor de Estefanía permanece en esa niñez que le impide superar su condición de hermanita, débil, caprichosa y dependiente.

Además, la violencia interpersonal se diluye en una atmósfera de violencia política que lo invade todo. Los movimientos en el espacio y las relaciones con los otros son el producto del miedo. Todas las acciones se rigen por temores inciertos.

En el capítulo tercero se ofrece un interludio en apariencia feliz. El divorcio de Magdalena y Enrique se inicia. Las hermanas continúan su huida hacia Suiza. Y en Ascona conocen a un grupo de vacacionistas alemanes y franceses. Viven allí experiencias como turistas ricas, van a las fiestas y cenas. Magdalena consigue tres novios, a pesar de ser una mujer casada. Pero la amenaza misteriosa de Enrique permanece presente.

Nuevos personajes entran en el relato, y las hermanas conocen a un profesor húngaro, Novicki, que iniciará a Magdalena en las lecturas marxistas y en la reflexión social. Único elemento que parece modificar su vida individualista, centrada en el miedo a Enrique, el marido.

En este capítulo se plantea una inversión en el sujeto de la crueldad. Ahora es Magdalena la que ejerce una violencia callada contra sus tres enamorados, en tanto no se decide por ninguno de ellos. La relación con ellos muestra la indecisión y frivolidad de Magdalena frente a una situación nueva, en la que Enrique es sólo una sombra.

En esa paz de las vacacionistas comienzan a ocurrir crímenes misteriosos. Se encuentra el cadáver de un supuesto contrabandista de armas y Paul, un amigo de las hermanas, es asesinado de manera sospechosa. La presencia-ausente de Enrique se intuye entre líneas, por sus posibles contactos con el contrabando. Las hermanas deciden el regre-

so a París, porque ya no tienen una esperanza en México. La familia
había huido de Justa y de Enrique, hacia los Estados Unidos.

El último capítulo replantea el tema del miedo. Ahora las hermanas
encuentran en el departamento de Magdalena una caja llena de documentos comprometedores. En la búsqueda de apoyos, van entrando en
situaciones más complejas y en vínculos con los opositores al gobierno.
Magdalena se reencuentra finalmente con Enrique, que desea obligarla
a acompañarlo. Estefanía intenta defender a su hermana de las agre-
siones de Enrique, pero sólo logra insultos que lo muestran como un
hombre inflexible: "-¡Cállate, imbécil! ¿Qué quieres decir con eso de que
aquí no estamos en México? ¡Pendeja! El mundo entero es México, Magdalena es ¡mi mujer! ¿No te has enterado?" (256).

Las hermanas logran escaparse con astucia de la persecución de
Enrique y, al final de la novela, opera una especie de *deus ex machina* o
de verdadero *tour de force*. El final feliz de la novela muestra la inversión
de la violencia, que corrige el maltrato emocional al que se somete al
personaje femenino y le augura un futuro en libertad. Aunque los amigos de las hermanas saben que la violencia social continuará generando
una violencia silenciosa. Es la violencia cultural, esa que se produce en
el ámbito simbólico y permanece por largo tiempo en el imaginario de
las sociedades.

Bibliografía

Carballo, Emmanuel. *Protagonistas de la literatura mexicana*. 2a. ed. México:
    SEP-ed. del Ermitaño, 1986.

Garro, Elena. *Andamos huyendo Lola*. México: Joaquín Mortiz, 1980.

___ . *La casa junto al río*. México: Grijalbo, 1983.

___ . *Felipe Ángeles*. Guadalajara: Cóatl, 1967.

___ . *Memorias de España 1937*. México: Siglo Veintiuno, 1992.

___ . *Mi hermanita Magdalena*. Pról. de P. Rosas Lópategui. Monterrey: Castillo,
    1998.

___ . *Los recuerdos del porvenir*. México: Joaquín Mortiz, 1963.

___ . *Reencuentro de personajes*. México: Grijalbo, 1982.

___ . *La semana de colores*. Xalapa: Universidad Veracruzana, 1964.

___ . *Testimonios sobre Mariana*. México: Grijalbo, 1981.

___ . *Un hogar sólido y otras piezas*. Xalapa: Universidad Veracruzana, 1983.

___ . *Y Matarazo no llamó...* México: Grijalbo, 1991.

Torres Falcón, Marta. *La violencia en casa*. México: Paidós, 2001.

Ana Rosa Domenella

Universidad Autónoma Metropolitana, Iztapalapa

Violencia histórica y virtudes "femeninas" en dos novelistas mexicanas en los 90: Brianda Domecq y Ágeles Mastretta

Estamos en el imperio del miedo
Hay niños que se extravían en invierno
Niños de brazos rotos y rostros cabizbajos.
La rabia es un alicante que los liga
(.....)
El viento de cristalinas alas sobrevuela
La frontera del miedo.
Nosotros estamos en la frontera
Y nos atraviesa el ecuador,
Nos atraviesa la amenaza,
Nos aclimata el odio
El tenso cavilar de la serpiente,
El pánico y la mordida del invierno.

Minerva Margarita Villarreal, *"El viaje"*

En este congreso dedicado, de modo tan inesperado y oportuno, al tema de la violencia y del patriarcado, que han marchado unidos a lo largo de la historia y las sociedades, me propongo analizar dos novelas publicadas en la década de los 90 en México y escritas por mujeres, dentro de los múltiples rostros que esta violencia adquiere en las escritoras estudiadas por un grupo de investigadoras del Taller de Teoría y Crítica Literaria "Diana Morán" en un libro colectivo, próximo a publicarse, titulado *Territorio de leonas. Cartografía de narradoras mexicanas en los 90*[1].

El término "patriarcado" se acuña a mediados del siglo XIX en torno a las nuevas disciplinas que emergen del positivismo, como la antropología y la sociología. El patriarcado, afirma Graciela Hierro, "es una estructura de violencia que se institucionaliza en la familia, se refuerza en la sociedad civil y se legitima en el Estado". (1998, 263-276)

Hay que recordar al respecto que la palabra " familia" viene de "famil", sirviente, esclavo, posesión; y la palabra padre, "pater", significa dueño, poseedor. El paterfamilias, que suele utilizarse con orgullo en la actualidad, era en la antigua Roma el poseedor de esclavos.

---

[1]Ana Rosa Domenella, coord., Juan Pablos, ed., *Territorio de leonas. Cartografía de narradoras mexicanas en los 90* (México: UAM Iztapalapa, 2001). Investigación colectiva realizada por las integrantes del Taller de Teoría y Crítica Literaria "Diana Morán".

Juliet Michell, en *Psicoanálisis y feminismo*, afirma que el padre se vuelve más poderoso en la muerte que en la vida y el padre simbólico muerto "es mucho más decisivo que cualquier padre viviente real que meramente transmite su nombre". Si al padre real se lo puede matar —y la literatura presenta ilustres ejemplos de parricidios—, al padre simbólico no porque desde siempre está muerto, lo que le otorga garantía y perennidad a la ley. Los efectos más destacables de dicha ley, desde la perspectiva lacaniana, serían: la organización simbólica, la diferenciación de los sexos, la diferencia de las generaciones y la fundación del deseo". Además, y esta propuesta es importante para nuestra lectura de las novelas escogidas, "la mujer está en el corazón de la contradicción del patriarcado".

Las antropólogas feministas proponen la existencia de una sociedad prepatriarcal, aunque no necesariamente un matriarcado, pero sí sociedades matrilineales que rendían culto a deidades femeninas y a las diosas madres, ya que los varones ignoraron por largo tiempo el papel que desempeñaban en la reproducción humana. Luego, en todas las sociedades estudiadas, se produce un desplazamiento hacia dioses masculinos (hijos o hermanos de las diosas primigenias) cuyo poder de creación es diferente al femenino (la voz, la palabra, que tiene su versión más acabada en el Génesis). Este desplazamiento devalúa la figura femenina de la diosa que metafóricamente crea desde la materialidad de su cuerpo.

Afirma Gerna Lerner que "la simbólica devaluación de la mujer en relación a lo divino se convierte en una de las metáforas fundadoras de la civilización de Occidente. La otra metáfora fundadora nace de la filosofía aristotélica, la que asume que las mujeres son seres humanos incompletos dañados"[2]. La internacionalización y canonización de esta simbología presenta como un orden "natural" el predominio masculino y patriarcal.

En el panteón mexicano la diosa madre era Coatlicue-Tonantzin, la de la "falda de serpientes", exaltada en los cantos celebratorios también como "nuestra madre, la guerrera", que correspondería a la "imago" de la madre fálica de los orígenes, dueña de la vida y de la muerte, en la perspectiva psicoanalítica. Sin embargo, al igual que las mujeres históricas, carga sobre sí con las tareas domésticas "barría y hacía penitencia" y también con el honor de la familia, como le ocurrió a Coatlicue cuando guardó en su seno la breve pelota de plumas que encontró y queda embarazada. La hija, Coyolxauqui, insta a los hermanos a matar a la madre por la afrenta, pero el hijo nonato le habla desde el vientre y la defiende, o sea que la antes poderosa diosa necesita de una figura mas-

[2]Gerda Lernes, *The creation of Patriarchy*. (New York: Oxford UP, 1986), cit. por Z. Nelly Martínez en "Introducción" a *El silencio que habla*.

culina, en este caso gestada en su propio cuerpo, para que la defienda y la vengue. En cualquier sino o cosmogonía que ocurran estos cambios el poder de la creación y la fertilidad se transfieren de las diosas a la diosa madre y a un dios masculino.

En cuanto a la violencia, como el cuerpo humano es la primera evidencia de la diferencia humana, la mujer ha sido -afirma Marta Lamas– el "otro" más cercano, después entran a la lid los colores de piel, las clases sociales, las lenguas, las costumbres y más allá las religiones, o el "factor Dios" como propone llamarlo José Saramago[3], las preferencias sexuales o las opiniones políticas. Marta Lamas afirma que en función de la forma en que se interpreta esa diferencia y su simbolización, se elaboran la angustia y el miedo que genera en los individuos. Luego añade que "de todas las formas más violentas de marcar la diferencia, el sexismo es la más arcaica y persistente" (1998, 191-198). Como sostenía Freud, "el odio es más antiguo que el amor", o el poeta Eduardo Lizalde que en su poema "Grande es el odio" escribe: "Nadie vacila, como en el amor, / a la hora del odio".

La forma paradigmática de la violencia, simplifica Bourdieu, es la lógica de la dominación de género y para oponerse a ella se debe trabajar y abogar por el establecimiento de relaciones equitativas; no pueden ser igualitarias por esas diferencias que subyacen y permanecen. El sexismo despliega su poder cotidiano a través de la violencia simbólica.

Desde una perspectiva filosófica la violencia es una especie de fuerza, "vis" en latín, "bias" en griego, energía, poder; pero existen —asegura Juliana González— formas no violentas de esta potencia, como lo es particularmente la "vis" de la virtud opuesta a la "vis" de la violencia" (139-146), como veremos en las propuestas de algunas de nuestras novelistas.

Lo específico de la violencia es esa fuerza avasalladora, que se aplica a la Naturaleza desbocada y a las sociedades y los individuos que exhiben su agresividad a través de las guerras, los sistemas opresivos y el terrorismo de todos los tiempos. Podrán encontrarse múltiples ejemplos, tanto en las llamadas sociedades "civilizadas" como en las consideradas "primitivas", porque, como ya escribía Voltaire en el Siglo de las Luces, cuna de la modernidad, "la civilización no suprime a la barbarie, la perfecciona".

Como los seres humanos suelen confundir la violencia con animalidad y, además, con la naturaleza, con el deseo. Georges Bataille, en oposición a Hegel, asegura que la violencia no ayuda a cumplir finali-

---

[3]José Saramago, carta abierta del Premio Nobel con el título de "El factor Dios" con relación a los atentados terroristas del 11 de septiembre de 2001 a las torres gemelas en New York y al edificio del Pentágono en Washington. Esta carta fue distribuida por correo electrónico.

dad alguna. Para el filósofo francés la violencia se haya siempre más allá del pensamiento, o mejor dicho, de la razón. "La razón, entre otras cosas, es el elemento que paraliza. De tal suerte la violencia es postulada como anti-razón, pero también la razón es negación de la violencia; Bataille propone otorgarle una supremacía en relación con la razón, es decir que la violencia es ante-razón, precede y excede a la razón."[4] En el mundo griego a la violencia se la relacionaba también con la "hybris", la desmesura o peligro demoníaco.

En el campo de la economía política, tanto para Marx como para Engels, la violencia está vinculada íntimamente con el Estado y, por supuesto, con el ejercicio del poder. Para el padre del psicoanálisis la violencia se relaciona con uno de sus descubrimientos más trascendentes, "la pulsión de muerte". George Sorel, maestro de José Carlos Mariátegui, en su clásico ensayo *Reflexiones sobre la violencia*, propone analizarla también como "arma para la libertad" y en esta línea se aplica a las revoluciones.

Dice Julieta González, y sus palabras resultan muy oportunas en estos tiempos de tempestades, que "la ética comienza cuando termina el círculo paralizante del Talión". Recordemos las prédicas sobre la no violencia de Gandhi y su sabia reflexión sobre el arcaico apotegma de "ojo por ojo y diente por diente" que sólo conduce a un mundo de ciegos y desdentados. Por lo tanto, la ética es un reto a la violencia y "la sociedad ética, para el filósofo Luis Villoro, sería la que hubiera eliminado toda traza de dominación. Este es el tema de todas las utopías" (165-178).

De santas, médicas y revolucionarias

> *No hay dioses —dicen los indios de Mackenzie— sólo hay medicina*
> Jean Chevalier y Alain Gheerbrant

Diccionario de símbolos

En nuestro recorrido por el "territorio de leonas" en la última década del siglo XX, contamos con una espléndida producción de escritoras desde las nacidas en la década de los 30 y que continúan escribiendo, hasta las jóvenes pertenecientes a las décadas de los sesenta y setenta con algunas obras que han merecido reconocimientos a través de premios o el apoyo del público lector y de editoriales tanto de la capital como de las provincias.

Muchas merecen formar parte del canon literario nacional si no fuese éste tan empecinadamente androcéntrico y discriminador.

---

[4]Ignacio Díaz de la Serna, tesis doctoral inédita.

Pero en este foro quiero detenerme en dos escritoras nacidas en la década de los 40, que publican dos novelas exitosas, con protagonistas femeninas fuertes y con un marco histórico violento, tanto por parte del Estado como de la sublevación revolucionaria; me refiero al otro final de siglo, los años terminales de la dictadura de Porfirio Díaz y la etapa armada de la Revolución Mexicana de 1910.

Las escritoras seleccionadas en esta ocasión son: Brianda Domecq (Nueva York, 1942), autora de *La increíble historia de la Santa de Cabora* (1990)[5] y Ángeles Mastretta, autora de *Mal de amores* (1996)[6], que mereciera el premio Rómulo Gallegos en 1997.

Fue la primera ocasión que este prestigiado galardón de las letras latinoamericanas le fuera entregado a una escritora y fue cuestionado por representantes de la "machocrítica", (neologismo acuñado por nuestra amiga y colega Luce Gutiérrez de Velasco) por los supuestos componentes de "literatura light" de la novela, que siempre buscan en la producción de mujeres y no suelen percibirlo en los otros escritores exitosos.

En una entrevista, Mastretta dice que desea pertenecer a la literatura mexicana a secas y no a la "literatura femenina mexicana porque todo lo femenino es considerado de segunda"(García Hernández 25).

La protagonista, Emilia Sauri, crece en una ciudad cargada de historia y de abolengo, la muy tradicionalista y clerical Puebla de los Ángeles, escenario del triunfo del ejército liberal juarista ante las tropas invasoras del imperio de Maximiliano de Hazburgo, quien fue finalmente derrotado, enjuiciado y condenado a muerte en el famoso Cerro de las Campanas. Puebla también es cuna de los revolucionarios hermanos Serdán que prenden la lucha contra Porfirio Díaz antes que en otros puntos del país.

El hogar formado por el yucateco Diego Sauri y la poblana Josefa Veytia es atípico por su liberalidad, armonía y respeto por las acciones y amores de su hija y de su extravagante tía, Milagros Veytia, personaje que pareciera formar parte de la galería de tías transgresoras de *Mujeres de ojos grandes* (1990).

En una entrevista con Marta Lamas, ésta le hace notar la importancia de construir un mundo naturalmente laico, incluso anticlerical, con personajes con sensibilidad social y que se ocupan de los demás y le pregunta por los rasgos autobiográficos de los escenarios y de los personajes femeninos. Mastretta contesta:

> Hay muchas características en Milagros Veytia que yo quisiera tener: es muy decidida, sabe bien que quiere, es muy contundente para

[5]Las citas textuales corresponden a esta edición.
[6]Las citas textuales corresponden a esta edición.

hablar, es muy audaz (...) Yo quisiera ser la mitad Josefa y la mitad Milagros. Por eso me di el lujo de construir un personaje armonioso que tuviera algo de las dos, que es Emilia. Claro que yo no sé si consiga, cuando tenga setenta años, la armonía interior que tiene Emilia. Estoy en busca de eso. (1996, 10)

Pero si Emilia Sauri (y el nombre está elegido en honor a la famosa propuesta pedagógica de Rousseau, que por supuesto pensó en un joven varón y no en una mujer), la protagonista de la novela de Domecq, Teresa Urrea es un personaje histórico que nació en Sinaloa en 1873 y vivió en la hacienda de Cabora en el estado de Sonora hasta su exilio en Estados Unidos, ordenado por Porfirio Díaz debido a los levantamientos indígenas que invocaban su protección llamándola "la santa de Cabora"; muere a los treinta y tres años en el pueblo de Clifton, Arizona.

La marca autobiográfica en este caso estaría presente en la obsesión que sufre el personaje de la escritora, "la escogida", en su búsqueda por México y Estados Unidos de las huellas del personaje de cuya existencia la autora real y extratextual, tuvo conocimiento en una nota de la famosa novela de Heriberto Frías, *Tomochic*, tras lo cual y debido a que la familia de su marido provenía de Sonora, se dedicó a investigar en fuentes periodísticas y orales durante más de una década.

Aralia López en su artículo titulado "La memoria del olvido: crítica y estética del indicio y del zurcido" afirma que el personaje tiene "un doble estatuto, el de la historia y el de la leyenda" Y ese doble estatuto nos lleva a un enfrentamiento "entre la razón dominante, la del orden logocéntrico y falocéntrico en la historia occidental; y otra forma de razón asociada a lo arcaico y femenino, descentrada, preedípica en la concepción del psicoanálisis, sumergida, que retorna y desafía al primero." (499-507)

Esta primera razón a la que se refiere Aralia está ligada a la "Ley del Padre" y al poder territorial del hacendado. La otra, la sumergida o borrada por la primera, está basada en el deseo, en el cuerpo erotizado y "sanador" que proviene de ese mundo materno negado a nivel social y simbólico. Porque Teresa era hija de Cayetana Chávez, indígena de catorce años violada por el patrón joven y abandonada tras de haberla despertado a la sexualidad, al igual que hiciera con otras adolescentes de la población dedicada al servicio de la hacienda. Se jactaba de no usar dos veces la misma mujer "así no las enviciaba" (15). Al final de su vida había procreado dieciocho hijos con varias mujeres.

Pero Teresa Chávez, entenada con su madre en la enramada de la tía Tula, no acepta la docilidad de Cayetana ni los reproches por su condición de bastarda, evidente en señales de su cuerpo: la piel blanca, los ojos ambarinos y el cabello rojizo que resultan insultantes para el orgullo de su tía. Se apodera de una imagen primero y de un nombre después, Teresa Urrea, que comienza a escribir en el suelo de la hacienda de Cabora, como marcando un territorio a conquistar después de quedar deslumbrada por la presencia del hacendado la primera vez que lo ve, durante la mudanza obligado por razones políticas, pero también por su vida desordenada, desde la propiedad en Sinaloa a la hacienda de Cabora en Sonora. Dice la voz narrativa:

> El iba al frente de todos, montado -recto y fuerte- sobre un imponente alazán. Aunque no era un hombre alto, a Teresa, desde la perspectiva de sus siete años, le pareció casi divino (...) Era rubio y su tez blanca resplandecía bajo el ala del sombrero. Tenía bigote y vestía un traje entallado lleno de adornos de plata que lo rodeaban de relumbres mágicos. Su seguridad y mando (...) le prestaba el aura de un "dios" benévolo cuidando a su rebaño (...) Se llenó de una sensación nueva, de maravillamiento, de pasmo, y deseó con toda su alma que aquel hombre se detuviera y la mirara, se diera cuenta de su existencia. (...) El jinete miró primero a Cayetana y después a ella; sonrió. Tenía los ojos verdes y claros como agua de manantial... (23-24).

Es la mirada edípica de la niña, deslumbrada ante la belleza y el poderío del padre. Desde ese momento quiere ser hombre, pero el cuerpo "la traiciona" (75), cuando le comienzan a crecer los pechos y se asusta con su menarca.

Es con el Nombre del Padre con el que se aplica la ley, en este caso Tomás Urrea, el que distingue el heredero del desheredado. Sin embargo sus hijos varones legítimos, concebidos sin amor con su esposa y prima Loreto, no heredan la amada hacienda de Cabora sino que el primogénito se apropia de ella cuando el padre es obligado, nuevamente, a marchar al exilio junto con su hija Teresa, para entonces conocida en todo el estado y el país como "la Santa de Cabora", por órdenes de un poder patriarcal superior al suyo, el del dictador Porfirio Díaz.

El concepto de desheredado, afirma Celia Amorós en su ensayo *Hacia una crítica de la razón patriarcal*, no existe sin " división del reino" y "es cómplice de las divisiones de clases, porque necesita clasificar, porque sin clasificación discriminatoria no hay herencia ni genealogía y el Nombre del Padre solamente funciona y significa en el contexto de un determinado sistema de distribución de Nombres"(78).

La hija bastarda, en la novela de Domecq, conquista un lugar en la propiedad del padre y en su cariño y protección gracias a su férrea voluntad de convertirse en sujeto de su propia vida y no objeto de las decisiones de los demás. "Don Tomás quería enseñarle todo lo que sabía: estaba encantado de tener don quién compartir sus opiniones"(121). La huella de la madre se va borrando y queda en la memoria de Teresa "la tibieza de Cayetana cuando se le repegaba en la madrugada" (21). Antes de su muerte, tras 17 años de separación, Cayetana visita a su hija, le besa la frente y no le habla; dice la voz narradora "con esa misma calidad de sombra entró al cuarto y se quedó repegada en la pared, mirando a la enferma" (378).

En esa ley distributiva y patriarcal de carencias y marcas se distingue al heredero del desheredado, pero también al verdadero del impostor. Y en la historia personal del hacendado también él jugaba un cierto papel de ilegitimidad e impostura ya que las propiedades las hereda de un tío rico sin descendencia, Miguel Urrea, porque su madre enviuda cuando Tomás tiene doce años y se lo entrega al cuñado para su educación y cuidado. Tomás nunca perdona el abandono aunque comprende que la renuncia materna lo benefició. Por decisión de su tía, Doña Justina Almeda y Zayas, quien desaprueba su vida desordenada, es obligado a casarse para asegurar su herencia. La poco agraciada, pero muy paridora esposa, Loreto, parece aceptar su lejanía e infidelidades, sin embargo no resulta ser tan sumisa pues cuando el marido la manda a buscar con sus hijos varones para compartir la enorme casa que construyó a su gusto, en Cabora ella se niega porque prefiere las comodidades de la ciudad y su vida social a la compañía de su marido en el campo; para afianzar su negativa cuenta con el obispo y la tía, como aliados. Entonces, Tomás Urrea lleva a vivir a la hacienda a la hija de otro hacendado vecino y amigo, Gabriela, porque extraña la compañía de una hija; es cuando Teresa, sólo un año menor que la joven concubina, se presenta reclamar su lugar junto al padre. Tomás Urrea ejerce su dominio sobre tierras y ganado y manda sobre sus mujeres, vaqueros y subordinados y establece acuerdos con la tribu yaqui para que no ataquen sus propiedades; mientras tanto la hija recobrada, Teresa, comparte su territorio y espacios privados y se permite invadir la hacienda con una muchedumbre de desarrapados que llegan en busca de salud y consuelo y que destruyen y ensucian la hacienda, llamándola Niña , Virgen y Santa. Teresa Urrea atiende sus "pacientes " y seguidores en un espacio alejado de la casa principal y cuando sobre un ataque de catalepsia, que ella llamará "su primera muerte", adquiere habilidades más allá de las enseñanzas recibidas por su maestra, la curandera y comadrona Huila, quien fuera la partera de Cayetana y forma parte del personal de la hacienda de Cabora.

He dicho que, por el contrario a Teresa Urrea Emilia Sauri no tiene un referente histórico extratextual. La joven poblana es hija deseada y única de una pareja que la concibe después de una década de feliz matrimonio. Recibe una cuidadosa educación laica en que se mezclan las novelas que lee su madre, con personajes como Ana Karenina, Julián Sorel y Ana Ozores (todos premonitoriamente luchando entre dos amores), y las noticias periodísticas que le lee el padre junto a las enseñanzas farmacéuticas en la botica familiar y las tertulias antirreleccionistas en casa del Dr. Cuenca, quien, además le enseña a tocar el chelo. Es en esa casa de los domingos sociales y políticos donde conoce y ama, desde niña, a Daniel Cuenca, huérfano de madre y protegido de su tía Milagros. Este amor turbulento, apasionado y correspondido (que se consuma, en la propia casa paterna a los diecisiete años de Emilia y veintiuno del novio) es vivido con intensidad e intermitencias, a causa de la vocación revolucionaria del joven abogado y periodista, unido a la inestabilidad política del país y las diferentes facciones que luchan por el poder antes y después del exilio de Díaz y la asunción a la presidencia y posterior asesinato de Francisco Madero.

Al estilo, o con el modelo literario, de Doña Sol (que, además, es el nombre de la mejor amiga de Emilia), la bella cocinera bahiana de Jorge Amado, la joven protagonista tiene una profesión y un segundo marido sin mediar trámites legales. El Dr. Antonio Zavalza, hombre de prestigio y abolengo poblano es el personaje con quien comparte un amor sosegado y fructífero, la pasión por la medicina y la constitución de una familia sólida, con tres hijos y posteriores nietos, sin dejar por ello de amar, con largos períodos de ausencia, a Daniel Cuenca. Cuando finalmente, después de sufrir por largo tiempo del "mal de amores" que da título a la novela y de luchar inútilmente contra la permanente y muy "masculina" necesidad de acción y cambios de Daniel, frente a su propia inclinación por el mundo familiar y el sosiego productivo, Emilia Sauri le confiesa a sus padres: "Soy bígama", su tía Milagros le responde: "El cariño no se gasta".

Por su parte, la agreste y voluntariosa Teresa Urrea no tiene ni la preparación ni la capacidad erótica de la singular burguesita poblana. No va a la escuela porque se aburre y es rebelde, pero decide aprender a leer con los periódicos viejos de Doña Rosaura y a escribir sola, (aunque nunca llega a dominar la escritura y ya adulta se vale de otras personas para enviar cartas a la familia); también aprende sola o simplemente observando a los vaqueros de la hacienda, a montar a caballo y a tocar la guitarra, con lo cual amenizará las tertulias de su padre. Pero su verdadera formación la recibe de Huila, la vieja curandera, comadrona, medio bruja, quien recuerda que Teresa nació con los ojos abiertos y rodeada de luminosidad, por lo tanto sabía que tendría una vida predestinada para "oler la vida y la muerte, escuchar las voces traídas por el viento y ver el futuro con la claridad del presente" (129). Se acerca a la Niña cuando la nota aburrida e inútil para las labores de la costura y la cocina y comienza a llevarla a sus visitas de enfermos.

Pero en amores Teresa no es afortunada, aunque gana el cariño de su padre (a quien siempre llamará "Don Tomás") llega virgen a los 27 años, aunque años atrás, se sintió enamorada por la presencia y los ojos oscuros del dirigente yaqui Cruz Chávez (el mismo apellido de su madre), quien muere en el asalto de las tropas federales al pueblo de

Tomochic defendido con la imagen de la Santa de Cabora. Cuando finalmente se casa en Arizona con Lupe Rodríguez, capataz de una mina, su padre se enoja y muere sin perdonarla. Sin llegar a consumarse la boda, el marido enloquece, lo ponen preso y se suicida. Finalmente, Teresa Urrea se embaraza y luego se casa, sólo para darle un nombre a la hija y no repetir la bastardía. El novio es John Van Order, el hijo mayor de su amiga mexicana de Solomonville, quien al igual que Don Tomás, tampoco le perdonará su "traición". El joven había viajado a Nueva York para servirle de compañía e intérprete en la empresa far-macéutica que la contrata como publicidad y promete hacerla recorrer Estados Unidos y Europa. El joven esposo, muy deseoso de recobrar la libertad y la soltería, cobra las "curas", cada vez más escasas, sin el con-sentimiento de Teresa a quien pronto abandona con dos hijas. Teresa muere a los 33 años acompañada por Gabriela, ya viuda de su padre, los hijos de ambos y sus propias hijas que dejará encomendadas a su fiel colaboradora Mariana, quien siempre deseó ser madre y Teresa le había prometido ese "milagro".

En una carta desde Nueva York le había resumido así su vida: "He sido de todo un poco: un poco santa, un poco virgen, un poco casada, un poco enamorada, un poco ilusa, un poco revolucionaria, un poco visionaria. ¿ Qué soy a fin de cuentas?"(374).

Integración de saberes. La "vis" de las virtudes femininas

> Soy la advenediza
> la perturbadora
> la desordenadora de los sexos
> la transgresora.
> Hablo la lengua de los conquistadores
> Pero digo lo opuesto de lo que ellos dicen.
>
> Cristina Peri-Rossi, *Condición de mujer.*

Tanto el personaje histórico de Teresa Urrea como el ficticio de Emilia Sauri dedican sus existencias al arte de curar, uniendo, "zurciendo" o entrelazando conocimientos de diversas procedencias: culto y popular, científico y milagrero, práctico y experimental, pero siempre alejados de los dominios eclesiásticos. De sus saberes y poderes dan cuenta enfer-mos de distintas clases sociales, aunque predominen los pobres, y de los que sufren males físicos, sociales o espirituales.

Sus padres biológicos son pacifistas declarados, y se oponen a la dictadura porfirista, como el boticario Diego Sauri, para quien "el heroísmo es un culto al asesinato" (201) (con su crítico apoyo a Madero); o se alejaron del escenario bélico, como el hacendado Tomás Urrea, amigo de Lauro Aguirre a quien se le adjudica una "revolución de papel" contra Porfirio Díaz desde el exilio. Por su parte, Jesusa Vieytia, la madre de Emilia, también receta tés para cualquier dolencia espiritual o física, le pide a su hermana Milagros que pronuncie unos conjuros mágicos ante la cuna de su hija y se encomienda a un "Dios", cuya filiación la familia ignora.

Teresa Urrea aprende a reconocer el olor de lo que su maestra denomina "la nata de la vida", junto a la memorización del uso de las hierbas y fórmulas para todo tipo de dolencias, aunque nada puede hacerse con los que no quieren vivir. Más tarde incorpora el poder curativo de sus manos, de su saliva y el manejo de un polvo rosado que busca de una cueva que parece simbolizar el principio materno, su huella primigenia olvidada en aras de la supremacía de la razón patriarcal.

Emilia Sauri que no nace predestinada, pero sí amada, aprende a reconocer hierbas, sustancias y recetas en la botica del padre y más tarde cambia las lecciones de chelo por las de medicina con el Dr. Cuenca; los adelantos científicos los estudia en Estados Unidos y los practica con el Dr. Zavalza en Puebla. Sus maestros son instruidos y sabios y ella logra conseguir acreditación universitaria y la admiración y fidelidad de sus pacientes. Sin embargo, reconoce que para curar tanto sirven las infusiones de Ombligo de Venus de la partera indígena, como la Pulsatilla de los homeópatas, y no dudaba en emplear desde el xtabentún yucateco, los masajes chinos en los pies y, por supuesto, el instrumental quirúrgico que les vende para el hospital el cónsul gringo en Puebla.

Nos enteramos en la novela del cariño que Emilia profesa por el "Geneve College", porque en 1847 recibe a la primera estudiante de medicina, cuando las demás universidades estadounidenses las rechazaban en sus claustros. Incluso se narra la curiosa anécdota de que el decano envió a sus alumnos una consulta escrita preguntándoles si aceptarían una condiscípula mujer y todos, creyendo que se trataba de una broma, contestaron afirmativamente. De ese modo anticonvencional Elizabeth Blackwell ingresó a la facultad de medicina y recibió con las más altas calificaciones de su generación. Resulta curioso que la autora, Ángeles Mastretta siendo poblana, no incluyera de algún modo el dato de la primera médica mexicana, Matilde Montoya que nació en Puebla de los Ángeles en 1839, de origen humilde y salud precaria que debía realizar las autopsias a solas y con cadáveres vestidos. En 1870 le permiten matricularse en la escuela de medicina y estudiar obstetricia, pero cuando regresa a Puebla, por problemas de salud, la muy conservadora sociedad poblana la rechaza acusándola de "masona y protestante" (otra vez la intolerancia en nombre del "factor Dios", del que habla Saramago y que ha ejercido su poder desde antiguo). Quiso viajar a Estados Unidos, pero no contaba con los medios económicos para hacerlo, como sí los tiene el personaje de Emilia. Se titula finalmente en 1887 como "médico cirujano" y es el "primer título científico profesional —escribe Laureana Wright de Kleinhans en sus biografías de "mujeres notables mexicanas", publicadas en l910— alcanzado a costa de una vida entera de trabajo, estudio, de amargura , de sacrificio, por la débil mano de una mujer que ha reivindicado los derechos de nuestro sexo elevándola por encima de una sociedad injusta por naturaleza y antagonista por sistema"[7].

Por el contrario, las protagonistas de las novelas de Domecq y Mastretta, a pesar de la oposición del clero conservador o de la "buena sociedad", ejercen su don de reparar cuerpos y almas a través de muy diversos procedimientos. Considero que, más que representantes de culturas híbridas propias del mestizaje étnico, estas mujeres integran, creativamente, los saberes que van adquiriendo a lo largo de su vida y los amores y lealtades que van conquistando en esta tarea cotidiana de vivir en plenitud.

Si en la Edad Media y hasta el siglo XVII se quemaron miles de mujeres acusadas de brujas porque el poder "fonologofalocéntrico", (al decir de Derrida), no aceptaba que poseyeran otros saberes y habilidades que no fueran los autorizados por el poder eclesiástico y patriarcal, en el siglo XIX estaba prohibido o era difícil para las mujeres estudiar y ejercer la medicina, como queda expresado con los casos de las primeras estudiantes de medicina de Estados Unidos y México.

Pero en el espacio de la literatura estos personajes femeninos decimonónicos pero creados a fin de siglo XX, parecen encarnar con sus capacidades innatas o adquiridas y su voluntad de independencia y libertad, la "vis" de la virtud en oposición a la "vis" de la violencia.

Bibliografía

Amorós, Celia. *Hacia una crítica de la razón patriarcal*. Barcelona: Anthropos, 1985.

Domecq, Brianda. *La increíble historia de la Santa de Cabora*. México: Planeta, 1990.

Domenella, Ana Rosa, coord. *Territorio de leonas. Cartografía de narradoras mexicanas en los 90*. Ed. Juan Pablos. México: UAM Iztapalapa, 2001.

Domenella, Ana Rosa y Nora Pasternac, coords. "Biografías femeninas y periódico de señoras." *Las voces olvidadas. Antología crítica de narradoras mexicanas nacidas en el siglo XIX*. México: PIEM COLMEX, 1997.

Díaz de la Serna, Ignacio. tesis doctoral inédita.

García Hernández, Arturo. "El premio no me hace ni mejor ni peor escritora: Ángeles Mastretta." *La Jornada* [México] 5 julio 1997.

[7]Ana Rosa, Domenella y Nora Pasternac, coords. "Biografías femeninas y periódico de señoras." *Las voces olvidadas. Antología crítica de narradoras mexicanas nacidas en el siglo XIX*, reimp. (México: PIEM COLMEX, 1997) 374-375.

González, Juliana. "Etica y violencia." *El mundo de la violencia.* Ed. Adolfo Sánchez Vázquez. México: UNAM FCE, 1998.

Hierro, Graciela. *De la domesticación a la educación de las mexicanas.* México: Ed. Torres Asoc., 1990.

___ . "La violencia de género." *El mundo de la violencia.* Ed. Adolfo Sánchez Vázquez. México: UNAM FCE, 1998.

Lamas, Marta. "La violencia del sexismo." *El mundo de la violencia.* Ed. Adolfo Sánchez Vázquez. México: UNAM FCE, 1998.

___. Entrevista a Ángeles Mastretta. "Perseguir el deseo." *La Jornada Semanal* [México] 10 noviembre 1996.

Lernes Gerda. *The creation of Patriarchy.* New York: Oxford UP, 1986.

López González, Aralia. "La memoria del olvido: crítica y estética del indicio y del zurcido." *Sin imágenes falsas, sin falsos espejos.* Coord. Aralia López González. México: PIEM COLMEX, 1995.

Mastretta, Ángeles. *Mal de amores.* México: Alfaguara, 1996.

Michell, Juliet. *Psicoanálisis y Feminismo. Freud, Reich y las mujeres.* Barcelona: Anagrama, 1975.

Sorel, George. *Reflexiones sobre la violencia.* Madrid: Alianza, 1976.

Villoro, Luis. "Poder, contrapoder y violencia." *El mundo de la violencia.* Ed. Adolfo Sánchez Vázquez. México: UNAM FCE, 1998.

Laura Cázares H.
Universidad Autónoma Metropolitana-Iztapalapa

La violencia en el ritual del matrimonio: *La sunamita*, de Inés Arredondo y *El tiempo justo*, de Aline Pettersson

> "Me busco sin hallar voz o figura
> o el borde de un espacio que sea mío"
> Aline Pettersson. *Cautiva estoy de mí.*

"La violencia ha sido siempre importante en nuestra literatura, como lo ha sido en nuestra historia", dice Ariel Dorfman[1], y a partir del naturalismo la violencia es eje de la narrativa, pues se descubre que nuestra realidad es esencialmente violenta. Claro que él se refiere a la lucha de los americanos, a su explotación por la oligarquía, a su debilidad frente a la tierra devoradora. Todo ello se inserta perfectamente en el campo de las que se consideran muestras de violencia: golpes, torturas, asesinatos, guerras.

Desde una perspectiva no literaria, Hacker opina que:

> La violencia se ha convertido en un hecho cotidiano, natural, trivial, en una insignificancia, y reclama en nuestras ideas y sentimientos el derecho de la costumbre, de lo tradicionalmente inevitable. Estamos ya tan insensibilizados que se precisa una considerable escalada de violencias o unos actos de brutalidad especialmente dramáticos para que salgamos de nuestra crasa indiferencia, nacida de una supuesta impotencia. *Lo fácil es acostumbrarse a la violencia, en tanto que resultado violentamente simplificado de unos procesos forzosos de habituación.* (19-20). (El subrayado es nuestro)

Con base en lo anterior podemos ver que se considera violencia a la manifestación abierta, casi siempre física, de la agresión; la cual también se produce con gran frecuencia en las relaciones entre los sexos. El sexismo consiste en "el proceso directo de violentar, oprimir y reprimir las oportunidades vitales de un ser humano (...) con base en su

---

[1]Ariel Dorfman, "La violencia en la novela hispanoamericana actual" *Imaginación y violencia en América* (Barcelona: Anagrama,1972) 9 - ss.

anatomía (el sexo)" (Lamas 193), y está más ligado a cuestiones de orden simbólico que a la anatomía, o sea que está más ligado al género. Acerca de éste dice la propia Marta Lamas:

Es la simbolización que los seres humanos hacemos de la diferencia sexual —el *género*— lo que reglamenta y condiciona las relaciones entre mujeres y hombres. Mediante dicho proceso de simbolización, la sociedad fabrica las ideas de lo que deben ser los hombres y las mujeres, de lo que se supone es "propio" de cada sexo. La cultura marca a los sexos con el *género* y el *género* marca la percepción de todo lo demás: lo social, lo política, lo religioso, lo cotidiano. (...) Así, establecido como "conjunto objetivo de referencias", el género estructura la "percepción y la organización concreta y simbólica de toda la vida social". (192)

Estrechamente ligados al género y al sexismo se pueden dar otras formas de agresión que no son brutales y evidentes, que son menos visibles y se producen bajo apariencia de suavidad. La violencia así entendida se expresa con frecuencia en la obra de Inés Arredondo y de Aline Pettersson, aunque yo sólo me detendré en dos cuentos: *La sunamita* y *El tiempo justo*, respectivamente.

Inés Arredondo

Nació en Culiacán, Sinaloa, en 1928 y falleció en la ciudad de México en 1989. Pertenece al grupo de escritores de la Generación de Medio siglo[2], escritores que "compartían [...] lecturas, intereses, anhelos y una misma voluntad de decir y decir libremente, fuera de los cauces convencionales y ajenos a las normas de una cultura establecida" (Pereira129). Y que colaboraron en las principales revistas y suplementos culturales del país, como: *Cuadernos del viento, La Palabra y el Hombre, Revista de la Universidad, Revista de Bellas Artes, Revista Mexicana de Literatura, México en la cultura* y *La cultura en México*.

La producción literaria de Inés Arredondo se reduce a tres libros de cuentos: *La señal* (1965), *Río subterráneo* (1979), con el que obtuvo el premio Xavier Villaurrutia ese mismo año, y *Los espejos* (1988); además publicó un estudio sobre el poeta Jorge Cuesta. Sus *Obras completas* aparecieron en 1988, un año antes de su fallecimiento.

El cuento *La sunamita* corresponde a su primer libro, *La señal*, y por su título y el epígrafe, la protagonista se relaciona intertextualmente con el personaje del Antiguo Testamento (*Reyes I*, 3-4), Abisag Sunamita, la joven que le entregan al viejo rey David para calentar su cuerpo. Luisa narra la historia de su regreso a la ciudad a causa de la enfermedad y

[2]Claudia Albarrán señala que el término fue utilizado por Enrique Krauze para referirse a las personas nacidas entre 1921 y 1935. en *Luna menguante. Vida y obra de Inés Arredondo* (123)

posible fallecimiento de su tío político, Apolonio, del matrimonio *in articulo mortis* para convertirse en heredera, y de la lujuria que lo posee y le prolonga la vida, convirtiéndola a ella en una mujer abyecta. Encontramos así, en este relato, un buen ejemplo de lo que José María Espinasa afirma de Inés Arredondo: "Sus cuentos buscan el umbral entre la sordidez y la pureza, entre el bien y el mal si se quiere, sabiendo que hay ese umbral en que, forzosamente, en algún momento, tuvieron que convivir y con ello sumergirnos en un vértigo ético."(100).

Con seis fragmentos de extensión diversa se construye el relato, siendo el primero una sola línea sugerente e inquietante: "Aquél fue un verano abrasador. El último de mi juventud."[3] A partir de ese momento, ya pasado, se reconstruirá el recuerdo de una etapa aparentemente feliz: ella, viviendo como hija de Apolonio y de Panchita, la hermana de su madre. También todo el proceso de su relación con Apolonio, desde el regreso, por la enfermedad de él, hasta el presente de su viudez: nuevamente un verano, que parece remitirnos a aquel con que se inició el cuento, dejando a la personaje atrapada en un círculo eterno: "Sola, pecadora, consumida totalmente por la llama implacable que nos envuelve a todos los que, como hormigas, habitamos este verano cruel que no termina nunca." (96).

Si bien el tema central en los diversos fragmentos es la relación de esa vida joven con esa otra que está a un paso de la muerte, en el recuerdo de su etapa como hija de sus tíos ya se plantea "la relación básica de la mujer con su cuerpo: ser de otro. (...) El deber estético de la mujer tiene el sentido de preparar su cuerpo (y su persona) esencialmente para el placer del otro (como destinatario), para lograrlo debe ser bella y atraerlo." (Lagarde 213). Para eso está preparándola su tía, quien le ordena que se haga un vestido nuevo y le presenta prospectos de matrimonio: "—« Bueno, hija, si Pepe no te gusta... pero no es un mal muchacho. »" (88) La joven Luisa no tiene más futuro que el matrimonio, primero con alguien acorde con su edad, pero tal parece que ella está buscando el amor; después con su anciano tío, quien, desde que llega a la casa, empieza a adjudicarle el papel "especial" de madresposa; no importa que no tenga hijos ni cónyuge, pues forma parte de una historia que, como a todas las mujeres, la conforma como tal: "— Sí, hija, sí (le dice Apolonio). Ahora descansa, toma posesión de la casa y luego ven a acompañarme (…) Comencé a cuidarlo y a sentirme contenta de hacerlo. La casa era *mi* casa y muchas mañanas al arreglarla tarareaba olvidadas canciones." (89).

Con base en su poder económico y en la libertad que le otorga su cercanía con la muerte, pues todo lo que hace no es mal visto, Apolonio

---

[3]Inés Arredondo, "La sunamita."*Obras completas* (México: Difocur-Sinaloa, Siglo XXI, 1988) 88. Todas las citas provienen de esta edición.

va tentando poco a poco a Luisa: ya la hizo dueña de su casa, después le obsequia las joyas de su tía. Como un demonio la va preparando para la atracción final: la propuesta de matrimonio. Apolonio impulsa a Luisa hacia una posición de hacer-hacer, a la cual ella responde con un querer-hacer, por eso puede hablarse de tentación, en el sentido de Greimas y Courtès. Para auxiliarlo en el logro de su objetivo, el viejo cuenta con el apoyo de dos instituciones, la familia y la iglesia:

> A mi espalda habló al sacerdote.
> -Don Apolonio quiere casarse con ella en el último momento, para heredarla.
> -¿Y tú no quieres? —preguntó ansiosamente la vieja criada—. No seas tonta, sólo tú te lo mereces. Fuiste una hija para ellos y te has matado cuidándolos. Si no te casas, los sobrinos de México no te van a dar nada. ¡No seas tonta!
> -Es una delicadeza de su parte...
> -Y luego te quedas viuda y rica y tan virgen como ahora –rió nerviosamente una prima jovencilla y pizpireta.
> -La fortuna es considerable, y yo, como tío lejano tuyo, te aconsejaría que...
> -Pensándolo bien, el no aceptar es una falta de caridad y de humildad. (92)

Poco a poco, Luisa va siendo cercada, convencida, tentada, y en ese cerco adquiere gran relevancia la voz del sacerdote, que si bien sólo se identifica en su primera participación, se hace perfectamente explícita por la manera que manipula a la joven en su sentimiento de culpa.

A pesar de que la narradora expresa su rechazo del convenio matrimonial, finalmente acaba aceptándolo, desde su perspectiva, presionada por los que la rodean:

> Desperté como de un sopor hipnótico cuando me obligaron a tomar la mano cubierta de sudor frío. Me vino otra arcada pero dije "sí".

> Recordaba vagamente que me habían cercado todo el tiempo, que todos hablaban a la vez, que me llevaban, me traían, me hacían firmar y responder. (92)

Así se presenta siempre como un objeto de los deseos y las opiniones de los otros. Y entra plenamente en lo que Rubin llama el tráfico de mujeres, ya que éstas "son entregadas en matrimonio, tomadas en batalla, cambiadas por favores, enviadas como tributo, intercambiadas, compradas y vendidas. (Y) Lejos de estar limitadas al mundo 'primitivo', esas prácticas parecen simplemente volverse más pronunciadas y comercializadas en sociedades más 'civilizadas'" (54)

Luisa se adscribe a las "normas sociales y culturales que reproducen la asimetría genérica entre los cónyuges", menor edad, menos conocimientos, dependencia económica, virginidad, belleza y salud, comprensión, obediencia y bondad. Apolonio, en cierta forma, también cumple con estas normas, claro que con las características opuestas que al hombre se le exigen. Lo que causa el conflicto en su relación conyugal es su desventaja física, su vejez que no acaba de concretarse en la muerte. Como bien señala Graciela Martínez-Zalce, el "rito iniciático de la mujer, el matrimonio de Luisa con su tío lleva un signo maldito sobre sí: se realiza *in articulo mortis*. Ha violado dos veces el interdicto: se casa con un miembro de su clan y une su vida a la de un muerto (...) Pero no sólo es eso: se casa con el que fuera marido de su madre vicaria, simbólicamente comete incesto."[4]

La sensualidad y la sexualidad del personaje femenino parecen reducirse al contacto de sus dedos con las cuentas del rosario; con esas caricias entra en ella "ese calor ajeno y propio que vamos dejando en las cosas y que nos es devuelto transformado: compañero, hermano que nos anticipa la dulce tibieza del otro, (...)" (93). Pero la frialdad de la muerte no le permitirá el placer de esa tibieza, y menos cuando la lujuria convierta a Apolonio en ese muerto-vivo que la tortura con el afán de la posesión. Ella, como la rosa en que se simboliza, va experimentando el paso del tiempo. Primero está ahí, "con sus pétalos carnosos y leves, resplandeciente." Después sigue "plena, igual a sí misma", e intacta, "monta la guardia de la luz y del secreto". ¿Cuál secreto? ¿el de la pureza? ¿el de la vida y la muerte? Precisamente cuando la agonía le parece una mentira, busca la complicidad de la rosa, pero no la encuentra: "el sol la ha marchitado." (94)

Basándose en Bataille, Martínez-Zalce destaca "que la coincidencia de muerte con erotismo es diabólica" (100), y nos dice que por la infracción del tabú, Luisa se contamina y no tiene redención. Para Rose Corral, la joven es "diosa y virgen, respetada y venerada", en un primer momento; después se convierte   en lo opuesto:

> La experiencia que vive Luisa es la de la mancha, del mal, experiencia que rompe, profana, un orden sagrado anterior, orden hecho de pureza, altivez, respeto, y que la convierte de un modo definitivo en un ser impuro, degradado, "abyecto". Esa es su señal, la marca   indeleble e invisible que transforma radicalmente su ser y su percepción del mundo: ha perdido su integridad y su fuerza anteriores. (Corral   xii).

José María Espinasa considera que cuando, como en *La sunamita*, "el amor da vida y muerte, redime y condena, en ese momento estamos ante los vampiros. Don Apolonio cambia su muerte por la vida de Luisa. Se la chupa. No es un ser malvado en sí mismo (incluso Luisa lo

---

[4]Graciela Martínez-Zalce, *Una poética de lo subterráneo: la narrativa de Inés Arredondo* (México: CONACULTA-Fondo Editorial Tierra Adentro, 117,   1996) 102-103. Véase en este libro todo lo referente al erotismo.

recuerda bondadoso), sino un hombre enamorado, diabólicamente enamorado. Y no es la edad lo que vuelve diabólico ese amor, es la proximidad de la muerte. El amor (y el amor es deseo y lujuria, y está bien que lo sea) libera a Fausto del infierno, pero aquí Fausto/Apolonio se salva a cambio del infierno de Luisa" (104).

Infractora del tabú, diosa-virgen que es profanada, sangre joven que alimenta al tío-vampiro, casi siempre a Luisa se le considera un cordero de sacrificio. Víctima de la lujuria de su tío, su conocimiento del mal no causa mayor conflicto desde los parámetros del género; el mismo sacerdote hace caso omiso de su queja por la lujuria de Apolonio y la incita a volver con su marido moribundo, porque ése es su deber:

> Fui a ver al confesor y le conté mi historia.
> -Lo que lo hace vivir es la lujuria, el más horrible pecado. Eso no es la vida, padre, es la muerte, ¡déjelo morir!
> Moriría en la desesperación. No puede ser.
> -¿Y yo?
> -Comprendo, pero si no vas será un asesinato.
> Procura no dar ocasión, encomiéndate a la Virgen, y piensa que tus deberes...
> Regresé. Y el pecado lo volvió a sacar de la tumba.   (96)

Sin descartar las diversas lecturas, considero que debe tomarse en cuenta el hecho de que la historia llega a nosotros a través de la personaje-narradora, y desde esa perspectiva se destaca la consecución de los otros personajes en el matrimonio. Pero ¿cuál es la responsabilidad de Luisa? Ella desempeña perfectamente el papel para el cual la han preparado y su matrimonio, como resultado de la tentación a la que la somete Apolonio, parece ser una respuesta motivada por la codicia. Ella no quiere, pero finalmente acepta. Ella desea los bienes que le proporciona la relación conyugal y tiene casi la certeza de que no deberá cumplir sus deberes de esposa. Es entonces cuando el cuento da un vuelco interesante, la historia se desautomatiza y la personaje queda atrapada en una perversa relación amorosa. Esto explicaría quizá la dureza con que se refiere a su "carne corrompida" y a su papel, más que de esposa, de prostituta. Luisa ha alcanzado un estatuto social, un rango, pero mercantilizando su cuerpo como objeto erótico. Es una transgresora, pero a la vez se encuentra atada a las exigencias de género, por eso muestra tanto desprecio por sí misma y se convierte en mujer-objeto mirado y deseado: "Pero yo no pude volver a ser la que fui. Ahora la vileza y la malicia brillan en los ojos de los hombres que me miran y yo me siento ocasión de pecado para todos, peor que la más abyecta de las prostitutas" (96).

Aline Pettersson

Nació en México en 1938 dentro de una familia, por el lado paterno, de origen sueco. Su producción literaria es bastante amplia, ha escrito poesía[5], novelas[6], literatura infantil[7] y cuentos. De estos últimos ha publicado dos libros: *Más allá de la mirada* (1992) y *Tiempo robado* (2000). Para Aline "escribir es un acto mágico, porque da la oportunidad de vivir al mismo tiempo tantas vidas, y no sólo vivirlas, sino percibir y juzgar todo lo que nos rodea apoyados en diversas perspectivas."[8]

En sus narraciones es muy frecuente una estructuración basada en los personajes femeninos, la violencia que en las relaciones cotidianas se produce y el problema de la comunicación interpersonal. Un ejemplo de ello es *El tiempo justo*, el cual aparece en su primer libro de cuentos y es muy breve, apenas dos páginas y media.

En este cuento tenemos un solo personaje, innominado, una mujer que, moribunda, va a rememorar su secreto. ¿Cuál es el tiempo justo? ¿el de la muerte? No, es el de tener un cuerpo, desde el punto de vista de los otros, listo para entregarlo en matrimonio: "Vi con miedo cómo se me iban hinchando los pezones y las lunas llegaban puntuales, inevitables. Vi cómo se me sombreaba el vientre y cómo me seguían los ojos de mis padres a la espera del tiempo justo. Vi cómo cambió la mirada de los hombres,..." (84). Violentamente, la niña es desposeída de su cuerpo, ya no le pertenece; y no siendo suyo, debe cuidar en él como un tesoro aquello que deberá entregar como primicias en la noche de bodas, aquello que le dará a "su cuerpo" un propietario único: la virginidad. Pero ni la virginidad ni el secreto son la base de la estructura del relato, lo es la confrontación con unas leyes que la protagonista considera injustas. De ahí la relevancia de que el adjetivo justo (o su variante) aparezca cuatro veces en el relato, una en el título y las otras tres al principio, en medio y al final del texto: "Las palabras justas", y yo me pregunto, para decir qué; "el tiempo justo", para hacer qué; "el cauce justo", para llegar a dónde.

Consciente de que "lo justo" puede ser terriblemente injusto, la protagonista decide apropiarse de su cuerpo, desvirgarse, y de esa manera romper con la ley. El hecho es violento, porque se trata de un acto de

---

[5]Dentro de este género ha publicado: *Cautiva estoy de mí* y *Enmudeció mi playa*.

[6]En el conjunto de su obra, son muy relevantes las novelas: *Círculos, Casi en silencio, Proyectos de muerte, Sombra ella misma, Los colores ocultos, Piedra que rueda, Querida familia, Mistificaciones y Eulalia, La noche de hormigas*. Recién se publicó *Colores y sombras. Tres novelas*, donde reaparecen *Círculos, Sombra ella misma* y *Los colores ocultos*.

[7]Tiene una producción breve muy amplia: *Ontario, la mariposa viajera, Fer y la princesa, El papalote y el nopal, Renata y su gato, Renata y sus curitas, Clara y el cangrejo*; también un relato extenso: *La princesa era traviesa*.

[8]Aline Pettersson, "Las historias de mis personajes no son noticia de ocho columnas" en *Ruptura y diversidad* (México: UNAM-Serie Diagonal, 1990) 61-62.

protesta, no de un acto de placer.[9] Sin embargo, como la mujer no es considerada dueña de su cuerpo, "ese acto último de libertad, (...) que selló (su) tiempo" (85) no trasciende como tal, se convierte en un conflicto en el cual un hombre le arrebató a otro las primicias de un cuerpo femenino. Pero quién puede dilucidar la verdad; únicamente el objeto del conflicto. De manera que la mujer-objeto se convierte en sujeto de enunciación. Su palabra volverá a poner todo en orden. Y es entonces cuando la protagonista lleva a cabo su supremo acto de rebeldía, la segunda y definitiva transgresión de la ley: como sujeto, ella decide no decir, porque hacerlo implica volver a ser propiedad de los otros. A la virginidad, considerada un tesoro por los demás, la ha desechado; mientras que el secreto toma su lugar: "Nunca dije que con la cuchara de madera que iba a mover la tarta de almendras de la boda, yo decidí ensayar primero el camino" (85). Ese es su más preciado tesoro, lo único que le permite continuar "una vida con (su) fardo". Como señala Steiner: "El silencio 'tiene un decir distinto del decir ordinario', pero de todos modos se trata de un decir significativo" (84). Con su silencio, ella violenta nuevamente el orden social y religioso, y hace visible lo injusto de ese orden. El silencio se convierte así en una alternativa.

Tanto en *La sunamita* como en *El tiempo justo*, dos personajes femeninos rememoran su historia en el espacio de su intimidad. La apropiación de sus cuerpos por los otros, que Luisa acaba por permitir y el personaje innominado rechaza completamente. La violencia está ahí, soterrada, terrible e ignorada; y los personajes femeninos, tanto sometiéndose como rebelándose, acaban totalmente en la marginalidad, incomunicados. Por eso su historia la cuentan a nadie y a todos, por eso están inmersas en el silencio; y éste se convierte en un arma más terrible que el canto, como ocurre con las sirenas kafkianas: "Aunque no ha sucedido, es quizás imaginable la posibilidad de que alguien se haya salvado de su canto, pero de su silencio ciertamente no" (Steiner 84).

Bibliografía

Arredondo, Inés. "La sunamita."*Obras completas*. México: Difocur-Sinaloa Siglo XXI, 1988.

Corral, Rose. "Inés Arredondo: la dialéctica de lo sagrado." en Inés Arredondo, *Obras completas*. México: Difocur-Sinaloa Siglo XXI, 1988.

Dorfman, Ariel."La violencia en la novela hispanoamericana actual."*Imaginación y violencia en América*. Barcelona: Anagrama, 1972.

---

[9]Para Lady Rojas-Trempe: "estaríamos frente a un caso patológico de rechazo de la sexualidad genital." en "Formas del goce femenino en *Más allá de la mirada*." *Sin imágenes falsas, sin falsos espejos. Narradoras mexicanas del siglo XX*, coord. Aralia López González (México: PIEM-El Colegio de México, 1995) 451. En mi opinión la personaje no es una enferma, sino una rebelde.

Espinasa, José María. "La expulsión del paraíso." *El tiempo escrito*. México: Ediciones Sin Nombre, 1995.

Greimas, A.J. y Courtés, J. *Semiótica. Diccionario razonado de la teoría del lenguaje*. Trad. Enrique Ballón Aguirre y Hermis Campodónico Carrión. Madrid: Gredos, 1990.

Hacker, Friedrich. *Agresión*. Trad. Feliu Formosa. Barcelona: Grijalbo, 1973.

Krauze, Enrique. *Luna menguante. Vida y obra de Inés Arredondo*. México: Casa Juan Pablos, 2000.

Lamas, Marta, "La violencia del sexismo." en Adolfo Sánchez Vázquez. Ed. *El mundo de la violenci*a. México: UNAM-FCE, 1998.

Lagarde, Marcela. *Los cautiverios de las mujeres: madresposas, monjas, putas, presas y locas*. México: UNAM, 1993.

Martínez-Zalce, Graciela. *Una poética de lo subterráneo: la narrativa de Inés Arredondo*, México: CONACULTA, 1996.

Pereira, Armando, "La Generación de Medio Siglo." *Juan García Ponce y la generación del Medio Siglo*. México: Universidad Veracruzana, Xalapa, Veracruz, 1998.

Pettersson, Aline, "Las historias de mis personajes no son noticia de ocho columnas." *Ruptura y diversidad*. México: UNAM,1990.

___. "El tiempo justo." *Más allá de la mirada*. México: Joaquín Mortiz, 1992.

Rojas-Trempe, Lady. "Formas del goce femenino en *Más allá de la mirada*." en Aralia López González. Coord. *Sin imágenes falsas, sin falsos espejos. Narradoras mexicanas del siglo XX*. México: PIEM El Colegio de México, 1995.

Rubin, Gayle, "El tráfico de mujeres: notas sobre la 'economía política' del sexo." en Marta Lamas. Comp. *El género. La construcción cultural de la diferencia sexual*. México: PUEG UNAM Miguel Angel Porrúa, 2000.

Steiner, George. "El silencio y el poeta." *Lenguaje y silencio. Ensayos sobre la literatura, el lenguaje y lo inhumano*. Trad. Miguel Ultorio. México: Gedisa, 1990.

Maricruz Castro Ricalde

Tecnológico de Monterrey, Campus Toluca, México

Violencia y género: el cine mexicano de la década de los ochenta

Entre 1980 y 1990, la industria cinematográfica mexicana presenció un fenómeno que comenzó a anunciarse en la década anterior: la presencia de realizadoras de largometrajes. Aún cuando en décadas anteriores había habido intentos femeninos por expresarse a través de la dirección cinematográfica, sólo los esfuerzos de Matilde Landeta habían rendido sus frutos, con cuatro películas en su haber. Antes, Cándida Beltrán Rendón, Adela Sequeyro y Eva Limiñana habían estado también al frente de distintos proyectos fílmicos.

El inicio de dos escuelas de cine (el Centro de Capacitación Cinematográfica y el Centro Universitario de Estudios Cinematográficos) en México, comenzaría a formar generaciones de mujeres capacitadas formalmente para dicha tarea. A partir de la década de los ochenta se rodaron y exhibieron varias películas dirigidas por mujeres: *En el país de los pies ligeros. El niño rarámuri* (1981) y *Nocturno amor que te vas* (1987) de Marcela Fernández Violante; *El coyote emplumado* (1983), *Ni Chana ni Juana* (1985) y *Ni de aquí ni de allá* (1988) de María Elena Velasco, *"La India María"*; *Las amantes del señor de la noche* (1986) de Isela Vega; *El secreto de Romelia* (1988) de Busi Cortés y *Lola* (1989) de María Novaro.

Como nunca antes, casi todos los años de esa década contaron con un estreno cinematográfico de una realizadora mexicana. Si en ninguna de dichas películas, la violencia es el eje de las historias, sin excepción, en las ocho hay una carga de ella, sea física, sea simbólica. *Niño rarámuri* de Fernández Violante es la que expresa más claramente la denuncia y el señalamiento de la opresión hacia los indígenas mexicanos. Pero no podemos ignorar el planteamiento de María Elena Velasco en *Ni de aquí ni de allá*. Bajo un tono de comedia ligera y un afán de complacer a un espectador de corte popular, retrata el mundo de las indígenas que son contratadas como sirvientas por extranjeros y emigran de su país para ofrecer mejores condiciones de vida a su familia mexicana. En su discurso, entonces, subyace la dualidad del dominante y el dominado, el poderoso y el indefenso.

En pocos segmentos de estos productos cinematográficos realizados por mujeres se muestran hechos violentos y en todos ellos, los detalles son omitidos. Sin embargo, el espectador puede fácilmente identificar las razones y las repercusiones de este tipo de actos. A través del análisis de las películas de las realizadoras mexicanas de esta década es posible encontrar un subtexto referido a la concepción de la violencia y sus mecanismos, dentro de la sociedad mexicana. Los procedimientos empleados son, esencialmente, tres: la retórica, el silencio y la exposición.

La retórica de la violencia: *En el país de los pies ligeros.* *El Niño rarámuri* de Marcela Fernández Violante

Teresa de Lauretis acuñó el término "violencia de la retórica", al referirse a "la violencia que se ejerce en el lenguaje y a través de él. El lenguaje conlleva violencia en cuanto produce y reproduce (y así impone o pretende imponer) clasificaciones y definiciones constrictivas o degradantes del otro" (Melgar 23). En ello, hay una dimensión social que acepta y naturaliza la polarización, en donde el otro es dominado y menospreciado desde y por el lenguaje.

Marcela Fernández Violante expone el problema de la violencia de la retórica, a través de su cuarta película: *En el país de los pies ligeros. El niño rarámuri* (1981). En el título mismo, la realizadora procura integrar los dos mundos que retrata en su obra. Por una parte, al designar con la traducción del tarahumara el nombre de la región: El país de los pies ligeros. Por la otra, al introducir el vocablo que designa la lengua de los tarahumaras, el rarámuri.

Fernández Violante elige como protagonista a Manuel, un niño de doce años, cuyo padre trabaja como ingeniero en la sierra Tarahumara. Desde las primeras tomas, que se posan en picada sobre la ciudad de Chihuahua, se mezcla el paisaje montañoso, el de la sierra, con la urbe, pero también a los ciudadanos mestizos con los indígenas que caminan por la ciudad, integrados a ella. Como si fuera un texto de aprendizaje, la realizadora relata el viaje de Manuel y su familia a Creel, un poblado a los pies de esa sierra, y después al corazón de sus barrancas. En ese lapso, el pequeño convivirá con los tarahumaras, se interesará por su lengua, comenzará a aprenderla, y poco a poco irá apreciando su forma de vivir. Así, Manuel mezclará su vestimenta occidental con la étnica, comerá sus guisos y los preferirá por encima de los sandwiches preparados por su madre, se curará los pies heridos o el estómago con hierbas, según los consejos de Benito, su amigo indígena, y expresará su deseo de quedarse a vivir en el lugar.

Desde las secuencias iniciales, el receptor se entera de una subtrama que es la que sostiene la visión colonizadora de occidente. Un grupo de hombres, alentados por otros de la capital, la ciudad de México, están interesados en establecer un aserradero, en una zona boscosa y protegida como reserva natural. Ellos conocen la oposición de los indígenas a que sigan invadiendo sus tierras. En contextos donde predomina este tipo de lenguaje, generador de una violencia en contra del indígena, las mujeres o cualquier otra minoría, el concepto de Teresa de Lauretis "en-gendered", el engendrado a partir del género, "resulta útil para relacionar la agresión interpersonal, por ejemplo, con la estructura social", sostiene Lucía Melgar (23).

En el diálogo de los mestizos, al referirse a los indígenas, se detecta la violencia de un discurso desde la perspectiva de quien domina y el establecimiento de una falsa jerarquía:

> Los tarahumaras son peor que los animales: se aferran a su lengua y a sus costumbres. Deben integrarse o desaparecer. Los aserraderos a diestra y siniestra serían la solución.
> Los indios son como niños, hay que regenerarlos, integrarlos, ayudarlos y ayudarnos, ¡qué caramba!

En el intercambio verbal anterior, Fernández Violante plasma dos visiones, igualmente sustentadoras de esa retórica de la violencia. Una de ellas opta por la anulación del otro, quien es distinto. La lengua y las costumbres le recuerdan al hombre de occidente la diferencia, la cual no es tolerada. Así, la naturaleza de los aserraderos es también una metáfora del aparato civilizador que arrasa y extermina. El segundo personaje ilustra la concepción paternalista en relación con los pueblos indígenas. Menores de edad, es preciso educarlos, pero a la manera del blanco. En la medida en la que se integren a la civilización occidental, serán mejores y, al mismo tiempo, el mestizo se verá beneficiado.

La jerarquía social en esta película es asociada con clase social y etnia. La familia de Manuel, encabezada por un padre ingeniero, con un trabajo estable en Creel, y mestizo sería lo opuesto a la de Benito, indígena tarahumara, sin estudios ni empleo fijo. No obstante, el antagonismo no radica en el enfrentamiento de ambas familias, con lo cual se establece la posibilidad de tender puentes entre ambas culturas. El epílogo del texto cinematográfico lo confirma. Más bien, el enfrentamiento de los dos mundos y con él, la generación de una violencia simbólica e, incluso, física, proviene de los grupos mestizos corruptos. De sus vicios se desprende no sólo la incomprensión hacia otro colectivo humano, sino la destrucción de un hábitat que es de todos. Marcela Fernández Violante, pues, deja claro que la violencia es ciega, irracional y desoladora.

A través de su texto cinematográfico y mediante la historia de Manuel, la realizadora va mostrando las costumbres y las ceremonias, cuenta las leyendas e ilustra las creencias tarahumaras. El viaje del infante con sus amigos indígenas al corazón de la sierra, sin la presencia de ningún otro hombre blanco, le permitirá ir adentrando al espectador a ese país de los pies ligeros, en donde los individuos no sólo son ligeros de pies, sino de todo lo material. Están despojados de cualquier signo que en occidente es sinónimo de opulencia: ropa, alimento abundante y propiedades. Para los tarahumaras, plantea Fernández Violante, la riqueza descansa en otro lugar: el íntimo contacto con su entorno y con ellos mismos, por ejemplo. El hombre blanco aprovecha esta cosmovisión y la toma como pretexto para propiciar la miseria socioeconómica de estos grupos étnicos. El conflicto detona, en el momento en el que, al quitarles sus tierras, les arrebatan también los factores esenciales que los constituyen.

Con el viaje de Manuel a lo profundo de la sierra, la retórica occidental va diluyéndose y con ella, la violencia simbólica de las primeras secuencias de la película. En su lugar, tomas generales ilustran la placidez del paisaje, en donde los niños se empequeñecen aún más ante la apertura del plano, aunque también debido a la magnificencia de las formaciones rocosas, las cascadas y los ríos. Los diálogos también se adelgazan, sin temor alguno hacia el silencio.

Los tarahumaras, a través de su lengua, también clasifican al hombre blanco, según sus características y con una estructura de pensamiento diferente a la de la lengua española, la lengua de quien domina. Las personas no son distintas entre sí por su color, su origen o su lengua, sino son sus actos los que las diferencian. Así, quienes roban la tierra de los indígenas tendrán una designación lingüística especial, que los separa del resto y los marca. El uso de los apelativos también indica una percepción múltiple, más integradora. De esta forma, el niño tarahumara, estrechamente unido a Manuel por lazos de amistad, se llamará Uaru, Jesús o Pablo, según el día. Uno es su nombre rarámuri, con el otro fue bautizado en una ceremonia tarahumara y el último es el de su bautizo católico. La designación, entonces, se flexibiliza, de acuerdo con las necesidades del individuo y deja de ser una imposición del orden social.

Fernández Violante inicia el cierre de su texto, cuando la violencia simbólica y discursiva da paso a la física. Los taladores clandestinos se ven descubiertos por Manuel y deciden asesinarlo, simulando un accidente. Los grupos, el de los defensores de los indígenas y el de los depredadores, se enfrentan a golpes. En tanto, el niño huye con su amigo Jesús hacia la sierra, con la convicción de que desea crecer en el lugar y no regresar a la ciudad, como es el deseo de sus padres. Éste es el desenlace de la película, pues concluye así el ciclo de aprendizaje de Manuel: en el arranque, su persona gira en torno del núcleo materno. Después emprende el primer viaje hacia la sierra acompañado por un adulto, lo cual implica un doble desprendimiento: del círculo familiar y lo conocido por él como civilización. Finalmente, al huir hacia el entorno agreste, se valdrá por sí mismo, con la amistad como necesidad única. Esto impulsará a sus padres a comprender que no era un capricho, sino un deseo real el quedarse a vivir en el espacio tarahumara.

La película, así, anula la violencia, temporalmente al menos, al dejar entrever que los taladores no son más un peligro; prioriza el entendimiento entre culturas diversas y proyecta los reflectores sobre dos colectivos a los que usualmente se les ha negado la palabra: los niños y los indígenas.

El silencio frente a la violencia: *El secreto de Romelia* de Busi Cortés

Ann Kaplan, en su texto "El silencio como resistencia femenina en *Natalie Granger* (1972) de Marguerite Duras" (1998: 169-190), aborda "la política del silencio, como estrategia femenina para contrarrestar el impulso destructivo del varón que le urge a articular, analizar, diseccionar." (1998: 176) Silenciada e ignorada durante siglos, cuando la mujer habla corre el riesgo de reproducir el orden del patriarcado, a través de la lengua que ha sido uno de los principales instrumentos de su dominación. Desbaratar el discurso impuesto ha sido una de sus opciones. Otra, el silencio.

Kaplan cita a Claude Herrmann, al afirmar que "la única posibilidad que le queda a una mujer es hallar el espacio vacío, la tierra de nadie que, al menos pueda llamar suya, y hablar desde él."(173). Romelia Orantes, la protagonista de *El secreto de Romelia* (1988) de Busi Cortés ha decidido refugiarse en el silencio, durante casi cuarenta años de su vida. El influyente médico Carlos Román la repudió ante su familia, una noche después de su boda, argumentando que no era virgen e insinuando que había sido Rafael, el hermano de las jóvenes Orantes, el responsable. Poco a poco, el espectador, junto con la hija y las nietas de Romelia, descubrirán que se ha tratado de una venganza.

Así, a través de unas cartas, Carlos Román comprende que su primera esposa, la bella Elena, no lo quiere. En realidad, ella es amante de Rafael. Al no poder seguir viéndolo, se deja morir y él se suicida. El deseo de venganza del ahora viudo Román se dirige hacia la joven Romelia, quien guarda como amuleto un breve recado escrito por Rafael, poco antes de dispararse en la cabeza. Por su parte, el médico esperará pacientemente a que Romelia crezca, se enamore y acepte casarse con él.

Derrotada ante la incredulidad de sus padres y sus hermanas, acerca de su inocencia, Romelia opta por el silencio, la huida y el secreto. Si las palabras no sirven para reivindicarla, si han sido ellas, a través de las cartas y el amuleto, las causantes de su desdicha, las que la han destruido, su estrategia, entonces, será distinta. Durante casi cuatro décadas, mantendrá en secreto lo sucedido, después de marcharse de su pueblo, junto con sus padres y hermanas. Antes de recibir el desprecio de la cerrada sociedad del lugar, prefieren perderse en el anonimato de la ciudad de México. Sin embargo, ella conserva, cuidadosamente, para heredarlas a su hija y sus nietas, las sábanas manchadas de sangre que demuestran su inocencia. La palabra hablada, por lo tanto, es despojada de su carácter de signo y son los objetos los que la sustituyen, los que se convierten en ese signo negado, en el símbolo de su virginidad.

Callarse, para Romelia, es también otra manera de decir. Como en el caso de los tarahumaras, el silencio es una cuestión de elección que se lleva hasta la puesta en escena. En *El país de los pies ligeros*, la secuencia final es larga y se basa casi en su totalidad en cantos rarámuris e imágenes, mostrando la asimilación del pequeño Manuel a la cultura tarahumara. En la película de Busi Cortés, el plano inicial es el de una Romelia anciana, muda, detrás de una ventana. Sus diálogos son escasos, en comparación con el bullicio de sus nietas o la desenvoltura de su hija Dolores. La historia de la venganza es contada no por Romelia, sino por la voz en "off" del viudo Román, a través de su diario, descubierto por las niñas.

El discurso del viudo Román que escucha el espectador y leen sus nietas es frío y calculador. Es la voz del orden y la violencia simbólica sobre Romelia que carga con las culpas de su hermano. En cambio, las palabras no son necesarias entre la ahora anciana Romelia y la más pequeña de sus nietas, quien se llama como ella. Ambas pasean juntas, tomadas de la mano, se acompañan, sólo con el intercambio verbal justo. De esta manera, Busi Cortés establece una genealogía femenina: Romelia abuela fue también la más pequeña de las tres hermanas Orantes. Romi nieta es la menor de las hijas de Dolores. La ausencia de intercambios verbales, a lo largo de algunas escenas, la comprensión entre ambas, apunta hacia ese vínculo callado, en el que el silencio es una manera diferente de hablar.

Al silencio se une la carencia de movimiento. No es sólo su edad la que determina la pasividad de Romelia, sino una especie de voluntad por continuar habitando en un espacio distinto al de un presente que pudiera haber sido de otra forma. En repetidas ocasiones, ella estará ensimismada, como en la primera, larga, toma estática de la película. Los personajes que la rodean la sacarán de su mundo y ella insistirá en regresar a él. Tal pareciera, entonces, que el planteamiento de la realizadora apunta hacia una abstracción de la realidad, como una manera de protestar en contra de un sistema social excluyente y cruel. No obstante, en la adaptación cinematográfica del texto original de Rosario Castellanos[1], Cortés añade personajes que indican un presente y un futuro. Afirma Ann E. Kaplan:

> No está claro, en lo absoluto, que el lenguaje sea tan monolíticamente masculino que sólo nos conceda la opción de la dominación o el silen-

---

[1] La película está basada en la novela corta *El viudo Román* de Rosario Castellanos, incluida en su libro *Los convidados de agosto*.

cio. Por motivos prácticos que están claros, el lenguaje debe ser nuestra herramienta de cambio. Si creemos que el orden simbólico está fijo, el cambio es imposible para las mujeres. (189)

Dolores es distinta a su madre. Ella levantó la voz, durante las protestas estudiantiles del 68, es divorciada y está a punto de involucrarse amorosamente con un antiguo compañero de la escuela. Por su lado, las nietas de Romelia, a través de la palabra, conocen la tragedia de la protagonista y se asombran de las diferencias entre una época y otra. Ambas han comprendido que no sólo a través del silencio es posible actuar, pues incluso el relato cinematográfico de Busi Cortés es generado gracias a la ruptura del silencio: debido a la confesión y el arrepentimiento del viudo Román con que empiezan las acciones del filme.

La exposición de la violencia: *Lola* de María Novaro

Olivier Mongin advierte sobre los riesgos de esa violencia cinematográfica en donde la violencia ha perdido un rostro y una razón de ser; se torna en indeterminada, "omnipresente y difícilmente localizable" (27). En las películas mexicanas analizadas, en cambio, cuando la violencia aparece en pantalla, está encarnada por algún personaje definido que bien puede ser el representante de un sentimiento social generalizado.

En *Lola* (1989) de María Novaro, el título de la película alude a su protagonista. Madre soltera, vendedora ambulante, se ha acostumbrado a vivir a salto de mata, acosada por los policías que persiguen a quienes carecen de licencia para comercializar los productos que vende. Una violencia simbólica ejercida por el orden social permea todo el filme: es la que la obliga a vivir su maternidad de una forma, a trabajar de otra, a conservar una relación amorosa con una pareja irresponsable e intentar mantenerla a como de lugar.

La ciudad de México, arrasada por el temblor de 1985 y las crisis económicas de la década, "acaba convirtiéndose en una prisión" (Francisco Millán 62). Lola huye hacia el espacio abierto, hacia los márgenes, hacia la costa veracruzana. Ahí, se debate entre dejar a su pequeña hija al cuidado de su madre o regresar a la urbe para asumir la responsabilidad de la maternidad. Con el agua del mar hasta las rodillas, Lola llora y bebe tequila, en el momento en el que Mario, un pretendiente, se le acerca. Él la abraza, la besa, la chupa, sin hacer caso a los sollozos de la mujer, quien le busca la mirada. Mario la evita, pero sigue tocándola. Lola intenta separarse y al no poder, forcejea, mientras él ríe, pensando que es un juego:

> Le sujeta la mano a Lola y se la pone sobre su sexo erecto.
> Mario: Esto es lo que necesitas...

Lola intenta darle un rodillazo en los huevos. Él la sujeta por la entrepierna y la tira al agua. Luego se le tira encima. Ella lo patea, se levanta, grita. Mario sigue sonriendo, como si estuvieran jugando, pero sujeta a Lola con violencia. (102-103)

El intento de violación por parte de Mario es respondido agresivamente por Lola, en un acto que Marta Peixoto designa como violencia mimética[2], fruto de un sistema social en donde hombres y mujeres se enfrentan, en sus papel de victimarios y víctimas, respectivamente. La protagonista de María y Beatriz Novaro rechaza el rol de víctima, al herirlo con la botella de tequila. Él debe ser llevado al hospital para coserle la herida, mientras Lola sigue llorando y temblando de miedo.

Lo presenciado por el espectador en una de las últimas secuencias de la película de Novaro, termina de posicionar a su protagonista como una mujer que se está construyendo a sí misma. No sólo busca una nueva definición de lo que significa ser madre, sino también de lo que implica ser mujer. En el momento en el que se da cuenta de que es un mero objeto físico para él, Lola lo rechaza. Ir tras su mirada es una manera de sellar un encuentro entre sujetos. Ella no opone gran resistencia, mientras hay la posibilidad de encontrar algunas de las respuestas que necesita en él. Lola balbucea, intentando ser escuchada. El joven, en cambio, le dice:

> Mario: ... nos gusta el reventón... (chupándola, besándola con violencia)... rolar, chupar, coger... no tener que querer a nadie... (102)

El deseo del encuentro corporal de él contrasta con la necesidad de ser apoyada, escuchada, de ella. Esa discrepancia de actitudes da como resultado el enfrentamiento físico. Dice Lucía Melgar que "en donde prevalece el machismo 'la violación es contextualmente propiciada, incluso aunque las leyes formales la pueden castigar'" (18). Así, para Mario es natural tratar de someter a la mujer que opone resistencia. Sobre esta situación, observa Francisco J. Millán:

> Cuando intenta violarla, se comporta como un macho dominante que reclama su derecho por haberse acostado anteriormente con ella, sin respetar la voluntad de la mujer y humillándola en público. (65)

En ningún momento de la escena hay un titubeo de su parte, en cuanto al empleo de la fuerza para consumar el acto sexual, si Lola se

---

[2]Ésta es definida como "the representation of dominating or aggressive interaction between men and women, often set in the family or placed within larger systems of social and even racial oppression." En Marta Peixoto. *Passionate Fictions. Gender, Narrative, and Violence in Clarice Lispector.* (Minneapolis: University of Minessota Press, 1994) xiii.

opone a ello. El espectador, de esta manera, ve cuestionado un discurso normalizado socialmente y traducido en la naturalidad de Mario, en cuanto al uso de la violencia. En este momento del filme, no se trata de invitar a tomar una postura que apoye a quien intenta violar o a la atacada, sino de interrogarse sobre las actitudes que rodean un acto de este tipo.

La reacción de Lola detiene súbitamente los engranajes de la violencia que se reproducen y se retroalimentan de distintas maneras, al desfigurar la situación en donde la víctima débil es impotente ante el victimario poderoso. Con su actitud, ella expone la posibilidad femenina de construirse un destino. Lola no está sola: tiene un pequeño grupo de amigos incondicionales que la apoyan en ese momento. Éste también es otro recurso, en el nivel de la historia, que permite romper con la victimización de la mujer: si para Mario ella es el objeto de su deseo, su materialización y su corporeidad, Lola no pierde de vista los aspectos de la conciencia, la emoción y la subjetividad. Es imposible negar su condición física, de cuerpo a través del cual ella existe. Precisamente por esto, ella es vulnerable, en la medida en la que la materialidad corpórea puede cercarse y ser dañada. Sin embargo, esa vulnerabilidad queda en suspenso (sin ser anulada), en la medida en la que la subjetividad no se debilita. La violación y cualquier agresión física acaban por aniquilar al individuo, si se desmayan el cuerpo y la voluntad de manera conjunta.

La crítica de la violencia política y social es atendida por la gran mayoría de las películas mexicanas dirigidas por varones en ese lapso. Recordemos los casos de *Campanas rojas* (1981) de Serguei Bondarchuk, *Nocaut* (1982) de José Luis García Agraz o *Bajo la metralla* (1982) de Felipe Cazals. En estas cintas, los títulos aluden ya a una problemática general, histórica y característica de un contexto. En ellas, la violencia sí es el eje o uno de los que vertebran cada película[3]. En cambio, no se percibe un interés por la representación crítica de la violencia sexual contra la mujer, como es el caso expuesto del filme de María Novaro o bien, en la de Isela Vega. En *Los amantes del señor de la noche*, la historia arranca cuando un hombre mata a su esposa ante la sospecha de que ella le es infiel. Al crecer, la hija de ambos decidirá tomar venganza en contra de su padre. Evidentemente, la historia rechaza el asesinato de una persona del género femenino, a causa del ejercicio de su sexualidad (por demás, ella es inocente, víctima de una confusión). Incluso, va más

[3]*Campanas rojas* gira en torno de la vida del periodista John Reed, durante los años en que vivió en México, en plena Revolución Mexicana. *Nocaut* trata de un boxeador que asesina a un empresario corrupto y, por lo tanto, se ve obligado a huir. Por su parte, *Bajo la metralla* aborda el tema de la guerrilla urbana en México, a través de la historia de un secuestro que provoca, finalmente, el aniquilamiento del grupo.

allá: cuestiona la autoridad del padre y propone también a la mujer como agente de la violencia.

Para concluir, deseamos apuntar unos cuantos rasgos comunes a las películas realizadas por mujeres en México, durante la década de los años ochenta. Primero, se percibe, en los textos cinematográficos analizados y en unos con mayor profundidad que en otros, la ausencia de una estructura social excluyente. Mujeres, niños y niñas, e indígenas protagonistas están presentes en las ocho películas realizadas por directoras en la década de los ochenta. En todas, es posible escuchar las historias de quienes usualmente permanecen callados, en un intento de comprender esas otras maneras de decir y estar en el mundo.

Segundo: se enfatiza menos en la violencia física y, en cambio, se resalta la violencia simbólica, manifestada incluso en una de tipo verbal. En ésta, hay una naturalización del uso lingüístico que habla de un aceptación social generalizada de los presupuestos ideológicos que conlleva. Así, los indígenas son como niños (con lo cual se normaliza la minusvalía de éstos) y peor que animales. Esto entraña una jerarquización, en donde se implica la presencia de un dominador y un dominado, un victimario y una víctima.

Tercero: los procedimientos mediante los cuales se generan procesos de resistencia son múltiples. Desde la huida hacia los márgenes de Lola o hacia el anonimato de Romelia hasta la creación de espacios propios y diferenciados, como el de ésta o el de los tarahumaras. En ambos, el silencio también puede ser otro procedimiento que devela la violencia ejercida en su contra. Renunciando a ejercer el discurso ajeno, los dos lo cuestionan y lo convierten en anómalo. Y, por último, en los tres textos cinematográficos estudiados, las realizadoras afianzan los vínculos familiares y amistosos. No importa cuán adverso sea su presente, Lola cuenta con el cariño de su pequeña hija, Manuel es apoyado por su familia y aceptado en la comunidad tarahumara, y Romelia es arropada por cuatro mujeres: su hija y sus tres nietas. Frente a la violencia de la palabra, la simbólica y la explícita, se generan propuestas de vida basadas en otro tipo de instancias que apelan a signos más amables y esperanzadores.

Bibliografía

Kaplan, E. Ann. *Las mujeres y el cine. A ambos lados de la cámara*. Madrid: Cátedra Universidad de Valencia Instituto de la Mujer, 1998.

Martínez de Velasco Vélez, Patricia. *Directoras de cine. Proyección de un mundo obscuro*. México: Imcine Coneicc, 1991.

Melgar, Lucía. *Violencia y silencio en obras selectas de Elena Garro*. Tesis de doctorado. Chicago: Universidad de Chicago, 1996.

Millán, Francisco J. "Rostros de mujer con paisaje al fondo. La mirada femenina del cine de María Novaro." *Cine y mujer en 2001*. Teruel: Ayuntamiento de Teruel, 2001.

Millán, Márgara. *Derivas de un cine en femenino*. México: PUEG Miguel Ángel Porrúa, 1999.

Mongin, Olivier. *Violencia y cine contemporáneo*. Barcelona: Paidós, 1999.

Novaro, Beatriz. Novaro. María. *Lola. Guión cinematográfico*. México: Plaza y Valdés CONACULTA, 1995.

Peixoto, Marta. *Passionate Fictions. Gender, Narrative, and Violence in Clarice Lispector*. Minneapolis: University of Minessota Press, 1994.

Julia Tuñón

Dirección de Estudios Históricos-INAH

Domando a la naturaleza: La violencia hacia las mujeres en el cine de Emilio Fernández

Cada sociedad cuenta con un conjunto de ideas que sostienen sus formas de vida y sus instituciones sociales. Las que atañen a los géneros sexuales y la relación entre ellos son fundamentales. Sin embargo, como bien lo ha planteado Roger Chartier, las ideas no pueden ni conservarse ni transmitirse en el nivel de la abstracción, y es necesario que se materialicen en representaciones.

Las películas son representaciones sociales y en ellas se expresan en lenguaje fílmico[1] los conceptos con los que viven los hombres y las mujeres. Al proyectarse en una pantalla, se reafirman, por lo que a menudo se ha considerado a las películas una arma peligrosa que influye sobre la mentalidad de los espectadores, inermes ante sus dictados. Sin embargo es claro ya que la relación entre las audiencias y los filmes es más compleja, es mucho más que un simple proceso de emisor a receptor. Como toda representación, en las películas se re-escenifican los dilemas que conforman la vida de sus públicos, y esto es un requisito imprescindible para lograr su identificación y por ende el éxito comercial del filme. Por otro lado los espectadores resignifican lo que miran de acuerdo a sus propias experiencias. Así las cosas no debemos culpar al cine de los pecados de la sociedad.

Sin lugar a dudas el séptimo arte es uno de los espectáculos más importantes del siglo XX, y en México fue determinante durante los años cuarenta y cincuenta para los sectores populares, ávidos de entretenimiento. Se trata de la llamada "Edad de Oro"[2]. Las películas trasmiten ideas y valores a sus audiencias, forman parte de su educación sentimental, pero insisto, también representan en lenguaje fílmico la cultura que se vive, con todas sus contradicciones y ambigüedades. El hecho del uso y abuso de estereotipos[3] les ha valido ser acu-

---

[1]O sea, el constituido por imágenes en movimiento, proyectadas y asociadas al sonido, organizadas mediante la edición y el ritmo. Imágenes que cuentan historias y que tienen un carácter simbólico y metafórico evidente.

[2]*Grosso modo* entre los años treinta y cincuenta, en que el cine tiene éxito comercial y se convierte en un modelo cultural para los sectores populares.

[3]Estereotipo como simplificación de la realidad representada sea por omisión o deformación.

sadas de frivolidad y simpleza, pero al analizarlas observamos que no evaden los problemas de su sociedad. Estos aparecen en pantalla más o menos deformados, imaginados de diferentes formas, explicitados o soslayados, en forma clara u oblicua, pero aparecen.

Las películas, entonces, pueden convertirse en una fuente para el análisis de algunos problemas humanos, en particular del imaginario acerca de esos problemas. La deformación es, en sí, significativa y a través de las ficciones cinematográficas, podemos comprender mejor la sociedad de la que surgen y algunas de sus estructuras veladas, pues el cine muestra de manera contundente o velada, pero discernible, tanto las ideas de la ideología como las de la mentalidad de quienes lo hacen. A veces las películas resultan irritantes, pero esto se debe a la gran fuerza que irradian esas imágenes que se mueven y hablan en la pantalla, y que a menudo re-presentan los aspectos que disimulamos, que no querríamos ver en nuestra vida cotidiana. Uno de ellos es el de la violencia y la violación en las mujeres.

Las películas mexicanas de la edad oro surgen de una cultura en que la diferencia social entre hombres y mujeres es muy acentuada y está fuertemente jerarquizada. En pantalla, *grosso modo* se les asigna a los varones la actividad y la defensa de la honra, la contención y el equilibrio emocional y se les acepta la violencia y la vida sexual diversificada, mientras que a las mujeres se les demanda pasividad y modestia, tolerancia, capacidad de entrega y sumisión a su destino que destaca la exclusividad sexual o, al menos, afectiva a un solo varón (para salvar a la buena prostituta). A ellas se les permite la efusión lacrimógena y sentimental. Es importante no confundir la realidad con las películas y este modelo no es un retrato fiel de la vida, sino una representación a medio camino entre los hechos y los deseos. Las películas son siempre una construcción cultural.

Sin embargo, la violencia y la violación contra las mujeres sí son parte de la vida cotidiana en México, a lo largo de su historia. Se trata de una realidad que se quiere eludir y se considera de mal gusto mencionar. Milán Kundera explicaba lo *kitsch* como una representación de la realidad que omite algunas de sus características, aquellas que resultan inadmisibles para el ser humano(254). Podemos decir que respecto a los diversos tipos de violencia, sucede exactamente eso: querríamos negarla, evitamos nombrarla con lo cual se fortalece. Analizar la representación que hacen las películas o la literatura respecto a los temas delicados de nuestra vida aumenta nuestra comprensión al respecto.

Aquí me ocuparé de la violencia y violación en las películas de Emilio Fernández, apodado el *"Indio"* y considerado por muchos el autor del cine mexicano por antonomasia, que construyó un estereotipo del país. Ha sido considerado también un defensor a ultranza del machismo. Su cine se apoya en el cine institucional mexicano.

El cine institucional y la representación de la violencia

Distintos autores coinciden en destacar como las dos figuras predominantes de nuestro cine a la madre y a la prostituta, que responde al esquema de "buena-mala", en que coincide el drama hollywoodense y los prototipos de Eva y María de la cultura católica, sin embargo, yo considero que las diversas imágenes femeninas velan apenas una idea de *La Mujer* como ente abstracto, que uniforma al género con una esencia de corte zoológico que suprime a las mujeres sus características de índole social. Para poder narrar las historias fílmicas los arquetipos de la mujer esencial se disocian en una serie de estereotipos, entre los que Eva o María son tan solo dos caras de un mismo modelo (Tuñón 1998). Las películas ofrecen múltiples imágenes, a menudo contradictorias entre sí, como lo es la cultura a la que expresan y así pueden ser interpretadas de formas diversas por sus distintos públicos. Es así que las imágenes del cine mexicano, además de lo dicho antes, a menudo muestran la fuerza femenina, colocan a las mujeres en el centro de la narración y vulneran la idea de que ellas son pasivas, simple objeto de la mirada "*voyeurista*".

La violencia y la violación en el cine institucional mexicano de la edad de oro están muy presentes (Tuñón 1989, 57-67). Se trata de un cine de *film-makers*[4], hecho con rapidez y pocos medios económicos y técnicos pero que, sin embargo, tiene una recepción de privilegio entre las audiencias populares de los años cuarenta. La razón de eso no es banal: al cine se va para divertirse, y para eso es necesario poder identificarse y, también, poder imaginar otros mundos posibles. Estos dos mecanismos los permite sobradamente el cine clásico mexicano, pero además, a menudo estos filmes presentan problemas básicos, de esos del orden mítico que expresan los dilemas sin solución que desvelan a los seres humanos, los que remiten a los mitos y a los arquetipos[5]. Cuando es el caso conmueven y obligan a reflexionar a sus audiencias.

Las películas baratas y de mala calidad, los llamados "churros" tienen para el historiador la ventaja de que expresan la mentalidad de una manera notable. Seguramente lo hacen en forma más precisa que las películas cuidadas, que cuentan con mayores recursos técnicos y económicos, y en las que a menudo accedemos a las obsesiones de sus autores. Es el caso del cine del "*Indio*", que no sólo expresa la mentalidad de la que participa sino también sus propias obsesiones y fobias, esas que lo hacen indudablemente un autor cinematográfico.

---

[4]Término que refiere a todos aquellos que participan de la elaboración de una película, desde el director hasta los miembros del "*staff*".

[5]Arquetipo como modelos de larga duración que remiten a pulsiones básicas de los seres humanos.

La violencia y la violación son temas de difícil análisis, en parte porque se asocian al erotismo que, en gran medida, es precisamente su opuesto, pero también porque plantea una tensión del mundo humano: la de ser animales racionales, con la contradicción y el conflicto consecuentes.

Hombres y mujeres compartimos el mundo aún desde las diferencias que nos identifican como tales y que permean todas las áreas de nuestra vida. En el erotismo entramos a un tema delicado, porque ignoramos hasta donde ciertos rasgos radican en la cultura y son adquiridos o derivan de la naturaleza humana, esa de índole zoológica que también nos constituye. En todo caso, es evidente que el sistema de género patriarcal reafirma algunas de las diferencias biológicas. El erotismo de unas y otros es diferente, según Alberoni. Si las mujeres, por lo general, requieren de confianza, rituales preparatorios y cuidado para el disfrute sexual, el erotismo masculino se ha asociado a la agresión y al dominio de la pareja. En nuestra cultura a ellos les toca poseer y a ellas ser poseídas. La sexualidad masculina se considera avasallante, irrefrenable y activa, mientras la femenina se observa provocativa y receptora. "El es hombre", hemos oído todos alguna vez a guisa de disculpa. Este punto se hace muy evidente en las películas por el uso y abuso de los estereotipos, símbolos contundentes, necesarios para la comprensión fílmica (Tuñón 1998).

El tema de la violencia y la violación están atravesados por esta situación, pero también aparece el deseo de evasión del que hablé antes. La tónica, aparentemente conciliatoria, es mostrarlas como si de situaciones diferentes se tratara. La violencia, en la que se incluye el maltrato verbal y físico, se presenta como algo "normal" en las relaciones de pareja, parte del amor, sin mayor importancia, mientras que la violación aparece como algo "monstruoso", que viola la norma del cuidado que el más fuerte debe al más débil y que subvierte el orden debido de las cosas. No pretendo decir que la violación no sea algo monstruoso, ni homologarlo sin más a la violencia, pero sí considero que en ambos casos la agresión abreva del mismo terreno: ambas son manifestaciones que surgen de un sistema de género en el que las características asignadas a unos y a otras son excluyentes y que implica una jerarquía mayor de los hombres, que se imponen sobre las mujeres, un sistema.

En el cine institucional mexicano, la violencia del hombre a la mujer, así sea verbal, es común hasta cuando se supone que él es el "bueno" de la película. Existe la idea de que se trata de parte de los rituales que hacen al amor, que otorga a los varones el control de la situación y entre líneas se nos muestra que ellas lo provocan para sentirse atendidas. El cine mexicano nos dice de múltiples maneras que a la mujer le gusta la violencia y anhela la llegada de un hombre que se lo haga saber. La violencia cotidiana se considera casi un piropo.

La violencia la ejercen todos. La violación sólo los villanos. Cuesta aceptar que el perfil del violador en la vida real es el de cualquier hijo de vecino. La violación se presenta pocas veces en las películas, siempre dramáticas y, cuando se hace, es de manera oblicua: no se nombra con claridad, porque es algo brutal y de mal gusto. Lo correcto es simbolizarla, como en *El rebozo de Soledad* (Gavaldón 1952), en el que un jinete acorrala con su caballo a la protagonista bajo un puente, y después de un *"fade"* vemos el rebozo en el piso, sucio y desgarrado, o con el manido recurso de presentar una flor pisoteada por la bota del hombre que se retira. En cambio, la violencia se presenta a menudo, en películas cómicas y en dramas, en decires y en haceres. Las mujeres de la "vida ligera" aprenden a ejercer la violencia y las vemos rompiendo botellas y arañando a los contrincantes, mientras las muchachas "decentes" solo se defienden administrando dignos bofetones. Cuando ellas los golpean de otra manera se presenta como algo cómico y se pasa al género de comedia: solo se pueden romper las convenciones del género en plan de broma. La violencia debe presentarse como algo que a nadie ofende y que, incluso, gusta a las mujeres. Solamente los límites de la violencia son horrorosos, y se evade que ambas sean situaciones de la misma pasta, soslayando que se trata de una diferencia de grado más que de fondo.

La violación se presenta como un accidente, como quien recibe de pronto una pedrada. La mujer víctima es la muchacha "buena" de la película. En caso de ser la seductora o la cabaretera, no se la considera tal, pues supuestamente lo tiene merecido: ella se ha salido previamente del orden moral debido. La violación conyugal no se menciona siquiera: es claro que no se concibe como tal. Sin embargo, aun cuando quien sufre esta agresión sea la "buena mujer", no se observa como algo contra su dignidad humana, sino como "daño a su honor" o "atentado al pudor", de manera que el más lastimado es el varón que cuida de ella: padre, hermano, novio o marido. Si acaso la mujer no tiene a su lado un hombre que la defienda, haya sido violada o seducida inicia la consabida ruta a la prostitución camino señalado con nitidez por *Santa* (Moreno 1931) y *La mujer del puerto* (Boytler 1934).

En *Allá en el Rancho Grande* (De Fuentes 1936), el tema aparece como un aspecto de la tradición: "el derecho de pernada". La película muestra la supuesta vida idílica en una hacienda mexicana, en donde el amo y el caballerango son amigos de infancia, cómplices de travesuras y hasta compañeros de sangre (el dueño de la hacienda recibió una transfusión sanguínea de su subalterno). Felipe (René Cardona), el joven hacendado, desconoce los amores de Crucita (Esther Fernández) con Francisco, su caporal, y cuando descubre la belleza de la muchacha decide apropiársela. Da a los criados la noche libre, con lo que ellos adivinan que piensa llevar a su casa a alguna muchacha de la hacienda, como sucede con frecuencia. Eso los divierte y deciden espiar para pasar un buen rato. Cuando Crucita es llevada por su madrina, que la ha vendido al patrón, el conflicto de honor para Francisco queda sellado. Crucita se desmaya oportunamente ante la ofensiva de Felipe, y menciona en su delirio a José Francisco, con lo que el amo cancela sus intenciones, pero el honor de Francisco ha quedado en entredicho. Solo cuando está a punto de vengar su honor en un duelo con Felipe se entera de que nada pasó. Crucita le dice: "El tuvo lástima de mí", como si efectivamente tuviera un derecho sobre ella y la intención no fuera importante, y entonces los hombres se abrazan y siguen siendo grandes amigos. No se censura en ningún momento la conducta sexual de Felipe, sino que se considera parte de su papel de patrón. Se critica que Doña Ángela haya vendido a Crucita, pero a lo largo del film se exculpa al hacendado. En la película está en juego el problema de la amistad varonil y la conciliación entre las clases sociales, y ambos resultan salvaguardados, pues los hombres continúan con la amistad y se casan con sus respectivas novias en la misma ceremonia.

Doña Bárbara (De Fuentes 1943) presenta un caso particular, en el que puede destacarse la fortaleza y peligrosidad de La Mujer. Basada en la novela de Rómulo Gallegos, la cinta está protagonizada por María Félix, que se apropia del talante de la protagonista para su aureola de estrella y lo ejerce en sus papeles subsecuentes, haciendo gala del carácter dominante y destructor del personaje, al grado de recibir el sobrenombre de "La Doña". En la película, la joven e inocente mujer es violada por la tripulación del barco en que viaja y entonces se convierte en una dura y despótica devoradora de hombres, que no sólo los usa sexualmente sino que los explota laboralmente haciéndose dueña de grandes latifundios. Doña Bárbara ejerce la venganza y destruye todo aquello que la desvía de su camino de poder. Podría decirse que ella es un personaje machista, como lo es la estrella María Félix. Julianne Burton-Carvajal considera que la violación se presenta en el cine como un momento fundante del orden, origen de la identidad o de la nación y analiza el caso de Doña Bárbara en este sentido (258-268, 262-263).

Se apuntan en estos filmes aspectos en los que convendría profundizar pero, haciendo un balance del modelo fílmico, puede decirse que la violencia y violación se ven en el cine institucional mexicano como cosas diferentes: la primera es un mal menor, natural en la relación hombre mujer y que propicia situaciones que ambos gozan. La violación es un delito aislado, terrible, que nunca se entiende bien a bien, cometido por alguien fuera de toda ley, la humana y la natural. La violencia es algo molesto que resulta seductor si la ejerce el hombre al que una mujer quiere: le da la seguridad de la fuerza. La violación es algo remoto y monstruoso, de cuyo arreglo deben encargarse los hombres de la familia, porque es un ataque al honor. Entre lo natural y lo monstruoso se abre un abismo que impide comprender que ambas abrevan de la misma fuente, que las diferencias son de grado, más no de fondo, y con esta perspectiva se soslaya la crítica social que el tema hubiera podido implicar.

Emilio Fernández y su actitud hacia las mujeres

Firmemente apoyado en el cine institucional mexicano, Emilio Fernández, puede ser considerado un autor: tiene temas y obsesiones propias, un estilo personal de filmar y tesis reconocibles[6]. Su intención explícita es aprovechar la pantalla para transformar al país y sus personajes muestran en forma didáctica las formas humanas ideales para ese proyecto. Las tesis del *"Indio"* se expresan en todos sus filmes: el agrarismo, el nacionalismo, el indigenismo, la necesidad de la educación laica, pero el tema del amor entre hombre y mujer estructura siempre sus tramas. La imagen de las mujeres muestra lo que él quisiera que fueran en realidad.

El *"Indio"* encabeza la llamada "Escuela Mexicana de Cine" y, en su mejor período, integra a un equipo de gran calidad[7]. Emilio Fernández filmó 41 películas entre 1941 y 1978. Su cine trascendió porque fue reconocido por la crítica europea a partir de 1946, en el Festival de Cannes[8] por lo que puede decirse que películas como *María Candelaria, La perla, Flor silvestre, Pueblerina, Maclovia* o *Río Escondido* han sido el rostro de México en todo el mundo.

Emilio Fernández se convirtió en una encarnación y un símbolo del machismo mexicano, pero en su momento de esplendor se consideró por algunos que, con sus películas, hacía un "hondo homenaje a la mujer, así esté caída o levantada, sea ella buena o esté calificada como mala"(Cagliostro 1947). Ciertamente las mujeres son parte medular de su universo fílmico, la simple mención a los títulos da cuenta de su protagonismo. Según cuenta su hija Adela Fernández (38) siendo un niño mató al amante de su madre. Probablemente esta experiencia pauta su mirada de ellas.

Es conocida su obsesión por mantener controladas a las mujeres de su casa y de su vida. Ellas debían asemejarse a obras de arte. Adela Fer-

---

[6]Para un acercamiento a su cine y a su persona véanse las obras relacionadas con este director en la bibliografía final.

[7]Gabriel Figueroa (fotografía), Mauricio Magdaleno (guiones), Gloria Schoemann (edición) y sus fulgurantes actores: Dolores del Río, María Félix y Pedro Armendáriz

[8]Ese año el festival no tuvo un carácter de competencia y once películas compartieron la Palma de Oro con *María Candelaria*. En 1947 obtuvo tres premios en el festival de Locarno, véase Emilio García Riera. *Emilio fernández. 1904-1980.* (Guadalajara: U de G. CIEC, 1987) 55.

nández recuerda que tanto ella como Columba Domínguez eran miopes y él les decía:

> No importa que ustedes no alcancen a ver, lo fundamental es que quien las mire las encuentre primorosas y esos lentes echan todo a perder [...] el caminar casi a ciegas nos daba 'estilo', lentitud y prudencia al andar, suavidad al tomar y mover los objetos además de cierta vaguedad melancólica en la mirada (131-32).

Ellas debían "[...] recorrer la casa y quedarse quietas en los rincones más hermosos, como si fueran una escultura, una pieza de arte"(116). Al parecer, una de sus obsesiones era construir una mujer ideal que pudiera calificarse de obra de arte. Cuando visitó en París el museo del Louvre, decía:

> "Me enamoré de la Venus de Milo... y cuando había tipos que se quedaban viéndola, tenía ganas de pelearme con ellos... y había unos indiferentes que nomás se pasaban, me daban ganas de agarrarlos del cuello y decirle: Fíjate en ella. Era una mezcla de celos y de alcahuetismo. [Le llamó la atención] por una perfección, y además siempre me causó un enigma tremendo los brazos, porque con brazos no sería la Venus de Milo. La Venus de Milo es perfecta sin brazos... ¡es tan perfecta así como está!".

Es perfecta así: quieta como estatua, manca, sin moverse, sin poderse ir de su lugar en el Louvre. Para Emilio Fernández "La mujer es el alma de un pueblo, es la inspiración, es todo, ¿no? [...] Además, uno vive para cuidarlas y para sentirse orgulloso de ellas" y como su cine tiene carácter didáctico muestra a las mujeres:

> "[...] haciéndolas femeninas, demandándoles una moral, un vibrar, cierto orgullo, cierta dignidad, naturalmente, ¿no? pero siempre las quiero tener como perros fieles, sumisas al hombre y el hombre digno de matarse por la defensa y el honor de su mujer [...] y [por] la construcción de una familia"(Tuñón 1982).

Cuando conversaba con Magdaleno, su guionista, "[...] yo le sacaba ciertas virtudes [de las mujeres] decía: -Pero las mujeres no son tan virtuosas así, Emilio -Me decía-, -Le digo- Pero vamos a hacerlas -Le decía- Vamos a construirlas" (Tuñón 1982). Esto tiene que ver con su incomprensión de ellas: "No sé como son realmente las mujeres. Son caprichosas, muy egoístas, muy posesivas y celosas de algo que no deben tener celos"(Tuñón 1982). Ante esto, las dota de las que él considera virtudes.

La idealización de la mujer implica, necesariamente, la del hombre: si ella es sumisa, obediente y abnegada, él la protege, consuela, dirige y controla. En el recuento de las virtudes masculinas, se le asocia a la luz y a la fuerza del sol. Este ideal de hombre medido, calmado, seguro de sí mismo, "respetuoso sobre todo", que nunca alza gratuitamente la voz tiene muy poco que ver con el propio Emilio Fernández, o con Pedro Armendáriz, su amigo y principal figura artística, famoso por sus enfados violentos. Para él es claro que "todos nosotros ... nos estamos viendo a nosotros mismos en lo que uno quisiera haber sido, entonces uno lo hace en otra persona" (Tuñón 1988, 76). Sus héroes son pacíficos pero a menudo violentos con las mujeres. El *"Indio"* lo justifica, sin hacerlo explícito, por su concepto peculiar de lo que son los hombres y las mujeres.

Mujer-naturaleza y hombre-cultura

Una de las señas de identidad en el cine de Emilio Fernández es el conflicto siempre presente entre naturaleza y cultura[9]. La primera aparece como una estructura básica y avasallante, sin lógica ni tiempo, a la que le suceden, sin afectarla demasiado, los acontecimientos sociales, políticos, militares. Todas las ideas por las que Emilio Fernández lucha con entusiasmo (la educación, el agrarismo, la Revolución), que dan sentido a las tramas de sus películas, acaban por estrellarse contra esta naturaleza de carácter sagrado que sólo se muestra en síntomas y símbolos. No hay en ella un proceso, menos aún un progreso. La naturaleza tiene, si acaso, un tiempo cíclico, al que caracteriza la repetición, por eso en ella actúa la fatalidad: es el territorio del destino.

Parte de esta naturaleza son los seres humanos, personas-paisaje que están insertos en una realidad que poco responde a los criterios de la historia o del cambio social. Se trata de una naturaleza terrible, que no cede ante los ruegos de sus héroes para trascenderla, que no les da tregua y que los obliga a confundirse con la inmanencia, a renunciar a la ambición y a la lucha. Parte medular de sus tramas es la lucha de sus héroes por trascender esa inercia, y ahí el *"Indio"* muestra un problema arquetípico de los seres humanos, la tensión entre el destino y la libertad.

En el marco de este conflicto observamos que si bien todos sus personajes son naturales, *"La mujer"* aparece identificada de manera esencial con esta naturaleza de Fernández, que es inclemente y dura. Sólo puede pasar a un estado superior de ella misma con la ayuda de su pareja, el varón, que es el agente de la cultura y de la historia, el que

---

[9]He trabajado el tema en Julia Tuñón. "Un regard derrière les grilles." *Le cinéma mexicain*. Ed. Paulo A. Paranagua. (París: Centre Georges Pompidou, 1992) 213-217. De este artículo existen traducciones inglesa por el London Film Institute) y española en *Los rostros de un mito. Personajes femeninos en las películas de Emilio "Indio". Fernández.*

lucha por trascender. El mundo moderno, occidental, se caracteriza, entre otras cosas, por el control de la naturaleza y el desarrollo de la técnica. La cultura controla a la naturaleza, lo que ha sido nombrado como la lucha entre civilización y barbarie. Los hombres, entonces, están destinados a dirigir a las mujeres y a modelarlas como si fueran barro, para hacer con ellas una obra de arte. El medio para lograrlo es el amor.

Por ser naturaleza, las mujeres son las encargadas de mantener la tradición, la inercia, la liga con la tierra, con la que están identificadas. No quieren moverse de su territorio y la ambición no forma parte de sus afanes. Ellas aceptan al destino y las caracteriza la intuición. La naturaleza es bella en la medida en que remite al nacimiento de la vida y la nutrición. No en balde aparecen frecuentemente preparando u ofreciendo comida a sus hombres. Sin embargo, su liga con la vida implica un aspecto amenazante: la posibilidad de negar su don, ligada a la capacidad de dar muerte[10]. Y su dependencia del destino es una forma de muerte.

La esencia femenina para Emilio Fernández es, entonces, de índole natural y no cultural o social, lo que es un lugar común respecto a los géneros sexuales, pero su concepto de naturaleza es peculiar, y surge de su cultura aborigen[11]. La inmanencia de lo cíclico y lo amoral tiende a absorber y a nulificar los cambios que procura la historia, el progreso y el orden. Los personajes del *"Indio"* están inermes ante los designios de la vida, de la naturaleza, se identifican con ella, pero aspiran a trascender y construir su propio destino. Por eso son conmovedores. Se trata de una lucha de orden cósmico y para ganarla es importante que las mujeres se subordinen. Sólo así se logrará un mundo más elevado, en el que la justicia social sea posible.

Sus personajes femeninos solo pueden trascender mediante su vínculo con los hombres. Si la mujer es barro, el hombre será su alfarero. Él puede trocar esa materia informe, carente de valores y proyectos en una obra de arte. La pareja permite la completud, porque si la mujer es naturaleza y por serlo carece de límites, pudiendo ser feroz, en la relación con el varón encuentra contención y proyección: el hombre hace marchar a la historia y provoca los cambios mientras que la mujer sostiene al mundo. El amor de dos busca, entonces, recuperar el paraíso, que es la completud, pero siempre se ve dificultado por la aparición de un tercero, que puede ser de índole diversa. La idea del amor de Fernández remite a los orígenes, al mundo mítico de lo cerrado, completo y abso-

---

[10]Mujeres dadoras de muerte las vemos en *Río Escondido* (1947), *Salón México* (1948) *Víctimas del pecado* (1950), *Cuando levanta la niebla* (1951), *Islas Marías, Paloma herida, Un dorado de Pancho Villa* (1966), *La Choca* (1973). Casi todas lo hacen a balazos, aunque a Mercedes en *Salón México* el azar le puso un cuchillo en las manos.

[11]La madre de Emilio Fernández era india Kickapú.

luto que es invadido por un tercer elemento externo que lo destruye. La adversidad rompe esa unidad primigenia, absoluta, única, prenatal, que requiere de "la abnegación de la mujer con el hombre...a donde va él, va ella, como una sombra enamorada, y está atrás y adelante y al lado y al frente. Eso, a mí, me parece divino"(Tuñón 1988). Y sí, es divino más que humano: porque sólo lo divino es absoluto y debe parecerse mucho al mundo de una matriz, que es lo que él describe.

El ideal del director es la simbiosis amorosa, unidad que suprime la independencia o libertad de cada integrante, aunque en su discurso:

> La dedicación absoluta de un hombre a una mujer y de una mujer a un hombre es divina, ese matrimonio jamás se quebrará. Si hay una devoción y una entrega absoluta y que sepa que esa es su vida y esa es su misión, ahí llegó a la culminación de su felicidad: el ser responsable de una mujer y tener una mujer que se sienta responsable de uno, ¿no? (Tuñón 1988)

La violencia

Emilio Fernández no valora a la mujer por su capacidad de procrear y ser madre, como es usual en el cine mexicano de los años cuarenta y cincuenta, lo que también se basa en una identificación entre la mujer y la naturaleza (Tuñón 1998), sino que teme su fuerza y otorga al varón la posibilidad de domarla y convertirla en obra de arte, se dijo antes: si ella es barro, él será su alfarero.

La naturaleza carece de moral y ante eso lo primero que hace la cultura es poner prohibiciones. Un tema presente en su cine es el incesto, porque la naturaleza no sabe de reglas y el tabú que quiere imponerles es de carácter cultural. El tema es presentado de manera discreta y metafórica por el director. El ejemplo más frecuente es el de la hija que cumple el papel de pareja del padre, viudo desde el nacimiento de ella, que se parece tanto a su difunta y amada madre. Sus películas no muestran una relación sexual abierta, lo que tampoco permitiría el código estético de Fernández, sino un cariño sublimado que propicia también violencia, al impedir a la hija consumar sus propios vínculos amorosos.

Para lograr controlar en todos los aspectos la fuerza femenina y obtener la simbiosis amorosa que la neutralice se valen los medios violentos. Es notable la frecuencia de bofetones, golpes y empujones que reciben las mujeres en sus películas, de parte de sus parejas. Ellos no reciben crítica alguna. En algún caso su gesto puede ser censurado por algún comparsa, pero no merman el prestigio de quien los realiza. La música y la cámara secundan el dramatismo de la escena, pero la trama demuestra que, casi siempre, la violencia del hombre contra la mujer rinde el fruto deseado. Se presenta como una estrategia necesaria para un fin mayor, pues la naturaleza tiene que ser controlada, y lo es por la cultura. Lo vemos en *Flor Silvestre* (1943), *La perla* (1945), *Enamorada* (1947), *Siempre tuya* (1950), *La red* (1953), *El rapto* (1953) y *Erótica* (1978), entre muchas otras.

A menudo se da la violencia verbal o son otros hombres los que las golpean, como el padre de Margarita en *Las abandonadas* (1944). Las prostitutas también son frecuentemente maltratadas por sus clientes o padrotes, lo vemos en *Salón México* (1948), *Víctimas del pecado* (1950), *La tierra de fuego se apaga* (1955) y muchas otras. El entusiasmo que ponía Emilio Fernández en los golpes era motivo de comentarios en la prensa de cine: durante las filmaciones el pedía mayor verisimilitud y se provocaron algunos accidentes en el *"set"*: fue célebre la golpiza que recibió Marga López por Rodolfo Acosta en *Salón México*.

La respuesta de ellas es el silencio y la pasividad. Las secuencias que le siguen y las tramas completas de la película demuestran que esos hechos no modifican el aprecio de ellas hacia sus hombres, ni tienen consecuencias de gravedad, antes bien, permiten el alivio y hacen marchar la historia: se pasa a otra secuencia sin problema. Amalia en *Bugambilia* (1944) expresa con nitidez su deseo de encontrar "Un hombre que solo con mirarme me dominara, de esos hombres que no piden jamás, porque todo les pertenece. Un hombre fuerte. Un hombre que, a su lado yo me sintiera pequeñita". Es claro que un deseo así implica dominio. Ricardo Rojas, el gallero plebeyo que cumple sus expectativas no tiene tiempo de ser agresivo con ella: cuando se acaban de casar es muerto por su suegro, que no acepta el romance a causa de la diferencia de clase social, pero también, seguramente, porque era un viudo y su hija se parecía demasiado a su difunta esposa.

El caso más notable de violencia hacia la mujer es en *Enamorada*. Esta película llama la atención desde que se empieza a filmar, por el hecho de juntar a dos monstruos sagrados: Emilio Fernández y María Félix, ambos con fama de violentos y arbitrarios: existe expectación por ver cuál de ellos lo será más. Durante la filmación ambos fueron un dechado de prudencia, pero el *"Indio"* incluyó varios golpes a la protagonista, como hará en las otras películas que filma con la estrella.

El filme va como sigue: el general José Juan Reyes (Pedro Armendáriz) llega a ocupar Cholula durante la Revolución y conoce a Beatriz Peñafiel, la brava, incontrolada e incontrolable hija de uno de los principales del pueblo (el argumento se ha considerado una versión de *La fierecilla domada* de Shakespeare). En el primer encuentro él piropea de manera burda sus piernas y recibe dos bofetadas. Queda irremisiblemente enamorado y comienza a seguirla, recibiendo desprecios recurrentes. En una secuencia memorable la alcanza en el atrio de la iglesia y tienen una discusión: él defiende a las soldaderas que la muchacha desprecia.

No son mujerzuelas esas soldaderas a las que usted desprecia porque no las conoce, pero yo sí las conozco. Son humildes y abnegadas, saben trabajar, sufrir y morir sin esperar nada, nada más que el cariño del hombre que quieren [...] y si le hubiera tocado nacer sin ninguna ventaja, como nacieron muchas de esas mujeres, ¿qué clase de mujer hubiera sido usted?... ¿una... mujerzuela?

Lo dice sonriendo con ironía muy cercana al desdén, ella le da dos bofetones, él la agarra del pescuezo y le da un golpe que la tira al piso. La cámara los encuadra en contrapicada y los enmarca en la puerta que da al atrio de San Francisco Acatepec. La gravedad del asunto parece derivar, más que de los actos violentos del hecho de hallarse en lugar sagrado. También el padre Sierra (Fernando Fernández) recibirá un bofetón. El sacerdote le pregunta a Beatriz, conociendo su talante agresivo, que le dijo para provocarlo: la trama muestra que la muchacha es impulsiva y gusta de ofender al general y el sacerdote la culpa de provocar la violencia masculina. Son las mujeres las culpables de la violencia que reciben.

Las secuencias que siguen muestran la conversación del cura con Beatriz en la iglesia, cuando le informa de la delicadeza cotidiana del general y de la devoción que siente por ella, y la triste borrachera de José Juan en la cantina, en donde es aconsejado por un viejo ("El Nanche" Arozamena). Estas secuencias preparan al espectador para asistir a la serenata que el hombre lleva, arrepentido, a la mujer: ella despierta mostrando sus maravillosos ojos fotografiados por Gabriel Figueroa. Es claro que la duda empieza a aparecer en su ánimo: el retrato de Mr. Roberts, su novio, parece reprocharle algo. ¿Fueron acaso las palabras del cura?, cabe dudarlo. La actitud de Beatriz empieza a cambiar: su naturaleza busca el cauce que el varón otorga: él ha demostrado su contundencia, la capacidad de violentarla *ergo* la posibilidad de domarla.

Los siguientes encuentros que tiene la pareja carecerán de virulencia y tendrán un tono triste y grave y, al final de la película, el general verá consumado todos sus anhelos llevando a Beatriz como una soldadera sumisa y feliz que camina atrás de su caballo. La vuelta de tuerca la permitió su agresividad hacia ella: fue el instrumento para domar a esta mujer en que su natural naturaleza se expresaba como altisonancia y pérdida de control. Jean Franco plantea que este final restaura el orden natural de la superioridad masculina pero también implica el paso al nuevo orden social revolucionario que permite el nacimiento del nuevo México (Franco 194).

El rapto (1953) es una cinta que emula a *Enamorada* en cuanto al tema de doma de la mujer, rebelde, que se resiste a entrar al orden impuesto por el director. Es también interpretada por *La Doña* y es también una comedia. El primer conflicto de la pareja tiene al río como escenario: Aurora (María Félix) quiere cruzar y Ricardo (Jorge Negrete) le avisa que en la parte por donde ella quiere hacerlo es peligroso. Cuando ella cae y se empapa, el ríe y la ayuda a salir, entonces Aurora lo jala para tirarlo al agua. Pronto habrá un motivo más grave para la rencilla: la casa abandonada por Ricardo para irse a los Estados Unidos ha sido comprada por Aurora.

Las autoridades del pueblo se muestran vacilantes en la administración de justicia. En un momento decisivo Aurora debe abandonar la propiedad. Ella trata de abofetear a Ricardo y él la empuja. Ella se queja: "-¡Maldito!, ¡Pegarle a una pobre mujer débil como yo!": ella no es todavía *su mujer*. El director juega con la falsa debilidad de la figura, encarnada por la poderosa María Félix y enunciada con su espesa voz, no hay que olvidar que se trata de una actriz que encarna la ambigüedad de la fuerza varonil, con voz de hombre en una hermosa mujer, y que este es un elemento clave del mito María Félix.

Aurora empieza a imaginar su defensa: inventa una agresión y sugiere, incluso, la violación. Lleva el asunto a los tribunales en donde se da un juicio largo y confuso. En el salón todo el pueblo está expectante y se escuchan frases significativas: "Si estuvieran casados, aún bueno, pero... pegarle a una desconocida...", un marido replica a su esposa: "El caso es que cuando no te pongo la mano encima andas diciendo que no te quiero". Aurora explica con lujos de detalle el ataque y conmueve a la concurrencia. Las autoridades deciden que deben casarse. A Ricardo le dicen: "tu cortaste la rosa de ese místico rosal y ahora, aunque tengas la mano toda espinada, te casas". La lucha por la casa seguirá entonces un cauce conyugal. La violencia de Ricardo alternada a su cautela ayuda para el final feliz, pero lo interesante es el juicio, pues en él se ponen sobre el tapete las ambiguas concepciones respecto a la violencia de género y la incapacidad de los administradores públicos de administrar justicia.

La agresividad no parece lejana de la excitación sexual. En *La Choca* (1973) la protagonista se entrega con placer al asesino de su marido una vez él la ha doblegado a golpes. Choca tiene todavía sangre en la boca cuando cierra provocadoramente la cortina de su cama, incluyéndolo en ella y excluyendo a los espectadores. Al día siguiente *su vestido rojo* y la flor que adorna su cabello dan cuenta de su plenitud sexual. La agresividad de Fernández en la vida real era comentada a menudo en la prensa. Edmundo Domínguez Aragonés le pregunta si acaso es verdad que golpeó en el *"set"* a Dolores del Río, a lo que el director contesta tajante:

"No. Esto lo he hecho yo nada más con mis esposas y con mi madre. Son falsos. Nada más [...] yo le tengo el respeto más grande no solamente a Dolores del Río y no solamente a las actrices, ya sean las estrellas o las más humildes extras, a los hombres también siempre los trato en forma respetuosa" (Domínguez Aragonés 172)

Paco Ignacio Taibo hace un compendio de las opiniones de Emilio Fernández respecto al sutil arte de golpear como parte del ritual amoroso (108-109). Las imágenes de celuloide parecían más inocentes, pero ¿acaso lo serían?.

La violación

Muy de acuerdo con el cine institucional mexicano, Emilio Fernández presenta la violación como un episodio monstruoso que destroza la vida de las mujeres y de sus hombres, pero, en su cine, tiene que ver con la ruptura del orden debido. Los hombres deben de proteger a sus mujeres y la violación significa la ruptura de este propósito trascendente y, además, la afrenta al honor. En la violación el varón pierde los atributos de contención necesarios para que la cultura triunfe sobre el instinto. Con ese acto los hombres están vencidos de entrada, convertidos en pura naturaleza, sin moral ni ley.

El tema aparece en varios de sus filmes. En *Río Escondido* (1947) el cacique se propone violar a la maestra Rosaura y promete a cada uno de sus secuaces su participación en el atentado. Con eso pretende lograr que sea su amante: "Ya verán como luego viene de rodillas a pedirme que la reciba", pero Rosaura lo recibe a balazos y lo mata, instaurando un nuevo orden social. En este filme excepcional, la mujer representa a la cultura y el hombre a la naturaleza avasallante, pero se debe a que Rosaura no es una mujer normal: en este filme María Félix simboliza a la Patria. *En Paloma herida* (1962) el ladino Danilo Zeta, interpretado por el mismo Emilio Fernández, doblega a los indígenas de Guatemala y viola a sus mujeres, una de ellas habrá de asesinarlo, aunque cuide amorosamente al hijo que le dejó.

La película más representativa al respecto es *Pueblerina* (1948). Paloma ha sido violada por el cacique del pueblo y su novio Aurelio trató de vengarse del que había sido, además, su mejor amigo, por lo que fue encarcelado durante seis años, al cabo de los cuales es liberado y regresa a su pueblo. Declara: "Vengo a trabajar la tierra y a casarme con Paloma, que es inocente de lo que pasó". Su amigo le dirá: "¡De veras que eres muy macho!". Recibe ese piropo (para Emilio Fernández eso es un piropo) porque hacerlo significa enfrentar el código no escrito de que la mujer violada está manchada y pertenece a su violador. Ese es también el esquema de Paloma, que se ha marginado de todos, se dedica a lavar ropa ajena y vive con su hijo en una choza del cerro, "como cabra arisca". Aurelio se presenta en su choza y le dice que ha vuelto a buscarla: "He llorado y soñado contigo seis años enteros, con sus días y sus noches", pero Paloma parece odiarse por haber sido violada. Cuando Aurelio la busca y le declara su amor ella responde llorando y concluye: "Haz de cuenta que me encontraste enterrada". Busca que el cura le ayude a desanimarlo: "...dígale que se fije en una que lo merezca y lo haga feliz, él es digno de que lo quiera la más alta de las mujeres [...] yo también lo quiero, y por eso me da horror de que se manche conmigo". El cura, como buen comparsa del cine mexicano, es sensato: "No seas cruel contigo misma ni con quien bien te quiere. Tú eres inocente y no debes martirizarte de esa manera".

Teniendo de música de fondo la guitarra de Bribiesca, Aurelio insiste y ella también:

> No quiero que nadie me tenga lástima [...] ¿Qué quieres?, ¿mancharte tú también? [...] tengo un hijo de otro, un hijo que no pedí [...] A cada palabra que digas te estarán gritando que soy una mujer manchada, una que tuvo un hijo a la fuerza, una que tiene vergüenza hasta de su sombra, porque debió morir [...] Mátame si quieres, pero no me pisotees con tu lástima, ni me recuerdes que soy una basura. De cualquiera podría soportarlo, menos de ti.

Aurelio remarca que ni está manchada ni le tiene lástima: "Si alguna vez Dios Nuestro Señor hizo algo puro acá abajo eres tú [...] Te pido que seas mi esposa". La densidad de las palabras de Paloma es abrumadora e impregnan la pantalla: parecen no dejar resquicio posible: dan cuenta del estigma y del sufrimiento que provoca la violación, pero lo que sorprende es el sentimiento de culpabilidad que se observa en Paloma. Sin embargo Aurelio no ceja: declara con suave firmeza que se casarán, su hijo vivirá con ellos y que el jueves irán juntos a la fiesta del pueblo. Aparentemente Paloma lo rechaza, pero acude a la cita. Aurelio ha ganado todos los premios de la feria popular cuando ella se presenta con su hijo y se abrazan. Las órdenes resultaron más eficaces que la labor de convencimiento. Cuando Aurelio y Paloma se casan, ella empieza a vestir de colores claros y aparecen algunas sonrisas en su cara. Todavía habrán de enfrentar bastantes desgracias hasta que Aurelio se otorgue justicia y futuro por su propia mano.

Aurelio es el personaje masculino ideal de Emilio Fernández: fuerte pero contenido, que sabe soportar el daño y marchar adelante con entereza, que cuida a la mujer y le enseña el camino del orden y la dignidad. La violación, a diferencia de la violencia, no es para Emilio Fernández un medio para organizar el idilio entre hombres y mujeres, pero su gravedad proviene de que es una batalla perdida en la lucha por establecer el orden frente al caos, una derrota de la cultura frente a la naturaleza, aquí ejercida por los varones.

Para concluir...

En las películas de *"El Indio"* Fernández el machismo se representa como una estrategia para lograr el paraíso. Al analizar sus películas accedemos al mito de la lucha original entre la naturaleza desbordada y la aspiración de los seres humanos de alcanzar el orden. Es por eso que la presencia y la trasgresión del tabú es fundamental en todos sus filmes: coloca a sus héroes en el tiempo del origen, momento fundante, eternamente convocado, cuando los opuestos se fundieron para crear el mundo.

"El Indio" construye sus historias a partir de la diferencia entre hombres y mujeres, que el considera esencial, y de ella deriva el papel subordinado que ellas deben tener en la sociedad. Quiere volver a un tiempo mítico. Su discurso no es acorde con la práctica social de la mitad del siglo XX, pero en el universo de las ideas y los símbolos culturales estos desfases son comunes y, además, el cine a menudo remite a los grandes dilemas humanos.

Sus enamorados construyen un centro cerrado y absoluto. En sus parejas no pueden existir dos personas, porque su sentido es precisamente la fusión de dos principios: el de la naturaleza (femenino) y el del orden (masculino). Se produce, entonces una simbiosis que funde las diferencias, pero que requiere, de entrada, de la sumisión absoluta de las mujeres y por consiguiente son aceptados los métodos violentos.

Sus estereotipados personajes femeninos cubren una función en la trama y sorprenden e irritan por su pasividad y sumisión: las mujeres son domadas con brutalidad para ser convertidas en una creación masculina, en una obra de arte. Lo femenino está inacabado y sólo el hombre lo puede completar. La forma de representarlo es excesiva, a menudo grotesca. La construcción que hace Emilio Fernández de los géneros sexuales se apoya en la cultura de su tiempo y en el cine institucional mexicano, pero por su temperamento exaltado nos permite mirar con lupa, exagerados, distorsionados y excesivos, sin pasteurizar, los conceptos velados y muchas veces disimulados en la sociedad, como son la violencia contra las mujeres, el deseo de que sean como sombras que se borran por amor y se funden simbióticamente a su pareja. En realidad, *"El Indio"* transmite, escondida en la devaluación, su miedo a la fuerza femenina y su desconocimiento de las mujeres reales.

Sin embargo, con su cine expresa también el problema humano por ser tanto naturaleza como cultura y por anhelar tanto la fusión cuanto la trascendencia. Para *"El Indio"*, romántico irredento, esta contradicción sólo puede superarse en la relación amorosa, aunque estas siempre fracasen. Sus mujeres de celuloide se suprimen para el amor pero, en cambio, el principio femenino que organiza el mundo, que avasalla, nutre y devora, acaba por imponer sus reglas. Es el destino y la lucha

siempre se reinicia. Al final de cuentas el principio femenino, esa naturaleza salvaje, desproporcionada y feroz es la que triunfa en casi todas
las películas.

Bibliografía

Alberoni, Francesco. *El Erotismo*. México: Gedisa, 1986.

Burton-Carvajal, Julianne. "Regardines Rape. Fictions of origin and film Spectatorship." *Mediating two worlds. Cinematic Encounters in the Americas.* Ed.
John King, Ana López y Manuel Alvarado. London: British Film Institute,
1993.

Cagliostro. "Mi querido Indio Fernández". "De lunes a domingo." *El cine gráfi-
co* [México] XV, n. 732, 22 junio 1947.

___ . "Un regard derrière les grilles." *Le cinema mexicain.* Ed. Paulo A.
Paranagua. París: Centre Georges Pompidou, 1992.

Chartier, Roger. *El mundo como representación. Historia cultural entre prácticas y
representaciones.* Barcelona: Gedisa, 1992.

Domínguez Aragonés, Edmundo. *Tres extraordinarios. Luis Spota, Alejandro
Jodorowsky, Emilio "Indio"Fernández.* México: Juan Pablos Editor, 1980.

Fernández, Adela. *El Indio Fernández. Vida y mito.* México: Panorama Editorial,
1986.

Franco, Jean. *Las conspiradoras. La representación de la mujer en México.* Versión
actualizada. México: El Colegio de México FCE, 1994.

García Riera, Emilio. *Emilio Fernández. 1904-1980.* Guadalajara: U de G. CIEC,
1987.

Kundera, Milan. *La insoportable levedad del ser.* México: Seix Barral, 1986.

Reyes Nevares, Beatriz. *Trece directores del cine mexicano.* México: SEP, 1974.

Rozado, Alejandro. *Cine y realidad social en México. Una lectura de la obra de Emilio
Fernández.* México: U. de G. CIEC, 1991.

Taibo I., Paco Ignacio. *El Indio Fernández. El cine por mis pistolas.* México:
Joaquín Mortiz Planeta, 1986.

Tuñón, Julia. *Mujeres de luz y sombra en el cine mexicano. La construcción de una
imagen.* México: El Colegio de México Imcine, 1998.

___ . "Entre lo natural y lo monstruoso: violencia y violación en el cine mexicano de la edad de oro." *Estudios de género y feminismo I.* Eds. Patricia Bedo-
lla Miranda, Olga L.Bustos, et al. México: UNAM Fontamara, 1989.

___ . *Los rostros de un mito. Personajes femeninos en el cine de Emilio Fernández.*
México: Imcine Conaculta, 2000.

___ . *En su propio espejo. Entrevista con Emilio "El Indio" Fernández.* México:
UAM-Iztapalapa, 1988.

Shelley Godsland

Royal Holloway, University of London

Mujeres 'Malas': the representation of the female criminal in Spanish women's crime fiction as a response to discourses of gendered violence

The most prominent features of Spanish women's crime fiction of the past two decades have been not only the consolidation of the textual position of the female sleuth, but also, and more significantly, the protagonisation of women criminals. Narrative of this type belongs to several sub-genres: the Spanish re-formulation of the hard-boiled model known as the novela negra which was a cultural response to the early years of the "Transición," the police procedural which seems to be a by-product of full democracy, and the psychological thriller which tracks the ratiocinative processes and explores the motives of the criminal herself, as well as assessing the causes and consequences of crime. This literary "penchant" for female crooks shows no sign of abating, and in my opinion serves to reflect and comment on, and develop a wider social, media and academic interest in the violent or delinquent woman and the gendered nature of aggression in both the Spanish and international contexts.

My aim in this paper, then, is to assess the junction between women, criminality, and patriarchally-engineered violences as they are conceptualised in a number of representative crime fictions by Spanish female writers. I want to show how they function to articulate concerns about sex and aggression, how they reflect and ponder discourses of gendered deviance, and how their authors respond to the concerns and desires of their (female) readers through the textualisation of these issues. The works selected for analysis conform to the characteristics of a number of sub-genres of the types mentioned above, and all feature at least one female criminal and, in some cases, a woman sleuth as well. A brief survey of the types of crimes committed by their protagonists reveals the powerful pull of women who kill on the popular and media imaginations, for homicide is the crime featured in *¡Es tan fácil matar!* (1991), Julia Sáez-Angulo's collection of unusual murder tales, *Asesinando el pasado* (1997) by the lawyer and feminist thinker Lidia Falcón, and is at the centre of *Ritos de muerte* (1996), *Día de perros* (1997), *Muerte en el* *gimnasio* (1998), and *Muertos de papel* (2000), police procedurals penned by Alicia Giménez-Bartlett which introduce police inspector Petra Delicado and which have proved immensely popular and have been adapted for television. The first of Giménez-Bartlett's crime novels also centres on an unusual case of a girl rapist, and *Antípodes* (1988) and *El sol que fa l'anec* (1994) by the Catalan writer Maria-Antònia Oliver also focus on women's participation in sex crimes. Oliver's first novel, *Estudi en lila* (1987), and *Amanda* (1998) by Isabel-Clara Simó, another Catalan writer, centre on female castrators, while Matilde Asensi's best-selling *El salón de ámbar* (1999), and *Escapa't d'Andorra* (1988) by Assumpta Margenat both protagonise highly successful female thieves.

This notion of "success" in criminal terms inevitably functions to introduce a further central feature of women's crime fiction which characterises female miscreants — that of the author's stance towards the deviant and her activities — and it is this writerly position that further elucidates their reaction to other discourses of gendered law-breaking. Broadly speaking, in contemporary woman-authored crime fictions from Spain, the "success" of the female criminal is discernible from the consequences of her actions; on one hand, some women crooks escape justice, become fabulously wealthy, or carry off some other "prize" such as a "Prince Charming" or enhanced personal freedom as a result of their foray into law-breaking. Others of these fictional miscreants, however, are chastised at the hands of their literary creators, and their punishment for transgression is death, imprisonment, or some other legal sanction, thus following a pattern established in male-authored hard-boiled fiction in the US and in Spain (Walton and Jones 192-93, Young 97). This division in turn corresponds fairly closely to the type of crime committed by the female deviants; if violence or illegal behaviour are directed towards the male body or possessions, or an institution of patriarchy, then writers deal gently with their characters. If they target their criminal energy against other women or children, however, then retribution will be harsh, although this twofold vision is thwarted somewhat by Giménez-Bartlett whose siting of her female detective as a member of the police in fact functions to disrupt this duality, as I shall discuss later.

Fictional female felons who manage to skip "justice" outnumber those who are sanctioned for their misdemeanours. Elena, the protagonist of Falcón's *Asesinando el pasado* appears to be a happily-married member of Barcelona's middle class. Her past, however, comes back to haunt her in the form of her first husband who blackmails her with the threat of revealing to her present spouse that her first marriage was never annulled and that she is therefore a bigamist, and that the young girl Elena's friends and relatives believe to be her sister is in fact her daughter, offspring of the blackmailer. In order to protect her child,

Elena kills her first husband, a crime to which she confesses, but is not believed by the police who deem her admission of guilt to be the rantings of a middle-aged female attention-seeker. Not only does she thus escape imprisonment, Falcón goes so far as to reward her character's incursion in homicide with a rather traditional "happy ending" in the arms of Félix, her true love, with whom she will spend the rest of her days in a tropical paradise redolent with overtones of a redeeming primitive innocence. This pattern is also apparent in two stories contained in Sáez-Angulo's anthology *¡Es tan fácil matar!*, both of which feature women who kill husbands whose laziness and lack of consideration are a source of veritable torture for their spouses. Covadonga, protagonist of "Un luto deseado" pushes her unfaithful, good-for-nothing partner from a sixth floor window, while in "Mañana de domingo" Bibiana stabs her mate in the back as he sits eating toast. Whereas the open ending of the second narrative fails to furnish commentary on Bibiana's fate following the homicide, she is certainly rewarded with personal freedom and a return of her artistic flair, while Covadonga escapes any punishment because her husband's death is attributed to an unfortunate accident while fixing a window blind.

The castrators portrayed in *Estudi en lila* and *Amanda* also clearly direct their violence against men, but both women evade detection, in the first text because the feminist-minded detective, Lònia Guiu, feels justified in allowing the castrator to escape the clutches of the law because the men upon whom she weilded her scalpel had raped her, and in the short story due to police incompetence. Impunity is also the textual response to robbery on a grand scale as both Rossi, who steals the month's takings from her unpleasant boss at the supermarket in which she works in *Escapa't d'Andorra,* and Ana, a member of a phenomenally successful international art gang at the centre of *El salón de ámbar,* evade detection and enjoy a materially enhanced lifestyle as the inevitable outcome of their activities.

Apart from unpunished woman-authored criminality, these texts also have in common the sex of their victims: their deviance is directed against the male body or genitals, male private property, or the material assets of a patriarchal institution, such as the Russian Orthodox church from which an icon is stolen before the opening of the narrative sequence related in *El salón de ámbar.* Equally significantly, these fictions seek to justify the criminal acts of the female protagonists, and culpability is always attributable to the male. Thus, Elena's husband is killed because he is a blackmailer who endangers her daughter's well-being, and in five of the nine short stories collected in Sáez-Angulo's anthology despotic, lazy, philandering spouses are meted out the punishment their wives and the author assert that they deserve, and die at the hands of the woman whose only error was to have married them. Even castration is justifiable in these fictions. In *Amanda* Mercedes castrates her husband and then feeds his fried testicles to him as retribution for his affair with a former girlfriend, while Elena Gaudí, the protagonist of Oliver's *Estudi en lila*, views castration as the appropriate punishment for the three men who raped her, her uncompromising stance serving to underscore the significance of the novel's title which alludes to graffiti daubed on walls across Spain during the 1980s which proclaimed "Against rape, castration" in lilac paint. The causal agent of theft is also shown to be male, for Margenat's character, Rossi, steals a signficant sum of cash from her boss not only to ease her own and her sister's economic position, but also because her manager is an abusive "machista" who harasses his female employees. While Rossi views her crime as thus entirely justified, Ana's criminal activities are revealed in *El salón de ámbar* to be ethically admissible because those from whom she steals are rich men, the unwritten moral of the tale being that theft from a wealthy male to fund the lifestyle of a young woman is permissible, particularly as it is a mechanism for overcoming female economic marginalisation by patriarchy.

Fictional justification of female delinquency directed against the male body and male property reflects an explanatory tendency also apparent in both specialist and popular discourses of female criminality. The Spanish criminologist Marisol Donis asserts that

> la mujer siempre ha estado muy presionada socialmente y, en muchos casos, ha pasado del maltrato del padre al maltrato del marido. Además, muchas veces está frustrada, tanto si trabajaba como si no, y casi ninguna tiene las mismas oportunidades respecto del hombre. Una frustración tras otra puede llevar a la desesperación, y la desesperación puede terminar en caos. (Vázquez 26)

Her view is reflected in a recent text by the Spanish journalist Francisco Pérez Abellán. Although the title of the work, *Ellas matan mejor. 50 crímenes cometidos por mujeres*, reveals its rather sensationalist nature, its author points out that among the cases he researched

> La mayoría de los crímenes de las mujeres son para liberarse del acoso o del terror al que las someten los varones. Matan a sus maridos porque las maltratan, les dan mala vida o amenazan a los hijos. En general se defienden de agresiones continuas o de situaciones insoportables.
> Bajo la presión de la sociedad, llegan a enloquecer [...] Sus condicionantes biológicas las deprimen y enloquecen. (15).

In an international context Margaret Shaw has asserted that victimisation of the female can provoke a criminally violent response (115-16), and Anna Motz notes that the woman faced with annihilation of some part of her self may exteriorise "the enactment of a primitive defence mechanism" (217), although Shaw does warn about constructing the female delinquent as a product only of her victimisation, and stresses that other socio-environmental factors must also be considered as causal agents (120, 125-126).

In Spain, this justificatory and explanatory discourse also pervades the media and the popular imagination and was made manifest in the press's frenzied response and prominence given to the case of Teresa de Jesús Moreno Maya, known as "Tani," a gypsy woman who in 1995 shot dead her husband after seventeen years of abuse at his hands. When, five years into her fourteen year sentence "Tani" was transferred to the Alcalá-Meco prison in Madrid, the daily *El Mundo* described how between 2,000 and 3,000 demonstrators had gathered at the gates of the jail to demand the assassin's immediate pardon and release (Tristán). Rosa Tristán's article reporting these events functions to condone the sentiments expressed by the campaigners, as it opens with the words "« Libertad ». « Libertad ». « Libertad ».", a linguistic device which makes clear the journalist's stance, if not the newspaper's editorial policy too. In a further piece which appeared in the quality daily *El País*, Alicia Giménez-Bartlett, one of the crime writers whose fiction I analyse in this paper, also underscores popular perception of 'Tani's' crime as a justified one to which the judicial system should have responded with sympathy when she notes that the murderess had been the victim of "golpes, humillaciones y terror" at the hands of a husband the writer classifies as a "torturador." Both Tristán and Giménez-Bartlett are women, however, and while their journalistic production may reflect attitudes undoubtedly "en vogue" in the fictions of contemporary Spanish female crime writers, the male legal standpoint was represented in a further article in *El País* in which Hermenegildo Altozano, a Spanish lawyer, argued that "Tani" had been tried and imprisoned as a natural, judicial consequence of the seriousness of her crime, alleging further that "(e)l sentimiento popular no debe ser el criterio que rija la administración de Justicia."

This discrepancy between the 'official' patriarchal or specialist perspective and the popular media or fictional response to women who are provoked to commit crimes is not the only divergence manifest from an analysis of the two discourses. Both Donis and Pérez Abellán whom I cited earlier clearly suggest that the female killer is psychologically unstable, perhaps not genetically, but that her 'madness' or destabilisation can be a product of the social conditions in which she lives or of her biology. With the single exception of Sáez-Angulo's story "Mañana de domingo" which suggests that Bibiana's pre-menstrual state is an important factor in her decision to rid herself of her husband, none of the other novelists who justify female criminal violence so much as hints that their protagonists are in any way really deviant, either morally or psychologically. Indeed, portrayal of the women crooks is generally positive, thus permitting identification between reader and character, readerly complicity in the crimes that are committed, and a vicarious readerly enjoyment of the felons' exploits. Ana and Rossi, the accomplished thieves, are portrayed as intelligent and daring and have attractive personalities, and the reader of *El salón de ámbar* and *Escapa't d'Andorra* is skillfully induced to consider theft as entirely justifiable when it functions to fulfil the material aspirations of such pleasant girls who as young women would otherwise be economically marginalised in a nation where the collective female income is only 18% of the national total (Falcón 2000:9). Reader response is perhaps assured through a simple mechanism: a parallel between the perceived financial status of the potential consumer of the text and that of the fictional robbers were they not to successfully pull off their heists. The texts not only respond to readers' escapist monetary fantasies, however, they also reformulate the academic and sociologically constructed motivation for female-authored theft. The very title of Pat Carlen's *Women, Crime and Poverty* (1988) evokes the need of many women to steal to provide essential amenities for themselves and for their families, while in a specifically Spanish context Andrés Canteras Murillo (209-17) and Paz de la Cuesta Aguado (undated) both identify a link between crime and poverty and other forms of social marginalisation and exclusion, although they both note that the relationship is not necessarily a causal one. Similarly, the authorial viewpoint advanced in *Estudi en lila* and *Amanda* clearly functions to engage the reader with the justifiability of castrating men who perpetrate sexual violence or sexual misdemeanours, and neither Mercedes nor Elena Gaudí are shown to be unusual or "abnormal." They do not reveal any symptoms of "madness," nor are their lives chaotic; they carefully plan and skilfully execute their crimes because they are women who are pushed by men beyond all limits of tolerance and exact retribution, much as are the female killers of Falcón and Sáez-Angulo, women for whom the reader is encouraged to feel sympathy, if not to openly identify.

Generation of such an empathetic response from the reader is founded in her identification of the fictional female criminals as victims of individual men or of patriarchal institutions, of their aggression as a response to their victimisation, and acknowledgement and recognition of her own victim status, essential to readerly comprehension of the protagonists' criminal motivation. In *Sisters in Crime. Feminism and the Crime Novel* (1988) Maureen Reddy notes that within the genre "women are far more likely to be victims than murderers" (35), an assertion confirmed in the Spanish social context by the observation that in the collected proceedings of two large international conferences on gender and violence held in Valencia in 1996 and 1999, every paper focuses on male violence against women and / or children (Generalitat Valenciana 1997 and 2000). Although the authors analysed here re-write this norm in that their narratives feature female criminals whose victims are men, their protagonists are also victims of male physical, psychological or sexual terror, or of economic and social marginalisation prior to their engagement with law-breaking, as I have already shown.

This concern in female-authored Spanish crime fictions with violence against women serves to reflect academic and popular preoccupation with the phenomenon which the lawyer and feminist Lidia Falcón (2000) characterises thus:

> en los finales de los noventa y principios de 2000 la violencia contra las mujeres se desencadenó como un tifón, como un vendaval, como un maremoto, por parte de maridos enfurecidos al encontrarse de pronto ante la situación inesperada e inaceptable de ser despreciados en su papel de machos jodedores y fertilizadores, de patriarcas obedecidos y admirados, de haber sido despedidos incluso del hogar conyugal, la casa que ellos habían pagado y que era su hogar indiscutible, a la vez que se les negaba el derecho a tener los hijos consigo y a veces hasta de visitarlos. (131-32)

Falcón's words echo those of the novelist Francisco Umbral who, in an article provocatively entitled "Pegar a una mujer" proffers a similar explanation for the current wave of male violence against women, although it should be noted that neither author considers that their reasoning can possibly justify male actions of this kind:

> Estamos viviendo una oleada de violencia contra la mujer, contra las mujeres. [...] En la violencia contra la mujer uno ve toda la inmensa frustración masculina, la energía represada de millones de hombres a quienes a su vez abofetea la vida, maltrata la sociedad. [...] Se pega a la mujer porque no se puede pegar al jefe, al amigo, al enemigo. (Umbral)

In an earlier work, *Violencia contra la mujer* (1991) Falcón had explored the phenomenon in Spain in greater detail, and had collected a chilling selection of articles from the national press which detailed an array of crimes against women. The worrying trend she identifies does not seem to have abated, and headlines such as "Cerca de 650.000 españolas son víctimas en la actualidad de malos tratos" (Hernández Velasco), "Unas 34.000 alumnas sufren acoso sexual en su instituto" (Simón) or "El tráfico de mujeres extranjeras se ha duplicado en España" (Jiménez) function to highlight the multiple ways in which women in Spain are victimised. My own observations during this year also show the extent of media interest in this issue. A random sample of a week's copies of *El País* that I purchased during a visit to Spain during February revealed that every issue contained articles on Spanish women's status as victim, and headlines reported "Asuntos sociales critica a los jueces por su escasa protección a las mujeres maltratadas" (Nogueira), "Detenido un hombre por matar a cuchilladas a su mujer en Getxo" (*El País* 13 Feb. 2001), amongst others.

Public concern was made even more apparent during a further visit to Spain in early July of this year. The city centre of Valladolid, a large provincial capital north of Madrid, was plastered with posters headed "Ningún agresor en cargos públicos. Ninguna agresión sin respuesta" which advertised a demonstration to be held in Ponferrada on the 7th of July to call for the sacking or resignation of Ismael Álvarez, the local mayor, on the grounds of his alleged sexual harrassment of Nevenka Fernández, the former "concejala" of Ponferrada. Breadth of outrage at Álvarez's aggression of his colleague was apparent from the rotund denunciation of gendered violence issued by the young people of both sexes whom I met as they posted the bills, and from the range of political and women's groups — from the trades unions and established political parties, to housewives groups and feminist associations — that sponsored the demonstration. Possibly as a response to media outrage, or perhaps with an eye on the female vote, political support of female victims of male and patriarchal violence has been more apparent in the very recent past. In 1999 the Spanish president, José María Aznar, encouraged abused women to report their tormentors (*El Mundo* 5 Oct. 1999). Earlier this year the Consejo General del Poder Judicial took the decision to sanction a judge whose refusal to acknowledge reports from Mar Herrero of stalking and harassment by her former partner resulted in the young woman's murder by the ex-boyfriend (Torres), and in the same month the regional government of Madrid for the first time brought charges for domestic violence when it constituted itself as plaintiff against a man who had stabbed his wife twenty times (Barroso and Aguirre). While media and public interest, and increasing political engagement with violence against women enhances visibility and awareness, it should also be remembered, however, that such aggression is not always perceived of as criminal, as the authors of the report "La victimología y las mujeres" (no date) report:

> la mujer es colocada en la condición de víctima, pues se lesionan bienes jurídicos importantes suyos y se le ocasiona un grave perjuicio, cuanto menos comparativo. Pero en la medida en que tales conductas no están jurídico penalmente desvaloradas no se puede hablar de "víctima" desde un punto de vista jurídico penal pues aquí la conducta que crea la victimización no es un delito. Más bien al contrario, los victimizadores actúan cumpliendo las normas del rol social que desem-

peñan.(http://members.ripod.com/fmuraro/victimologia_y_feme-nismo.htm)

Increasing media sympathy and public and political outrage at the apparently unceasing victimisation by men of women in Spain, and the authorial glee of female writers who attempt to invert the situation by means of a protagonisation of women victimisers and male victims take a very different turn, however, when female violence and criminal activity are directed at other women or at children. Where Tristán's and Giménez-Bartlett's articles, cited earlier, employ a vocabulary intended to induce a sympathetic reaction to "Tani" the husband killer, the press deploys no such subtleties in cases of female aggression against another woman. An article published in *El País* detailing the high-profile murder in Andalusia of Rocío Wanninkhof by Dolores Vázquez highlights the editorial view of the assassin as vicious, cowardly, and unjustified in her actions by pointing out that she was "enemistada" with her victim, whom she *"golpeó y atestó ocho puñaladas por la espalda"* (L. G., my italics). A further piece from El Mundo reports on the criminal activities of the "Bandas de las Vanessas", teen girl gangs that savagely attacked and robbed other young girls in Barcelona, and in focusing on what he perceives as their "actos de violencia gratuita e indiscriminada," the journalist emphasises his view of the gang's members as abnormal and indefensibly violent (de la Cal). Such notions enjoy international currency, as Anna Motz signals:

> The move from idealisation to denigration can be seen in the sentimental regard with which women and children are held, and the rage which is evoked when their aggressive or sexual impulses appear to become out of control or dangerous. There is then a punitive backlash which has a ferocity that may alarm those who attempt to understand aggressive behaviour. It can be seen in the public fury when mothers display aggressive or perverse behaviour, and appears to be a manifestation of rage and disappointment that these women have failed to conform to powerful stereotypes of them as nurturing and gentle creatures. The backlash against these women reflects the depths of the disappointment and anger that they do not conform to these sentimental notions and reveals the strength of the taboos relating to maternal incest and violence. (259-60).

In the fictions selected for analysis in this paper this position is apparent in a small number of texts, specifically Oliver's *Antípodes* and *El sol que fa l'anec* which feature, respectively, female participation in gangs dedicated to the slave prostitution of women and a paedophile ring, and in Giménez-Bartlett's first crime novel, *Ritos de muerte* which recounts the story of a young girl who rapes others with an old-fashioned door handle prior to murdering them in order to avert suspicion from her fiancé. The most prominent female members of the gangs portrayed in both of Oliver's novels are punished, either by the legal system or by their own death, while Giménez-Bartlett's policewoman, Petra Delicado, feels no compunction at incarcerating the female rapist, and experiences more horror and disgust upon her discovery of the sex of the attacker than she exteriorises sympathy for the victims of the male rapist. It should be noted that Giménez-Bartlett's police procedurals all differ very significantly from other contemporary women's crime writing from Spain in that female criminal activity and deviance are never justified, are never pardoned, and are certainly never afforded the positive narrative treatment that characterises the novels of other writers. All of her female crooks — even those whose victims are male victimisers — are apprehended by the police, and are dealt with judicially according to the dictates of "the law," or meet with a violent end. While on one hand Petra Delicado's response to women criminals is conditioned by her position as a member of the Policía Nacional, as I discuss elsewhere Giménez-Bartlett's manifestly postfeminist vision which negates the feminist assumption that all women are victims of the patriarchy inevitably functions to deny the possibility of a justified or justifiable female criminality (Godsland 2002).

Postfeminism need not, however, necessarily thwart the project of most of the authors whose crime fictions I study here, and whose manifest aim is to furnish a female readership with fantasies of contesting victimisation while also articulating the extent of violence against women. The individualism, materialism, and search for what, with reference to a popular women's magazine, could be termed a "Cosmo" lifestyle, signal Asensi's *El salón de ámbar* as a postfeminist text that ponders the potential of "girl power." Nonetheless, it is one of those cultural products that justifies female criminality as a means to an end and proffers a positive textualisation of its law-breaking protagonist. Despite the contradictions inherent in the increased media attention in and visibility of violence against women within the context of a postfeminist economy which purports to deconstruct and deny the feminist notion of universal female victim status, Spanish women's crime fiction is engaging with gendered aggression and re-writing its paradigms. For this reason, postfeminism, or at least the rejection of feminism, will not necessarily be the death knell for these narrative inversions of gendered relationships to crime and aggression, particularly because the female public continues to buy and to read these texts which are escapist fictions in at least two senses of the term.

Bibliografía

Altolozano, Hermenegildo. "Un grave precedente." *El País* 29 Oct. 2000.

Asensi, Matilde. *El salón de ámbar.* Barcelona: Plaza y Janés, 1999.

Barroso, F J and B Aguirre. "El gobierno ejerce la acción popular por primera vez en un caso de violencia conyugal." *El País* 20 Feb. 2001.

Cal, J C de la. "Las bandas de las «Vanessas» atemorizan a las niñas de Barcelona." *El Mundo* 5 Feb. 1997.

Canteras Murillo, Andrés. *Delincuencia femenina en España.* Madrid: Ministerio de Justicia, 1990.

Carlen, Pat. *Women, Crime and Poverty.* Milton Keynes: Open University Press, 1988.

Cuesta Aguado, Paz de la. "Perfiles criminológicos de la Delincuencia Femenina." http://comunidad.derecho.org/icapda/Perfiles.htm.

"Aznar anima a las víctimas de malos tratos a que denuncien." *El Mundo* 5 Oct. 1999.

"Detenido un hombre por matar a cuchilladas a su mujer en Getxo." *El País* 13 Feb. 2001.

Falcón, Lidia. *Violencia contra la mujer.* Madrid: Vindicación Feminista, 1991.

——. *Asesinando el pasado.* Madrid: Vindicación Feminista Kira Edit, 1997.

——. *Los nuevos mitos del feminismo.* Madrid: Vindicación Feminista, 2000.

Generalitat Valenciana. Consellería de Bienestar Social, Dirección General de la Mujer. 1as Jornadas: sobre la violencia de género en la sociedad actual. Valencia: 1997.

Generalitat Valenciana. Consellería de Bienestar Social. Jornadas. La violencia de género en la sociedad actual. Valencia: 2000.

Giménez-Bartlett, Alicia. *Ritos de muerte.* Barcelona: Grijalbo, 1996.

——. *Día de perros.* Barcelona: Grijalbo, 1997.

——."Muerte en el gimnasio." *Historias de detectives.* Ed. Ángeles Encinar. Barcelona: Lumen, 1998. 199-224.

——. *Mensajeros de la oscuridad.* Barcelona: Plaza y Janés, 1999.

——. *Muertos de papel.* Barcelona: Plaza y Janés, 2000.

——. "Sin teorizar." *El País* 29 Oct. 2000.

Godsland, Shelley. "From Feminism to Postfeminism in Spanish Women's Crime Fiction: The Case of Maria-Antònia Oliver and Alicia Giménez-Bartlett", *Letras Femeninas,* XXVIII:1 (2002): 84-99.

Hernández Velasco, Irene. "Violencia doméstica / primeros datos de una macroencuesta a 20.000 mujeres. Cerca de 650.000 españolas son víctimas en la actualidad de malos tratos." *El Mundo* 4 Feb. 2000.

Jiménez, David. "El tráfico de mujeres extranjeras se ha duplicado en España." *El Mundo* 11 Nov. 1998.

"La victimología y las mujeres."http://members.ripod.com/fmuraro/victimologia_y_femenismo.htm

L. G. "El fiscal pide 14 años para la supuesta asesina de Wanninkhof." El País 24 Mar. 2001.

Margenat, Assumpta. *Escapa't d'Andorra*. Barcelona: La Magrana, 1988.

Motz, Anna. *The Psychology of Female Violence. Crimes Against the Body*. Hove: Brunner-Routledge, 2001.

Nogueira, Charo. "Asuntos sociales critica a los jueces por su escasa protección a las mujeres maltratadas." *El País* 15 Feb. 2001.

Oliver, Maria-Antònia. *Estudio en lila*. Trad. de Manuel Quinto. Barcelona: Vidorama, 1989.

___. *Antípodas*. Trad. Manuel Quinto. Barcelona: Vidorama, 1990.

___. *El sol que engalana*. Trad. Manuel Quinto. Barcelona: Thassàlia, 1998.

Pérez Abellán, Francisco. *Ellas matan mejor. 50 crímenes cometidos por mujeres*. Madrid: Espasa Calpe, 2000.

Reddy, Maureen. *Sisters in Crime. Feminism and the Crime Novel*. New York: Continuum, 1998.

Sáez-Angulo, Julia. *¡Es tan fácil matar!* San Fernando de Henares: Editorial Bitácora, 1991.

Shaw, Margaret. "Conceptualizing violence by women." *Gender and Crime*. Ed. R.E.Dobash, R. P. Dobash, and L Noaks. Cardiff: University of Wales Press, 1995. 115-31.

Simó, Isabel Clara. "Amanda." *Historias de detectives*. Ed. Ángeles Encinar. Barcelona: Lumen, 1998. 117-32.

Simón, Pedro. "Unas 34.000 alumnas sufren acoso sexual en su instituto." *El Mundo* 30 Nov. 1999.

Torres, Maruja. "Al fin." *El País* 15 Feb. 2001.

Tristán, Rosa M. "Piden su indulto. Miles de personas acompañan a « Tan i» a Alcalá-Meco." *El Mundo* 25 Oct. 2000.

Umbral, Francisco. "Pegar a una mujer." *El Mundo* 26 Sept. 1998.

Vázquez, Montaña. "Asesinas natas." *Blanco y Negro*. Ella suplemento 9 Jun. 2001. 26-30.

Walton, Priscilla L., and Manina Jones. *Detective Agency. Women Rewriting the Hard-Boiled Tradition*. Berkeley: University of California Press, 1999.

Young, Alison. *Imagining Crime. Textual Outlaws and Criminal Conversations*. London: Sage, 1996.

Georg Schmid

University of Salzburg, Austria

Patriarchal Structures and Female Resistance in Films by Carlos Saura: *Ana y los lobos, Deprisa, deprisa, Taxi de noche*

During the last three decades, historical developments in Spain have demonstrated an astonishing rapidity; one is tempted to refer to the respective "social exposure" of the Spanish population by using the title of the French language dubbing of one of Saura's films: *Vivre vite* (Fast living). This rapidity certainly has subjected the Spaniards to a tremendous amount of stress (*Stress es tres, tres* is the title of an early Saura movie from 1968), a stress implying some sort of a cultural shock, perhaps a collective sensation of vertigo, but also an experience of catching up with the rest of Europe in a spectacular fashion. It is not easy any more to conceive of a passably backward Spain from only about a little more than a generation ago, since the country nowadays counts among the most dynamic ones in the European Union.

But let us not be misled by stereotypes of backwardness either. To mention just one nearly always overlooked (yet nonetheless spectacular) fact, one should also take into consideration that Spain, in the 1930s, was the only country where fascism was actively combated from the very beginning. The legitimate democratic political system was crushed solely by military action; and had it not been for the intervention of Nazi Germany, Spain — it can well be argued from an "alternate history" point of view — would have remained a democracy. Thus, it would have been, apart from the United Kingdom and possibly the Benelux countries the only Western European nation to remain democratic; France, following the Nazi occupation, chose to "collaborate" with the victorious conqueror, although there would have been the possibility to continue the war effort, be it in Africa or other overseas territories, as de Gaulle's Free France movement has proved. Around 1940, continuing to fight, to defy and to oppose the oppressor, the illegitimate régime, the occupying power, in short: perpetuating resistance throughout Europe would have resulted in an utterly different history. The least that can be said is that it would have made it considerably more difficult for Germany to annihilate democracies such as Czechoslovakia or at least to corrupt them to a more (Switzerland) or decidedly less patent degree (Sweden). Whether in the longer run, given this "alternate" situation, Spain would have been able to prevail vis-à-vis a "Teutonized Europe" is, alas, questionable: strictly speaking, no one has done it in Continental Europe — apart from the aforementioned cases.

It is useful to think of such facts when attempting to analyze works of art in order to be able to situate them in historical and sociological contexts. It seems to be irrefutable that Carlos Saura's films mirror recent Spanish history and contemporary Spanish reality in a nearly perfect way. Thus, his *oeuvre* represents an historical source par excellence. Well-known dialectics or feedback-systems within a given society come into play: artists seem to be influenced by their perception of specific realities and consequently express themselves in their works; they, in turn, influence and eventually co-determine collective outlooks and behavioral patterns within the same society that has exercised its influence upon them.

Hence, a longitudinal profiling of Saura's *oeuvre* seems to be enlightening. As the title of this article suggests, I propose to analyze violence in his movies specifically with regard to women characters, how they react to it, in which ways they revert to violence themselves and, generally, to what an extent and in which ways certain patterns may change. Spain is, indubitably, an excellent example as far as problems of male dominance and, indeed, machismo are concerned. These behavioral patterns seem to amplify fascist collective attitudes in Spanish society as well as a certain inherent violent streak in general and vice versa. Moreover, Spanish history, particularly recent history, is a superb paradigm for the longevity of collective memories, in this instance specifically with regard to the Civil War.

However, as far as the basic thematic conundrum — patriarchy and violence — is concerned, we will also have to recognize that there are underlying matriarchal structures to be diagnosed, thus reminding us of the never-ending mockeries of Mediterranean type mother-figures without whose tacit acceptance — or often active participation — the respective sociological system and its "symbolic" superstructure could never function. We can most plausibly illustrate the reproduction of such a system and its *mise en scène* by psychoanalytical models of explanation. Indeed I shall, at least implicitly, revert to those methods and techniques repeatedly for two reasons: on the one hand, they play a major role in Saura's earlier films, and on the other psychoanalysis always takes into account the sociological determinants.

An additional — technical — remark does seem appropriate, be it only as a reminder. It is incontrovertibly impossible to just write about film, to solely describe scenes and sequences, to express the multidimensional sum-total of a stupendous number of codes which finally make up an individual movie or "film" in general by only using words, by merely reverting to text, be it a particular one or "text" in general, "generic text," so to speak. But while mere "verbalization" is decidedly not sufficient, there is, at least for the moment, with the exception of complicated multimedia methods of representation, no other way.

Be it as it may, here are my arguments, developed textually. I will begin with Saura's *Deprisa, deprisa* (DP), released in 1980. One sequence depicts the heroine's "initiation" in the world of guns as her boyfriend teaches her how to make use of one. The male "governs" the gun; it is obvious that it belongs to his segment of the symbolic universe in which he has, in his individual existence, most likely been initiated indirectly, but early and decisively. Nevertheless, he only condescendingly hands down his "discrete knowledge" to his girlfriend or we should rather say: female partner, as it is interesting to note that those young people are shown to behave in a passably "non-sexist" way. A second sequence, however, reveals clearly that the initiative has been transferred to the young woman: following one of the hold-ups by the group of small-time young criminals it is the young woman who fires deadly shots at the driver of a money transport van which they had assaulted.

In many, indeed most ways this film is of an astounding actuality. This is not only due to the fact that juvenile delinquency is, sadly, so actual; rather, DP still feels so veracious because it depicts a universe without purpose, significance and depth. These young people are quite pleasant. Apart from their, at least in the beginning, rather petty crimes they seem to bear no ill intentions, yet they are not equipped with any perspective for a future. The three male figures simply live on a day-to-day basis; the young woman's vision seems to consist principally in the aspiration to an apartment of her or their own — a rather petit-bourgeois ambition — and to go to the sea once in her lifetime.

The movie clearly implies that this is not the "fault" of those young people, that there are no specific personal shortcomings to be diagnosed; rather, it is this one-dimensional world into which they have been projected which should, in a sense, be held responsible for their outlook — or rather the lack of it. It is also of interest to itemize the absence of significant elements in this film. This becomes much more evident when one attempts to compare it to Saura's earlier works which show an enormous wealth of such elements: their richness, often bordering on the opulent, and always presenting profound and numerous sets of meaning, renders the impoverishment of this value-stripped Madrid suburb all the more patent. There seems to be no way out.

The woman's eventual getaway in DP's final sequence is of a dismal ambivalence. Her companions are dead, even the cultivated-looking elderly doctor whom she bribes to take care of her fatally wounded boyfriend because he cannot possibly be transported to a hospital due to a previous bank robbery. Everyone is gone, dead as she grabs the money and walks into an uncertain future, which Saura does not even attempt to sketch. This getaway thus seems to be presented all the more depressingly. She leaves the mediocre apartment building, walks into the typical sounds of a lower-class paltry existence with shouting, cheap music and suburban trains: it is impossible to see what the future might hold for her — if she is to have one at all. This flat, dull and bleak universe, this "world with no mercy," lacks so severely any guiding idea, ideal or principle that it is hard, if not altogether impossible, to perceive any chance of a qualitative amelioration of the existence the woman had led. This, then, is what "the world" has come to: although a violent place — violent because of this absence of any guideline what-soever, hurling everyone into the abyss of non-perspective —, this world is also a place where, in a sense, nothing happens any more because nothing really matters. There is simply disheartening doom, failure and carnage, perfectly exemplified by the boyfriend's hours of a terrible struggle against his own death.

Such is the world the fathers have made. In *Ana y los lobos* (AL), made some eight years earlier (and before the re-establishment of democracy in Spain), there were still "fathers," symbolically represent-ed by the lecherous bourgeois, the religious monomaniac and the bloodthirsty officer. While it would be wrong to perceive AL only under the auspices of symbolization, there certainly is an emphatic symbolic component. Still, a definite realistic dimension must not be disregarded. I would like to present the ultimate sequence of AL in French, as a sub-stitute for viewing, by quoting some portions of the description of that very sequence as rendered by the excellent, alas defunct, journal *L'a-vant-scène cinema*. It refers to the scenes following Ana's attempt to quit the strange household where she had been living and which represents a symbol of a certain Spain, dominated by the three pillars: bourgeoisie, military and Catholic religion — and certainly manipulated by a domi-neering mother-figure:

> Ana sort de la maison et traverse la terrasse, sa valise à la main. [...] Brusquement, les trois frères se dressent derrière les buissons et se jet-tent sur Ana. [...] José lui donne une terrible gifle [...] Juan (plan moyen) [...] se couche sur Ana, tenue par les deux autres frères. Mal-gré tout Ana continue à se battre. Juan la viole. [...] Mais ce n'est pas fini. José la pousse, l'oblige à s'agenouiller, puis lui passe des menottes. Les mains d'Ana sont liées derrière son dos. [...] Fernando [...] se penche vers la jeune femme [...] lui coupe les cheveux presque à ras, [...] de plus en plus excité. [...] José, un pistolet à la main, vise Ana à la tête. [Ana asks for pity.] José tire. Ana s'écroule. José tire une deux-ième fois, sur le cadavre d'Ana. Puis il contemple le cadavre avec une

satisfaction sensuelle (gros plan). Le cadavre martyrisé [...] est la dernière image du film. (*L'avant-scène cinéma* 35)[1]

Obviously, even the best, most circumspect description is no substitute for viewing the sequence in question. The brutality depicted here — much less bearable when actually seen and not just read — is certainly archetypical for certain phases of Spanish society. It is, however, also allegorical to a high extent. The surrealistic (or super-realistic) technique has made more than one think of the influence of Buñuel on Saura's films.

In any case, it is obvious that the strategies of presentation have changed profoundly in the decade between AL and DP. Psychoanalytically speaking, the frightening and objectively insupportable super-father —as embodied or typified by Franco — has disappeared; the resulting freedom, though, has to be made commensurable with an apparent collective feeling of loss, void, and absence.

I remember that many a critic voiced concerns as to the presumed growing lack of inspiration in Saura's *œuvre* after the downfall of the franquist régime. If one considers it necessary for a film to consist mainly, if not exclusively, of symbolic opulence, this might, to a certain extent, even be true. This would be a fairly superficial viewpoint, though. But when concentrating on the portrayal of the central female figures by Saura it quickly becomes evident that he merely shifts his strategies of presentation to other realms. Moreover, despite affirmations of the contrary, films such as *Flamenco* or *Tango* contain an impressive amount of well-hidden or, rather, not so prominently positioned political encoding which indeed has to be deciphered — and it may pose a problem of a certain "undecipherability" for people who are not very familiar with Spanish and/or South American history. Let us not forget the fact that the tango was forbidden in most South American military dictatorships — presumably because of a certain corrosive potential.

Major portions of Saura's films seem to be induced by reflections about male-dominated and male-oriented patterns — possibly even up to notions as to how films have to "behave" dramaturgically and aesthetically. Still, by emphasizing our topic, it becomes rather evident that Saura, although certainly somewhat eclipsed by a younger generation

---

[1] "Suddenly, her three brothers come out from behind the bushes and jump at Ana. José slaps her violently. Juan lies down on Ana who is held by the other two brothers. Still, Ana continues to fight. Juan rapes her. But it isn't over yet. José pushes her, forcing her to kneel down and binds her hands. Ana's hands are bound behind her back. Fernando leans over the young woman and cuts her hair very short while he is getting more and more excited. José, with a gun in his hand, aims at Ana's head. [Ana asks for pity.] José pulls the trigger. Ana falls. José pulls the trigger a second time at Ana's corpse. Then he contemplates the corpse with a sensual satisfaction. The martyrized corpse is the last picture in the movie" (*L'avant-scène cinéma* 152 [Nov. 1974]: 35).

of Spanish or Hispanic directors, has created specific methods of his own,[2] and he has certainly understood better than many others the necessity of adapting to ever-changing social realities. While it is undoubtedly adequate to revert to techniques of "symbolization" in Spain of the early 70s, a new reality, in a way cruder, though not necessarily structured in a less confused way, made Saura obviously feel that analyzing violence from 1975 onward could or should be made according to a different fashion or pattern.

In *Taxi de noche* (TN) there are three rather gruesome sequences at the beginning: first, the body of a young woman is pushed out of the car by the "familia" of taxi drivers (including another woman) because she seems to be a drug addict. In the second sequence, another young woman, the witness from the first sequence, confronts her father with her intention not to concur with her family's (petit-)bourgeois aspiration to study at the university whereupon he simply hits her. In this brief scene, it becomes clear that paternalistic authority and domination still exist and that it seems necessary for the young woman to let herself be subdued, at least for the time being. In the third sequence a skinhead-like young male taxi driver insults and mistreats a cultivated gentleman of African descent, despite his first-class Spanish. We are also confronted with a brief scene in which some young people spray the words EUROPA BLANCA on a brick wall, as a sort of graffiti or mural "painting."

Going a step further than merely rendering the "contents" of a given film, it seems quite conceivable that it is "globalization" — having "opened up" Spanish society — which unleashes a new variant of violence. Or is it an additional one? By hitting his daughter the father endorses a very old "social program." The new variant I am referring to is violence against alterity. Drug-addicts, "foreigners," especially people of color, unknown (or not so familiar) traits of societal developments — these and similar factors lead to radical and indeed murderous reactionary tendencies. By calling them "reactionary," I am also referring to the fact that they manifest an obvious reaction in the sense of "conditioned reflex."

The relatively uncommon term of alterity, adopted from psychoanalytical and specifically French parlance — with a Lacanian undertone — should simply be understood as a way to refer to "minor models" which, one way or another, can be distinguished from the "main models" or notions, in short, as the mainstream or "middle of the road" of the dominant type. It is elementary to understand that different forms of violence, and the ways in which they are handled — and, symbolically, "rendered" — by male dominance correspond to either general/

---

[2] It would be an interesting question to examine to what extent Saura's earlier "partner," Geraldine Chaplin, might have contributed to those modifications.

main models or fairly specific, minor ones, thus delineating complementary structures and sub-structures of society. The criterion or standard thus is the white (or "Aryan", "Caucasian") male, preferably Anglo-Saxon, potentially and under certain circumstances a member — it is indeed comparable to the membership in an exclusive London club which does not allow women on its premises — of another old, cultured nation or, rather, cultural tradition, be it Spanish, Italian, French etc. In any case, the key word is "white" as I have already demonstrated by alluding to the racist radicals spraying the words "EUROPA BLANCA" on a wall, words accompanied by a swastika.

There is no place for anyone who is considered to be less or more "different," "other," according to the tendency: "alien." Eventually, step by step, the young woman in TN finds out about the "true nature" of her petit-bourgeois family. Let us remember that she has already disavowed the ideal of social ascent by not continuing her studies. Disoriented as she might be, she seems to have comprehended her parents'/father's request to engage in some university studies as a hypocritical ambition to highlight and supplement her family's presupposed social position and their future. She doesn't mind driving a taxi through Madrid; what she does mind, however, is being forced to do it in a certain way which should make her understand that she is doing this because she has rejected certain paternalistic rules. But what finally really annoys her is the fact that her boyfriend too has succumbed to the fascist ideology resurging in this milieu in a specific yet fairly generalizable way since fascist elements and components are to be found everywhere and anywhere. This resurrection of fascism manifests itself mainly in its most basic form of racism — always the example par excellence of even more and worse things to come: at first there is the verbal blueprint, the "parole" of hatred, followed by physical violence, which tends to get more and more out of hand and ultimately leads to genocide. This sequence can be encountered or detected globally, but there are also, so to speak, indigenous configurations.

Once the young woman has comprehended what she is confronted with — by gradually finding out the base ideological make-up of this caricature of a "Men's World" in which killing the allegedly unfit or not-(quite-)adapted and the "aliens" is considered a virtuous accomplishment — the showdown can't be far. Hence the dramatically active fight against violence — and I am consciously choosing this somewhat problematic phrasing, as there is hardly any pacifism in Saura's oeuvre (a fundamental proposition to which I can subscribe) — is successful: not only is the young woman able to prevail this time, she also pulls off the trick to win her boyfriend back from his fascist entanglement, and finally even literally saves his life. This is compellingly shown in a sensational final sequence reminiscent of the finale of an Italian opera.

It seems a long way from the raped and murdered Ana to this figuration of the late 90's. Although murderous misogyny and machismo persist, be it — sarcastically put — in a modernized form; although women, too, actively participate in the respective occurrences, it is possible to have a chance to fight those behavioural patterns. In 1980 one could, as a woman, just get away. Not bad. In 2000 the woman can fight back. So much for an, after all, positive outlook.

Films by Saura discussed above
with a brief description of the storyline

Ana y los lobos (1972): prod.: E. Querejeta, written by Saura & R. Azcona, director of photography: L. Cuadrado, actors/actresses: G. Chaplin, F. Fernan-Gomez, J. M. Prada, José Vivo, R. Aparicio.

A young female teacher from a foreign country gets a job as a governess in a well-to-do Spanish family who reside in an intriguing large mansion in the country. Apart from the domineering mother, overweight and half-paralysed, there are three sons: the sex-obsessed introvert, the homicidal authoritarian and the religious fanatic. As Ana becomes more and more involved in the three men's phantasms her chances of survival seem to diminish. (However, her brutal murder seems to be "revoked" in a sequel from 1979, entitled *Mamá cumple cien años*.)

Deprisa, deprisa (1980): prod.: E. Querejeta, written by Saura and Querejeta, photography: T. Escamilla, musical score: Los Chunguitos, Lole y Manuel, Los Marismeños, actors/actresses: B. Socuéllamos-Zarco, J. A. Valdelomar, J. M. Hervás Roldán, J. Arias.

A small gang of young petty criminals (car theft etc.), soon joined by the young waitress Angela, lives on a day-to-day basis in the outskirts of Madrid. A somewhat more consequential coup, the robbing of a bank, miscarries miserably: with the exception of Angela who, finally moving on to an uncertain future, is trying to save her boyfriend, they all die.

Taxi (de noche) (1997): producers: TVE, Saura, Canalplus, written by Saura, photography: V. Storaro, music: Manu Chao, actors/actresses: Ingrid Rubio, Carlos Fuentes.

A gang of taxi drivers from Madrid, clearly fascist and about to be integrated in a totally racist neo-Nazi organization, does away with drug addicts, transsexuals and foreigners. As the daughter of one of the members of the gang finds out about what's going on, she also realizes that her boyfriend is about to be "recruited" by the paramilitary neo-Nazi conspiracy. In the end she is able to redeem the young man by killing the instigator of the fascist organization.

Rocío Silva Santisteban
Boston University

Cuidado zona de deslizamientos
La cuestión de la estética y el poder en la recepción de los debates sobre "literatura femenina" en el Perú

> Pretendo, simplemente,
> desplazar algunos milímetros las cosas,
> pero verán que unos pocos milímetros
> pueden introducir un gran desplazamiento.
> Es decir que si en la perspectiva inicial
> hay una pequeña brecha, a medida que se avanza,
> la separación respecto de lo que estamos
> acostumbrados a percibir será cada vez mayor.
> Jacques-Allain Miller, *Los signos del goce*.

Preámbulo

Considerando la estética de lo corporal o lo que llamaré la *posición políti-ca desde el cuerpo femenino* como espacio específico de la producción de mi discurso crítico, y partiendo de un método que tenga como punto de partida la propuesta de la crítica como *deslizamiento*, me propongo analizar la recepción del debate sobre literatura femenina[1] en el Perú. No obstante, esta intención tiene que circunscribirse a la realidad de las pocas páginas de una ponencia y a la restricción del tiempo de la inves-tigación, por lo tanto, sólo me limitaré a iniciar mis pesquisas.

Debo señalar y hacer explícito, pues será evidente en las próximas páginas, que mi interés oculto pero prioritario es en realidad desarro-llar el concepto *posición política del cuerpo femenino* y plantear el método del *deslizamiento* como posibilidad teórica real y factible para investigar desde "sujetos subordinados" los debates que tienen origen en esa

---

[1] El término "literatura femenina" ha sido debatido desde diversas instancias dentro de la crítica literaria feminista, desde las propias propuestas de las escritoras y desde otras entradas literarias, teóricas y críticas. Se trata, por supuesto, de un término muy polémi-co que muchas veces reduce el problema de la producción textual de las mujeres para homogeneizarla. No es un término que me parezca, personalmente, feliz para hablar del complejo problema de la textualización desde la *posición política del cuerpo femenino*, no obstante, lo uso puesto que con esa nomenclatura ha entrado al debate en el medio peruano.

misma subordinación. En otras palabras: la propuesta de investigación y lectura crítica es sólo el pretexto para lo anterior. Por lo mismo, mi interés al acercarme al debate sobre la literatura femenina o la literatura escrita por mujeres y su recepción desde la prensa y la academia es desmadejar el uso subliminal del poder a través de cánones propuestos como hegemónicos (sobre todo en la construcción del canon literario peruano) así como descifrar y entender por qué, en determinado momento, la crítica abre sus puertas hacia la presencia, por lo menos, del debate y deja de invisibilizarlo aunque convierte en gueto la producción cultural de las mujeres[2].

Por razones de espacio en esta ponencia sólo he considerado tres discursos receptivos en torno a ese debate: el de José Carlos Mariátegui; el de José Miguel Oviedo y algunos artículos periodísticos aparecidos en diarios de circulación nacional y firmados por distintos escritores y críticos como el propio Oviedo, Antonio Cisneros, Ronaldo Menéndez y un texto anónimo.

La razón por la cual he privilegiado estos tres espacios de recepción es por la importancia que considero tiene cada uno en distintas instancias y registros. Es José Carlos Mariátegui uno de los forjadores del canon literario peruano a través de su ensayo *El proceso de la Literatura* (181-ss). La periodización que propone ha sido prácticamente recogida por todos los historiadores literarios posteriores y a pesar de mis pesquisas, no tengo información sobre alguna crítica pormenorizada que analice los supuestos desde los que parte para hablar sobre las mujeres y la literatura[3]. Por lo tanto, me parece imprescindible rastrear este tema en sus artículos y ensayos.

Por otro lado, José Miguel Oviedo, más allá de la importancia que tiene como crítico literario, hoy es uno de los últimos autores de una de las más extensas y ambiciosas historias literarias. Se trata de la *Historia de la Literatura Hispanoamericana*, editada en cuatro tomos por Alianza Editorial durante el año 2000. No es difícil imaginar que este texto se convertirá, al igual que otros análogos anteriores de autores con similares propuestas críticas, en una de las fuentes de información sobre literatura, obras y autores más consultada por estudiantes y profesores de ambas orillas y, sobre todo, de los centros de producción teórico-literaria de los Estados Unidos. En este sentido lo que Oviedo propone

---

[2]En relación con el tema del *gueto* se han planteado desde diversos espacios críticas a la formulación de esta propuesta. Doris Moromisato y otras escritoras consideran que no se trataría simplemente de un gueto en tanto, también, ha sido una construcción de las propias autoras.

[3]Sara Beatriz Guardia en *Voces y cantos de las mujeres* (CEMHAL, 1999) esboza un acercamiento a este punto; sin embargo, me parece que confunde la propuesta de Mariátegui en relación a la forma cómo usa los términos "poetisa", "poesía de mujeres" y "poesía de hembra".

como historia de la literatura es en rigor una propuesta canónica: recoge, escoge y excluye. Mi interés radica en saber en qué medida ha incluido y cómo lo ha hecho a las escritoras pero, más que eso, cuál es su visión sobre "la literatura femenina", así como su posición en lo relativo al debate que la literatura femenina genera.

También me interesa rastrear en qué momento del debate sobre la literatura femenina nos encontramos y analizar las resistencias de la prensa nacional o su supuesto aliento y curiosidad. Considero que hoy en día el espacio de difusión de la crítica cultural en los medios de comunicación es una de las formas más rotundas de consolidar el "reconocimiento" de un canon literario. Es decir, el capital simbólico que prima en las marchas y contramarchas del campo literario en nuestro país (en términos de Bourdieu), no se da básicamente dentro de la denominada "academia" (en el Perú "la universidad") sino en las páginas de los periódicos y de las revistas no-especializadas. Es así como la reafirmación del propio campo de la literatura se va consolidando, no en las aulas como antes, sino en la vitrina pública de las páginas de revistas, diarios y otras publicaciones efímeras. Por eso me parece sumamente importante analizar lo que los diversos críticos y glosadores o simplemente comentaristas, afirman o niegan en torno a este debate. Generalmente la inmediatez y la exigencia de actualidad son los peores consejeros a la hora de intentar colocar algunas ideas en relación con un libro, un autor o una propuesta estética en este tipo de escritos; sin embargo, esta presión por la actualidad también "suelta la pluma" de algunos comentaristas periodísticos que en otras circunstancias tal vez encorsetarían sus ideas dentro de los parámetros de lo "políticamente correcto" (supongo que esta es una de las razones de comentarios tan gruesos argüidos por diversos columnistas).

Entonces, según mi entender, el canon literario en el Perú se construye desde múltiples espacios: pero desde los periódicos se reafirma, se aseguran los muros que le dan autoridad, se levantan las celdillas internas y, paradójicamente, desde cierto sector de la academia (tantas veces marginal dentro de los mismos muros institucionales) se intenta descentrarlo, minándolo, ampliándolo, repudiando sus lógicas, sacándolo de encuadre, luchando desde los bordes (como, por cierto, es el caso de este mismo seminario). No obstante, las resistencias en la crítica periodística permiten dar cuenta también de la renuencia de algunos críticos, teóricos e investigadores frente a las propuestas de la hermenéutica feminista o a la perspectiva de género aplicada a la crítica cultural que pueden encontrarse en distintos espacios de la aparentemente renovada academia/universidad. Desgraciadamente en este breve espacio es imposible desarrollar este punto que, por otro lado, es sintomático de nuestras propias posiciones discursivas.

Talud /alud /deslizamientos
(metáforas geográficas y análisis crítico)

La imagen física del talud continental es la forma que condensa los significados de lo monolítico, lo denso, la verticalidad. El talud continental es aparentemente inmutable y eterno, y siempre frente a él nos percibimos pequeños, insignificantes e impotentes. Su forma tradicional es la de una rampa (en el caso del Perú con 4° de declive), pero, a veces, en las zonas de la costa, se "corta" y cobra la forma de una inmensa muralla, una pared de tierra de dimensiones increíbles, que va a componer lo que llamaremos "el terreno que pisamos". Vivimos, sufrimos y gozamos, generalmente, sobre este final del talud continental (la plataforma continental) y no nos damos cuenta de la fuerza de su presencia, de su magnitud. Sólo advertimos su verdadera proporción cuando, gracias a situarnos al costado de uno de esos "cortes", desde una playa o desde el mar, podemos percibirlo en un ángulo inferior a él; mientras nos encontremos encima es simplemente el lugar de la disposición de nuestras casas y de nuestros cuerpos. Pero si por algún motivo podemos "percibirlo" en su exacta dimensión nos pasma porque parece omnipotente. Sin embargo, no siempre es así: a veces, por ciertos movimientos internos, el talud continental puede desprenderse. Es más: puede caer por completo arrasado por las lluvias que lo convierten en un huayco costero, en un alud.

Talud y alud: se trata de dos formas de localizarnos frente al mundo y de dos estrategias de entender y percibir. Junto a la unidad, el dominio, la transparencia existe la posición contraria: la fragmentariedad, lo performativo, la opacidad. Los deslizamientos son, entonces, maneras, menguadas, de afirmarse en el eje simbólico del alud: desprender, deconstruir, desterritorializar.

Mi propuesta es plantear aquí que, en el plano cultural, *un deslizamiento es una estrategia discursiva para descolocar las significaciones y relocalizarlas según nuestro propias propuestas y tal vez según nuestra propia disposición*. El deslizamiento puede convertirse en una forma de lectura y en una base para sustentar una nueva propuesta crítica. El deslizamiento plantearía como impulso vital el salir de la esfera de lo monolítico y emplazar las búsquedas en un ir directo hacia un terreno por conocer (lo no-nombrado). La propuesta no es el abismo sino la ruta que lleva de un lugar definido a otro por definir.

En este sentido —en el sentido de los caminos entre la absolutamente conocido y constatado y los caminos por definir— considero que las propuestas feministas vinculadas con la crítica cultural o lo que algunos denominan la perspectiva de género dentro de lo literario y lo estético, permiten deslizar con cierto énfasis algunos de los supuestos y presupuestos monolíticos y adentrarnos en las nuevas formas de percepción y conocimiento de la "modernidad reflexiva", para plantearlo en términos de Giddens (1999) y, particularmente, de esta modernidad reflexiva y contradictoria que es la peruana (con sus grandes embalses premodernos).

Si la modernidad hoy nos propone pensar la representación como un acontecer, como un discurrir, como un devenir (Deleuze) y ya no como algo definitivamente dado, la crítica como exégesis o la crítica como interpretación no nos permitirían reflexionar sobre las nuevas representaciones. En las arenas movedizas de las sociedades actuales, la crítica estética podría ser, asimismo, en tanto que deslizamiento de sentido, una forma de constatar los "otros deslizamientos" del arte contemporáneo, es decir, una forma de abordar el quiebre inexplicable que se produce desde una experiencia sensible.

Es así que la crítica como deslizamiento de sentido, es decir, como relocalización de las propuestas estéticas y políticas de los productos culturales[4], permite ya no el "juicio" que cierra un texto desde un veredicto de validez sino el deslizamiento que "abre" el texto a múltiples lecturas desde la suya propia, que por cierto, será siempre provisional.

En este sentido recuperamos lo que propone Gadamer sobre la crítica estética, que no puede pasar —como la crítica del gusto— por un "convencer con argumentos", sino que debe compartir el riesgo estético del propio texto (su abismarse más allá del talud). "Esto es el arte: crear algo ejemplar sin producirlo meramente por reglas. Y no se puede separar en esta relación la creación del genio y la cogenialidad del receptor" (63-64). Se trata del más provocador desafío y hay que tomarlo o claudicar.

Por otro lado, continuando con el riesgo, enfatizamos que el carácter específico de esta crítica como deslizamiento de sentido se concentraría en reorganizar las significaciones de un producto cultural en "otros terrenos": relocalizar los supuestos "universales" en su particular dimensión histórica y, por supuesto, sacar a flote y analizar aquellos elementos[5] que constituyen el *inconsciente político* del texto (Jameson)[5].

Por otro lado, dentro de la desterritorialización y su posterior reterritorialización en un espacio marcado, Susana Reisz plantea abiertamente reterritorializar lo íntimo y propio como lector/crítico/analista/comentarista creativo y especificar la localización del sujeto con la

---

[4]Productos culturales y ya no "obras de arte". Productos culturales en la medida que están instalados históricamente y su lectura será siempre localizada, situada. Las "obras de arte" están enmarcadas desde una estética que se pretende metafísica cuya validación es eterna y universal, cuestión con la que discrepamos.

[5]"... en semejante sociedad [de la imagen y del espectáculo], saturada de mensajes y con experiencias 'estéticas' de toda clase, las cuestiones mismas de una vieja estética filosófica necesitan ser historizadas radicalmente y puede esperarse que se transformen en el proceso de manera irreconocible" (12).

finalidad de plantear una propuesta subversiva de análisis crítico. Siguiendo las propuestas de Silvia Molloy sostiene: "desfamiliarizar la escena demasiado familiar de la lectura crítica impersonal y de crear en los lectores una incomodidad que favorezca la percepción de la 'duplicidad' de los textos analizados, es decir, de las suturas, lagunas, contradicciones y puntos ciegos a lo que un estudio supuestamente objetivo y despersonalizado no suele prestar atención" (48).

Propongo que la crítica como deslizamiento, en resumen, sea una forma de ejercer resistencia política ante la ilusión de unidad y hegemonía de los textos, en principio, y de los sistemas simbólicos en última instancia. La perturbación de la inercia vital (el *impromtu estético* al que se refiere Kant) es el inicio de la experiencia estética que, por cierto, no se circunscribe a una experiencia de lo bello sino a otra suerte de experiencia de lo sensible: ¿la experiencia de la intensidad?, ¿del goce[6] y por lo tanto de lo temible?, ¿de lo pulsional?, ¿una forma de simbolización desde lo trasgresor e innombrable? En todo caso una crítica estética "deslizada" sería una forma provocadora de abordar lo perturbador del arte.

2. Estética corporal: la voz del sujeto del discurso crítico

La experiencia estética es producto de un cruce entre lo cultural, es decir, lo inherente a la estructura de nuestra experiencia humana y lo sensible (sensitivo). Pero, ¿es posible arrancar lo específico cultural de la experiencia sensible? La experiencia directa de los sentidos incluso está marcada también por un campo simbólico aprendido, por lo tanto, y en mi opinión, no existe universalidad de lo estético. Sin embargo, en la medida que nuestras experiencias corporales pueden ser bastante próximas y bastante diferentes en tanto que somos mujeres y hombres, ¿cómo se puede entrar en un análisis estético desde la experiencia sensible corporal femenina?, ¿cómo escudriñar los resquicios no cubiertos por la cultura de los mandatos "universales" androcéntricos?, ¿existe algún pliegue, borde, resquicio que pueda producir el deslizamiento que esperamos?

Considero que existe un espacio teórico, de extrema franqueza subjetiva, que puede permitir ese deslizamiento o en todo caso "acomodar el terreno" para que el deslizamiento suceda. Este espacio teórico consiste en asumir (o afrontar, como se quiera) la subjetividad del hablante

---

[6]Me refiero por cierto al goce según Lacan, es decir, a aquello que resulta intolerable al organismo, que está fuera de la simbolización y cuyo sentido es constante y vuelve siempre al mismo lugar para provocar perturbación (sufrimiento/satisfacción). Para Zizek el goce es un factor político cuyo estatuto está ensamblado desde el discurso ideológico.

de un texto desde su corporeidad en tanto que somos hombres o mujeres, es decir, desde el cuerpo engenerado (Lauretis).

Una estética anclada en lo corporal es de alguna manera una estética que regresa al eje materialista para generar posturas sobre nuestra relación con la cultura. El cuerpo es, en definitiva, junto con la muerte, la única certeza que nos resta. Es lo dado y lo construido, al mismo tiempo.

Entonces nos encontramos ante dos posibilidades corporales: masculino y femenino (es necesario remarcar aquí que tanto cuerpo masculino como cuerpo femenino son dos referentes simbólicos). El cuerpo masculino es el cuerpo del discurso y de la Razón (del que hablan y al que se refieren), así como el cuerpo de la construcción de tecnologías del yo (Foucault) y de prácticas del micropoder. Dentro de la tradición se trata de una posición localizada como dominante, colonizadora y fálica en tanto que *detentadora del poder del símbolo*. Esto no significa, por cierto, que el cuerpo masculino no haya sido el centro de prácticas subalternas, pero, en primera instancia y dentro de la cultura occidental, es uno de los espacios de producción de poder simbólico. En la cultura escrita, por ejemplo, desde la Epopeya de Gilgamesh o desde la Biblia, el cuerpo masculino ostenta la práctica de centrar sobre sí y en sí todas las victorias, todos los relatos, todos los discursos (el ejemplo más claro es el discurso crístico de la resurrección en cuerpo y alma)[7].

Hoy y aquí en el Perú el cuerpo masculino —las "boloñas", lo "testiculado y hormonado"— continúa en ese mismo eje falocéntrico, aunque desacreditado, sin posibilidades de resignificación, encorsetado por sus propias ambiciones simbólicas de una erección permanente que no lo lleva al placer sino a la tautología: el vacío de sentido.

Para la mujer, por el contrario, el cuerpo femenino generalmente ha sido *deshabitado* porque, tras las presiones de las miles de representaciones sociales que la obligan a ser la referencia de la belleza por antonomasia, la mujer ha vivido su cuerpo como ajeno, como "perteneciente sin pertenencia" (García Canal 1996), como un "otro" para sí misma. Es por este motivo, por la presión de una "estética basada en el mandato de la belleza para el cuerpo femenino" que muchas mujeres han optado por negar el cuerpo fugando de lo sólido: la anorexia nerviosa es una manera de escapar de la gravedad hacia la levedad de un cuerpo imposible.

Pero hoy en día desde muchos espacios, feministas o no, el cuerpo femenino es resemantizado para otorgarle *sustancia*. Esto ha sucedido en el arte desde la literatura, la plástica, el cine y la danza moderna. Esto

---

[7]"Pues aquí se nace sin unión física, ni deseo carnal, ni querer de hombre: éstos han nacido de Dios. Y el Verbo se hizo carne y habitó entre nosotros, hemos visto su gloria, lo que corresponde al Hijo Único cuando su Padre lo glorifica" Juan 1, 13-14

ha sucedido también en la teoría: Hélène Cixous y otras autoras europeas anclan sus textos no sólo en la exacerbación de la presencia del sujeto hablante (yo cognoscente) como un ser localizado en un cuerpo femenino sino también en las posibilidades que el cuerpo femenino por sí mismo (cavidades, hondonadas, depresiones, huecos y los juegos de represión-resistencia en torno a esta geografía corporal) podría permitir en la construcción simbólica del pensamiento, ya no sólo artístico, sino hermenéutico. La llamada teoría corporal de la escritura pública según el calificativo de Mariaca (1999).

En tanto que la realidad es un efecto de significación, la posición desde el cuerpo femenino (*loci corpori femminae*), que no implica necesariamente que se deba poseer un cuerpo de mujer para asumirla, permite proponer diferentes/otros códigos de estructuración de sentido que escapan a la construcción hegemónica de lo simbólico y pueden representar una fuerza libidinal o pulsional totalmente enérgica y propositiva. Esta experiencia de la marginalidad simbólica de este nuevo *cuerpo femenino con sustancia* puede subvertir la economía patriarcal (la sedimentada racionalidad "universal") para privilegiar la experiencia subjetiva y el conocimiento por otras vías alternas (intuitivas, emotivas, pragmáticas) en equilibrio con el pensamiento reflexivo.

El cuerpo femenino o el cuerpo de la mujer ha creado desde una nueva forma de gestión, autopercepción y autorepresentación simbólica que disiente de la representación tradicional una nueva posición discursiva y, por lo tanto, una disposición política que sería lo que he venido llamando la *posición política del cuerpo femenino*. Si bien es cierto que la construcción y origen de este nuevo espacio ha partido de la exploración corporal en la mujer no se queda en lo somático sino que deviene en simbólico para, esta vez, abrir un nuevo espacio de representación. Por este motivo, porque lo somático permanece atrás, no es necesario ser mujer para gestar una obra creadora o crítica desde la *posición política del cuerpo femenino* o desde esta estética corporal. En este sentido asumimos y reciclamos para nuestros propósitos lo que señala Iris Zavala en relación a la propuesta lacaniana de la imposibilidad de un "universal" Mujer en el orden de la cultura:

> "Pero si permanecemos en la tesis de Lacan, quien se alinea en el lado femenino puede ser anatómicamente hombre o mujer y todo debiera conducirnos a un proceso de desidentificación y desfalicización. Y ello tendría consecuencias importantes en el orden ideológico y político" (Zavala 2001, 57)

La *posición política del cuerpo femenino* como localización política no sería excluyente pues no deviene de una naturalización de las diferencias ni de un temor a la alteridad. La *posición política del cuerpo femenino* es una opción simbólica que hace mucho ha sido asumida como propia por diversos productores culturales. En el Perú podemos mencionar a tres como los más representativos dentro de la literatura: César Vallejo en algunos de sus *Poemas Humanos*, Jorge Eduardo Eielson en *El cuerpo de Giulia-no* y César Moro en sus *Cartas a Antonio*[8].

"Teorizar el cuerpo tanto como corporizar la teoría pasa por afirmar el valor táctico de un conocimiento situado [...] Gracias a la politización del cuerpo femenino, entonces, los mecanismos de la representación colonial están pudiendo ser explicados y derrotados a través de esa extraordinaria estrategia de guerrilla simbólica" (Mariaca 34).

Precisamente esta es la doble intención de esta ponencia: localizar (situar) el conocimiento y la producción del análisis y plantear una estrategia guerrillera. La imagen a la que echa mano Guillermo Mariaca para canalizar su entusiasmo por este tipo de estrategia dentro de los discursos literarios en América Latina es bastante elocuente. En todo caso, hiperbólica o no, explica en sí misma la forma cómo se percibe en relación con su despliegue: la guerrilla es focalizada, sostenida, fragmentada, planteada como una red, organizada sin centros, en "células" y pequeños piquetes y avanza lentamente por todos los flancos. Pero en realidad el punto más interesante de su propuestas no es sólo la homologación con las tácticas guerrilleras, sino la oposición a los mecanismos de colonización.

El deslizamiento desde lo corporal femenino —aventura hacia el abismo— podría vincularse con la propuesta de la estética nómada que plantean algunas feministas como Rosi Braidotti. Ella sostiene que los desplazamientos nómades designan un estilo creativo de transformación, pero para evitar que las estrategias del nomadismo se ritualicen y pierdan de este modo su "efecto de sentido" es imprescindible corporizar las propuestas.

> "El punto de partida de mi esquema del nomadismo feminista no es sólo un movimiento de oposición crítica contra el falso universalismo del sujeto, sino también la afirmación positiva del deseo de las mujeres de manifestarse y dar validez a las formas diferentes de subjetividad femenina. El punto de partida de este proyecto (teórico y creativo) es la necesidad de situar a las mujeres de la vida real en posiciones de subjetividad discursiva. Aquí los términos claves son la corporización y las raíces corporales de la subjetividad" (Braidotti 185).

Considerando que "la naturaleza de la obra de arte no es una cuestión de por qué sino de dónde" (Zizek 2000), me parece impres-

---

[8]Excedería la intención de estas páginas la explicación de por qué propongo a estos tres autores, pero como ejemplo, planteo que en las *Cartas a Antonio*, Moro asume una posición subalterna en relación con el objeto amoroso de la lírica tradicional y arma, asimismo, su poética y erótica desde una situación en la que opta por calificar al otro de "hombre" en la medida que el sujeto de la enunciación se resiste a la tradicional moralidad.

cindible el ejercicio de localización corporal para definir nuevos términos de análisis. Planteo, entonces, retomando la propuesta del inicio, un análisis desde mi peculiar condición de observadora participante de estos debates en torno al tema "literatura femenina" desde mi *posición política del cuerpo femenino*, sin ningún disfraz y con ninguna pretensión de objetividad equilibrada y distante. Este trabajo forma parte de una lucha simbólica, la única diferencia entre mi postura y la de los autores que analizo, es que yo la hago explícita.

3. El corpus

3.1. Mariátegui

No obstante que es Mariátegui quien plantea explícitamente una localización política como sujeto crítico dentro del texto analítico mucho antes que mi tímida confesión de propósitos anterior, no asume en la praxis de su construcción textual su posición discursiva y al final del famoso ensayo sobre la literatura peruana sigue erigiéndose como el detentador de la autoridad y proponiendo un canon que excluye de un solo olvido a un grupo importante de escritoras y, asimismo, evalúa la producción literaria de la Colonia con una mirada en exceso homogeneizante.

Mariátegui *localiza* su entrada al análisis como un testimonio de parte y admite que trae al debate sus "pasiones e ideas políticas" (asumimos que también sus prejuicios). Sostiene Mariátegui en la introducción a *El Proceso de la Literatura*: "mi concepción estética se unimisma, en la intimidad de mi conciencia, con mis conceptos morales, políticos, religiosos y que, sin dejar de ser concepción estrictamente estética, no puede operar independientemente o diversamente" (182).

Esta propuesta la plantea para advertir (y guiñar al lector) y enfrentarse a críticos como José de la Riva Agüero. El objetivo de Mariátegui con este ensayo es buscar el momento de inicio de la "literatura peruana" como tal, más allá de las propuestas colonizadas y epigonales de la literatura virreinal (que él consideraba española). Al margen de qué podemos discrepar o no con su propuesta (a la luz de los estudios poscoloniales contemporáneos sus afirmaciones resultan poco penetrantes), es necesario dejar en claro que su proyecto político cultural asume una instancia materialista y obviamente clasista para considerar sus jerarquías y organizar su periodización. Sin embargo, no por ello, es un proyecto contracultural y antihegemónico, pues mantiene las mismas reglas que las propuestas tradicionales de la época —blandidas precisamente por sus contrarios ideológicos (Riva Agüero, Clemente Palma)— sólo que protagonizadas por autores más cercanos a su propia propuesta estética rupturista (indigenistas y vanguardistas).

En relación con el debate sobre la literatura femenina, Mariátegui omite y excluye la presencia y los textos de las autoras pertenecientes a la denominada "primera generación de mujeres ilustradas en el Perú" (Denegri). No se refiere ni dice nada sobre Clorinda Matto de Turner, ni sobre Mercedes Cabello de Carbonera, ni sobre Juana Manuela Gorriti. No debe de tratarse de desconocimiento, pero en todo caso, excluyó de su propuesta en este "proceso literario" a autoras que compartían con él algunos de sus ideales y por lo menos su anticlericalismo. La única mujer a la que incluye Mariátegui en su "proceso" es a una autora contemporánea suya: Magda Portal (1903-1989). Considera Mariátegui que con el advenimiento de Portal "al Perú le nació su primera poetisa", excluyendo, tal vez porque consideraba al período colonial como un momento no-peruano, a las poetisas anónimas de la colonia: Amarilis y Clarinda, consignadas por Ricardo Palma en sus *Tradiciones peruanas*.

Mariátegui sostiene que antes de Portal sólo habían habido "mujeres de letras" y que recién con ella surge una verdadera poetisa. No especifica la diferencia sustancial entre unas y la otra, pero se deduce que sugiere una diferencia de "rangos" o "jerarquías" en relación con la seriedad del propio oficio o la profesionalización del autor. Sin embargo, más adelante sostiene que: "La poetisa es hasta cierto punto un fenómeno de nuestra época. Las épocas anteriores produjeron sólo poesía masculina. La de las mujeres también lo era, pues se contentaban con ser variación de sus temas líricos o de sus motivos filosóficos" (Mariátegui 1968, 255). Parecería que intuitivamente Mariátegui en estas líneas logra captar uno de los problemas centrales de la producción literaria de la mujer a lo largo de la historia: su travestismo lírico, que no consiste en adscribirse simplemente a usar seudónimos masculinos, sino en revestir la producción de una mujer en estrategias marcadas por lo masculino entendido como "universal".

Más adelante Mariátegui continúa con esta reflexión: "La poesía [antes] no tenía el signo del varón, no tenía el signo de la mujer —virgen, hembra, madre—. Era una poesía asexual. En nuestra época, las mujeres ponen al fin en su poesía su propia carne y su propio espíritu. La poetisa es ahora aquella que crea una poesía femenina. Y desde que la poesía de la mujer se ha emancipado y diferenciado espiritualmente de la del hombre, las poetisas tienen una alta categoría en elenco de todas las literaturas. Su existencia es evidente e interesante a partir del momento en que ha empezado a ser distinta" (255)

La diferencia en la producción cultural de las mujeres, ese problema que hoy es refrendado por las feministas posestructuralistas y el feminismo de la diferencia, es entendido por Mariátegui como el elemento que permite una creación propia y no apropiada, y como un aporte singular que precisamente le da un énfasis especial a la producción femenina.

Asimismo, Mariátegui hace algunos comentarios generales sobre Juana de Ibarburu, Delmira Agustini, Gabriela Mistral y Blanca Luz Brum, demostrando una vez más que se trataba de un crítico sumamente informado. Luego concluye "la poesía un poco envejecida en el hombre, renace rejuvenecida en la mujer" (256). Pero, ¿cuáles son las características de este rejuvenecimiento según el Amauta? Aquí Mariátegui no se salva de caer nuevamente en los tópicos vinculados con lo femenino. Sostiene "la poesía que en los poetas tiende a una actitud nihilista, deportiva, escéptica, en las poetisas tiene *frescas raíces y cándidas flores*. Su acento acusa más elán, más fuerza biológica" [subrayado nuestro] (256). Una vez más lo femenino se mantiene dentro de la órbita de la naturaleza y lo biológico, es decir, Mariátegui continúa planteando las tradicionales dicotomías entre masculino y femenino, aquellas dicotomías tantas veces analizadas y deconstruidas por todos los discursos feministas y de género. Sin embargo, Mariátegui comenta que lo nuevo, lo renovado, es el ingreso de este "elán" natural y biológico al ámbito de la cultura. En eso consistiría la diferencia y el aporte de las mujeres para el autor.

Más adelante analiza la obra hasta entonces publicada de Magda Portal y en una clara estrategia para que su poesía califique "a pesar de" la saca de lo femenino (del mismo modo como Octavio Paz "sacó" a Blanca Varela de lo femenino llamando a su poesía "valerosa y mujeril"). Mariátegui la califica como "esencialmente lírica y humana". El calificativo de "humano" lo plantea para emparentar su propuesta con la de Vallejo, sosteniendo una posible genealogía a través de la piedad (no obstante, la forzada genealogía no se propone para vincular a un poeta reconocido con una poetisa aún poco conocida, pues Vallejo en ese entonces no tenía la importancia que adquirió posteriormente). Mariátegui vuelve a sus anteriores planteamientos sobre la originalidad y renovación de lo femenino: "Exenta de egolatría megalómana, de narcisismo romántico, Magda Portal nos dice: 'Pequeña soy...!'" (256) En realidad la humanidad a la que apunta Portal según Mariátegui es muy distinta de la humanidad vallejiana: esa piedad está centrada en la propia nimiedad del yo poético, en su escasa "megalomanía" y en su afán de pasar inadvertido, pequeño, insignificante. "En su poesía Magda Portal nos da, ante todo, una límpida versión de sí misma. No se escamotea, no se mistifica, no se idealiza" (257). No, claro que no, porque en realidad se ninguna, se empequeñece. Los juegos del poder vuelven a echar carga sobre este comentario y Mariátegui no se libra de sus propios prejuicios: la "limpia versión" de una mujer es la humildad, el ninguneo, la pequeñez.

En el comentario sobre Magda Portal, luego de analizar e incluir dos estrofas largas de sus versos, termina Mariátegui afirmando sobre las "otras" posibilidades de la autora: las potencias oscuras de su poesía y las oscuras contradicciones de su alma. Finalmente, en un remate elegante, Mariátegui deja abierta la posibilidad de una cierta mayor heterogeneidad de los versos que, según él y desde entonces, planteaban muchas y nuevas posibilidades de renovación de la literatura peruana. Sus pronósticos no tuvieron mayor acierto en relación ya no a las posibilidades estéticas del discurso de Magda Portal sino a la realidad artística de su obra: no fue renovadora, no creo discípulas, no planteó estéticamente una ruptura con el orden y permaneció, aunque desde los bordes, dentro del ámbito de lo femenino tradicional (me parece que no hay que confundir su propuesta política vanguardista y rebelde con sus planteamientos y aportes estéticos).

Pero Mariátegui se ha adentrado nuevamente en el debate sobre la literatura femenina desde una propuesta menos orgánica que su ensayo sobre la literatura peruana. Es un artículo sobre temas italianos incluidos en sus *Cartas de Italia* que sirve de presentación e introducción de difusión de la literatura escrita por mujeres en Italia. En "Mujeres de Letras en Italia" Mariátegui glosa la obra de la poeta Ada Negri. En este comentario Mariátegui nuevamente entra a analizar en detalle el tema de la diferencia entre "mujer que escribe poesía" y poetisa, precisamente para considerar que la propuesta artística de Negri no es la de una "poetisa" sino la de una "mujer que escribe". Y paso a citar en extenso el párrafo:

> "Su poesía ha sido siempre la poesía de una mujer pero no la poesía de una poetisa [...] Y es que los versos de las poetisas en general no son versos de mujer. No se siente en ellos sentimiento de hembra. Las poetisas no hablan como mujeres. Son en su poesía seres neutros. Son artistas sin sexo. La poesía de la mujer está dominada por un pudor estúpido. Y carece por esta razón de humanidad y de fuerza. Mientras el poeta muestra su "yo", la poetisa esconde y mistifica el suyo. Envuelve su alma, su vida, su verdad, en las grotescas túnicas de lo convencional..." (192).

Mariátegui, una vez más, logra centrar el debate precisamente, aunque no lo hace explícito, en los escenarios vinculados al poder de la palabra. Las poetisas "envuelven", es decir, sepultan el poder de su propio gesto detrás de los ropajes de lo convencional: no logran romper con el cerco patriarcal que coloca al centro el discurso del hombre. Esconden su sexo, entonces, no logran construir un verdadero yo como sí lo plantean los poetas. Mariátegui es claro cuando lo advierte: se trata de una cuestión de arte e identidad. La construcción del yo, de la voz del poeta y de la enunciación, pasa específicamente en el caso de las mujeres por sexuar su voz y despojarla de las neutralidades agradables a una forma de entender el mundo excluyendo lo que cada mujer lleva de hembra. Podríamos entender, nuevamente, que para Mariátegui es imprescindible que la voz de una mujer asuma su propia identidad. No obstante, la identidad de la mujer y el hembrismo que reclama como parte integrante de ella se reduce a las pautas y roles tradicionales.

3.2. Oviedo

José Miguel Oviedo, como lo señalamos en la introducción de este trabajo, es uno de los críticos literarios peruanos más conocidos a nivel internacional — sobre todo por sus trabajos sobre la narrativa de Vargas Llosa— y con una producción bastante importante publicada en editoriales internacionales y en periódicos de la región. Su última obra es la *Historia de la Literatura hispanoamericana* (2001). De los cuatro tomos de la obra hemos escogido los dos últimos para el análisis: se trata del tomo 3 que incluye Posmodernismo, Vanguardia y Regionalismo y el tomo 4 que se titula de "Borges al presente".

En ambos tomos Oviedo revisa una serie de obras de escritoras, desde Delmira Agustini y las escritoras de comienzos de siglo afincadas en la cuenca de La Plata (Storni, Ibarburu), así como Gabriela Mistral hasta autoras contemporáneas tan disímiles como Diamela Eltit, Zoé Valdés y Gioconda Belli (aunque este último estudio es uno de los más breves del libro en su conjunto). En relación con las opiniones e información que Oviedo incluye sobre las diversas escritoras, sólo vamos a relevar las que se refieren directamente al debate sobre la literatura femenina o de mujeres, por lo tanto, su opinión en relación con la propia producción de las autoras, esto es, su análisis concreto de los textos, no lo vamos a tomar en cuenta (a menos que dé luz sobre el tema en cuestión).

Habría que señalar que Oviedo, aunque implícitamente lo hace (sobre todo en un artículo publicado en un diario peruano), no se plantea a sí mismo como otro polemista dentro del debate sobre literatura femenina. Al hacer alusión a las escritoras, sobre todo en el tomo 3 de su Historia, hace referencia directa a una especie de polémica oculta con cierta crítica literaria feminista pero no especifica cuál ni a quiénes pretende refutar. El entiende que se tratan de verdades gruesas que circulan dentro de los ambientes académicos pero también entre los lectores no especializados.

Para empezar habría que mencionar que Oviedo considera que la inclusión de escritoras en antologías e historias literarias se ha vuelto un pulseo entre lo que se considera políticamente correcto (para la academia estadounidense, se entiende, y dentro de ella probablemente para los *Women Studies*) y cierta verdad que detentan las propias obras. Para él las feministas y las críticas literarias exageran en lo relativo a este juego de inclusiones/exclusiones. En otras palabras: plantea que la omisión de las mujeres de las historias literarias no se debe simple-

mente a que los críticos no hayan valorado sus obras, sino a que la producción de las mujeres ha sido escasa; no obstante, Oviedo señala claramente la razón de esa escasez: la dedicación de la mujer a la reproducción humana y su dificultad para ingresar en otras esferas más allá de
lo doméstico. Por otro lado insiste en señalar que las pocas autoras que
han detentado una obra importante siempre han sido incluidas en his-
toriografías literarias (como Sor Juana o las mencionadas poetas río-
platenses) y antologías, aunque también señala que estas inclusiones
han estado marcadas casi en su generalidad por los estereotipos clásicos vinculados a las mujeres (dulzura, maternidad, sensibilidad) y que
esto se debe básicamente a la pereza de la crítica. Por otro lado, a pesar
de la gruesa exclusión de Mariátegui con relación a las escritoras de la
primera generación de mujeres ilustradas, Oviedo no la menciona.

En un artículo publicado en *El Dominical* del diario *El Comercio*,
Oviedo sostiene que existen dos mitos "relativos al trabajo literario en
el que están empeñadas las mujeres". El primer mito sería el de la
negación, es decir, el que la literatura escrita por mujeres esté históricamente negada u olvidada. Y el otro mito es la presunta exclusión que
sufrieron las mujeres en el campo literario como otra manifestación de
discriminación. Oviedo reitera que las autoras no han sido ni excluidas
ni olvidadas ni subordinadas y más bien, insiste en que la literatura está
más allá de los problemas de género y sexo:

> "La literatura no tiene en sí misma sexo específico, no porque excluya
> a los sexos o a lo sexual sino porque los incluye a todos de manera
> inevitable. Cuando escriben las mujeres no lo hacen sólo como
> mujeres, lo hacen como seres humanos cuya visión, sensibilidad e
> interés son particulares; igual sucede con los escritores hombres sin
> que nos animemos a hablar de por eso (pues sería ridículo) de una lite-
> ratura masculina" (Oviedo 2: 2001).

Planteados en esos términos parece sumamente coherente decir que
la literatura no tiene sexo (o que tiene los dos). No obstante, a mi parecer, se trata de *otra* posición falogocéntrica[9], en la medida que la plurali-
dad planteada de esa manera es el otro lado de la moneda de la neutralidad anterior porque no reconoce las marcas genérico-sexuales en
los textos entendiendo que los textos son productos de algún sector
"universal" o plurisexual del ser humano.

---

[9]Falogocentrismo es un término acuñado por el filósofo argelino Jacques Derrida para
demostrar la estrecha unión entre el logos paterno (el discurso de lo universal) y el falo
como significante privilegiado. Como lo sostiene el propio Derrida entrevistado por
Cristina de Peretti: "Debido a que la solidaridad entre logocentrismo y falocentrismo es
irreductible, a que no es simplemente filosófica o no adopta sólo la forma de un sistema
filosófico, he creído necesario proponer una única palabra: falogocentrismo, para sub-
rayar de alguna manera la indisociabilidad de ambos caracteres" en Cristina de Peretti,
"Entrevista a Jacques Derrida". *Debate Feminista* 1 v. 2 1990.

"Me he pasado la vida pelándome con quienes caballerescamente me explicaban que no existe literatura de hombre o de mujer, sino que existe literatura a secas, o mejor, Literatura de Ser Humano con mayúsculas, engañosas mayúsculas, pensaba yo, trampa de lo ideal [...]Los genocidios antipáticos —quema de brujas, quema de judíos, esclavización de negros— fueron seguidos por los genocidios simpáticos 'Todos somos iguales, es decir, todos ustedes son iguales a mí'..." (Dujovne 28-30).

Es por este hecho que diversos autores (Culler, Derrida, de Lauretis, Showalter, Cixous) señalan que la mujer debe aprender a escribir como mujer saliéndose de las reglas del logos androcéntrico. Reisz es aún mucho más enfática cuando afirma imperiosamente que "insisto, pues en que escribir (o leer) como mujer es una opción política y que, cuando se la asume, el producto de tal actividad ingresa en un sistema literario que se puede caracterizar como en relación de intersección con el sistema dominante, es decir, que en parte coincide con él y en parte lo erosiona o lo desborda". (Reisz 1996).

Si bien es cierto que escribir como mujer es una actitud política sobre todo porque permite construir diversas variables de textualización desde múltiples ángulos —y esto, por supuesto, no significa que sea necesario marcar el yo del texto con el accidente gramatical correspondiente al femenino— a pesar de que muchas mujeres eviten señalizar sus textos desde la diferencia genérico-sexual, ellos llevarán las huellas de sus cuerpos. Esta huella aparecerá en el momento menos previsto y en múltiples formas de simbolización. La toma de una actitud "política" frente al texto en realidad está vinculada con la conciencia de parte de la autora del "gesto de la escritura" como un gesto de alto rendimiento frente a las estructuras tradicionales de poder. (Reisz 1996).

Como hemos visto el alcance de Oviedo no entra a analizar, discutir o nombrar las innumerables polémicas al respecto, ni da cuenta de lo más serio de la crítica literaria feminista. Es más, por cierto, cuando se refiere a ella siempre insiste en decir que es una falacia que "cada sexo tenga capacidad para describirse sólo a sí mismo", "esa idea de las lectoras y la crítica femenina de que una escritora sea importante sólo por el hecho de ser mujer" y otros clichés de los cuales él mismo no puede abstraerse. Oviedo polemiza, en realidad, con un fantasma que él imagina es la crítica literaria feminista pero que en realidad sólo es una sombra mal armada de clichés y frases hechas que no deben haber sido extraídos de las propuestas más conocidas sobre el tema (Moi, Showalter, Kristeva, Irigaray, Cixous y en América Latina: Olea, Ortega, Lamas, Reisz entre otras).

Por último Oviedo regresa al tema de las esencias: "Esto nos lleva a otro asunto, que apenas si podemos tocar: el de la existencia de una 'literatura femenina'. Sabemos que existe una 'sensibilidad femenina', aunque sea imprecisa, pero es todavía menos seguro que su representación literaria sea menos cabal (o superior) si la hace una mujer [...] La lógica indicaría que la simple afirmación de una 'literatura femenina' implica la de una 'literatura masculina' (para no hablar de la homosexual) que a nadie se le ocurre plantear como categoría crítica." (251)

Luego de haber realizado un análisis histórico sobre las pésimas condiciones de producción cultural de las mujeres en América Latina, Oviedo regresa a las indagaciones metafísicas en torno al arte, la cultura y la literatura. Oviedo confunde, como suele suceder, género con sexo y aún más, con opción sexual, simplificando al máximo una asunto sumamente complejo[10].

Es cierto que la propia crítica literaria feminista no tiene una sola posición al respecto[11] pero sí ha desarrollado una sólida interpretación en torno a la deconstrucción de las esencias, la vinculación entre texto y posición genérica sexual y ha otorgado complejidad al tema de la autoría, la firma, la producción cultural y las forma cómo se organiza el poder simbólico dentro del campo literario (subordinaciones-dominaciones). Oviedo no registra, ni en su artículo ni en su texto historiográfico, una revisión de estos puntos, no obstante que en su bibliografía se encuentran autoras que definitivamente parten de este marco teórico (como Sylvia Molloy o Lucía Guerra).

La literatura no tiene sexo (ni clase, ni género, ni propuestas políticas implícitas) es una sentencia que vincula la excelencia literaria con una suerte de metafísica más allá de cualquier base histórica o social. La

---

[10]El género es la construcción cultural de la diferencia sexual. En tanto es cultural y no biológico o esencial, sobre el "género" pesan las dominaciones y subordinaciones. Cuando se habla de lo masculino y de lo femenino no necesariamente se habla de lo que inherentemente está vinculado a hombres y a mujeres sino que nos referimos a categorías organizadas desde diversos estatutos de poder y que atraviesan todos los campos de la realidad social, sobre todo, el simbólico. Para teóricas como Iris M. Zavala el género no corresponde con lo biológico sino con una posición discursiva, para ella el proceso de sexuación no proviene ni de la biología ni ampliamente de la cultura, sino del lenguaje (Zavala, 1991).

[11]Dentro de la crítica feminista y no-feminista que trabajan el tema de la literatura escrita por mujeres existen diversas posiciones heterogéneas. Las críticas de la escuela norteamericana, con Elaine Showalter a la cabeza, insisten en enfocar los análisis de la escritura de mujer o el "texto femenino" como el producto de un grupo subalterno al dominante, es decir, dentro de relaciones de poder Opresor-Oprimido. Por otro lado dos críticas de la escuela francesa, Heléne Cixous y Luce Irigaray, construyen sus postulados a partir de un recorrido corporal por la mujer, pero continúan planteando que "lo femenino" y "lo masculino" estaría vinculado a ciertos rasgos esenciales. Por el contrario, la propuesta de Julia Kristeva , también del grupo de las teóricas francesas, estaría por recuperar lo anterior a la construcción simbólica falogocéntrica —lo innombrable pero que posee sentidos— para desentrañar los elementos construidos de lo femenino.

neutralidad de lo literario es un tema ampliamente trabajado, criticado y superado, hoy sólo sostenido desde la más tradicional y conservadora propuesta literaria que, desgraciadamente, tiene un eco poderoso en los debates peruanos, sobre todo, a través de la prensa.

3.3. La prensa nacional

No es nueva la forma cómo desde los periódicos y las revistas se va consolidando un canon literario. Definitivamente lo mismo sucedía con *El Mercurio Peruano* en el s. XIX y con la revista *Amauta* a comienzos del s. XX. En ambas se registraban críticas de libros y de autores, pero sobre todo, formas de entender lo que es y no es la literatura peruana (por ejemplo, el debate sobre el indigenismo tuvo como tribuna privilegiada a la revista de Mariátegui). Pero no es éste el espacio para hacer esa pesquisa, simplemente partimos de un hecho consolidado: la prensa peruana ha reafirmado el canon literario, asegurando los muros que le dan autoridad, levantando las celdillas internas que diferencian a unos y a otros, excluyendo, ignorando, olvidando, relegando y, en otros casos, aplaudiendo y promoviendo.

En estos momentos en Lima existen muchos espacios donde se ejerce la crítica periodística. Uno de los más importantes es el diario *El Comercio* y sus múltiples y diversos secciones (cultura, las columnas de opinión, las revistas adjuntas como *Somos* y *El Dominical*). Le siguen *Domingo* del diario *La República* y también la sección diaria de cultura del mismo periódico; la sección de cultura de *Caretas*; las diversas secciones de *El Peruano*; los comentarios de Ismael Pinto en *Expreso* y otros más en diarios a veces efímeros (como fueron *El Sol*, *El Mundo*, etc.). Todos y cada uno de los espacios mencionados han participado, directa o indirectamente, del debate sobre la literatura femenina.

El alcance de esta ponencia no puede comprender un análisis pormenorizado de este debate ni un seguimiento al detalle (tal vez esa tarea sea para un desarrollo posterior). Por este motivo he optado por un corte temporal: los artículos aparecidos durante el año 1999 cuando Lima se convirtió en la sede de tres encuentros que convocaban a escritoras: Se trata en primer lugar del Encuentro Nacional de Escritoras organizado por la Red de Escritoras Latinoamericanas y patrocinado por Woman's World (22 y 23 de julio). En segundo lugar la asociación SIC organizó el I Encuentro de Narradoras Latinoamericanas en el Museo de la Nación (18 y 21 de agosto) y en noviembre la Universidad de Lima organizó el Encuentro Internacional La Mujer en la Literatura. A propósito de estos encuentros — a propósito sólo de la convocatoria de estos encuentros— aparecieron diversos artículos que reaccionaban a sus planteamientos implícitos pues no se referían a ninguna de las ponencias que se presentaron, ni a ninguna de las propuestas que se debatieron en ellos; a excepción de un artículo firmado por Ana María Portugal y publicado por FEMPRES "Narradoras Iberoamericanas: el riesgo de escribir" (2001).

El primero fue un artículo anónimo publicado en el *El Dominical* 25 de julio titulado "¿Un Club Literario?". En él se da cuenta del congreso de Mujeres Narradoras organizado por SIC y se considera que tanto los encuentros como los certámenes de mujeres escritoras hacen énfasis en el hecho extra-literario del sexo del autor desvirtuando la esencia de la literatura: la calidad estética. Parecería irrelevante precisar, aunque lo voy a hacer, que la mayoría de encuentros literarios siempre juegan con otra variable al margen de la literaria: nacionalidad del escritor, origen del texto, etc. Si un encuentro de escritoras pone énfasis en el género, los encuentro de escritores latinoamericanos ponen énfasis en una condición geográfica-política, esto es, también extra-literaria. Los escritores y críticos que opinan lo mencionado líneas arriba han asistido sin mayores problemas de conciencia a diversos encuentros, congresos y simposios "latinoamericanos" o de "jóvenes escritores", etc.

Sobre el mismo tema también opina Ronaldo Menéndez en su "Columna de Sansón" de la sección "Luces" de *El Comercio* titulada "Teología Ecuestre": "... no existe la teología ecuestre, aunque a Santo Tomas de Aquino le gustaran los caballos. Tampoco existe la literatura femenina, aunque a las feministas le gusten los congresos" y más adelante agrega "Aunque vale todo (para organizar congresos de escritores) hay diversos grados de legitimidad: no es lo mismo reunir mujeres narradoras que escritores latinoamericanos. Y es que existe un espacio lingüístico que es Latinoamérica que sirve para explicar la cualidad cultural de una diversidad de obras. Me pregunto para qué sirve definir un espacio sexual dentro del campo literario que no sea para satisfacer voluntades partidistas y beligerantes". (Menéndez 2: 1999).

El columnista cubano jerarquiza pero no explica las razones de sus propias jerarquías, simplemente apunta a la validez de un tipo de encuentros por la ¿unidad lingüística? de América Latina (en realidad debió de plantear una unidad política pues no tenemos ni siquiera la misma lengua en Brasil, las Antillas o Haití). La única manera de ser consecuente con el inmanentismo radical de la literatura pura — bandera que levantan muchos de los comentaristas y columnistas de periódicos — sería organizar un "encuentro de textos". Divertido pero absurdo. Por otro lado descarta de plano que la relación entre sexo y texto no se construya sobre un puente lingüístico hecho que en estos momentos tiene fundamental importancia para la crítica cultural como lo he señalado líneas arriba al mencionar los trabajos de Iris M. Zavala.

En una columna del mismo periódico el poeta Antonio Cisneros, con algo más de humor pero la pluma igualmente empapada en una especie de indignación frente a los "usos y abusos de alguna laya de feminismo mal entendido" ataca también el tema de la reunión: "La próxima semana se inaugura en Lima un encuentro de narradoras (narradores abstenerse). Al mismo tiempo las instituciones del Estado, las empresas y hasta los "talk shows" con cuotas exclusivas para las mujeres tienden a multiplicarse. Y me parece que, como van las cosas, los varones de buena fe (Tobis y Manolitos aterrados) sólo tendrán cabida en los viriles oficios de chofer y guachimán".

Las razones de Cisneros son, a pesar de la acritud, de otra índole: el mencionado párrafo se encuentra dentro de un artículo que reclama contra las cuotas para las mujeres en otros espacios más allá del literario (los cargos públicos). Pero, además, su intención es absolutamente transparente: "aterrado" por saber que hay recursos legales y simbólicos que las mujeres usan (y a veces abusan, es cierto), se imagina un futuro en que la fuerza de la virilidad masculina sólo permita a sus portadores protagonizar oficios subalternos. La increíble transparencia del miedo de enfrentarse a la subordinación como condición -disfrazados de indignación e ironía, sus referencias a los chóferes y guachimanes son explícitas- nos revela una vez más las increíbles formas de recibir este debate en torno al quehacer político y cultural de las mujeres. Cisneros sabe que el mundo "facilitado" para los hombres dentro de la cultura está retrocediendo en términos simbólicos y abriéndose de manera cada vez más importante a la presencia femenina. Por eso reclama la igualdad absoluta: ¿por qué favorecer a las mujeres que ya lo están copando? Su propuesta sin duda se trata de una manera de luchar[12], la última que le resta a este discurso: el humor, la ironía, la aparente intolerancia graciosa y pizpireta (para usar un término caro a Vargas Llosa).

Menéndez, en cambio, no propone nuevos recursos en relación a esta lucha, apuesta por lo seguro: la literatura está más allá del bien y del mal. En la misma página comentada, sostiene que la única forma de llegar al "valor profundo de una obra literaria está más allá de una verificación física: literalmente pertenece al reino de una metafísica". Menéndez no tiene la ironía de Cisneros ni su visión más desenfadada de sus reclamos; él juega en serio y me parece que en este punto están concentradas la mayor cantidad de resistencias de los críticos: ver el hecho literario como metafísico, transhistórico y hasta místico (Menéndez luego compara la profesión del escritor con la del místico, ambos "son elegidos").

Sobre este asunto el artículo anónimo del *Dominical* sostiene que: "revisando la lista de las invitadas al Congreso, hay que notar que algunas tienen una obra importante pero otras no habrían sido invitadas si

---

[12]A propósito, es indispensable señalar aquí que tanto Antonio Cisneros como Ronaldo Menéndez son dos importantes escritores reconocidos internacionalmente, con diversos premios internacionales y publicaciones en el extranjero.

se tratara de un congreso que mide la calidad de la obra y no el género de los autores".

Sostener que lo importante es escribir bien o la calidad de la propia obra de los participantes es una propuesta muy simple que plantea un "falso dilema": excelencia literaria vs. argumentos extra-literarios. No creo que sea posible encapsular a la literatura para vaciar de ella todo lo que no le pertenece por antonomasia. En otras palabras, *la literatura pura no existe*, aún cuando ciertos críticos sigan machaconamente apostando por sus cualidades "esenciales, transhistóricas, metafísicas, divinas". Por lo tanto, lo extra-literario no lo es *per se*, sino dentro de una óptica determinada por patrones culturales que a su vez marcan los valores estéticos. El valor de un producto cultural depende de un entramado muy complejo en el que entran a jugar la ideología, la posición de clase, el género, la etnicidad, la subordinación de los productores y de los receptores, en suma, el poder simbólico

En realidad el argumento del "falso dilema" intenta demarcar el terreno de lo literario para sostener lo que es y no es literatura. Es la típica estrategia que ya ha analizado Pierre Bourdieu como las luchas simbólicas dentro del campo literario. La lucha simbólica en este aspecto se referiría al intento de cambiar categorías de percepción y de apreciación del mundo, de estructuras cognitivas y evaluativas, de sistemas de clasificación, en otras palabras, las bases del código que construye la realidad social (las palabras, los signos, los símbolos, los mitos y la formas de racionalidad) y obviamente las resistencias que se producen contra ese cambio. Para realizar estos cambios es preciso primero cambiar las bases en donde se sustenta la posesión del capital simbólico y la eficacia simbólica de ese capital, pero, como los dice claramente Bourdieu, hay que considerar que el poder simbólico es el poder de hacer cosas con palabras. Establecer una nomenclatura, por ejemplo, o un metalenguaje científico, otorga a los que usan esta nomenclatura un poder simbólico que viene con la palabra pero que puede ir más allá de ella.

En este sentido sostener que "esto no es literatura" o "estos elementos son extraliterarios" es la forma más corriente de lapidar los movimientos renovadores y de ruptura, pero sacar del campo simbólico una propuesta no sólo implica rechazarla, sino incluso excomulgarla e ignorarla. Por otro lado, las luchas dentro del campo literario se dan en dos sentidos: los reaccionarios, aposentados en el campo, fijos, incólumes, luchando por asegurar los muros que le dan autoridad a su campo desde el propio campo y aduciendo lógicas formales e instrumentos racionales (la literatura es neutra/ la estética es universal) y por el otro lado, los revolucionarios, perforando los muros desde los bordes, desde los márgenes, desde lo subalterno, *desterritorializando* el campo, minándolo, ampliándolo, repudiando sus lógicas pero asumiendo su razón, o repudiando su razón y asumiendo su lógica (estrategia guerrillera).

La polémica en torno a la literatura femenina o la escritura de las mujeres revela este viejo combate de la lucha por el reconocimiento, esto es, por ese capital simbólico que moviliza todas las marchas y contramarchas del campo literario. Ese reconocimiento que no reside en el éxito comercial, ni en la consagración ni en la notoriedad sino en algo muy particular, indefinible, pero perceptible por los demás miembros del grupo: una singular forma de prestigio.

Considero que, en este sentido, la lucha está siendo ganada. Estos discursos de recepción en torno a la literatura escrita por mujeres lo han puesto de manifiesto con sus ambigüedades, unos, y sus autoritarismo, los otros: la reacción es producto de una necesidad imperiosa de aferrarse a un momento anterior en que todo era explicable a través de la metafísica o de la fe o de la hegemonía simbólica. El deslizamiento se ha venido produciendo pausada y constantemente, y durante aquellos días de 1999 con la realización de estos irritantes encuentros, se desató un alud de dimensiones considerables que, probablemente, tuvo como efectos inmediatos cortes y heridas narcisistas en los distintos observadores; algunos de los cuales reaccionaron utilizando la pluma como los australopitecos utilizaron la cachiporra. Esa es la única explicación que encuentro para un párrafo tan grueso escrito por Ronaldo Menéndez: "¿para qué ponerle faldas a la literatura y atribuirle una supuesta y nueva sensibilidad? La literatura no necesita que la vistan ni que la maquillen, sino que la escriban. Y es que esta nueva sensibilidad ha abierto la brecha a una sensiblería que se vende como pan caliente. [...] Las mujeres venden, quién lo duda, ¿Acaso a ellas no les corresponde el oficio más antiguo de la humanidad?" (Menéndez 2: 1999).

Putas: es la forma en que los chicos de los barrios insultan a las chicas cuando salen con otros, cuando les ganan al fútbol, cuando no los miran, cuando empiezan a descubrir que pierden el piso. La metáfora, puesta de esta manera en la columna de un periódico para hablar de la producción textual de las mujeres, surge evidentemente del goce que se abre paso, como un géiser, desde lo canónico literario hacia el espacio de la tribuna pública, para evidenciar una vez más la economía política de la institucionalidad estética y sus recursos desesperados. Este texto anecdótico e ilustrativo, me sirve personalmente para cerrar con una evidente muestra de debilidad de parte de los escritores que siguen suponiendo que la entrada, posicionamiento y fortaleza de las mujeres dentro de la literatura resta en lugar de sumar.

Bibliografía

Bradotti, Rosi. *Sujetos Nómades. Corporización y diferencia sexual en la teoría feminista contemporánea*. Barcelona: Paidós, 2000.

Bourdieu, Pierre. *Las reglas del arte. Génesis y estructura del campo literario*. Barcelona: Anagrama, 1995.

de Peretti, Cristina. "Entrevista a Jacques Derrida." *Debate Feminista* 1 v. 2 1990.

Cisneros, Antonio. "Déjenla que ella baila sola." *El Comercio* [Lima, Perú] 18 agosto 1999.

Denegri, Francesca. *El abanico y la cigarrera. La primera generación de mujeres ilustradas en el Perú*. Lima: Flora Tristán IEP, 1996.

Dujovne Ortiz, Alicia. "El cuerpo transparente." *FEM* Vol. IV, n.21 febrero-marzo 1982.

Gadamer, Hans-Georg. *La actualidad de lo bello*. Barcelona: Paidós ICE-UAB, 1996.

García Canal, María Inés. "Las metáforas del cuerpo." *Debate feminista* Vol.14, n. 7 octubre 1996.

Giddens, Anthony . "Lecture 1 Globalisation." *Runaway world: The Reith Lectures Revisited* 10 November 1999.

Guardia, Sara Beatriz. *Voces y cantos de las mujeres*. Lima: CEMHAL, 1999.

Jameson, Fredric. *Documentos de cultura, documentos de barbarie*. Madrid: Visor, 1989.

Mariaca, Guillermo. "El cuerpo de la obra" en Prada-Ayllón-Contreras. Diálogos sobre escritura y mujeres. Memoria del seminario. La Paz, noviembre 1998.

Mariátegui, José Carlos. *El proceso de la Literatura. Siete ensayos de interpretación de la realidad peruana*. Lima: Amauta, 1968.

___. *Cartas a Italia*. Lima: Amauta, 1987.

Menéndez, Ronaldo. "Bajo las faldas de la literatura." *El Comercio* [Lima, Perú] 7 febrero 1999.

___. "Teología Ecuestre." *El Comercio* [Lima, Perú] 15 agosto 1999.

Oviedo, José Miguel. *Posmodernismo, vanguardia, regionalismo*. Madrid: Alianza Editorial, 2001. Vol. 3. de *Historia de la Literatura Hispanoamericana*.

___. *De Borges al presente*. Madrid: Alianza Editorial, 2001. Vol. 4. de *Historia de la Literatura Hispanoamericana*.

___. "Mujeres de Letras. ¿Existe Literatura Femenina?" *El Comercio* [Lima, Perú] 21 enero 2001.

Portugal, Ana María. "Narradoras Iberoamericanas: el riesgo de escribir." www.nodo50.org/mujeresred/escritoras-peru.html.

Reisz, Susana. *Voces Sexuadas. Género y poesía en Hispanoamérica*. Lleida: Universidad de Lleida-Asociación Española de Estudios Literarios, 1996.

___. "Teoría y subjetividad: una extraña pareja." *Quimera* 153-154 diciembre-enero 1996-1997.

Zavala, Iris M. "Las siete plagas y sus paradojas (2).". *Quimera* 204 junio 2001.

___. "Lo otro de la posmodernidad: El feminismo radical." *JCLS/CIEL* 2, 2 1991.

Zizek, Slavoj. "The Matrix o las dos caras de la perversión." *La Insignia, periódico alternativo* octubre 2000.

Lady Rojas-Trempe
Concordia University, Canadá

Violencia político-sexual del Estado, trauma y la historia de una victima en *La fiesta del Chivo* de Mario Vargas Llosa*

La canción popular de República Dominicana titulada, "Mataron al Chivo", sirve de epígrafe de los veinticuatro capítulos que conforman la novela *La fiesta del Chivo* (2000) e invita al lector a preguntarse por qué el escritor Mario Vargas Llosa retoma una copla del merengue que testimonia el carácter festivo del asesinato de uno de los más sangrientos dictadores del Caribe y de las Américas, Rafael Leonidas Trujillo Molina (1891-1961), tirano septuagenario que cayó muerto después de un reinado absolutista de más de tres décadas en el poder. El clima oscurantista de la época y las confesiones de personajes que conocieron al Chivo se acentúan y confirman que la violencia se infiltra en todos los relatos dándole al contenido de la obra un sabor amargo. Sin embargo, en el capítulo veinticuatro que llamo "Mataron a la inocencia" porque se lee como si fuera una elegía a la pérdida de la pureza, una mujer acaba de relatar en un tono vindicativo cómo la violaron. En efecto, Urania Cabral presenta la violación política de sí cuando era adolescente trazando pistas narrativas para que se comprenda por qué cuenta en diálogos entrecortados que dibujan sólo pinceladas de un secreto guardado desde 1961 hasta 1996. El misterio de su desaparición de Ciudad Trujillo comenzó después de que Urania, a la edad de catorce años, acudió a una fiesta rara porque era la única invitada y debía obedecer todas las órdenes del anfitrión. El peor mandato de la autoridad máxima del país era que la joven se echara en su cama y abriera sus piernas para que él empezara su ritual orgiástico. Urania impotente ante la brutalidad del Chivo, "sentía sus músculos y huesos triturados, pulverizados. Pero la asfixia no evitó que advirtiera la rudeza de esa mano, de esos dedos que exploraban, escarbaban y entraban en ella a la fuerza. Se sintió rajada, acuchillada; un relámpago corrió de su cerebro a los pies. Gimió, sintiendo que se moría." (508-9). La narradora expresa elocuentemente, mediante la selección apropiada de un léxico verbal, adjetival y nominal, la violencia física que usa un hombre cuando viola, la sensación de muerte que trastorna a la joven violada, su desamparo

* "Violencia político-sexual del Estado, trauma y la historia de una victima en *La fiesta del Chivo*", En: Forgues, Roland (ed.), *Mario Vargas Llosa. Escritor, ensayista, ciudadano y político*. Lima: Editorial Minerva, diciembre 2001, 537-552.

ante ese personaje monstruoso y bestial que le mata toda ilusión, perpetrando el peor crimen contra las mujeres: la violación sexual.

En este trabajo me concentro a analizar el crimen de la violación como violencia política y el trauma físico-psicológico que soportó una de las víctimas de su Excelencia Trujillo, experto en pedofilia, el Generalísimo Padre de la Patria Nueva. Según la antropóloga Françoise Héritier, en su obra *De la violence* (1996), la etimología de violencia viene del alemán "Gewalt", término que une el acto violento al poder y a la fuerza del que violenta a su prójimo. De su lado, Michel Foucault esclarece el contenido de la violencia cuando indica que la libertad no se entiende sin la resistencia popular al poder. Dicha resistencia política engendra a su vez una contra violencia. Vargas Llosa marca en su obra, esta asociación entre abuso de poder y violencia, mediante la tensión narrativa en la historia dramática de la hija del ex-senador Agustín Cabral. Muestra las fuerzas complejas, opuestas y asimétricas de las relaciones humanas en un sistema vertical en el que el Jefe Trujillo, en su papel de macho predador, se apropia ilícitamente del cuerpo de las mujeres dominicanas: esposas legítimas, hijas vírgenes de sus principales colaboradores o esbirros, logrando los fines abyectos de humillar a los maridos y de deshonrar a las mujeres; mostrándoles quién detiene la autoridad fálica en su territorio, quién reglamenta la vida político-sexual, en función de quién actúa y por qué decide la muerte o la expulsión de muchos vasallos.

Asociaciones semánticas que ligan violación y violencia ilustran la manera en la que Vargas Llosa organiza, en el universo de su novela, la evolución de la política caribeña y cómo se modelaban los códigos socio-culturales machistas en función del gobierno de un tirano que manejaba a sus fieles siervos de República Dominicana mediante el terror, los chantajes y los sobornos, legalizando así una época represiva, xenofóbica y misógina que la Historiografía denomina la Era de Trujillo. Integraré luego, en la primera isotopía de la violación y violencia, la semantización irónica de dos acciones, festejar y matar, cuyos significantes y significados se oponen, al menos lingüísticamente, pero que en los hechos prácticos de muchos países de las Américas se alían y ponen de relieve el carácter carnavalesco y trágico de la historia latinoamericana. Me interesa sondear en la novela vargallosiana, el discurso sobre el impacto de la violencia estatal cuando arremete contra los opositores femeninos; pero especialmente los efectos devastadores en Urania Cabral, "una criatura tan dulce y tan bella" (347) en su niñez, que se transformó adulta en "un témpano de hielo..., remilgada, indiferente, frígida" (211), y que sobrevivió en el destierro estudiando y trabajando en los Estados Unidos. Después de tres décadas y media de vergüenza y humillación por la violación de su cuerpo y la transformación de sí, se atrevió a recordar y contó a su familia, en una lengua sugerente y fragmentada pero reveladora que el Chivo era el agente y la causa de su mal-estar físico, afectivo, social y psicológico.

Retomo la perspectiva psicoanalítica y de género que comunican un sentido crítico al trauma de esa mujer dominicana y un sentido reparador al asesinato del criminal Trujillo. Una narradora audaz y homodiegética confronta el discurso entrecortado de Urania y un narrador heterodiegético orienta el cauce narrativo de *La fiesta del Chivo* hacia el grupo de conspiradores que preparan el tiranicidio. Ambos narradores provocan el suspenso en los lectores sugiriendo ciertos motivos familiares al regreso de Urania que debe posicionarse de nuevo, mediante el recuerdo, en un contexto socio-político de terror y atrocidades políticas en República Dominicana que negó, bajo la égida de Trujillo, los derechos humanos a la población y las libertades a las mujeres. También acompañan a la Doctora Urania Cabral cuando llega de su viaje de Nueva York a Santo Domingo en 1996, luego de treinta y cinco años de ausencia y de exilio, de silencio y de olvido. Muchas preguntas me interrogan como lectora empática y sensible al crimen político de la violación y a sus efectos devastadores en la conformación identitaria de los sujetos: ¿De qué manera Urania reconstruirá su historia, cómo saldrá de la depresión, cuál será su actitud ante la complicidad del padre en su violación, ante la justificación de la tía Adelina de que se trataba de "otros tiempos", de que era posible que su padre haya sido manipulado por el celestino Manuel Alfonso de Trujillo? ¿La víctima de un trauma político se recupera recordando y contando su propia historia como lo sugirieron los psicoanalistas y la paciente Anna O. de Joseph Breuer? ¿Urania reabrirá la cicatriz del abuso político-sexual y revivirá en el discurso, el crimen en el que la Bestia ultrajó su virginidad y la integridad de su ser?

En *La fiesta del Chivo*, Vargas Llosa acude con maestría y tacto a las funciones mnemonísticas y creadoras de la lengua española con las que Urania, profesional soltera de cuarenta y nueve años, arma los entramados de su violación y se auto representa a sí para saber quién es en interacción con su padre, el celestino, el tirano y su familia. Por medio del recuerdo de sí y el conocimiento histórico, que proviene del material escrito y leído sobre el trujillismo, la mujer se transporta al pasado, a la escena del crimen, tantea con suspenso y vacilación, el origen del mal que la aqueja e identifica al criminal que la violó y a sus aliados. La doctora se siente "extraña" en su país de origen, como si no perteneciera a la sociedad dominicana, espacio de la tiranía en el que reinaban: el despotismo, el ultraje, el abuso y las delaciones para quienes no comulgaban con la ideología dogmática y la práctica criminal del Chivo. La identidad de Urania se desdobla para recuperar ese pasado, se habla a sí misma en tanto Tú, sujeto de sus actos, y Yo que la interroga sobre la veracidad de los hechos del pretérito y la propiedad del sondeo interior actual.

Me atengo al planteamiento psicológico de Donald Winnicott en *Jeu et Réalité* (1975), que sostiene que el Yo narcisista de los seres humanos se asocia con el Mí que integra las normas sociales. Sin embargo, en el presente narrativo el Mí de Urania rechaza los papeles que Trujillo y la sociedad designaban a las adolescentes como hembras forzadas a ofrecer al poderoso jefe, sus cuerpos intactos. La identidad individual genérica de Urania no fue respetada por su padre ni por el tirano, por ello la instancia psicológica de su identidad, el Sí verdadero no logra juntar el Yo con el Mí, ni puede armonizar el cuerpo con la psiquis. Los padres se forman una imagen del cuerpo de los hijos, los aceptan como seres placenteros o los rechazan como seres alienados. La primera mirada maternal y paternal, en la infancia y la adolescencia es muy importante porque forja la calidad de la representación del Sí en el avenir. En la identidad de Urania, huérfana de madre, la mirada y los cuidados del papá Agustín Cabral sostuvieron la estima de sí de la niña, hasta el momento en que el padre le impuso ir a una fiesta y la obligó, con engaños, a entregarse al Jefe. El cuerpo de Urania se redujo a una mercancía de intercambio político. El amor y la traición de su padre Agustín, personaje aliado fiel del Chivo, originan en ella dos emociones opuestas, "Por eso lo habías querido tanto. Por eso te había dolido tanto, Urania" (22). El Sí falso que se forjó la niña Urania cuando se sometió a las exigencias del progenitor biológico y a las del progenitor de la Patria Nueva, suscita en la Doctora en leyes, mujer adulta, un sentimiento de vacío, de insatisfacción emocional y una actitud defensiva frente a todos los hombres.

Desde el punto de vista legal, semántico y narrativo la isotopía de violar implica una infracción física en el cuerpo de una víctima por parte del violador que debería pagar su crimen para restaurar la justicia. La investigadora feminista Susan Brownmiller confirma en su clásico libro *Le viol* (1983) un elemento de suma importancia para entender el sistema de impunidad en el que fue violada Urania, cuando dice, "Tout viol est une manifestation de force, mais certains de ceux qui violent ont un avantage qui est plus que physique. Ils opèrent au sein d'un cadre institutionnalisé qui fonctionne à leur bénéfice et dans lequel une victime a peu de chance de voir réparé le tort qui lui a été fait" (311). Fue la situación de las jóvenes víctimas como Urania y de esposas dominicanas bajo el trujillismo. De un lado, Urania y otras víctimas huyeron del país porque sus padres, funcionarios políticos, tenían las manos sucias y los espíritus atados servilmente a su endiosado Jefe. De otro lado, la sociedad domesticada no las apoyaría para denunciar al verdugo, aplicar justicia y reparar las faltas. Héritier en su concepto incluye los efectos abominables del agravio que conoció Urania Cabral, "Appelons violence toute contrainte de nature physique ou psychique susceptible d'entraîner la terreur, le déplacement, le malheur, la souffrance ou la mort d'un être animé; tout acte d'intrusion qui a pour effet volontaire ou involontaire la dépossession d'autrui, le dommage ou la destruction d'objets inanimés" (I, 17). La violación engendra según la psiquiatra Judith Herman en *Trauma and Recovery* (1997), el "Psychological trauma [que] is an affliction of the powerless. At the moment of trauma, the victim is rendered helpless by overwhelming force... When the force is that of other human beings, we speak of atrocities. Traumatic events overwhelm the ordinary systems of care that give people a sense of control, connection, and meaning. They confront human beings with the extremities of helplessness and terror, loss of control and threat of annihilation" (33).

En el primer capítulo de *La fiesta del Chivo* una narradora sugiere que la cólera y el impulso de vengarse de la traición y la trampa del senador afectaron la psiquis de Urania con una severa depresión que la agobia desde que descubrió que su padre aceptó que la Bestia la violara. Así lo advierten las preguntas y el enunciado que siguen, "¿Lo detestas? ¿Lo odias? ¿Todavía? «Ya no», dice en voz alta. No hubieras vuelto si el rencor siguiera crepitando, la herida sangrando, la decepción anonadándola, envenenándola, como en tu juventud, cuando estudiar, trabajar, se convirtieron en obsesionante remedio para no recordar. Entonces sí lo odiabas. Con todos los átomos de tu ser, con todos los pensamientos y sentimientos que te cabían en el cuerpo" (14). A lo largo de la novela, Urania se da cuenta de la significación sacrificial de su desfloramiento por eso testimonia con lujo de detalles, en el capítulo final, acerca de su condición de víctima política de una autoridad coercitiva, que le infundió la parálisis, el miedo y la muerte despiadada de su infancia. La desesperación y el terror del mal que sintió Urania, lo recuerda la joven violada como una situación límite inaguantable, "Pensé tirarme por la ventana. Pensé ponerme de rodillas, rogarle, llorarle. Pensé que tenía que dejarme hacer lo que él quisiera, apretando los dientes para poder vivir, y, un día, vengarme de papá" (501). Cada uno de los gestos sexuales, que excitan al monstruo político, se contamina de bestialidad y destrucción, ya que la atracción de la niña se hace de manera mañosa con el fin de que ella caiga como una presa en la trampa de la fiesta-muerte y él guste el bocadillo de su virginidad sin resistencia. Los ojos lascivos del macho despiertan la sensación de una metamorfosis total en la niña que cuenta, "esa mirada me vació, me dejó puro pellejo. Ya no fui yo" (502). La pérdida de la inocencia de Urania se agudiza con el discurso falsete del viejo alcohólico que la piropea, juega al enamorado, le recita "El poema 15" de Pablo Neruda –el que elogia la pasividad y el silencio del ser femenino-, la hace bailar preparándola para el asalto, la besa con su lengua, "viborilla húmeda, fogosa", en la boca. La joven violada habla de su "cuerpo muerto" signo de su analfabetismo sexual, —propio de la educación— desnudamiento físico, obediencia total, desamparo e inmovilidad que provocaron una reacción violenta en el macho cabrío, que deseaba sobre todo ratificar su potencia animal, "con un güevo todavía capaz de ponerse tieso y de romper los coñitos vírgenes que le pusieran delante" (508).

La perversión político-sexual que utilizaron el Chivo y su hijo Ramfis para violar a las jóvenes dominicanas o seducir a las esposas de sus ayudantes políticos en sus propias casas ocasionaron efectos nocivos en la identidad de las mujeres. Tomo la figura novelística de Urania Cabral, paradigma de la joven violada, que se siente en 1996 agredida por la bulla del medio dominicano, por la mirada viciosa de los hombres y se muestra intolerante frente a la actitud melodramática de las mujeres de su familia. El contraste y la perspectiva le permiten reconocerse como una mujer sin complejos intelectuales, ser diferente que entra sin quererlo en un proceso liberador de auto-análisis narrativo que la insta a jalar del olvido, palabra por palabra, acto y contra-acto, agresión sexual e indefensión, una página oscura de su historia que no se entiende sino se la ubica dentro del entramado caribeño violento del Trujillismo que duró de 1930 a 1961. Según el discurso de Urania los códigos culturales que rigen la conducta del senador Agustín Cabral, cuando entrega a su "niña normal y sana" (351) como "ofrenda viva" (501) a su ídolo Trujillo, no provienen de rezagos rituales de los pueblos Incas o Aztecas que sacrificaban a las vírgenes o enemigos para que el sol siguiera su ruta celeste. Provienen de su exclusión política del grupo de los "elegidos" después de treinta años de servicios a su Benefactor. Cabral reduce a su hija a un papel de hembra conciliadora entre dos machos. Ambos ven en el sacrificio del cuerpo inmaculado de Urania el medio de conseguir: para Agustín Cabral, el perdón del Amo y su inmediata reintegración en la política; y para el Chivo, la práctica del derecho feudal de desfloración. La acusación que lanza Urania a su padre así lo confirma, "Habías perdido los escrúpulos, la sensibilidad, el menor asomo de rectitud. Igual que tus colegas. Igual que el país entero, tal vez. ¿Era ése el requisito para mantenerse en el poder sin morirse de asco? Volverse un desalmado, un monstruo como tu Jefe" (137). Las reglas políticas, sociales y culturales se imponían por el sacrosanto poder del falo y del gobierno falocrático que lo sustentaba, determinando la inferioridad de las mujeres, su "invisible" e "inexistente" ser (367, 510).

Según Paul Ricoeur en *La mémoire, l'histoire, l'oubli* (2000) la fenomenología de la remembranza comporta el objeto —qué se recuerda—, el sujeto —quién lo hace— y la manera —cómo se recuerda— (3-4). En el discurso de la doctora en leyes con el que Vargas Llosa inicia y termina la novela, Urania Cabral busca sistemas de significación históricos que tracen un contexto colectivo a su victimización impregnada de afectos y rencor a su padre, de odio al Chivo y al manipulador alcahuete Manuel

Alfonso, de rupturas familiares porque creen en la inocencia del padre y la mentira de la violada, de exilio en los Estados Unidos y de rudeza con los machos. Urania imprime el ritmo fragmentado y la cadencia dubitativa de su enunciación, como sujeto que indaga la violación de su cuerpo y de su ser en el primer y cuarto capítulos; revela, en el séptimo, el toque angustioso y dubitativo cuando su Yo le ordena, "cállate, deja de escarbar esas llagas, de resucitar esos recuerdos" (136); se afirma a sí misma como hija violentada cuando enfrenta a su padre y le increpa su cobardía; y conversa con su familia en el décimo, décimo tercero, décimo sexto y vigésimo cuarto capítulos en los que desmonta, primero, la bondad del senador Agustín Cabral mostrando más bien su vileza como padre; y, segundo, el propósito violento de la fiesta del Chivo. Por medio de la anamnesis se configura mentalmente cómo se quiebra el microcosmos inocente de Urania, un pivote neurálgico del macrocosmos violento de la novela de Vargas Llosa.

El cuerpo abusado de la niña por un adulto cruel, encuentra su voz y la fuerza para restaurar, tal vez, la conexión entre lo privado y lo público, entre el individuo y su familia, entre su cabeza y sus sentimientos. Al huir de La casa de Caoba donde el Generalísimo criminal la viola, Urania escoge el refugio de su colegio y la protección de las religiosas, pero ya se encuentra con una severa depresión: se siente "desasida del mundo y de sí misma" (209), sin ningún apego por su país ni por su familia, con "el asco que le inspiran los hombres en quienes despierta deseos" (211). La narradora le dice a Urania, "detrás de esa fortaleza que te admiran y envidian, tienes un corazoncito tierno, asustadizo, lacerado, sentimental" (12). A pesar de que Urania no se considera enferma, sus síntomas conforman el pos-traumático desorden que puede, según Judith Herman, constituirse en la base de un relato o "talking cure". Para Herman, "Rape is an atrocity. Feminists redefined rape as a crime of violence rather than a sexual act... as a method of political control, enforcing the subordination of women through terror" (30). Si la persona violada cuenta su verdad escondida y la comparte con una persona que le da confianza, la dialéctica del trauma se transforma: el secreto pierde su fuerza y naturaleza represivas, y la palabra se constituye en el primer índice para que la víctima recupere la estima de sí y el cuerpo violado como parte de su historia personal, haga el duelo de su sufrimiento y retome su existencia. Por medio del monólogo interior, del soliloquio con su padre "muerto en vida" o del intenso diálogo con su tía, primas y sobrina, la víctima Urania reconoce su historia de mujer violada, "—Me molesta, me da vómitos... Me llena de odio y asco. Nunca hablé de esto con nadie. Quizá me haga bien sacármelo de encima, de una vez. Y con quién mejor que con la familia" (339). Con su vida de víctima, que se vuelve relato, Urania reconstruye una historia fatal que la traumatizó cuando apenas entraba en la adolescencia; y puede iniciar su curación.

Resulta sumamente ilustradora la lucha interna que Urania como hija debe librar con la vieja tía Adelina que no solamente niega la participación del senador Agustín Cabral en el plan del asalto sexual, sino que le pide callarse y rezar. Sólo cuando Urania da el paso iniciático y desentierra del olvido un pasaje siniestro, se reivindica como sujeto de sí misma y de una historia que también compartieron otras jóvenes y mujeres dominicanas. Con ese propósito Urania trata de entender lo incomprensible, verbaliza lo prohibido, termina con el silencio y el lenguaje elíptico, cuenta la "historia que laceraba tu memoria" (196) y escondía, en el significante "aquello", un relato de horror que cambiaría su vida. De acuerdo a Ann Burgess y Lynda Holmstrom los efectos del "síndrome del trauma de la violación" comprende: "a life-threatening event, having generally feared mutilation and death during the assault" (Hermann 31). A partir de las vivencias del presente narrativo, Urania inicia un viaje elocutorio, simbólico y evocador de restauración identitaria con su pasado. Su pesquisa interior le recuerda la trampa y el sentido de la fiesta trujillista urdida por el celestino y aprobada por su padre, en mayo de 1961, en vísperas del tiranicidio.

De acuerdo al relato de Urania, la estrategia seductora y la escena de los crímenes del Chivo son simples, invita a su presa a una de las "fiestas" que organiza en sus casas de campo. Su hábito de violar "a las mujeres más bellas de este país" (74) continuó hasta el día de su asesinato. Su lema: "haré chillar a una hembrita" (234) lo retrata como triunfador sexual ante la Otra, rival perdedora que le confirma la eficacia de su arma sexual en la que radica su poder político, libidinoso y punitivo. El Chivo "un padrillo reproductor de gran alzada" (32) no necesita de perífrasis cuando asalta a Lina Lobatón o a la esposa de Froilán Arana en su propia casa, ni cuando su celestino Manuel Alfonso planifica que su Amo goce "tirándose" a las jóvenes dominicanas. Entre ellas cuentan: Yolanda Esterel de diecisiete años, hija de Terencia Esterel que tuvo el mismo fatídico destino en su juventud, Moni y Urania Cabral ofrendadas por su respectivo padre. La tendencia del Jefe para violar con el visto bueno de los familiares no se entiende sin el apoyo tácito de una sociedad aletargada que no le pone freno a la práctica de, "La receta de Petronio y del rey Salomón: un coñito fresco para devolver la juventud a un veterano de setenta primaveras" (382). Dicho poder agresivo que Trujillo centra en la capacidad todopoderosa de sus genitales y en el deseo sexual insatisfecho, se la hereda a su hijo Ramfis, ser descrito como "gran singador, macho cabrío, feroz fornicador" que tampoco asume la responsabilidad de sus actos porque su padre lo protege. Ramfis y sus amigos copian el patrón del Padre de la Nueva Patria, abusan sexual y colectivamente de la joven estudiante Rosalía Perdomo, "hija de un coronel del Ejército", y la tiran como a un animal cuando ésta se desangra. Los actos perversos se banalizan y se ocultan en la sociedad encubridora, pero el narrador subraya repitiendo, "el frenesí fornicatorio, la necesidad de tumbar mujeres en la cama para convencerse de su virilidad" (129). De tal manera, el reino del misoginismo político-militar se impuso en la comunidad trujillana atacada de pánico, intimidación, ceguera y complicidad con el dictador Trujillo. Ciertas mujeres valientes y conscientes del significado real y simbólico de la invitación a la fiesta trujillista, como la esposa del funcionario Pedro Henríquez Ureña o la activa dirigente comunista Minerva Mirabel, que no estaban para fiestas, no acudieron a la ceremonia del Chivo, debían exilarse del país; sino corrían la tragedia de ser asesinadas con perversión, con el propósito de infligir daño físico a "mujeres indefensas ¡sin que nadie hiciera nada!" (314) como replica furiosamente Antonio Imbert. La historia del asesinato macabro de las hermanas, luchadoras antitrujillistas, Minerva, Patria y María Teresa Mirabal que cayeron muertas exigiendo libertad, despertó la conciencia de gente allegada a Trujillo. Entre ellos destaca el militar Imbert que asumió la resistencia contra el tirano.

Ciertos términos, como fiesta y muerte, pierden su valor etimológico debido a la función socio-cultural que se les atribuye en un contexto histórico concreto. Vargas Llosa registra las discordancias que la palabra fiesta propone en el nivel elocutorio traduciendo una desviación en el nivel práctico. Por un lado, cuando Trujillo ordena organizar fiestas y que le lleven ciudadanas jóvenes para subvenir a sus pulsiones sexuales y lo hace como si la violación fuera un evento festivo y rememorativo significa que su poder político trasunta el exceso de una violencia abusiva, perversa y planificada. Por otro lado, cuando parte de la sociedad utiliza la contra violencia para atajar los desmanes del estado tirano significa que todos los canales de la democracia y del diálogo entre el gobierno y el pueblo se han cerrado. De ahí que *La fiesta del Chivo* eche mano de la ironía popular y se ría de la muerte sexual y política del hombre que mató sin piedad a sus ciudadanos. No existe mayor ironía cruel en la novela de Mario Vargas Llosa que la que Urania descubre cuando acude a la fiesta que conmemora la muerte de la inocencia femenina y presencia la derrota fálica del mito Trujillo cuyo "pequeño sexo [estaba] muerto" (511). Los sentidos literal y lúdico de la expresión descriptiva contrastan con el pensamiento trujillista cuya dialéctica del poder residía en la fortaleza física y la erección del símbolo político masculino. Gracias a esa protuberancia anatómica, Trujillo actuó más de treinta años con prepotencia, se sintió indemne al paso del tiempo y se consideró conquistador de los núbiles cuerpos femeninos y de su país caribeño. No obstante, la orden para que la niña le masturbe el pene, lo ponga en erección en su boca, el hecho de que su apetito sexual crezca pero que se sirva de los dedos y viole así a Urania, indican que el Chivo, al final de su vida, era impotente, estaba obsesionado por su arma sin valor y los achaques de su cuerpo senil. Esta venganza narrativa mueve a risa y nos reconcilia con el triunfo de la vida sobre las muertes injustas, la esperanza sobre el caos y la confesión sobre la impunidad. En el retrato literario del fiero Trujillo abundan trazos de sus debilidades e impotencias: perdió el control físico del cuerpo de las mujeres, sufría de fobia de su suciedad y de la sangre de sus víctimas, era inflexible e intolerante ante la raza negra y manifestaba una personalidad delictiva. Ello explica por qué se sentía acomplejado antes de la batalla de cacería sexual y rogaba la ayuda de Dios para que su verga penetrara a las vírgenes. El cuerpo juvenil de Urania fue el espejo puro y límpido que le reflejó al macho cabrío su incapacidad eréctil, su incontinencia urinaria y su impotencia política-sexual.

Mario Vargas Llosa pinta con acertado brío, mediante las conmutaciones de niveles narrativos, los cruces de enunciaciones de varios personajes y los saltos espacio-temporales la voluntad de los conspiradores de un comando militar de asesinar al "verdugo de los dominicanos" (237) y derrumbar la dictadura trujillista. Novela con lucidez y desencanto las taras humanas diabólicas que empujan a toda una sociedad a sufrir en la opresión. De acuerdo con ese punto de vista Urania se arriesga a desvelar la bajeza inmoral de su padre y a confesar con espanto a su familia los meandros de un sistema podrido que aprueba sin chistar los asaltos y desmanes político-sexuales de Trujillo, su hijo y sus allegados al poder. Vargas Llosa también nos remece con esa lengua que deslumbra porque cuestiona los absolutismos de grandes y pequeños traidores, porque tambalea los secretos y mentiras de las familias, pero sobre todo porque su palabra habla directamente de la complicidad del pueblo dominicano amordazado que colaboró para que el espacio nacional se convirtiera en gran prisión, las casas en prostíbulos y las doncellas en presas, trofeos gratuitos por las hazañas militares y los méritos políticos del cazador. Es evidente, que sirviéndose de la posición e inmunidad políticas, los dictadores del siglo XX: violadores, asesinos, pedófilos y ladrones de alto calibre han legado a América Latina, una larga historia de crímenes, pobreza, pérdida de valores, violencia sistemática y ultraje a los derechos y libertades fundamentales de los seres humanos. Sólo después de la organización del movimiento feminista durante los setenta, la violencia machista contra las mujeres será ampliamente reconocida, denunciada y novelada como actos públicos. En ese sentido, *La fiesta del Chivo* de Mario Vargas Llosa contribuye a que la historia traumática de Urania Cabral y de otras mujeres ultrajadas, ninguneadas, violadas y traumatizadas por la violencia estatal del Chivo Trujillo en República Dominicana remueva nuestra indiferencia ante crímenes políticos de perversión sexual que se siguen cometiendo en el mundo actual gracias a los cimientos, la ideología machista y los actos de servilismo que sustentan los poderes corruptos.

Bibliografía

Brownmiller, Susan. *Le viol* [1975]. Trad. Anne Villelaur. Pref. Benoîte Groult. Montreal: Éditions Stock, 1983.

Héritier, Françoise. *Séminaire de la violence*. París: Éditions Odile Jacob, 1996. I v.

Herman, Judith. *Trauma and Recovery*. New York: Basic Books, 1997.

Ricoeur, Paul. *La mémoire, l'histoire, l'oubli*. París: Seuil, 2000.

Vargas Llosa, Mario. *La fiesta del Chivo*. Madrid: Alfaguara, 2000.

Winnicott, Donald. *Jeu et Réalité*. París: Gallimard, 1975.

Paolo de Lima

University of Ottawa

Aspectos de la violencia en la poesía de dos autoras peruanas de los años ochenta: Dalmacia Ruiz-Rosas y Rocío Silva Santisteban

1980 es un año clave en la historia de la república peruana. Dos hechos de suma importancia se dan cita en este año. Por un lado la llegada de la democracia formal con la asunción al poder del populista Fernando Belaunde Terry luego de doce años de dictadura militar. Por el otro, el inicio de las acciones armadas por parte de "Sendero Luminoso". En una entrevista, Rocío Silva Santisteban da cuenta del clima en el cual las jóvenes poetas mujeres de inicios de esa década empezaban su tránsito dentro de la institución literaria peruana:

> [...]vivimos nuestra primera entrada a lo literario en la dura década del 80, escuchábamos las bombas, nos cayeron las esquirlas, atravesamos [la Universidad de] San Marcos en la época del caos administrativo y de la politización a forro [...] No conseguíamos chamba, sobrevivíamos por aquí y por allá, conversábamos horas de horas, nos gustaba Lou Reed y David Bowie y Silvia Plath y queríamos sobre todo ser libres, que nadie `nos pise el poncho´. (Vargas 2000).

Y respecto a la visión que de su obra tenían los lectores y críticos de esos años, la otra autora objeto de este estudio, Dalmacia Ruiz-Rosas, en la misma entrevista afirma no creer "en el rollo de `literatura de mujeres´ y `literatura de hombres´" (Vargas 2000), y destaca que las poetas del ochenta: "Éramos fuertes, inteligentes, guapas y no nos quedábamos calladas... Éramos y somos, pero ha tenido que pasar un montón de años para que esos críticos se den cuenta de que al margen de lo erótico había en nosotras dedicación y consecuencia"[1]. (Vargas 2000).

---

[1]Ya que hemos adelantado el espinoso tema de las definiciones en torno a la "literatura de mujeres", citemos las siguientes opiniones de Carmén Ollé: "`¿Qué opinas sobre la denominada literatura femenina?´ `No me gusta el término de literatura femenina ni de literatura feminista. Pero cuando hablamos desde la literatura escrita por mujeres tenemos que darle un nombre a la producción de mujeres para diferenciarla de su entorno. Porque la literatura escrita por mujeres sufre: tiene problemas para publicar, problemas ante la crítica, problemas de ser guetizada o reducida a un tipo de literatura calificada

Como puede verse, ambas autoras hablan desde un "nosotras". Se refieren a las otras poetas que aparecieron paralelamente a ellas en el ambiente cultural limeño (y por añadidura, peruano). En unos cuantos párrafos podemos hacer un recuento de sus nombres; una breve historia que, para decirlo en términos del crítico argentino Noé Jitrik, ha ido conformándose desde las prelecturas que "[...] gravitan en la configuración de la lectura final; [y que] operan en cierto modo como una orden que proviene de la estructura global de la sociedad. [...] De modo que son la condición, si no también la garantía, de la lectura que efectivamente realizan los sujetos." (Jitrik 77)[2]. Todo esto desemboca en la conformación del canon de la poesía femenina (o practicada por mujeres) de las últimas dos décadas en el Perú.

Antecedentes

La historia la podemos iniciar con la aparición de los primeros textos de María Emilia Cornejo (Lima, 1940-1972). Tres poemas breves son los que le han valido la permanencia en la institución literaria. En uno de ellos confiesa, con una sinceridad muy directa, que "sola, / descubro que mi vida transcurrió perfectamente / como tú lo estableciste" (Escobar 177), eran los años del apogeo del narrativo-coloquialismo en la poesía peruana y latinoamericana en general. Tipo de escritura poética que prácticamente frecuentan, en distinta gradación, todas las autoras mencionadas en este estudio (exceptuando el caso de Magdalena Chocano). Las imposiciones del Otro masculino en las relaciones de pareja, y por extensión en las relaciones de poder dentro de la sociedad, se ven cuestionadas por esta conciencia opuesta a la voz convencional donde el "tú" también puede reflejar al canon literario.

En otro poema, el de mayor contundencia de los escritos por esta autora, la denuncia, el cuestionamiento y el quebrantamiento de las falsas hegemonías se ponen de manifiesto cuando se llama así misma "la muchacha mala de la historia / la que fornicó con tres hombres / y le sacó cuernos a su marido, / [...] soy la mujer que lo castró / con infini-

---

de una manera. Por eso, sí, existe una literatura producida por mujeres que se ve afectada por la crítica'" (Minardi 57). Se trata de una línea de pensamiento en la crítica feminista que viene de Virginia Woolf quien, como señala Raman Selden, "[c]reía que las mujeres siempre habían encontrado obstáculos sociales y económicos ante sus ambiciones literarias" (Selden 162).

[2]Jitrik explica que las prelecturas por el modo de la recepción configuran dos "grandes tipos de lecturas": "la lectura autorizada, que recupera las órdenes provenientes de las prelecturas, traduciéndolas o reconvirtiéndolas pero sin modificarlas sustancialmente [y que] se lee como quiere que se lea la red social que, en cada uno de esos actos, consolida su poder o su estabilidad. [Y] la lectura subversiva, que resiste las órdenes de las prelecturas y en la forma que construye intenta develar, justamente, el sentido que la red social quiere imponer a través de la autorizada" (Jitrik 77-8).

tos gestos de ternura / y gemidos falsos en la cama" (Escobar 178). Esta
sinceridad para contarnos su desafío a las normas sociales lamentable-
mente no llegó a cuajar en la actitud cotidiana y vital de Cornejo. Era un
grito demasiado temprano contra una sociedad pacata que no estaba en
condiciones de aceptar tan escandalosa provocación. Cornejo finalmente optaría por el suicidio como una vía de escape o de salida.

Sería Carmen Ollé (Lima, 1947), ex militante de *"Hora Zero"* (grupo
poético de mucha visibilidad durante los años setenta)[3], quien sí
lograría asumir plenamente su opción poética y vital liberadas de los
"tóxicos de la sociedad burguesa y patriarcal" y del "autoritarismo, los
prejuicios, las convenciones" (Pfeiffer 149). Aunque con los años Ollé se
ha revelado fundamentalmente como autora de textos narrativos: tres
novelas, un relato, y "tanteos con el cuento [dentro de] impresiones un
poco líricas" (Minardi 56), es su primer libro *Noches de adrenalina*, publicado en Lima en 1981, la obra que llega a ser considerada, incluso por
las propias autoras jóvenes aparecidas con posterior a ese año, como
un punto de referencia obligatoria, un hito en la poesía escrita por
mujeres peruanas[4]. El tono libertario y el desenfado en el tratamiento

---

[3]Ollé fue esposa de Enrique Verástegui, considerado por la mayor parte de la crítica literaria peruana como el poeta más interesante de esta agrupación. En una entrevista
reconoce abiertamente la influencia de Verástegui en su proceso de escritura: "Al principio, al escribir el libro [*Noches de adrenalina*], no tuve ninguna intención feminista.
Aunque recuerdo que mi ex-marido me sugirió que reivindicara las voces literarias de
las mujeres. Ya había citado yo a algunas (Victoria Ocampo, Virginia Woolf, Silvia Plath,
etc.). A partir de ahí pensé que eso podía tener algún sentido". Sin embargo, luego de
salir el libro de la cocina literaria, y siempre según el testimonio de Carmen Ollé, la actitud del "ex-marido" cambiaría de manera radical: "`¿Y él te daba ánimo para esto,
incluso te incitaba a hacerlo?´ `Cuando le enseñaba los textos me animaba a hacerlo. Lo
curioso es que cuando lo publiqué su reacción fue totalmente adversa *[se ríe]*´ `¿En qué
sentido?´ `El impacto del libro le resultó desagradable.´" (Pfeiffer 148). No obstante, nos
hemos topado con una declaración de Verástegui en la cual a propósito de *Noches...*
reconoce que "[…]se necesita cierto coraje para asumir el tema erótico frente a determi-
nados conocidos en tu mundo". (Ángeles 3). Y en una entrevista Rocío Silva Santisteban afirma que "[la Ollé de *Noches...*] estaba influenciada por Verástegui. Había llegado
a París y tenía influencia de Bataille y los franceses. Su propuesta era como la de
Verástegui, poemas largos y totalmente desenfadados." (Ramos 28).

[4]"Somos mujeres, pero también somos peruanas", declara enfáticamente Rocío Silva (Vargas 2000). Por otro lado, queremos resaltar las reflexiones de una jovencísima crítica
sanmarquina, Bethsabé Huamán, quien afirma que "[…]a diferencia de Blanca Varela,
Carmén Ollé no sólo contaba con un grupo de mujeres, que por cuestiones del azar también escribían en esa época y tenían proyectos similares al suyo, sino que había un contexto mayor: el del emergente feminismo y la lucha por los derechos de la mujer". También critica que a la poesía de Ollé "[S]e le ha[ya] relegado de esa ficción de la literatura universal [asociada más a lo masculino como construcción social y cultural] para ubi-
carla dentro del espacio de la poesía femenina y dentro del espacio de la poesía erótica,
donde se le ha otorgado un pequeño agujero donde descansar en paz". Finalmente, tras
reconocer que "[N]o existe una estrategia discursiva de género totalmente efectiva, pues
ello implicaría que se ha vencido el prejuicio y la discriminación", concluye que "[E]n

del tema del cuerpo femenino que se aprecian a lo largo del poemario son los factores fundamentales de su importancia. Tono y tema que posteriormente en un núcleo considerable de textos tratarían con igual o mayor atrevimiento Mariela Dreyfus (Lima, 1960), Patricia Alba (Lima, 1960) y Rocío Silva Santisteban (Lima, 1963), quien a propósito del poemario de Ollé nos dice:

> Con *Noches de adrenalina* [...] la poesía peruana cambia: el cuerpo, el erotismo pero también la racionalidad como elemento poético —la racionalidad, insisto— entran en el texto producido por una mujer. Y eso escandalizó. La excusa fue la onda erótica, pero el escándalo lo produjo el atrevimiento de escribir más allá de lo canónico. (Vargas 2000).

Este conjunto de autoras llegó a recibir denominaciones como la del "mini boom" de la joven poesía femenina (VV.AA. 14), un fenómeno que por lo demás coincidió con el surgimiento de diferentes movimientos de poesía escrita por mujeres en Latinoamérica y España. Mariela Dreyfus considera el término "mini boom" como una "categoría cuestionable", una estrategia crítica en la que el prefijo "mini" pretendería "acortar la importancia de la poesía de las mujeres de esa década aún más, como quien le sube la basta a una falda". (Dreyfus 2001)[5].

María Emilia Cornejo, Carmen Ollé, Giovanna Pollarolo (Tacna, 1953) y Dalmacia Ruiz-Rosas (Lima, 1957), aparecidas entre inicios y finales de los setenta, fueron perfilando una mirada alternativa a la canónica masculinizada que se profundizó con las mencionadas autoras de los ochenta, además de Rossella Di Paolo y Magdalena Chocano, cuyos lenguajes y temas ponen el énfasis en otros rumbos. Sin embargo, como hace notar Rocío Silva refiriéndose al conjunto de autoras de su generación:

> Nuestros estilos literarios son diferentes, sí, aunque yo jamás diría que radicalmente diferentes: hay una fuerte intertextualidad, pero cada quien le pone el énfasis a su propia obsesión. Y en esa diversidad está lo bacán. (Vargas 2000)[6].

---

realidad Varela es mucho más osada que Carmen Ollé si consideramos que se ha metido a la boca del lobo y ha acuchillado desde adentro sin que éste supiera de dónde venía la puñalada".

[5]En cualquier caso, por poner un ejemplo concreto, un poeta peruano de la generación posterior, Xavier Echarri, también opina que "la poesía femenina no ha tenido mayores logros estéticos por un pequeño problema que es más bien de orden sociológico: están demasiado marcadas por su, llamémosle así, `condición femenina´, en la que reabundan y reabundan en los poemas". Esto sin descontar que, dentro de su lectura, Echarri rescata a dos autoras, incluyendo a Dreyfus: "Hay, sin embargo, dos poetas que hacen de esta condición una cualidad estética: Mariela Dreyfus y Rossella Di Paolo". Como puede ver la propia autora, no hay que alarmarse tanto.

[6]En otra entrevista también afirmaba que "[L]o más interesante es que [en los ochenta] en poesía un grupo de mujeres comenzó a escribir, y ya no aisladamente sino como una

Veamos ahora con detenimiento a las dos poetas objeto de este estudio.

Dalmacia Ruiz-Rosas: "No quiero la paz ni la violencia"

Dalmacia Ruiz-Rosas es ya una autora madura y ampliamente conocida en el medio literario peruano cuando entrega a la imprenta *Secuestro en el jardín de las rosas* (1998), su primer poemario publicado pero el octavo en ser escrito. Respecto a este hecho la propia autora nos dice:

> Los siete libros anteriores aún permanecen inéditos. Por esos poemas, ya sea porque los he leído en público, porque con ellos he estado en algunos grupos como "Kloaka", "Hora Zero" o "La sagrada familia" o porque han sido publicados en revistas marginales y fanzines, es que la gente conoce más o menos mi obra. (Pita 1998)

La opción de Ruiz-Rosas a no publicar sus libros se debe, como señala Róger Santiváñez, "quizá a su vocación de ruptura: ir leyendo sus poemas, en vez de editarlos, como ha sido su práctica acorde con su concepto: `el recipiente cultural poema ha estallado'" (Santiváñez 1995). Ella misma lo confirma en un testimonio escrito: "el proceso de la escritura termina cuando acabo el poema. El resto es literatura." (Ruiz-Rosas 1997). Desde nuestro punto de vista, es una lástima que Dalmacia Ruiz-Rosas mantuviera esta actitud (tan legítima, por lo demás) durante tanto tiempo. Los poemas que publicó durante los setenta (cuando militaba en *"La sagrada familia"*) bien pudieron editarse en forma de libro; y ya no sería solamente uno sino dos los poemarios que marcarían el devenir de la poesía peruana escrita por mujeres[7].

"El resto es literatura". Esta frase se inserta muy bien dentro del viejo y conocido debate sobre el significado de la "literatura"[8]. La autora hace alusión al mismo desde una posición de rechazo. No le interesa: su única labor es la de producir poemas y ya. Listo. Y es que en los tex-

---

propuesta generacional [que consiste] un poco [en] el lenguaje del cuerpo y después, asumiendo lo confesional, tocar los temas femeninos como no se había hecho" (Ramos).

[7]Pero, como ella misma dice en una entrevista: "Pude haber publicado mi primer libro en el año 77, sin embargo, no tenía la necesidad" (Castro). Su segundo poemario édito, *Baile*, es del año 2000.

[8]En su libro *Poéticas del flujo*, José Antonio Mazzotti hace referencia al mismo: "[…]no es la literatura la que motiva un ejercicio crítico, sino que cada vez es más claro que los discursos críticos inventan un canon, seleccionando, clasificando y jerarquizando según una serie de pautas consideradas básicas para el entendimiento de los fenómenos verbales y específicamente impresos. En rigor, pues (y la idea no es una ocurrencia mía), la literatura no existe. Lo que existen son los libros, las revistas, los panfletos, que aspiran a ser articulados dentro de una categoría que será sancionada como "literatura" por un conjunto de letrados entrenados o no en esas labores".

tos de Ruiz-Rosas la expresión aparentemente sencilla, no elaborada, desprovista aparentemente hasta de imaginación, de pronto se destapa:

> "yo no sé qué es el amor / pero si sé que no es / solemne triste frágil o tramposo / ni apesta como las calles / suave como la cresta de una ola desde el acantilado / fresco como una noche a la intemperie". (*Baile* 29).
>
> "Yo, recién nacida / y olvidada ya de esa imagen de felicidad / canto en mis oídos y me hablo muy dulcemente / para pasar de largo ante los ridículos / la estupidez de los seres / es necesario poseer un secreto amor que el mundo no conozca" (*Secuestro...* 9).

Ella no demora sus poemas en los recuentos de sus relaciones de pareja, aunque es consciente de que "cuando las cosas te van mal a mí también me duele" (*Baile* 37). Más bien nos llega a transmitir su filosofía de vida, aprendida (esto lo intuye claramente el lector) luego de un largo recorrido vital. Para ella la poesía no es un desahogo "porque para desahogarme puedo hacer otras cosas. Puedo meter un puñete, puedo mandarte a la porra" (Pita 1998); si no que nos entrega la esencia de su visión, de su experiencia. Una experiencia y actitud tan particulares, que no resulta extraño que casi todas las personas que han escrito sobre ella se refieran a las mismas (Escribano 1998; Valcárcel 1998; Vargas 1998)[9].

En sus poemas, la violencia se expresa en forma de rechazo directo y frontal a los valores de la sociedad[10]. Si con Ollé hemos visto que la mujer se libera de los "tóxicos" sociales, es con Ruiz-Rosas donde se manifiesta el ejercicio de la libertad de una manera descarnada, sin lamentos: "el dolor es una melodía" (*Secuestro...* 23)[11]. Sus versos direc-

---

[9] Rocío Silva Santisteban, a propósito de la aparición de *Secuestro*, escribió este bello testimonio: "La primera vez que vi a Dalmacia, en el entrañable bar Wony del jirón Belén, allá en 1983, enfundada en una minifalda negra, lidiando con tirios y troyanos, alrededor de botellas tiernamente vacías, terca en su independencia y actitud contestataria, no pude dejar de sentir admiración[...]". (Silva Santisteban 1998b).

[10] Aunque sólo nos estamos centrando en los poemas de Dalmacia Ruiz-Rosas publicados en sus dos poemarios, no queremos dejar de mencionar los siguientes versos recogidos en la antología *La última cena*: "Madre violencia / tú haces grandes cosas que nosotros no entendemos / y aunque todos oyen tu voz / no pueden detenerte" (VV. AA. 43). Escritos (y publicados) durante el periodo de la violencia política vivida en el Perú (1980 – 1992), este poema, titulado "Amalia / Foto-poema de amor lumpen", marca claramente una de las direcciones ideológicas al interior de la poesía peruana de los ochenta. No es casual, por esto mismo, que despertara las más variadas suspicacias en un sector de la intelectualidad que se manifiesta a través del periodismo escrito de ese país.

[11] Ni siquiera en estos versos el sujeto poético se demora en transmitirnos lamentos, sólo nos expresa sus terribles y dolorosas (excesivas) constataciones: "nací bajo un mal signo / si no fuera por la mala suerte / no tendría suerte alguna" (*Baile* 37). Otro: "mi biografía / suma de terribles infortunios / que nunca / me sucedieron" (*Baile* 43). O sino este otro: "[...]nadie sabe dónde Estoy / y cuál es mi dolor / canto para nadie / acurrucado en mí / como la noche" (*Baile* 34).

tos y sin tapujos se pueden leer también como resultado de una actitud violenta en tanto que no hace las mínimas concesiones al entorno: "antes que en el poder / creí en un extraño valor llamado amigo / más duradero e incorruptible / plaf perdí la ingenuidad / el mejor canto es el de las monedas / adiós amigo"(*Secuestro...* 7).

Dentro de esta misma tónica, en otros versos se percibe un punto de contacto con el César Vallejo de *Poemas humanos* (1939). Mientras que este autor dice: "Quiero, para terminar / cuando estoy al borde célebre de la violencia / o lleno de pecho el corazón, querría / ayudar a reír al que sonríe, / ponerle un pajarillo al malvado en plena nuca, / cuidar a los enfermos enfadándolos, / comprarle al vendedor, / ayudarle a matar al matador —cosa terrible—", del poema "Me viene, hay días..." (324), Dalmacia expresa abiertamente su deseo de rechazo: "quisiera matar / destruir Exterminar / bonachonamente / no me importa / estoy taponeada de asco / y tras la calma / está la simpleza" (*Baile* 26)[12].

El rechazo es una manera de reafirmar su independencia, con los riesgos y excesos que ésta conlleva: "[...]No tengo hijos / pues tendría que abandonarse / la yerba para concebirlos y con ella / yo soy mi hijo. ¿Aberración? / En la vida uno escoge. Para mí el mundo / era otro antes de conocerla. / Lo dejo todo por ella / y ninguna otra sensación me entusiasma tanto, ni siquiera / la presencia de otro" (*Secuestro...* 27).

La violencia se ejecuta contra el propio sujeto poético, como en el siguiente poema:

Estoy segura que si me paro a coger un libro
se me caerán los ovarios al suelo
saldrán rodando
de mi cuarto hacia el jardín
no pararán hasta recostarse contra el pino
donde los encontrarán mis perros
y se pondrán a jugar con ellos

estoy segura que cuando baje de tu carro
voy a patear mi cabeza lejos

---

[12]Es decir que mientras Dalmacia Ruiz-Rosas entiende la violencia sólo como enfrentamiento o ataque, para Vallejo es fundamentalmente una forma de construcción. Esta comprensión de la violencia no se halla, salvo contados casos (poemas y no un balance general de sus obras), en los poetas peruanos posteriores a él. En ese sentido, hace falta una lectura más detenida de la posición que Vallejo tiene de la violencia respecto a la manera en que la asumen el resto de poetas peruanos. Esta visión vallejiana ya se avizora en "El pan nuestro", de *Los heraldos negros* (1919), y se desarrolla más acusadamente en el poema mencionado arriba, además de "Y no me digan nada...", "Marcha nupcial", "Palmas y guitarra", "El alma que sufrió de ser su cuerpo", "¡Ande desnudo, en pelo, el millonario!..." y "Los desgraciados" del mismo libro *Poemas humanos* (1939), sin olvidar por supuesto *España, aparta de mí este cáliz* (1939) donde Vallejo toma claramente una posición política desde la poesía ante la guerra.

mis pies
preferirán quedarse fuera de la casa
pues es muy largo el camino hasta mi cuarto
y el brazo derecho
quedará colgando del llavero

(*Baile* 9)[13]

La expresión aparentemente sencilla, no elaborada, desprovista hasta de imaginación se mantiene, pero sin embargo un nuevo elemento interviene en este texto: lo sobrenatural. Recurramos al estudio de Tzvetan Todorov sobre la literatura fantástica para clarificar nuestra idea:

> Si la red de los temas del *tú* proviene directamente de los tabúes y por consiguiente de la censura, lo mismo sucede con la de los temas del *yo*, aunque de manera menos directa. No es casual que este otro grupo nos remita a la locura. La sociedad condena con la misma severidad tanto el pensamiento del psicótico como el criminal que transgrede los tabúes: al igual que este último, el loco también está encerrado; su cárcel se llama manicomio. Tampoco es casual que la sociedad reprima el empleo de las drogas y encierre, una vez más, a quienes las utilizan: las drogas suscitan un modo de pensar considerado culpable.
> Por lo tanto, es posible esquematizar la condena que amenaza las dos redes de temas y decir que la introducción de elementos sobrenaturales es un recurso para evitar la condena. Se comprende ahora mejor por qué nuestra tipología de los temas coincidía con el de las enfermedades mentales: la función de lo sobrenatural consiste en sustraer el texto a la acción de la ley y, por ello mismo, transgredirla. (Todorov 1974 188-9)
> [...]la función social y la función literaria de lo sobrenatural son una misma cosa: en ambos casos se trata de la transgresión de una ley. [...]la intervención del elemento sobrenatural constituye siempre una ruptura en el sistema de reglas preestablecidas y encuentra en ello su justificación. (Todorov 1974 196)

Luego de repasar estas ideas de Todorov, nos parece claro que para expresar el desdoblamiento o la esquizofrenia, Dalmacia Ruiz-Rosas recurra en "Estoy segura..." a lo sobrenatural; sin embargo, este elemento está dicho de tal modo que para el lector resulta absolutamente real y atendible. En cambio, en los siguientes versos no interviene un elemento fantástico, sino que la hipersensibilidad de la autora enfatiza rasgos violentos en el Otro social, en este caso identificado con las fuerzas del orden: "mi cuerpo será cubierto con cal viva / 300 policías

---

[13]En una reciente llamada telefónica (octubre 2001), Róger Santiváñez (militante también en ese entonces de "La sagrada familia"), nos ha informado que este poema de Ruiz-Rosas fue escrito y leído en 1977. Una prueba contundente pues del valor tanto poético como temático de la poesía escrita por Dalmacia antes del año-hito de 1981.

/ lo arrojarán con sus sables / a una fosa abierta / en un cruce de caminos" (*Baile* 15).

Ante una sociedad que usa sus cárceles y sus manicomios, y que trata de instalarnos el sentimiento de culpa, el rechazo de Ruiz-Rosas se expresa abiertamente: "desprecio tu pálida idea de libertad / tu rechazo al odio no me excita / sexo drogas sólo una entelequia / (no sabía nada) / es una forma / de matar / sé / como eres / sé / víctimas irrecuperables / destruir el corazón nacional / —Me prendí fuego" (*Baile* 7). O, más concretamente: "la ENFERMEDAD / es los otros" (*Baile* 28). Y también: "vete a la miseria concha de ti misma / hija de ti misma / no dan ganas de olvidarlo todo por un plato de lentejas" (*Baile* 31).

Claramente, la propuesta poética de esta autora se erige en medio de lo caótico; una conciencia del deterioro, pero con esperanza de amor:

> "Tuve un amor oscuro / En noches como ésta pienso en él / Si él volviera / mi corazón habría vencido / a mis errores / Bajo la luna lo recuerdo". (*Secuestro...* 15).
> "[…]amo a mi gato y lloro cuando pienso / en los besos dados a un cuerpo" (*Baile* 16)
> "el amor que siento me da calma / el amor que siento me da paz y me limpia del odio" (*Baile* 19)
> "no quiero que me quieras / ni que sepas de mí / sólo en libertad / podemos encontrarnos / limpios del odio que es la vida / la falta de traición / brillará / como tú / entre la multitud / y el mar" (*Baile* 23)
> "sin esperar más tiempo / la expedición ambiciosa del amor / había llegado a mí / y ahora siento sus pasos echarse para atrás / no quiero la calma de la esclavitud o de la muerte / no quiero entenderme ni tranquilizarme / no quiero la paz ni la violencia / de la emoción la razón el corazón / que hoy está lleno / -y si se cae? / -reventará y hará volar mi tórax" (*Baile* 27)
> "el más extraño amor es el que se siente con furia de dolor" (*Baile* 31).

El escenario en el cual se desarrolla la poesía de Dalmacia Ruiz-Rosas es la ciudad de Lima, percibida como "un lugar opresivo, una ciudad sin mayores cambios" (Vargas 2000): "es que mi ciudad es sólo la soledad en los parques de los vagos / y los adictos / preguntas para una flor en medio del / concreto[…]" (*Baile* 32). Una ciudad que se mimetiza con su propio ser: "Descubrí que como todo lo que sirve para encerrar / no estaba construida de concreto / sino de un material leproso, que oscurecía el sol / y el aire y producía sueño". (*Secuestro...* 9). Sin embargo, siempre existen pequeños espacios para recobrar la calma, aunque estos se hallen asociados a la muerte: "–Qué lugar tranquilo sin la violencia de la urbe / que se desliza por el sendero al campo santo[…]" (*Baile* 31). No obstante, Ruiz-Rosas no deja de reconocer Lima como una "gran dama decadente, la figura literaria de [mi] poesía" (Vargas 2000).

Así como es consciente en reconocer que, a pesar de todo Lima da energía a su poesía, Ruiz-Rosas también sabe que aun todo su rechazo es poco o casi nada ante la contundencia de la realidad: "la droga es el dinero / esta ausencia me produce dolor / lo necesito para moverme comer y hasta dormir" (*Baile* 17). Es decir, el dinero no como un medio para cumplir los deseos o los sueños, sino como el inevitable elemento para seguir viviendo. El realismo de Ruiz-Rosas en ese sentido es contundente y plenamente afirmado. Ya lo dice en un poema: "hacer vivir a mi conciencia / es la libertad / la vida es (así) una exigencia moral"[14].

Su postura ante la sociedad también se ajusta a esa exigencia moral: "soy el orden / y buena presencia si se está de fiesta / pero siempre con una voz distante / que torna los actos en mentiras" (*Baile* 21). O sea, una poesía que no sólo expresa rechazo al entorno, sino que es también reflexiva con la necesidad de actuar para seguir viviendo. No obstante, su juego es calculado, ya que no quiere dejarse involucrar por los falsos valores a los que podría estar expuesta: "la felicidad / tiene un sabor extraño / igual se almuerza / y se habla Es / una trampa que me puede gustar / ante el asco" (*Baile* 35).

No sólo las trampas de la felicidad, existe otro tipo de exigencias que sortear: "el pasado es un alivio / un recuerdo / un sueño / Alguna vez me dijeron "Ahora" y apreté el gatillo / No fue por nada / sólo para ganarme una reputación / mi sexo es un frágil acróbata / mi corazón está frito" (*Baile* 38)[15]. Frito, es decir con el sentimiento comprometido. Pero su búsqueda de la libertad continúa, por eso se pregunta : "¿se puede ser feliz y estar atada?" (*Baile* 41)[16].

Lo importante es la opción final de permanecer en búsqueda, ya que nada al parecer tiene solución: "y estallará todo y se pondrá al revés comenzando de nuevo / y nada ha de pasar Todo tranquilo" (*Baile* 32). En el siguiente poema se resume esta opción; lo transcribimos completo y de paso dejamos la palabra final a la autora, a su explosiva poesía:

---

[14]Este poema pertenece al poemario inédito *Conjunto de objetos encontrados (detestables sentimientos de jóvenes ansiosos)*.

[15]Los versos anteriores pueden leerse también como de claro contenido político, acordes con la violencia social a la que hicimos referencia anteriormente. En otro poema la autora es todavía más explícita: "y trapos viejos en un país vacío y repulsivo voraz de hablar / gritando y atropelladamente Caen bombas y tiros Alguien cor- / re con armas en las manos / Así Sacándonos de los automóviles Golpeando nuestras cabe- / zas hasta sentir el ruido de los huesos bajo las cadenas" (*Baile* 31). El sujeto poético en este caso es quien sufre la violencia, reflejada no sólo en el tema sino en la escritura dislocada que produce los cortes de los versos.

[16]Como la respuesta es ociosa, leamos más bien esta elegía, que a nuestro entender se puede interpretar como una bella reformulación a esa misma pregunta: "Señor / Soy tan pobre / Que la única / Ofrenda / Que puedo traer / Soy yo" (*Secuestro* 29).

me están corriendo de esta morada
por la ventana el dolor abrazado a mi alma
quiero dar el último portazo
cortar mi única belleza
dejarlo todo en el grito final
y no volver no volver no volver   no ver
en el cielo de mi aldea el vuelo de los pájaros
devenir de mis células en la noche subcutánea
donde el aire es sangre y arena los huesos
acato pero no cumplo   *lo demás es silencio*

(*Baile* 46).

Rocío Silva Santisteban: "Voyeur del caos"

Al efectuar estos últimos días mi relectura en conjunto de la poesía de Rocío Silva Santisteban me he sentido interpelado en tanto lector masculino. Cierta cautela mientras borroneaba mis ideas, y el sentimiento de que con cualquier conclusión que extrajera de mis lecturas (o cualquier lectura en sí misma)[17] caería siempre en el juego de la poeta, en su clara oposición relacional, en su diferenciación en tanto autora mujer[18], fueron las primeras, rápidas llamadas de alerta que fui percibiendo. Sólo quiero dejar constancia de este hecho; el debate feminista, sabemos, es bastante amplio y largo, y no nos es ajeno. Yo sólo quiero expresar aquí libremente (hasta la idea de libertad la siento "genéricamente" relativizada) mis ideas e intuiciones en torno a la poesía de Rocío Silva. En principio, es obvio que esta lectura no agota las otras que uno va asimilando. He tenido que verme en la necesidad de enfatizar algunos rasgos (en principio, los que se anuncian en el título de este ensayo), ciertos poemas e incluso ciertos versos para ir construyendo mi discurso.

Autora de cuatro poemarios y de un libro de cuentos, periodista cultural y de opinión, editora de libros y revistas, y actualmente estudiante de Boston University, Silva Santisteban ha sabido ganarse un espacio dentro de la poesía peruana a secas. De las autoras surgidas durante la década del ochenta en el Perú es quien poética e intelectual-

[17]Respecto al tema de la lectura dice Todorov: "La primera operación de la lectura es trastornar el orden aparente en el que se constituye el texto: acercar las partes alejadas, descubrir repeticiones, oposiciones, gradaciones. Trastornar no quiere decir ignorar: el orden de encadenamiento no es indiferente, no es pura "forma" (nada lo es, en el texto), pero tiene significación tanto por lo que muestra como por lo que oculta. […]La lectura consiste precisamente en elegir ciertos puntos privilegiados: los nudos del tejido... Así se explica que la lectura no es una ciencia y que nunca podrá ser definitiva: los recorridos que pueden hacerse a través de la obra son innumerables." (Todorov 1971 12).

[18]Susana Reisz por ejemplo oye "resonar [en los poemas de *Mariposa negra*] el timbre característico de una voz de mujer en diálogo con una elusiva presencia masculina que es a la vez objeto del deseo y mudo juez" (119).

mente ha capitalizado mayor representatividad, además de desarrollar un trabajo de publicaciones de poesía mucho más sostenido (sin olvidar, nuevamente, a una poeta tan apreciable como Rossella Di Paolo, autora de cuatro poemarios de gran factura).

En cuanto al aspecto temático, esta poesía aborda el tema de la mujer en sus diferentes relaciones con el sexo opuesto, la visión de sí misma enfatizando la realidad del cuerpo y su propio ser, y, en los últimos libros, las preocupaciones maternales.

Los poemarios de Silva Santisteban están bien organizados, uno puede trabajar sobre la base de conjuntos de textos como una secuencia, centrándose en las diferentes partes que conforman su estructura. Por ejemplo, en "prioridad primera", primera sección de su primer poemario *Asuntos circunstanciales*, conformada por cinco poemas, se hace evidente la preocupación de una mujer joven en su ansiedad de amor:

> yo aliviaré la carga pesada de tus muslos
> despacio podré recorrerlos como cuando llego a una tierra buena
> y cerniré sobre ellos miles de polvos continuos
> para evitar que te desgastes
> tú giraras los grados precisos para hallarnos solitarios y hallarnos
> continuamente sin necesidad de repetirnos
> y yo podré tomar de tu cuerpo mucho más de cinco litros
> tu líquido dulcísimo, nunca empalagoso, arreciará con todo lo oculto
> como un tornado cambiará en un segundo las estaciones
> y tú podrás jadear eternamente más allá de toda energía
> nos veremos en un espejo agazapados
> cierra los ojos, ven ya, deshecha toda inconsistencia
> quémame con la espuma de tu sexo
> jadea, humedece mi naufragio
> y en el espejo de nuevo, penetrándonos.
>
> ("*Secuencia*")

Versos que además nos instalan perfectamente dentro de la onda erótica que incluyó a las distintas autoras mencionadas durante la década del ochenta. Sin embargo, y como sabemos muy bien, toda esquematización es empobrecedora, y en ese sentido la poesía de Silva Santisteban de ningún modo se agota en este tipo de referencias. Sus búsquedas son mucho más amplias, más personales, aunque el "énfasis [de] su propia obsesión", para usar sus propias palabras, esté centrado en estos temas. Y es que por lo demás, como también dice ella:

> [...]no es nada casual que, tanto las poetas mexicanas como las argentinas o las peruanas que irrumpieron en la escena literaria de la década del 80, escriba(mos)n prioritariamente sobre el cuerpo, ya sea desde el erotismo, desde el escarnio o desde la autocelebración. (Silva Santisteban 1998a 127).

En otra parte del mismo texto también escribe que "[e]l cuerpo es *nuestra* cárcel y *nuestro* templo, el lugar desde donde se contempla el mundo, [...] un primer grito y sólo a partir de este grito, es decir, de la puesta en juego de una corporeidad establecida en el propio nicho literario, la mujer puede centrarse, apoderarse del espacio" (cursiva nuestra).

Al leer esta poesía, no nos suena extraño que Rocío Silva señale la idea del "escarnio", o que generalice su visión del cuerpo como "nuestra cárcel" pero también "nuestro templo"; en un poema de *Condenado amor* precisamente se habla de "mi cuerpo aprisionado" (16). Y es que en su poesía la mente se halla invadida por la violencia más avezada contra el propio ser, un hecho que la convierte en sacerdotisa y víctima al mismo tiempo. Ya por ejemplo Carlos López Degregori, al escribir su lectura de *Ese oficio no me gusta*, ve específicamente en la sección segunda a una "mujer 'perseguida, amonestada, castigada, torturada', buscando su rol social y a sí misma". Y Susana Reisz también señala que a través de su "lenguaje poético articula sin inhibiciones la ardua experiencia de ser mujer en una sociedad autoritaria y represiva" (121).

En la mayoría de sus poemas de contenido sexual, el yo femenino se encuentra ajeno al momento del goce, del placer. Un sentimiento de inseguridad se presenta a través de preguntas y reflexiones diversas: "¿En qué pensará? ¿A qué mujer evocará cuando palpa mi sexo?" (*Ese oficio* 30). Otros versos del mismo poema, titulado "No es nuestra la guerra (Pero sí este combate)", también hacen patente este distanciamiento en el momento del acto sexual:

> Estoy pensando, no puedo concentrar mis esfuerzos en sus músculos
> vienen ideas de nombres, en fin, intentar otra posición, arriba me
> gustan tus hombros-
> y no puedo otras palabras, la ternura se escapa, no la detengo
> el dolor como la primera vez, agudo y constante
> sudar y callar, gemir por la estrechez del sexo
> un relincho y gozo, dejar una huella gris
> el sabor de la oreja, amarga, la lengua entre los dientes, bajo el paladar
> y grito y gimo y no miento tampoco
>
> (*Ese oficio* 32)

Pero no solamente distanciamiento del acto en sí se aprecia sobre todo en este poemario *Ese oficio no me gusta*. Hay un poema, de tono cisneriano, titulado "Diario de señorita recién casada", en el cual expresa no sólo distancia sino un tedio y un desencantamiento ante la nueva situación asumida. El poema concluye de este modo:

> Ah tiempos idos. Levantarse sola y sola revolverse entre las sábanas
> limpiarse las legañas, el fondo del oído, las partes íntimas, las
> telarañas.

Ah tiempos que se van, que se escapan como agua entre las manos
sin dejar marcas, ni fechas en las puertas,
ni óxido de navajas en los filos de los caños.
[...]
La papa rallada sobre los párpados, compresas de jazmín, té de la
                                                              India,
La fruta de las doce, toda la rutina,
toser con elegancia, fumar con el pulgar en la papada
y desvestirme como una puta cada noche.

(Ese oficio 56)

El verso final, violento e inesperado, refleja claramente un rechazo a la obligación, así sea de una institución tan respetada por la sociedad como la que se supone acaba de refrendar la "señorita recién casada" del poema. Podríamos multiplicar ejemplos de este tipo, pero de ningún modo queremos ahondar en este detalle[19]. Vayamos más bien a otro poema para contrastar el tipo de actitud que hasta este momento venimos apreciando.

El texto se titula "Hardcore", y está incluido en su tercer libro *Mariposa negra* (22). En él, la autora se ocupa del mismo tema pero desde una actitud de libertad asumida y que no sin cierto riesgo podemos suponer compartida por el sujeto masculino al que se hace referencia. La dedicatoria del poema está dirigida "para ti, loco", y el uso de esta jerga limeña utilizada preferente pero no exclusivamente entre los hombres jóvenes a manera de saludo coloquial, hace notar claramente esta actitud en el yo femenino. Evidencia además, aunque tampoco de modo concluyente, una relación mucho más libre, sin previas mediaciones sociales, en el juego sexual del que da cuenta el poema:

Desde aquí puedo decir:
Estoy lamiendo tus nalgas con desenfreno

Y las tías, puaj, y las muchachas, puaj,
Y nadie sabe qué sentir

Entonces te volteo
Y continúo
Lamiendo
Con desenfreno.

Ese "aquí" se puede interpretar como un espacio de representación frente a un público al que se supera. Y esta actitud de enfrentamiento se hace mucho más evidente con la manera casi fugaz con que desarrolla la acción ("Epigramas" se titula precisamente la sección en la que se

---

[19]Un verso de *Condenado amor* nos puede ayudar a resumir esta actitud: "Ese vértigo de dos cuerpos tratando inútilmente de fundirse" (11).

incluye este poema). A este mismo texto se refiere José A. Mazzotti, para quien "el `desde aquí´ del poema simboliza un espacio de libertad expresiva que sin duda provoca el rechazo onomatopéyico de la sociedad." (*Poéticas del flujo*)[20].

Veamos ahora otro aspecto de la poesía de Rocío Silva, el relacionado con el sujeto femenino que se aprecia y valora a sí mismo en tanto un cuerpo. Precisamente un poema se titula "Un cuerpo es un cuerpo y sólo un cuerpo" (*Condenado* 16). Y en el poema que presta título a su primer libro dice: "yo no soy quien para ser más / ni menos / soy la exacta imagen del espejo, pero al revés". Pero es en *Mariposa negra* donde nos topamos con el texto más violento en tanto rechazo de sí mismo (o sí misma) precisamente en tanto un cuerpo:

> No puedo más, no puedo.
> Pasé una hora agachada, recordando
> A los viejos amigos, a las muchachas, he sentido
> Vergüenza, he llorado,
> Las marcas sobre el ombligo
> La celulitis, las partes flácidas,
> Todo
> Y en mi caso no sé responder, nunca
> Me prepararon para malos tiempos.
> […]
> Esta culpa es mía.
> Mía la culpa de sentirme gorda y desquiciada,
> Con la papada al borde de la esquina
> Y los callos en las manos, mi excusa.
> Busco cantando una afilada hoja de afeitar
> Para dar comienzo al espectáculo:
> Desvestirme en silencio,
> Meterme en la tina
> Y rasgar con fuerza.
> […]
> -perdónenme, perdónenme-
> Sigo con las incisiones y ya no la hoja de afeitar
> Sino el cuchillo para el pan
> El pequeño verduguillo que guardé bajo la almohada
> -no quiero saber nada de nada-
> Entra el pequeño verduquillo como un pene, entra
> Y vuelve a salir porque no aguanto, no aguanto
> Y entra de nuevo y entra de nuevo y entra de nuevo.
> No más.   (61-2)

---

[20]Para un estudio más detenido de este poema, además de una apreciación general de la poesía de Silva Santisteban, véase José Antonio Mazzotti, *Poéticas del flujo. Migración y violencia verbales en el Perú de los 80* (Lima: Fondo Editorial del Congreso del Perú. En prenta).

7777777

La agresión contra el propio cuerpo, la automutilación, llega en este texto a su máximo expresión[21]. Sin embargo, y como en un acto de purificación, posteriormente se pasará a la aceptación en tanto conciencia de la "Maternidad", como se titula el poema que da pie a nuestro comentario:

> Este cuerpo viejo quiere reventar
> De calambres y dolores
> Este cuerpo
> Antiguo habitación de desencuentros
> Se agita e intenta inútilmente prolongar
> Pequeña mía
> Este tiempo en que somos
> Una sola.
>
> (*Condenado amor* 56)

Escrito "para [su hija] Sol", este poema luminoso de esperanza nos da una pauta de la nueva ruta hacia la que perfila su poesía Rocío Silva Santisteban. Aunque la idea implícita de esperanza ya se puede ver como propuesta no solo personal sino también colectiva (o al menos grupal) en el poema final de *Ese oficio no me gusta*.

Se trata de un "Fragmento de otra carta a sor Filotea de la Cruz (Extraviado adrede por la propia sor Juana)" (77-8). Una estrategia de la que se vale el sujeto poético como recurso para expresar ciertas cosas. Con la dedicatoria a Patricia [Alba], Tatiana [Berger][22], Mariela [Dreyfus], la autora pone en evidencia su juego y en ese sentido puede también tener mayor validez nuestra hipótesis.

La carta-poema en prosa acaba así: "Mas yo les repito: estrecho y largo es el sendero, la neblina lo circunda, al final los pies arderán, pero es necesario e insustituible llevarlo en marcha [...] la labor es dura, el

---

[21] En una entrevista ya mencionada la autora se refiere a la situación biográfica que enmarcaría este tipo de poemas: "`En *Mariposa negra* trasluce la Rocío subterránea, la *outsider*.´ `La experiencia personal te va a marcar siempre. Muchos de esos poemas fueron escritos en Cajamarca y acá en Lima a partir de una experiencia negativa que viví con el papá de mi hija. Era una época extraña en que trabajaba en *El Comercio* y me sentía como aprisionada por la familia, por los compromisos, por el trabajo.´ `¿Eres una depresiva existencial o una depresiva sentimental?´ `No, yo me consideraría una melancólica´". (Ramos 28).

[22] Otra autora aparecida en la escena poética limeña a fines de los años setenta, pero que recién dio a conocer su obra en forma de libro en 1998 (aunque su poemario *Preludio* lleva como fecha de imprenta 1996). Se podría decir que es un caso similar al de Dalmacia Ruiz-Rosas, pero con la diferencia que la escasa participación de Berger en recitales y publicaciones (además de los grupos poéticos, con los cuales sin embargo siempre tuvo una relación como compañera de ruta) le han merecido la permanente separación en la "lista" de poetas de los ochenta, a la que no obstante se ve ligada, como puede verse por ejemplo en este poema de Silva Santisteban, por múltiples motivos y afinidades varias.

gozo insuficiente...". No es que queramos finalizar señalando alguna apreciación específica de direccionalidad política en esta poesía, pero nos parece sintomático que precisamente en 1987, cuando "Sendero Luminoso" sentía mayor "heroicidad" en sus acciones, Silva Santisteban haya decidido concluir su poemario con estas palabras. Ella misma confiesa en una entrevista que luego "[del regreso a la democracia y todo eso] vino Sendero —la opción más radical— y después de los primeros —me imagino— entusiasmos, se vio la cosa en su verdadera dimensión." (Chueca 35). Nada impide pensar que esos "primeros entusiasmos" merodeasen su imaginación al momento de escribir ese poema. Por lo demás, son conocidas las múltiples y públicas manifestaciones de rechazo o por lo menos nula simpatía hacia "Sendero" por parte de Rocío Silva y las otras escritoras que se mencionan en este poema[23]. Sin embargo, hacemos hincapié en que una cosa es la posición ante un estado de cosas, y otra lo que un texto literario nos dice a los lectores.

En cualquier caso, acabemos con las propias palabras de Silva Santisteban transcribiendo la parte final de "Poética", el último poema de sus poemarios publicados:

> Busco esa sola palabra que lo diga
>   t o d o
> y al borde de tenerla entre mis manos
> se vuelve silencio.
>
> *(Condenado amor* 60)

Como en el caso de Dalmacia Ruiz-Rosas, Rocío Silva Santisteban atraviesa un largo camino de búsqueda personal, en medio de los violentos años ochenta y los también difíciles noventa para, como en el poema de Emilio Adolfo Westphalen, "[a]nsiar que los silencios incorporen y devoren el espacio — que se ahogue el tiempo en un charco de silencios" (204). Una forma quizá más sabia de asumir la violencia con la que todos convivimos de distintos modos.

---

[23]Por ejemplo, en esta reciente declaración de Dreyfus: "'¿Cómo te ha afectado la guerra, y a los estadounidenses en general?' 'En el momento en que el avión de la United Airlines atraviesa la segunda torre, no sólo se quiebra el paisaje urbano, sino la certeza de que Nueva York es vulnerable. Ahora nos toca vivir cotidianamente con el miedo al ántrax o a un nuevo ataque. Para los peruanos de aquí es como un sino: escapamos del terror senderista sólo para instalarnos en este nuevo peligro, más sofisticado e internacional.'" (Robles 2001).

Bibliografía

Ángeles L., César. Entrevista a Enrique Verástegui. "Hay que erotizar el pensamiento." *La República* [Lima, Perú] 20 noviembre 1988. 1-3.

Castro Obando, Patricia. Entrevista a Dalmacia Ruiz-Rosas. "Una rosa secuestrada por el amor." *El Comercio* [Lima, Perú] 5 diciembre 1998.

Chueca, Luis Fernando. Entrevista a Rocío Silva Santisteban. "Admiro mucho la intensidad de la vida." *Flecha en el azul* 2 [Lima, Perú] 1996. 34 – 37.

Dreyfus, Mariela. E-mail a Paolo de Lima. 10 marzo 2001.

Echarri, Xavier. "Revisión del poema." *El Sol* [Lima, Perú] 18 de abril 1997: 6B.

Escobar, Alberto. *Antología de la poesía peruana (1960 – 1973)*. Tomo II. Lima: Ediciones Peisa, 1973.

Escribano, Pedro. "Poesía secuestrada." *La República* [Lima, Perú] 5 noviembre 1998.

Huamán Andía, Bethsabé. "Dos estrategias de género: Blanca Varela y Carmen Ollé". Lima: inédito (septiembre 2001).

Jitrik, Noé. *Lectura y cultura*. 2ª. Ed. México: Universidad Nacional Autónoma de México, 1990.

López Degregori, Carlos. "Ese oficio no me gusta". *El Comercio* [Lima, Perú] 31 de julio 1988.

Mazzotti, José Antonio. *Poéticas del flujo. Migración y violencia verbales en el Perú de los 80*. Lima: Fondo Editorial del Congreso del Perú. (En prensa)

Minardi, Giovanna. "Entrevista a Carmén Ollé." *Hispamérica* 83 XXVIII (1999): 55 - 59.

Pfeiffer, Erna. Entrevista a Carmen Ollé. "Detesto el puritanismo." *Exiliadas, emigrantes, viajeras. Encuentro con diez escritoras latinoamericanas*. Madrid: Iberoamericana, 1995.

Pita Dueñas, César. "Dalmacia Ruiz Rosas. Historia de un secuestro." *Cambio* [Lima, Perú] 8 diciembre 1998.

Ramos, Helio. Entrevista a Rocío Silva Santisteban. "Yo me considero una melancólica." *Revista juvenil Escena 21* no.1 [Lima, Perú] noviembre - diciembre 1996. 27 – 28.

Reisz, Susana. *Voces sexuadas. Género y poesía en Hispanoamérica*. Lleida: Asociación Española de Estudios Literarios Hispanoamericanos y Universidad de Lleida, 1996.

Robles, Marcela. Entrevista a Mariela Dreyfus. "Poeta en Nueva York." *El Comercio* [Lima, Perú] 2 diciembre 2001.

Ruiz-Rosas Samohod, Dalmacia. "Testimonio." Lima: inédito (1997).

___. *Secuestro en el jardín de las rosas*. Lima: Hipocampo editores, 1998.

___. *Baile*. Lima: Hipocampo, 2000.

Santiváñez, Róger. "La poesía de Dalmacia Ruiz-Rosas". Lima: inédito (1995).

Selden, Raman. *La teoría literaria contemporánea*. 4ª reimp. Barcelona: Editorial Ariel, 2000.

Silva Santisteban, Rocío. *Asuntos circunstanciales.* Lima: Lluvia editores, 1984.

___. *Ese oficio no me gusta.* Lima: Ediciones Copé, 1987.

___. *Mariposa negra.* 2ª ed. Lima: Jaime Campodónico Editor, 1996.

___. *Condenado amor.* Lima: El Santo Oficio, 1996.

___. "Escrito con el cuerpo." *A imagen y semejanza. Reflexiones de escritoras perua-*
nas contemporáneas. Ed. Marcela Robles. Lima: Fondo de Cultura Económica, 1998a. 127-152.

___. "China Pop". *Somos* no. 622 [Lima, Perú] 3 de noviembre de 1998b.

Todorov, Tzvetan. *Literatura y significación.* Barcelona: Editorial Planeta, 1971.

___. *Introducción a la literatura fantástica.* Buenos Aires: Editorial Tiempo Con-
temporáneo, 1974.

VV. AA. *La Última Cena. Poesía peruana actual.* Lima: Asaltoalcielo / editores,
1987.

Valcárcel, Rosina. "Dalmacia Ruiz-Rosas Samohod, Poesía Killka: Secuestro en
el jardín de las rosas." *La República* [Lima, Perú] noviembre 1998.

Vallejo, César. *Poesía completa.* La Habana: 1988.

Vargas, Esther. "Dalmacia Ruiz Rosas: Desatarse a tiempo." *La República* [Lima,
Perú] 13 diciembre 1998: 36-37.

___. "Rocío Silva Santisteban, Mariela Dreyfus, Patricia Alba, Dalmacia Ruiz
Rosas, Tatiana Berger: Voces íntimas." *La República* [Lima, Perú] 2000.

Westphalen, Emilio Adolfo. *Bajo zarpas de la quimera. Poemas 1930–1988.* Madrid:
Alianza Editorial, 1991.

Alberto Villamandos Ferreira

University of Ottawa

Thamar y Amnón: recepción del tema bíblico del incesto en el Romancero, García Lorca y Maite Pérez Larrumbe

El objetivo de este trabajo es analizar brevemente la recepción de la historia bíblica del incesto de los hijos del rey David en la literatura española con tres calas, una introductoria en el romancero tradicional de fines del siglo XV, otra en la obra de Federico García Lorca y finalmente en la más actual de una poeta española contemporánea, Maite Pérez Larrumbe. Un mismo mito ha tenido tres lecturas diferentes, manteniendo los rasgos fundamentales pero variando el punto de vista y la finalidad.

La violencia en la literatura española se ha plasmado de manera múltiple, desde un enfoque político, social, discursivo... en muchos casos como un mal endémico en su historia. De entre los temas más tradicionales, uno de los más difundidos ha sido el del incesto. El contacto sexual entre miembros de una misma familia supone infringir unas leyes que parecen dictadas por el instinto y la sociedad, y que es causa de espanto para los receptores de esos textos literarios. Sin embargo su misma difusión nos habla de un interés o incluso de una atracción subyacente que complementan ese rechazo inicial. La historia trágica de Tamar y Amnón se extiende por épocas y autores, como un mito inamovible y perenne en su violencia terrible. Esta atracción se puede ver en los romances tradicionales, que actúan como válvula de escape de la pulsión sexual de la colectividad. De la misma forma que Bruno Bettelheim ha estudiado los cuentos de hadas desde una perspectiva psicoanalítica, las truculentas historias recitadas o cantadas de los romances que se han mantenido vivos hasta hoy nos muestran dentro de sus fronteras de lo ficcional los miedos y la atracción hacia lo moralmente penalizado que no podría ser verbalizado dentro de los parámetros de lo real.

Así, Lorca se servirá de la misma historia para expresar un yo poético torturado por la (homo)sexualidad reprimida o frustrada por la sociedad, mientras que Maite Pérez Larrumbe lo construirá sobre un discurso de búsqueda de identidad femenina.

El relato bíblico de Tamar y Amnón (*Libro II* Samuel XIII) es un ejemplo de cómo un texto casi marginal que servía de apoyo para narrar la historia de la Casa de David y la ascensión al trono de Salomón acaba tomando una autonomía inesperada en la literatura a la luz de otras circunstancias sociales, culturales, políticas de cuando fue enunciado por primera vez[1]. Es decir, que pierde su interpretación política e histórica para convertirse en un marco temático, en un *topos* que puede ser adaptado por los diferentes autores, pero manteniendo siempre el rasgo fundamental de la violencia sexual.

Amnón, hijo del rey David, se enamora de su medio hermana Tamar, y cae enfermo. Pide a su padre que mande a Tamar sola a su habitación para darle de comer. Ella acude y a pesar de la resistencia que opone es violada y posteriormente repudiada por su hermano. Tamar en señal de duelo se cubre de ceniza y se rasga la túnica y pide venganza a su hermano Absalón, que acaba matando al violador[2].

El relato bíblico tiene un amplio desarrollo en la literatura española de los Siglos de Oro, que se plasma en su vertiente popular, sobre todo, como el Romancero, aunque no falta en otros géneros como el dramático. Ejemplos de ello son *La venganza de Tamar* de Tirso de Molina y *Los cabellos de Absalón*, de Calderón de la Barca[3].

En cuanto a los romances el caudal parece inagotable: Manuel Alvar recoge 174 versiones peninsulares diferentes (*Romancero* 167-70)[4]. Dentro de la literatura sefardita, con no pocos poemas de inspiración bíblica frente a la literatura tradicional peninsular (221) también abundan los romances con el tema del incesto de Tamar y Amnón.

Tradicionalmente incluido dentro de los romances de tema bíblico parece olvidarse su carácter netamente novelesco. Una vez que han cambiado las circunstancias sociales, históricas, políticas, culturales, el texto va a sufrir cambios y cruces con otros con los que muestra algún

---

[1]En los romances del siglo XVI se ha perdido la interpretación política e histórica del texto bíblico. "The tale of Amnon's violent act and Absalom's revenge are treated as autonomous themes which could appear in any moral story." en Marguerite Mizrahi Morton,"'Tamar': Variation on a Theme." *El Romancero hoy: Poética. II Coloquio internacional University of California Davis.* (Madrid: Gredos, 1979) 306.

[2]Para una interesante versión del texto bíblico en traducción castellana del primer tercio del XV en Manuel Alvar, *Romancero. Tradicionalidad y pervivencia.* (Barcelona: Planeta, 1970) 163-4.

[3]"Ya antes […] la historia narrada en el *Libro II* de Samuel había tentado a otros varios: la *Tragedia de Absalón* […] y la *Tragedia de Amón* […] de Vasco Díaz Tanco de Fregenal (hoy perdidas), la *Tragedia de Absalón* de Juan de Mal Lara, y dos tragedias de *Absalom* pertenecientes al teatro de colegio de la Companía de Jesús" además del *Aucto de Thamar* de Diego Sánchez de Badajoz. En Mercedes de los Reyes Pena, "El *Aucto de Thamar* del Ms. B2476 de la Biblioteca de "The Hispanic Society of America": estudio y edición." *Criticón* 66-67 (1996) : 386.

[4]Manuel Gutiérrez Estévez reúne 1999 en "El corpus del romance de Tamar," *El incesto en el romancero popular hispánico. Un ensayo de análisis estructural*, vol. III (Madrid: Universidad Complutense, 1981) 609-809, citado en Reyes Peña 383.

punto de contacto[5]. Esto mismo se observa claramente en los nombres de los personajes: Amnón pasa a ser Amor, Anor, Atamón, Altamoro, Tarquino, Tranquilo, Don Alonso, Don Flores, Camilo, Pepito, Luisito[6]... Lorca también plasmará la variedad en las denominaciones de Tamar en una de sus lecturas públicas: "Los gitanos y en general el pueblo andaluz cantan el romance de Tamar y Amnón llamando a Tamar, Altas Mares. De Tamar, Tamare; de Tamare, Altamare; y de Altamare, Altas Mares, que es mucho más bonito."[7]

Estos cambios darán un texto con otros matices, con un desarrollo en lo melodramático. Detalles insignificantes en el relato bíblico gozan de una mayor trascendencia, hay un reconocible gusto por aumentar lo truculento, lo violento, lo sensual. Se olvida el hecho de que fueran sólo medio hermanos y ahora lo son de sangre: se intensifica el incesto. Se pierden las coordenadas culturales de la Biblia, ya que originariamente Tamar busca vengarse no por el hecho del incesto sino debido al repudio posterior. Se olvida también la venganza de Absalón en el Romancero, como hará después Lorca, y en algunas versiones Tamar incluso llega a dar a luz a una niña[8] en una versión andaluza que bien pudiera haber conocido el poeta granadino.

Se mantienen una serie de elementos. Entre ellos, la figura patriarcal del rey, aunque se vea transformado en "un tópico 'rey moro'" (Díaz-Mas 376) que acude a ver a su hijo enfermo, enamorado de su hermana. Mantiene también el rasgo de la *passio amoris* como desorden anímico y fisiológico, en donde la calentura presenta una dilogía de fiebre/ deseo sexual, relacionada con la teoría medieval de los humores.

Su padre le ofrece una "ave" o "una pechuguita de pava de esas "que se crían en casa." Como señala Díaz-Mas "todo el diálogo entre padre e hijo esta impregnado de ambigüedades y dobles sentidos, haciendo uso de un recurso de ironía trágica: el hijo le está comunicando la verdad de sus sentimientos, pero el padre es incapaz de entenderlo." (376). Al aceptar "comer el ave" Amnón ofrece un indicio de lo que ocurrirá a continuación. De esta manera se ofrece una imagen per-

---

[5]"Because the various resolutions [of incest in Tamar's story] are based on a world-vision that is concerned by tradition on the one hand and an ever-changing social reality on the other, the message of the narrative changes from one group of texts to another." citado en Mizrahi 305.

[6]Alvar *Romancero* 176-77; Díaz-Mas 376; Bénichou 114.

[7]Federico García Lorca, *Obras completas I,* ed. Arturo del Hoyo. (Madrid: Aguilar, 1973) 1090.

[8]"A eso de los nueve meses, tuvo una rosa temprana/y por nombre le pusieron hija de hermano y hermana." en Pedro M. Pinero, Virtudes Atero, eds. *Romancero andaluz de la tradición oral.* (Sevilla: EAUSA, 1986) 116.

278 *Alberto Villamandos Ferreira*

misiva del patriarca con las actitudes de su descendencia masculina y parece cerrar los ojos ante el delito[9].

Durante este breve dialogo entre padre e hijo se utiliza un lenguaje culinario como metáfora de la pasión amorosa[10]. Este lenguaje metafórico y la figura del padre desaparecerán en el texto lorquiano, que simplifica la escena eliminando aspectos de la tradicionalidad romancesca e innova en otros. Sin embargo, sigue manteniendo la importancia del tiempo en que sucede: el verano, del que dice que "siembra rumores de tigre y llama" (3-4). El calor estival acentúa la pasión y desnuda los cuerpos (21-2, 25, 29). En el romance tradicional Tamar aparece en escena con unas enaguas blancas, que simbolizan su virginidad. Esta imagen, propia de la poesía peninsular de tipo tradicional, funciona también como lenguaje figurado en el texto de Lorca, que señala que "Thamar estaba cantando/ desnuda por la terraza" pero Amnón, en un terrible gesto de violencia "ya la coge del cabello,/ya la camisa le rasga." (73-4). No hay contradicción: el símbolo se hace evidente.

En el romancero tradicional se da una oscilación entre lo eufemístico y lo escabroso. En las diferentes versiones abunda el detalle de la cinta verde para las manos o la boca, para que no grite Tamar. En estos textos parece que hay una delectación por explicar lo terrible, y al hacerlo por medio de objetos concretos se convierten estos últimos en simbólicos.

Tras el enorme auge del Romancero viejo y nuevo en los Siglos de Oro tenemos que esperar hasta 1927, con la versión definitiva del *Romancero gitano* de Lorca para recuperar de nuevo la trágica historia bíblica. Su interés por el relato ya lo demuestra el hecho de que hubiera proyectado escribir una trilogía dramática de tema bíblico: *La sangre no tiene voz, Thamar y Amnón, Caín y Abel*[11]. Incluso el primero de los títulos iba a desarrollar también el tema del incesto, "y si al saberlo se asustan los tartufos, bueno será advertirles que el tema tiene un ilustre abolengo en nuestra literatura desde que Tirso de Molina lo eligió para una de sus magnificas producciones."[12]

Se ha discutido si el romance de "Thamar y Amnón" tiene una base más culta (del teatro barroco del XVII) o más popular (del Romancero).

---

[9]"Incest no longer involves merely Amnon, but depends upon the cooperation of the father. The king, concerned for his son, unwittingly makes Tamar accesible to him: he becomes his son's 'adjuvant.'" en Mizrahi 307. Después añade que "Tamar at the request of her father, assumes the remaining functions of the missing mother," (308) aunque sea un juicio un tanto excesivo.

[10]En el texto de Tirso este detalle se intensifica. Véase Everett W Hesse, "The Incest Motif in Tirso's *La venganza de Tamar*," *Hispania* XLVII (1964) : 270, 275.

[11]Federico García Lorca, "Introducción." *Teatro 1*, ed. Miguel García Posada. (Madrid: Akal, 1980) 26.

[12]García Lorca "Una conversacion con Federico Garcia Lorca." *Prosa II*, ed. Miguel García Posada. (Madrid: Akal, 1985) 1027.

Manuel Alvar aclara este punto en su artículo "García Lorca en la encrucijada": Federico acompañó a Menéndez Pidal por Granada en una rebusca romancesca."[13]

Para Lorca este poema era "gitano-judío, como era Joselito, el Gallo, y como son las gentes que pueblan los montes de Granada y algún pueblo del interior cordobés."[14] El autor finaliza su poemario de universo andaluz y gitano con un romance de tema bíblico sobre el incesto, de una pasión violenta, irracional. De la misma forma que en su transmisión una parte del texto sagrado se vio transformado en relato novelesco, Lorca retoma el *topos* clásico como marco y fuente de inspiración y lo actualiza, lo adapta a su mundo poético.

Situado al final del poemario, su consideración dentro de la estructura del *Romancero gitano* es ambigua. El hecho de pertenecer al grupo de los "Tres romances históricos" le otorga una cierta autonomía frente al resto de los textos. Sin embargo podría señalarse que en lugar de un *corpus* independiente se consideraría la culminación de este universo poético lorquiano, en donde entran, a modo de conclusión lo popular/ culto, lo gitano/ clásico, lo tradicional/ vanguardista. Bajo este punto de vista en "Thamar y Amnón" se cifraría todo el Romancero, como señala Fabio Graffiedi en "El macrotexto del *Romancero gitano* de Federico García Lorca."

Comienza el texto con símbolos que anticipan la tragedia y crean el ambiente de fatalidad. Se repiten imágenes de sexualidad exaltada y frustrada ("tierras sin agua" (2) verano que "siembra amores de tigre y llama" (3-4), "nervios de metal" (6)). La tierra madre está cuarteada y "estremecida", abundan las imágenes de heridas, de dolor, asimilado a lo sexual frustrado, que viene a ser una transposición de los sentimientos de Amnón. A pesar del punto de vista externo, de tercera persona, el yo poético fluctúa entre Amnón y Thamar, aunque la identificación se dé en mayor grado con el primero. El personaje masculino observa a Thamar desnuda que canta, caracterizada por un vocabulario de frialdad, dureza, rechazo: "panderos fríos", "cítaras enlunadas", "agudo norte", "pide copos a su vientre", "granizo a sus espaldas." (13-21). Castillo señala que el poeta toma la imagen del desnudo no del relato de Tamar y Amnón sino de David y Betsabé (84).

El hermano traspasado por el instinto sexual "llena las ingles de espuma" (27) la observa, también desnudo, lo cual·acentúa el paralelis-

[13]Y cita al ilustre filólogo: "Recuerdo que cuando en 1920 hice un viaje a Granada, un jovencito me acompañó durante unos días conduciéndome por calles del Albaicín y por las cuevas del Sacro Monte para hacerme posible el recoger romances orales en aquellos barrios gitanos de la ciudad. Ese muchacho era Federico García Lorca, que se mostró interesadísimo en aquella para él extraña tarea recolectiva de la tradición llegando a ofrecerme él y enviarme más romances" en Alvar *Romancero* 240.
[14]García Lorca *Obras completas I* 1090.

mo entre los dos personajes. Se encuentran ambos en lugares altos: la torre, la terraza, solos y bajo el influjo de la luna, en cuya superficie puede ver el cuerpo de Thamar, una vez que la "flecha," como elemento clásico de un Eros latino, bíblico, gitano, se ha clavado.

Recoge Lorca el elemento tradicional de la enfermedad del protagonista masculino que se acuesta a la hora de la siesta, enfebrecido y torturado. Los signos se acrecientan: la luz dolorosa (41), la "linfa del pozo", como sustancia encharcada y venenosa, la "cobra tendida" que canta, como representación del pecado y de la tentación. Lorca elimina la presencia del padre y concentra la acción en los dos personajes. El diálogo entre ellos rezuma violencia simbólica ("mis hilos de sangre tejen/ volantes sobre tu falda." (59-60), "en tus pechos altos/ hay dos peces que me llaman" (65-66). Aparece la figura del caballo como representación de la pasión amorosa desbocada, como en *La casa de Bernarda Alba* y en *Bodas de sangre*. La tragedia es imparable, "ya la coge del cabello/ ya la camisa le rasga" (73-4), en una actualización de los motivos de la poesía de tipo tradicional y del propio romancero.

A partir de aquí se intensifica el ambiente gitano, con la *alboreá*, la forma calé del epitalamio clásico. El léxico del dolor y la herida llega a su culmen, a medio camino entre la reprobación a Amnón por el delito cometido y el apoyo al hermano incestuoso, como personaje que actúa con el instinto de libertad y de la sexualidad. Finalmente es perseguido, ya no está en la torre sino que desde allí le lanzan las flechas, y el rey David corta las cuerdas de su arpa con unas tijeras, en señal de duelo, de tristeza y de una cierta castración.

Según Graffiedi el poemario se divide en tres partes: una primera o A, con los seis primeros poemas de predominio femenino más el "Romance de la pena negra," "eje temático de todo el sistema" (58), un segunda parte o B de cinco poemas más la unidad que forman San Miguel, San Rafael y San Gabriel, de predominio masculino y la tercera parte o C, con los tres romances históricos, en donde se produce una conjunción de lo femenino y lo masculino, de lo instintivo y de lo racional, de la pena y de la muerte. Dentro de esta estructura "el episodio de Thamar y Amnón," que cierra el libro, "hace explícita la imposible dialéctica entre los dos sexos. La única síntesis posible está representada en un acto de violencia: el incesto." (Graffiedi 65). Vemos así que en este romance se cifra toda la carga pasional y poética del libro, en donde entran todos sus temas fundamentales: amor frustrado, destino trágico y muerte. Amnón, por efecto del punto de vista, acaba siendo un héroe trágico, no ya un príncipe melancólico, aunque caiga en una enfermedad furibunda. El incesto, a la luz de un tratamiento dramático que busca la catarsis, se desarrolla entre verbos en presente, inamovibles, sin tiempo, que ejecutan más que un relato, la descripción morosa de imágenes de tipo casi religioso. Se basa Lorca en el texto bíblico, en la tradición romancística, en las obras de teatro de Tirso y Calderón y crea algo diferente de todos ellos. El tema del incesto, como violencia sexual, le sirve como *topos* que asume ahora otra significación. El poeta parece buscar una relación sancionada y perseguida por la sociedad, una relación necesariamente frustrante, en la que el personaje de Amnón se caracteriza por un ansia de libertad y por la exaltación del deseo sexual. A la vista de estos elementos se podría señalar un correlato claro con la homosexualidad del poeta.

Maite Pérez Larrumbe publica en el año 2000 un poemario titulado *Mi nombre verdadero*, en el que se toman las figuras femeninas de la Biblia y hablan en primera persona. Esta fórmula se relaciona con la de otras poetas. Según Reisz "entre los procedimientos retóricos de más claro contenido contestatario y feminista se encuentra la reescritura de los grandes mitos de la tradición grecolatina y judeocristiana desde una perspectiva ignorada a través de los siglos: la de las protagonistas de esas historias paradigmáticas." (87). Entre esas voces que hablan se encuentra también la de Tamar:

TAMAR
    (*Libro II* de Samuel 13, 1-22.)

Creo que no sentí dolor
los días que me siguieron.
A la sexta mañana imaginé
que aquellos moratones
habrían de quemar para curarse
y les abrí mi pecho con toda mansedumbre.

Con parsimonia de niña enloquecida
retire la ceniza del cabello,
me lavé con vinagre.

Con la caricia de que sólo es capaz
una para sí misma
volvió la propiedad de aquella carne extraña.

Recuerdo, a veces, unas vigas de cedro
y un jadeo cercano.

Desde el título del libro ya se percibe la idea de la búsqueda o afirmación de la identidad personal, más allá del juicio reprobatorio de los hombres que narraron sus historias y más allá de los arquetipos femeninos de madre, virgen, prostituta, cautivadora... De alguna manera es una lucha contra la violencia discursiva a la que han sido sometidas.

El poema consta de verbos en forma personal, con un "yo" que duda, que no muestra una gran seguridad. La protagonista, marcada por el trauma y la violencia busca recuperar su voz y su identidad, su "nombre verdadero." La experiencia dolorosa, de la que no se nos dice apenas nada, pero que reconocemos en el imaginario cultural, se confronta con el olvido terapéutico, por rechazo o vergüenza. Se recuperan otros motivos bíblicos: "a la sexta mañana imaginé/ que aquellos moratones/ habrían de quemar para curarse," que se asimila al sexto día de la creación. Sin embargo, aquí el descanso es el olvido. Hay un constante ir y venir entre dos campos semánticos, del dolor (moratones, quemar, enloquecida) y del equilibrio (curarse, mansedumbre, parsimonia), como una tensión entre dos opuestos. La protagonista percibe el destino que la inmortaliza en su papel de hermana violada, pero hay una intención de escapar de ese *fatum*, por medio de la palabra. Según Luna "si ser mujer es culturalmente aceptar un destino de mujer, rechazarlo, rechazar ese pensamiento circular, significa sin remedio empeñarse en la búsqueda de otro, llamémoslo así, destino, identidad, personalidad o estilo, lo cual lleva la búsqueda inevitable de lenguaje." (16).

¿Qué hay en el poema de Lorca, del romancero, de la Biblia? El texto se basa primordialmente en el texto del *Libro II* de Samuel, pero se opone de alguna manera al romance lorquiano en el cambio del punto de vista, de Amnón pasa a Tamar, que había sido la gran olvidada, el medio por el cual se cumplía el delito, nada más. Luna señala que "frente a una representación masculina de autonomía del ser, como diría Berger, la representación de la mujer parece estar condicionada históricamente por un observador masculino que se constituye en uno de los elementos de dicha representación." (27). Ahora ella tenía voz y trataba de reconstruir su identidad perdida. Hay una búsqueda de las primeras fuentes de la historia, como se ve en la alusión a la ceniza del cabello como signo de duelo, que también aparece en las obras dramáticas del siglo XVII pero se añade un intimismo moderno, como la caricia "de que sólo es capaz/ una para sí misma." (10). Este gesto contrasta con la violencia a la que le ha sometido su hermano, única experiencia que ha tenido del "otro." De esta manera física recupera el control sobre su cuerpo y su vida, de "carne extraña" tras la violación pasa a ser ella misma. Finalmente, hay un vislumbre de recuerdo, siempre doloroso.

El cotexto que inicia el poema, en donde se señala la procedencia de la historia, nos pone sobre aviso de la tradición que recoge, sin embargo el texto solo nos habla de una mujer violada. Se desdibuja el *topos*, el marco tradicional que se había ido formando a partir del relato bíblico. Pero este no es un proceso repentino. Si en los romances tradicionales entraban en escena tres personajes (el padre "permisivo," el hermano incestuoso, la hermana violada) y se incidía en lo novelesco, sin darles una verdadera voz a su intimidad, en Lorca se pasaba a dos personajes solos, enfrentados en un deseo destructor, bajo un yo poético que fluctuaba. En el poema de Maite Pérez Larumbe nos encontramos con una primera persona, un solo personaje, que asimilamos a Tamar por el cotexto, pero que reúne las voces de las mujeres violadas. No hay venganza clásica, sino olvido, y de esta manera se enfrenta al texto bíblico en cuanto a que actualiza la historia desde el punto de vista femenino y evita los elementos novelescos de los romances y el concepto de amor frustrado de Lorca. El incesto aquí es dolor y violencia, sin posibilidad de perdón hacia el criminal, y en esta búsqueda de identidad sólo encontramos a Tamar, mientras que Amnón desaparece confinado a unos jadeos animalescos, de puro instinto egoísta y destructor.

Bibliografía

Alvar, Manuel. *Romancero. Tradicionalidad y pervivencia.* Barcelona: Planeta, 1970.

___. *El Romancero viejo y tradicional.* México: Porrúa, 1971.

Bénichou, Paul. Ed. *Romancero judeo-español de Marruecos.* Madrid: Castalia, 1968.

Bettelheim, Bruno. *The Uses of Enchantment.* New York: Knopf, 1986.

Calderón de la Barca, Pedro. *Los cabellos de Absalón.* Ed. Evangelina Rodríguez Cuadros. Madrid: Espasa Calpe, 1989.

Castillo, Abelardo. "Hesse, Poe, Lorca." *Cuadernos hispanoamericano* 459 Septiembre 1988: 79-86.

Díaz-Mas, Paloma. Ed. *Romancero.* Estudio preliminar de Samuel G. Armistead. Barcelona: Crítica, 1994.

García Lorca, Federico. *Obras completas, I.* Ed. Arturo del Hoyo. Madrid: Aguilar, 1973.

___. *Poema del cante jondo. Romancero gitano.* Ed. Allen Josephs y Juan Caballero. Madrid: Cátedra, 1977.

___. *Teatro 1.* Ed. Miguel García Posada. Madrid: Akal, 1980.

___. *Poesía 2.* Ed. Miguel García Posada. Madrid: Akal, 1985.

___. *Prosa 1.* Ed. Miguel García Posada. Madrid: Akal, 1994.

Graffiedi, Fabio. "El macrotexto del *Romancero gitano* de Federico García Lorca." *La Torre. Revista de la Universidad de Puerto Rico* 37 Enero-Marzo 1996: 55-83.

Hall, J. B. "Lorca's *Romancero gitano* and the Traditional *romances viejos* with Special Reference to San Rafael (Córdoba)." *Studies of the Spanish and Portuguese Ballad.* Ed. N. D. Shergold. London: Tamesis, 1972.

Hesse, Everett W. "The Incest Motif in Tirso's *La venganza de Tamar.*" *Hispania* XLVII, 1964: 286-76.

Luna, Lola. *Leyendo como una mujer la imagen de la Mujer.* Barcelona: Anthropos. 1996.

M. Pinero, Pedro y Virtudes Atero. Eds. *Romancero andaluz de la tradición oral.* Sevilla: EAUSA, 1986.

Mizrahi Morton, Marguerite."'Tamar': Variation on a Theme." *El Romancero hoy: Poética. II Coloquio internacional University of California, Davis.* Madrid: Gredos, 1979.

Pérez Larumbe, Maite. *Mi nombre verdadero.* Pamplona: Pamiela. 2000.

Reisz, Susana. *Voces sexuadas. Género y poesía en Hispanoamérica.* Lleida: AEECH, 1996.

Reyes Pena, Mercedes de los. "El *Aucto de Thamar* del Ms. B2476 de la Biblioteca de "The Hispanic Society of America": estudio y edición." *Criticón* 66-67 1996: 383-414.

Webster Cory, Donald. Ed. *Violation of Taboo. Incest in the Great Literature of the Past and the Present.* New York: The Julian Press Inc., 1963.

Elizabeth Meagle

University of Ottawa

Historia y autobiografía en *Urraca* de Lourdes Ortiz

Voy a comenzar esta exposición hablando sobre el objetivo de la novela histórica *Urraca*, de la escritora española Lourdes Ortiz, publicada en 1982. En segundo lugar voy a exponer la idea de crónica histórica y autobiografía como géneros que por sus propias características influyen en la construcción del individuo —como individualidad— en la novela. En tercer lugar, *Urraca* es tanto una crónica histórica (ficticia) como una autobiografía (ficticia), pero difiere de ambos géneros al insertar temas que tradicionalmente no son seleccionados por estos modelos literarios. El resultado de estas variaciones es un texto complejo que en última instancia refleja un concepto de sujeto histórico que no se ajusta al carácter que pretenden conseguir los géneros que esta obra, *Urraca*, revisa. El texto, por tanto, representa el intento de creación de un 'ser' 'yo'que surge fundamentalmente de dos realidades: es un ser complejo integrado en una red de subjetividades, a su vez complejas, y es el sujeto capaz de reconciliarse con aquellos elementos que una definición estática y unilateral consideraría opuestos.

Revisión histórica

Urraca, a través de su personaje principal, llamado también Urraca, reina española de Castilla y León durante el siglo XII, expone el objetivo de su escritura: la venganza —va a deformar los rasgos 'heroicos' con que la Historia conoce a los contemporáneos de Urraca— , y la justicia —que se resume en la necesidad de contar su versión de la Historia-; "sé que, antes o después, se me hará justicia" (11). ¿Por qué está indignada? Porque su voluntad —voluntad de poder, "will-to-power" (Nietzsche)— "se vio frustrada por la traición y tozudez de un obispo ambicioso y unos nobles incapaces de comprender la magnitud de mi empresa" (12) Esto significa que Urraca tenía un proyecto, que en la novela se presenta como la unificación de territorios y la creación de un Imperio bajo su nombre. Pero sus ideas encuentran la oposición de la Iglesia, de otros reyes y nobles españoles, que según Urraca no entendieron y no apoyaron el proyecto que ella quería dirigir. Básicamente, esto es lo que motiva la crónica de Urraca y es además una 'novedad', si comparamos lo que la reina nos cuenta a los documentos históricos oficiales. Según Mercedes Julia, el reinado de Urraca no se conoce en la historia oficial como un periodo a destacar, por ejemplo, la *Historia Compostelana*, donde se encuentran la mayor cantidad de datos sobre este reinado, está dedicada a ensalzar la figura del obispo Diego Gelmírez, y por otro lado, otros textos como *Las crónicas anónimas de Sahagún* tratan sobre la vida en la Abadía más que sobre el gobierno de la reina. Para Julia, otro documento más explícito es el del Enrique Florez, que hace una interpretación de las fuentes históricas y en el libro titulado *Memorias de las reinas católicas de España*, concluye, que al ser Urraca una mujer no podía ser buena administradora y por esto tuvo dificultad en su reinado.

Urraca, guiada por la documentación bibliográfica de L. Ortiz, es consciente de estas críticas y se queja sobre el futuro que le depara su propia historia; "Ellos escribirán la historia a su modo; hablarán de mi locura y mentirán para justificar mi despojamiento y mi encierro." (12) Como contrapunto, Urraca también es consciente de la manipulación que puede hacerse de los hechos, así, con un tono quizá irónico y que afecta tanto a su propio texto, como al de "ellos", dice; "quizá invento. Es difícil que pueda recordar aquella mañana." (13) Lo que sabemos de Urraca es que dejó de reinar y estuvo bajo custodia y, aunque de este hecho se podrían leer varias versiones, lo cierto es que sólo se conoce una voz en los documentos oficiales, que parece que afirman la opinión del obispo Gelmírez en la novela; "una mujer sólo es mediadora." (29)

Todos los hechos históricos que Lourdes Ortiz toma como referencia; la existencia real de Urraca, su reinado en Castilla y en León, las bodas con el Alfonso I de Aragón, la anulación del matrimonio, etc., son realidades anecdóticas que sirven de eje para estructurar la novela, y que permiten a Ortiz dar verosimilitud a la ficción, así como le ofrecen la oportunidad de ficcionalizar la historia, ya que hay muchas preguntas sin contestar sobre este momento 'dado'. Efectivamente, y en lo que coincide la crítica sobre la novela histórica, la novela histórica no está escribiendo Historia, sino que revisa la historia para, en el caso de Lourdes Ortiz, dar voz a un personaje fenomenológico, cuya versión, más allá del texto literario, va a afectar a aquellas tendencias que consideran ciertas descripciones como instituciones. De modo que aquí la novela se suma a la actitud que toma la posmodernidad sobre las verdades universales y las construcciones monolíticas. También sigue este análisis Robert C. Spires, cuando al hablar sobre *El cuarto de atrás* de Martín Gaite, afirma; "Indeed, the novel demonstrates that the reality of the Franco years cannot be apprehended by a static representation of dates, statistics and events; it cannot be reduced to a universal statement." En definitiva, es la manera de contar los hechos, la manera de relacionarlos con personas, o lugares, o con otros sucesos, el modo de explicar por qué, lo que determina una parte —quizá la ideológica— del perfil del texto.

Apologías de un individuo 'superior'

Si un texto tiene como objetivo representar figuras cargadas de cualidades sinónimas, destinadas a definir una imagen que para funcionar textualmente necesita eludir ciertos elementos porque enturbian el efecto que se pretende conseguir, y si este es el objetivo de una crónica, entonces, tal como dice Urraca, la crónica "debe ser contenida, respetuosa y atenerse sólo a sucesos y batallas." (81) Si los personajes deben presentarse como identidades seguras de su función, firmes y sólidas en sus actos y determinaciones, el lenguaje que debe utilizar el texto es un "lenguaje de alianzas" (100) con tono de "elegía, canto, glosa triunfal" (99). Habría que preguntarse, por qué funciona así la crónica? Porque existe una lógica que es la misma que dirige los pasos y las decisiones de Urraca en su "voluntad de gobernar" (163), esta "lógica implacable que mueve al soberano" (192) es "la razón de estado" (90), que a su vez gobierna el proceso de la selección de datos en la crónica histórica para dar imagen al líder de su razón. Esto produce que cierto tipo de documentos, como la crónica en este caso, consignan, con la imagen creada, deformar las proporciones del ser humano del que se está hablando para que aparezca como un 'ser' 'superior'. Como una consecuencia, estos seres se convierten en símbolos, en "nombres [que] son para él [Roberto] símbolos de una historia…" (76) Nombres que a su vez pueden servir para representar naciones o imperios, para justificar enfrentamientos, para exaltar la religiosidad, por ejemplo.

Por otro lado, la autobiografía tradicional, definida por S. Smith como "género androcéntrico" (100), se caracteriza por tener como protagonista a un individuo que "sin importar cuan duramente se vea constreñido por su sociedad ni lo comprometido que se vea en la lucha, puede reivindicar legítimamente una identidad autónoma que realiza plenamente su potencialidad única…" (Smith 100). La autobiografía de este modo construida, exalta el individualismo, el mismo que encontramos exaltado en la autobiografía de Urraca cuando nos habla de su determinación para reinar; "elegí el Imperio y me prepare para que todas las tierras reunidas por mi padre pasaran a mi, cuando su muerte llegara a producirse". (21) Es la voluntad de una conciencia que se reconoce independiente en su poder de 'ser', y capaz de realizar una función, en este caso, de liderazgo político. La autobiografía funciona para justificar o "dotar de sentido" (Gusdorf 17) una vida, y hacer un balance positivo a medida que analiza en una retrospectiva, lo que hace que el escrito produzca en el lector la sensación de estar leyendo "lo que su presencia [la del autobiógrafo] tiene de irremplazable" (Gusdorf 10), y Urraca piensa esto de su reinado y de sí, ya que reivindica contar ella misma su propia historia.

Pero los textos son el resultado de una selección y ordenación de datos. El escritor, en función de un proyecto estético o ideológico –o ambos asuntos al mismo tiempo-, manipula la información disponible, y no disponible (vacíos en la historia). Asimismo, el tono autobiográfico que le sirve a Urraca para escribir su autobiografía (ficticia), tono que sirve de guía a muchas otras novelas históricas escritas por mujeres y que B. Ciplijauskaité estudia en *La novela femenina contemporánea (1970-1985),* está sometido a la manipulación que la autobiógrafa hace de los datos que recuerda, y de los que no recuerda (vacíos en la memoria), independientemente de la existencia del llamado "pacto autobiográfico" (Lejeune), que en cierto modo controla tanto la libertad de invención del autor como la incredulidad del receptor.

Urraca sabe cuáles son las funciones de la crónica histórica, y así se lo da a entender a Roberto, su interlocutor cuando le dice; "yo me refugio en mi crónica y continúo" (100), lo que significa que excluye otras realidades como los "sueldos de miseria", "los ojos arrancados".(99) También sabe cual es el resultado de un escrito autobiográfico, porque "...Urraca, reina, no podía actuar de otro modo."(48). Ambos textos son el producto de unos criterios (filosóficos, ideológicos, estéticos) que influyen en la escritura —recrean personajes 'superiores'— y que producen un 'efecto cognitivo' en la lectura —el lector percibe el texto como 'la verdad'—.

El texto de *Urraca*

> "La literatura es un desafío a la lógica [...]
> no un refugio contra la incertidumbre"
> (*El cuarto de atrás*, Carmen Martín Gaite)

Podemos decir que Urraca tiene un serio problema en su relación con la escritura o con la misión que en principio se impone, es decir, ser cronista y seguir los criterios que hacen de un texto una crónica. Sin embargo, y aunque a medida que escribe va a ir exponiendo las características de la crónica y las de la autobiografía, Urraca no se muestra de acuerdo con las propuestas formales de estos dos géneros; linealidad cronológica, relación directa y única entre causa-efecto, estructura lógica acorde a la selección de datos y al proyecto ideológico de los géneros (crear sujetos exageradamente representativos, por ejemplo). La oposición de Urraca es coherente con su proyecto; la justicia y la venganza, porque para hacer justicia tiene que ejercer un nuevo 'orden', y para vengarse tiene que desvirtuar o desmitificar los símbolos.

La alternativa que propone Urraca es la de no exaltar una sola perspectiva y facilitar la exposición de la variedad de conexiones entre los elementos implicados en un momento 'dado', ya que estos son variables en relación constante. Esto hace que la escritura sea para Urraca una tarea aún más difícil de abordar; "Te das cuenta", le dice Urraca a

Roberto, "toda la historia puede reducirse a unas líneas" (115), que son para la reina un "recuento de batallas" (116). Otros asuntos, que Urraca considera interesantes, simplemente no pueden contarse, por ejemplo "el sexo", "las pasiones", "la envidia", "el deseo" (115).

Pero tampoco podemos engañarnos, porque el juego de Urraca con los registros de la autobiografía y de la crónica es sutil y algunas veces descarado, ya que si bien quiere poner en evidencia el proyecto de estos modelos, también los utiliza para configurar una imagen que reivindique la versión de Urraca sobre su presencia en la Historia española. Utiliza la crónica para configurar una imagen 'digna de una reina', y también utiliza la autobiografía para justificar sus acciones. Sin embargo, en busca de alternativas y siendo consciente que precisamente estos géneros van a oscurecer su futuro en la Historia, los va a subvertir es el aspecto formal y en la selección de sus contenidos; por un lado la 'discontinuidad' cronológica, variaciones estructurales 'ilógicas', anacolutos, interrupciones, etc., y por otro, la 'ascensión' a primer plano de elementos que normalmente son secundarios en la crónica y en la autobiografía, que en líneas generales es todo aquello que no debe contarse; el sexo, el miedo, las intrigas, aquello que anule la 'fachada' de personaje público, etc. Estas variaciones formales y de contenido, al imponerse al registro tradicional de la crónica y la autobiografía, hacen que los sucesos y los hechos oficiales sean la arqueología de la novela, es decir, justifican parte de la historicidad del texto. Así mismo, todos estos rasgos mencionados hacen que *Urraca* pertenezca a la llamada Nueva novela histórica.

Un ejemplo de la subversión de contenido se encuentra en la figuración de la pérdida de Toledo del rey Al-Qadir, donde se presenta a Rodrigo Díaz de Vivar, "El Cid", como personaje histórico y como héroe a los ojos de un pueblo que, según Urraca, se mantiene ignorante de las traiciones de las que su "santo justiciero" (138) fue protagonista. Pero, la exaltación histórica de los protagonistas de los sucesos no se elimina, sino que se presenta junto a otra realidad, por ejemplo la muerte, con la que se encuentra el padre de Urraca, cuando ya viejo trata de prepararse para morir pero, atemorizado, busca refugio en su propia apología; "nada quedaba ya de aquel luchador que yo había admirado y temido. Era sólo un viejo encogido [...] que citaba constantemente a Dios como testigo de sus "heroicas" victorias." (43)

Si he comentado antes que la crónica y la autobiografía tratan de construir un individuo "superior" al resto de los mortales, la pregunta que vendría a continuación sería, ¿cuál es el individuo que estructura la escritura de *Urraca*? Voy a tratar de esbozar una posible respuesta en el siguiente apartado.

El 'ser' 'yo' de *Urraca*

El concepto de sujeto es una de las razones que condicionan la configuración del 'ser' en un texto, y que hemos visto, a grandes rasgos, que sucede con el 'yo' autobiográfico y el 'yo' de la crónica histórica. En *Urraca*, la protagonista sufre una metamorfosis. Si comienza exaltando su *ego* y su voluntad categórica, "Yo era la hija del rey, Urraca, y aquellos también eran mis dominios" (13), acaba reconociendo que es el 'ser' de una indeterminación, "No hay una sola verdad, Roberto, sino muchas verdades." (193), –identidad sugerida por las dudas, las ambigüedades, las contradicciones. A medida que escribe, Urraca va percibiendo que no puede ajustarse a una definición útil para las demandas del relato, lo que le provoca una especie de insatisfacción, generada por la impotencia de comprender el 'ser yo' a través de estructuras previas, que además tiene a su disposición. Urraca le dice a Roberto: "Hubo probablemente muchas Constanzas, como también hay muchas Urracas y todas son verdad." (89), y esta es la única conclusión a la que se llega en la novela con respecto al concepto de 'ser'.

Según Keiji Nishitani, el pensamiento occidental se caracteriza por su carácter científico, es decir, "las cosas son normalmente recibidas como entidades objetivas [...] como realidades externas" , y así, percibimos la 'realidad', que produce por sí misma una 'otredad', que por definición quedaría fuera del "campo de conciencia", que tiene su centro en el *ego* (Nishitani 46). Así, nuestro *ego* imprime al contexto una naturaleza externa, que lo hace susceptible de objeto de estudio, y por tanto de ser aceptado o de ser falseado (rechazado). Un ejemplo puede verse en la mirada que Urraca, en un principio, dirige hacia su hijo, a quien ve como un "otro" (84) y por tanto susceptible de ser una amenaza para su corona, que es su *ego*.

Habría que cuestionarse, y contestar, si esta 'percepción' de la 'otredad' coincide con la manera en que el 'ser' se experimenta a sí mismo, o si por el contrario la dualidad sujeto-objeto es en sí misma agresiva hacia la realidad experimental del individuo, siendo esto último lo que provocaría que el 'ser' tuviera que adaptarse a unos variables imperativos teóricos. Y parece que esto último es lo que le sucede a Urraca en relación con la escritura, al afirmar que "las personas no se reducen a unos apuntes, a unas pinceladas trazadas con rapidez para redactar una crónica…" (70) Urraca llega a entender que existe multiplicidad de perspectivas, así que puede superar las definiciones categóricas en las que se refugia y dar un giro en la dirección de su pensamiento, más en concreto, invitar conceptualmente al 'ser' a, radicalmente, 'ser nada'. Esta vacuidad, que no tiene valor o categoría puede considerarse negativa, si se cree que una formalización da 'ser' al 'yo', es decir, que el 'ser', tras la negación necesaria de la vacuidad, va a reconocerse como 'yo' en la configuración resultante (Nishitani 94). Este es el 'ser yo' que representan el padre de Urraca, el obispo Gelmírez, y la reina misma en su primer encuentro consigo en la escritura.

Otra forma de observar este problema seria considerando que la 'nada' es el medio a donde el 'ser' pertenece y en donde, en cierto modo, debería permanecer, sufriendo así en un movimiento de configuración constante. (Nishitani 107) Sólo de esta manera puede realizarse la reconciliación y la separación necesarias de elementos que desde una perspectiva estática se consideran opuestos, y esto es, en definitiva, una de otras relaciones filosóficas que puede tener el individuo con el medio en que se desenvuelve, con el código. Esta posibilidad de 'ser yo' forma parte de las enseñanzas que Urraca recibe de Cidellus, un médico y alquimista judío. Enseñanzas que Cidellus alegoriza utilizando el código de la escritura; "juega con las letras, mézclalas, permútalas, trastócalas, [...] de esa combinación surgen cosas nunca antes dichas ni sabidas, cosas que jamás hubieras podido conocer gracias a la tradición..." (163)

Aquí también se aprende que no se trata de una 'deconstrucción' gratuita, sino de la posibilidad de crear, o como dice Cidellus, "tu forma es la voluntad" (162), lo que significa que no se trata de desear ser un *a priori* formal, sino de construir una forma que sería "la Obra" (170), el 'ser yo' de Urraca.

La 'conversión' que se ha producido en Urraca es en última instancia una metamorfosis en la naturaleza de la *voluntad,* un cambio que transforma la voluntad de poder, gobernada por la lógica de estado, en la voluntad de 'ser'. Al final de la novela y de la vida de la reina, a modo de paradoja, llega "el momento de comenzar la Obra" (198), una obra que para Urraca se encarna en el amor a la vida, "Ni un sólo muerto más para esta pira de cabezas cortadas." (204), dice Urraca, que puede servir como ejemplo de la transformación que sufre la protagonista, y de su gran acto final de seducción.

Para terminar, creo que la relación del individuo con el contexto, estudiada en sus rasgos filosóficos y en profundidad, puede dar algunas respuestas al porqué del perfil del texto *Urraca,* al carácter inconcluso, a las contradicciones, a las dudas y las insinuaciones, a las especulaciones sobre el futuro, etc., sin olvidar que también son rasgos vinculados al carácter estético de este trabajo de Lourdes Ortiz.

Bibliografía

Gusdorf, Georges. "Condiciones y límites de la autobiografía." *Anthropos* 29 (1991): 9-18.

Julia, Mercedes. "Feminismo, historia y posmodernidad: La novela *Urraca* de Lourdes Ortiz." *Revista Hispánica Moderna* LI (1998): 376-390.

Lejeune, Philippe. "El pacto autobiográfico." *Anthropos* 29 (1991): 47-62.

Nishitani, Keiji. *La religión y la nada.* Madrid: Ediciones Siruela, 1999.

Ortiz, Lourdes. *Urraca.* Barcelona: Puntual Ediciones, 1982.

Smith, Sidonie. "Hacia una poética de la autobiografía de mujeres" *Anthropos* 29 (1991): 93-106.

Spires, Robert C. "Intertextuality in *El cuarto de atrás.*" *From Fiction to Metafiction: Essays in Honor of Carmen Martín Gaite.* Ed. Mirella Servodidio y Marcia L. Welles. Society of Spanish and Spanish-American Studies, 1983.

Contributors

Sophie BOYER is Assistant Professor of German at Bishop's University in Lennoxville, Québec. She received her PhD in German from McGill University in 2000. She has since taught at Bishop's University. Her research areas are 19th and 20th century German literature, comparative literature and literary theory.

Christopher JONES is Senior Lecturer in German at Manchester Metropolitan University, UK. He obtained his doctorate from the University of Kent. His most recent publications have all been devoted to crime fiction in one form or another: an analysis of Swiss crime fiction in the 1990s; a comparative study of Agatha Christie and Sabine Deitmer; and an evaluation of the popular TV crime show "Kommissar Rex." His current research continues the investigation into the use of violence in crime fiction.

Jonathan LONG is Lecturer in German at the University of Durham, UK. He received his PhD from the University of Nottingham in 1997. His research area is contemporary German literature. His publications include *The Novels of Thomas Bernhard: Form and its Function* (Rochester: Camden House, 2001) and articles on Bernhard and other contemporary writers.

Gabrijela MECKY ZARAGOZA is currently a PhD student in the Department of German at the University of Toronto. She received her Magister Artium in German and Political Science from the University of Mannheim in 2000 and her MA from the University of Waterloo, Canada in 1999. Since 2000 she has been assistant editor of *The Germanic Review.* She has published several articles on the figure of Judith in German and Croatian literature.

Julia NEISSL is Research Assistant at the Austrian Society for Communication, University of Salzburg, Austria. She received her PhD from the University of Salzburg in 1999. As a member of the advisory board for women's studies since 1999, she has been promoting women's studies at the University of Salzburg. She is the author of *Tabu im Diskurs: Sexualität in Texten österreichischer Autorinnen* (Innsbruck, Wien, München: Studien Verlag, 2001) as well as of several articles on women writers.

Sigrid SCHMID-BORTENSCHLAGER obtained her PhD in 1974 from the University of Salzburg, Austria, where she is currently Associate Professor at the Department of German. She also studied in the USA and has been Visiting Professor at several universities (Graz, Paris VIII, Utrecht, Parix XII). Her main areas of research are 20th century literature and women's studies. She is one of the pioneers of women's studies in Austria and has contributed to the uncovering of the forgotten history of Austrian women's literature through the publication of numerous books, anthologies and articles.

Verena STEFAN is a Swiss born German author currently living in Canada. She became active in the New German Women's Movement through the women's group "Brot & Rosen" (Bread & Roses) in the early 70s. In 1975, she published the book that made her famous overnight and was called the "Bible of the German New Women's Movement:" *Häutungen* (*Shedding*). By the 1990s, it had sold over 300,000 copies and had been translated into several languages. Stefan is also an author of poetry, short stories, and essays. She also teaches creative writing.

Reinhild STEINGROVER received her PhD from the State University of New York at Buffalo in 1997. She is currently Assistant Professor in the Humanities Department of the Eastman School of Music, University of Rochester. Her publications include *Einerseits and Andererseits: Essays zur Prosa Thomas Bernhards* (2000) as well as articles on contemporary German and Austrian writers. She has also translated Kerstin Hensel's novel *Tanz am Kanal* into English. She is currently co-editing a volume of critical essays on Afro-German history and culture as well as pursuing a research project on the last DEFA feature films 1990-92.

Audrone WILLEKE received her PhD from Stanford University in 1972. She is Professor of German at Miami University in Oxford, Ohio, USA. She has previously taught at the University of Minnesota. Her publications include *Georg Kaiser and the Critics: A Profile of Expressionism's Leading Playwright* (Columbia: Camden House, 1995). She has published numerous articles on German and Lithuanian literature as well as on media-assisted language learning.

Georg SCHMID is a retired Associate Professor (History and Film) from the University of Salzburg. He has also taught as Visiting Professor at the University of Paris VIII, Innsbruck, and Vienna. He is the author of several books, the most recent being *Die Geschichtsfalle: Über Bilder, Einbildungen und Geschichtsbilder* (Wien, Köln, Weimar: Böhlau, 2000). He is also an editor, together with Sigrid Schmid-Bortenschlager, of the series NHS (*Nachbarschaften. Human-wissenschaftliche Studien*) at Böhlau-Verlag. He has written numerous articles on various historical, literary and cinematographic topics.

Luzelena GUTIÉRREZ DE VELASCO. Mexicana. Doctora en literatura hispánica por El Colegio de México. Profesora titular de El colegio de México, fue directora del Centro de Lenguas del ITAM y del Programa Interdisciplinario de Estudios de la Mujer de El Colegio de México. Es coautora de los libros *Las voces olvidadas. Antología crítica de narradoras mexicanas nacidas en el siglo XIX* (1991) y *Describir la infancia* (1996).

Ana Rosa DOMENELLA. Argentina. Doctora en letras hispánicas por El Colegio de México. Profesora titular de la Universidad Autónoma Metropolitana de Iztapalapa. Coordinadora del Taller de Teoría y Crítica Literaria Diana Morán. Es autora del libro *José Ibarguengoitia. La transgresión por la ironía.*(1989) y coautora *De la ironía a lo grotesco* (en algunos textos literarios hispanoamericanos) (1992), y coordinadora de *Territorio de leonas* (2001), entre otros. Es investigadora nacional desde 1990.

Laura CÁZARES. Mexicana. Es maestra en letras españolas por la Universidad Veracruzana. Es maestra e investigadora de la Universidad Autónoma Metropolitana de Iztapalapa. Es coautora de *Las voces olvidadas. Antología crítica de narradoras mexicanas nacidas en el siglo XIX* (1991) y autora de numerosos artículos publicados en revistas, entre ellos "Nellie Campobello, novelista de la Revolución" y " El examen de maridos de Juan Ruiz de Alarcón".

Maricruz CASTRO RICALDE. Mexicana. Doctora en Letras Modernas por la Universidad Iberoamericana. Profesora titular del ITESM Campus Toluca. Es autora de los libros *Razón y placer: Alfonso Reyes* (1994) y *Ficción, narración y polifonía. El universo narrativo de Sergio Pitol* (2000), entre los más recientes. Tiene publicados varios artículos en revistas especializadas y antologías dedicadas a autoras mexicanas.

Julia TUÑÓN. Mexicana. Doctora en Historia por Universidad Nacional Autónoma de México. Es investigadora de tiempo completo en el Instituto Nacional de Antropología e Historia. Es autora de *Los rostros de un mito. Personajes femeninos en las películas de Emilio Indio Fernández* (2000), *Mujeres en México. Recordando una historia* (1998), entre otro libros. Ha publicado numerosos artículos y ediciones sobre mujeres mexicanas y sobre el cine mexicano.

Rocío SILVA SANTISTEBAN. Peruana. Graduada en Derecho y Ciencias Políticas por la Universidad Católica de Lima. Escritora y periodista en *El Comercio* (Lima). Obra poética: *Ese oficio no me gusta* (1988), *Mariposa negra* (1993) entre otras obras. Ha escrito narraciones, *Condenado amor* (1995) y numerosos artículos en publicaciones de organizaciones dedicadas al desarrollo humano y a la defensoría del pueblo en Lima. Actualmente hace estudios de doctorado en la Universidad de Boston.

Shelley GODSLAND. Inglesa. La doctora Godsland es profesora del Royal Holloway de la University of London. Es autora de numerosos artículos sobre literatura española de finales del siglo XX y escritura de mujeres en la España Posfranquista. Entre ellos, "From Feminism to Postfeminism in Spanish Women's Crime Fiction: The case of María Antònia Oliver and Alicia Giménez-Bartlett"(2002) y "Piadosa en la urbe: visión zenogandiana de Nueva York". Últimamente su investigación está orientada hacia la novela policiaca de autoras españolas actuales.

Lady ROJAS-TREMPE. Peruana. Doctora por la Université Laval (Canadá). Es profesora titular de la Universidad Concordia de Montreal. Fundadora de la asociación de Crítica Canadiense Literaria sobre Escritoras Hispanoamericanas. Su libro más reciente *Alumbramiento verbal en los 90. Escritoras peruanas: signos y pláticas* (1999), es coeditora de los volúmenes, *Poéticas de escritoras hispanoamericanas al alba del nuevo milenio* (1998) y *Celebración de la creación literaria de escritoras hispanas en las Américas* (2000). Ha publicado numerosos artículos sobre escritura de mujeres hispanoamericanas.

Elizabeth MEAGLE. Española. Licenciada en filología hispánica por la Universidad de Málaga y M.A. en español por la Universidad de Ottawa. Es actualmente becaria de la Facultad de Estudios Superiores y Posgraduados y candidata al doctorado por la Universidad de Ottawa. Su investigación se dirige hacia las nuevas formas de la novela histórica escrita por mujeres en la España actual.

Alberto VILLAMANDOS FERREIRA. Español. Licenciado en filología hispánica por la Universidad de Navarra y M.A. en español por la Universidad de Ottawa. Es actualmente becario de la Facultad de Estudios Superiores y Posgraduados y candidato al doctorado por la Universidad de Ottawa. Ha publicado poemas en revistas españolas de poesía joven. Su investigación se dirige hacia el papel del intelectual en la literatura española del siglo XX.

Paolo de LIMA. Peruano. Poeta. Ha realizado estudios de derecho por la Universidad de San Martín en Lima y de Creación Literaria en la Universidad de Texas en El Paso y en la univesidad de Ottawa. Ha publicado los poemarios *Cansancio* (1995) y *Mundo arcano* (2002) y numerosos poemas en revistas peruanas especializadas en poesía joven. Actualmente es estudiante graduado en la Universidad de Ottawa.